Life is Elsewhere

A volume in the NIU Series in
SLAVIC, EAST EUROPEAN, AND EURASIAN STUDIES
Edited by Christine D. Worobec

For a list of books in the series, visit our website at cornellpress.cornell.edu.

Life is Elsewhere

Symbolic Geography in the Russian Provinces, 1800–1917

Anne Lounsbery

Northern Illinois University Press
an imprint of
Cornell University Press
Ithaca and London

First published 2019 by Cornell University Press

ISBN 978-1-5017-4791-5 (cloth)
ISBN 978-1-5017-4792-2 (pbk.)
ISBN 978-1-5017-4794-6 (pdf)
ISBN 978-1-5017-4793-9 (epub/mobi)

Cover design by Yuni Dorr
Composition by BookComp, Inc.

Librarians: A CIP record is available with the Library of Congress.

La vraie vie est absente. Nous ne sommes pas au monde.
—Arthur Rimbaud, *Une Saison en Enfer*, 1873

CONTENTS

ACKNOWLEDGMENTS

M any, many people have helped in the writing of this book.
My profound gratitude goes to Rebecca Stanton, a remarkable scholar and intellect who read and re-read every word of the manuscript and offered transformative advice. She has been this book's perfect critic.

Kate Pickering Antonova, Ilya Vinitsky, and Vadim Shneyder read the entire manuscript and provided invaluable suggestions. Susan Smith-Peter, Cathy Popkin, Bella Grigoryan and Valeria Sobol read chapters (sometimes more than once) with expert eyes. Sarah Krive offered editing help at a crucial moment, as did Liza Ivanova; Anastassia Kostrioukava and Diana Greene provided excellent research assistance. Ornella Discacciati, who shares my improbable interest in all things provincial, introduced me to a lively group of European colleagues as well as to the many pleasures of Italian academia. The editors at Northern Illinois University Press showed me what it's like to work with a team of truly collegial professionals—thank you, Amy Farranto and Nathan Holmes.

So fortunate have I been in my colleagues and friends at New York University that I fear it's not possible to thank them adequately. Ilya Kliger, Antonia Lant, Crystal Parikh, and Cristina Vatulescu have provided warm and inspiring models of friendship and intellectual generosity; Jane Burbank and Yanni Kotsonis have patiently answered questions and shared ideas; wonderful students like Mina Magda have helped me hone arguments in seminars and conversation. Finally, and in a category of their own, Eliot Borenstein and Frances Bernstein have offered endless sustenance in all forms—where would I be without you?

I'm grateful to my dear friends from childhood and youth who've willingly subjected themselves to a crash course in how academic publishing works. Jeri Thys Berlin, Pamela Cloyd Lighaam, Heidi Skuba Maretz, Jamie Persellin, and Shelley Willig—here it is at last!

Fellowships from the National Endowment for the Humanities and New York University's Remarque Institute allowed me precious time to write, and I am grateful for a subvention from NYU's Jordan Center for the Advanced Study of Russia.

Portions of chapter 4 appeared as "'No, this is not the provinces!' Provincialism, Authenticity, and Russianness in Gogol's Day," *Russian Review* 64 (April 2005): 259–80; portions of chapter 9 as "Dostoevskii's Geography: Centers, Peripheries, and Networks in *Demons*," *Slavic Review* 66, no. 2 (Summer, 2007): 211–229; and portions of chapter 12 as «Россия и 'мировая литература'» ("Russia and 'World Literature'"), Вопросы литературы (*Voprosy literatury*), no. 5 (September–October 2014): 9–24.

My closest family members, John, Will, and George, have responded to this project with a healthy mix of intellectual curiosity and happy distraction, for which I'm deeply grateful.

Having reached a moment in life when I'm acutely aware of my great good fortune in being born to loving, generous, and curious parents, I dedicate this book to Kenneth and Dorcas Lounsbery. No thanks could be sufficient for all they've given me.

NOTE ON TRANSLITERATION
AND TRANSLATION

When transliterating from Russian to English, I have used the Library of Congress system, modifying it on occasion to conform with customary English spelling (for example, I have left out soft signs in names of people and places). In parenthetical notations, endnotes, and bibliography, I have adhered precisely to Library of Congress standards. Unless noted, all translations are mine. When citing existing translations, I have sometimes made small changes in the interest of clarity and accuracy.

· CHAPTER ONE ·

Geography, History, Trope:
Facts on the Ground

Начинается земля, как известно, от Кремля.

The world begins, as is well known, from the Kremlin.
—Vladimir Mayakovsky, 1927

In Chekhov's story "On Official Business," a young government official—originally from Moscow but assigned to serve in a more or less remote district of an unspecified Russian province—is sent out to investigate the unexplained suicide of another official. In a miserable village (which is given a name—Syrnia—but no discernible location), the young man is forced to spend hours in a dark hut alone with the suicide's corpse, a blizzard raging outside. But he is not afraid: and the reason he is not afraid is that nothing here is *meaningful* enough to be frightening. Chekhov's bureaucrat muses, "If this person had killed himself in Moscow or someplace near Moscow . . . then it would have been interesting, important, even frightening . . . but here, a thousand versts from Moscow, all this was somehow seen in a different light, all this was not life, not people . . . it would leave not the least trace in the memory and would be forgotten as soon as he departed."[1]

Everything in this "remote" place, he thinks, is "alien," "trivial," and "uninteresting." In this character's estimation, what is wrong with the provinces is that things here do not mean anything: "everything here is accidental [*sluchaino*], there can be no conclusion drawn from it." Over and over he returns to the thought that "here there is no life, but rather bits of life, fragments; everything here is accidental." Thus he longs for the *kul'turnaia sreda*, the cultural center—a place "where nothing is accidental, where everything is in accordance with reason and law, where . . . every suicide is comprehensible and one can explain why it is and what significance it has in the general scheme of things."[2]

What strikes Chekhov's Moscow official as most painful about the hideous event he is investigating is precisely *its distance from the center*: it is this distance that somehow renders phenomena unbearably trivial. What he finds intolerable is not the awful suicide, the intractable poverty, the dirty hut, the snowstorm, or the injustice; it is, rather, the fact that this backwater has no power to confer significance on any of it. The way he sees it, the meaninglessness of anything that might happen in this place is an inevitable consequence of the place itself.

"On Official Business" both reproduces and critiques a powerful and powerfully distorting set of images that have often shaped how Russian literature represents the nation's physical space. This symbolic structure takes shape around the enduring binary of *stolitsa* vs. *provintsiia* (capital vs. provinces): as Chekhov's bureaucrat thinks to himself, "our homeland, the real Russia, is Moscow and Petersburg, but here is just the provinces, the colonies" (*rodina, nastoiashchaia Rossiia—eto Moskva, Peterburg, a zdes' provintsiia, koloniia*).[3] According to the schema implied in the story, only those phenomena that fall within range of the capitals' ordering powers (including even, say, an unexplained suicide) will be rendered legible, significant; everything else will slip into chaos or insignificance.

Of course, Chekhov is not endorsing his character's patently bizarre belief that "to live, you have to be in Moscow."[4] In fact at the end of the story he has the young man struggle to articulate a vague sense that there may exist "some tie, unseen but meaningful and essential, between all people," which would imply that "even in the most desolate desert, nothing is accidental."[5] But the belief that Chekhov's character seems momentarily to renounce—the seemingly discredited conviction that all significance and coherence are located in the center, and thus that "real" life can be found only in the capitals—is nonetheless an organizing principle that returns to haunt the narrative, much as it haunts Russian literature's geographic imaginary.

This book analyzes how nineteenth-century Russian high culture conceived of the nation's symbolic geography, the geography of Russia not as an empirical reality but as "a powerful symbol conveniently located outside of historical time" (to borrow Maria Todorova's characterization of "the Balkans").[6] While numerous studies have addressed the symbolic resonances of Russia's imperial borderlands, and while its two capitals, Moscow and Petersburg, have been endlessly described and redescribed in terms ranging from the sociologically precise to the mystically evocative, the meanings of "provincial" European Russia have remained less examined in scholarship. And even as the label "European" has been contested and the borders of European Russia repeatedly redrawn, the designation *provintsiia*—all those nonexotic, non-borderland, "native" spaces outside of and symbolically opposed to Petersburg and Moscow—has generally been allowed to stand unchallenged. This silence has served to reinforce the persistent image of Russia's provinces as mute, illegible, culturally barren, and indistinguishable from one another.

Circles and Grids

Mayakovsky taught Soviet schoolchildren the words, "the world begins, as is well known, from the Kremlin" (*nachinaetsia zemlia, kak izvestno, ot Kremlia*).[7] Clearly, Mayakovsky is assuming a symbolic geography with a *middle*, the kind of landscape we find in the enduring spatial model of Russia as a series of concentric circles centered on Moscow. Leonid Gorizontov has chronicled the process by which Moscow came to be seen as Russia's center or heart, its nucleus, seed, or core, the most fundamental, inner, and middle bit of the country (to cite some recurring vocabulary from nineteenth-century sources).[8] Indeed, according to one nineteenth-century ethnographer, Moscow's absolute centrality was "no accident": the city lay "at the very center of Rus'," he claimed, its position so *perfectly* central that it corresponded to Russia's "middle" with what he termed "mathematical precision." In the words of the memoirist F. N. Glinka, Moscow is Russia's "central sun, around which other towns appear like planets."[9] Of course the boundaries of "central" Russia were redrawn many times as the shape and extent of the empire changed, but the idea that Russia had a middle, a space that was both interior and central—along with the assumption that this space was uniquely important—was rarely challenged.

Consider an 1808 postal map of central Russia (figure 1): here Moscow is situated at the center of a web-like system, the hub of a wheel with spokes extending out to the perimeter.[10] This perimeter forms a ring with stations or towns every 20–30 versts or so—with 8 or 9 spokes stretching out from the center, and from there going out further in all directions toward the empire's borders. This arrangement is characteristic of the coach relay system that connected the empire: if you were to take a compass and set the foot in the center of Moscow, and then dial rings that were 25, then 50, then 75 kilometers out, you would likely find a pattern of settlement rings. And in fact if you look at a road map of Russia to this day, you will see more or less the same thing: all roads lead back to Moscow. (Petersburg, by contrast, is supported by just one road, the one that Alexander Radishchev made famous in the late eighteenth century.)

The second map (figure 2) is linked to Thomas Jefferson's 1785 "land ordinance," the U.S. congressional legislation that provided a mechanism for selling and settling tracts of land in the western part of the continent.[11] This map represents the landmass of North America, but more importantly, it also represents a plan for colonizing, organizing, and governing this land (territory that was of course seen

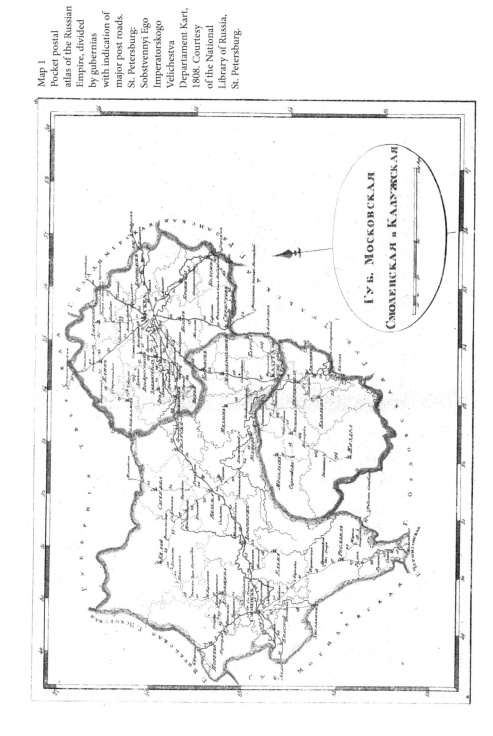

Map 1
Pocket postal
atlas of the Russian
Empire, divided
by gubernias
with indication of
major post roads.
St. Petersburg:
Sobstvennyi Ego
Imperatorskogo
Velichestva
Departament Kart,
1808. Courtesy
of the National
Library of Russia,
St. Petersburg.

Detail of Map 1.

as more or less "empty," in the sense that it was uncultivated and had few white people in it). If we compare the land ordinance map to the Russian postal map, we are immediately struck by the fact that Jefferson's map has *no center*. This difference has enormous implications for how both countries imagine their geographic space. Instead of rings, Jefferson's map lays down "a mechanical grid over the surface of America": it invites us to see the continent as a series of interlocking and essentially interchangeable one-mile-square Lego-like sections. Each of these sections can be either subdivided (so as to yield farms of so many acres) or endlessly extended (so as to define state borders "that look as though drawn with a ruler": the state borders we see when we look at a map of the American Midwest today). I draw here on an analysis of Jefferson's map by the American cultural critic Philip Fisher, who argues that the image can be read as an expression of what he calls "Cartesian social space"—space that is "identical point to point and potentially unlimited in extent," with "no clear logic of limitation."[12]

In space that is imagined as a grid, all parts are in essence identical—and therefore, as Fisher notes, *any* part "can stand for or represent the whole."[13] In theory, Kansas City, Missouri, or Fresno, California, has the same claim to meaningfulness and representativeness as does New York, Los Angeles, Boston, or anyplace

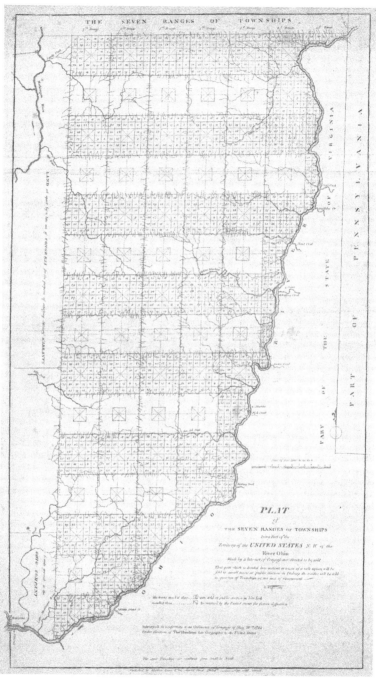

Map 2
"Plat of the Seven Ranges of Townships Being Part of the Territory of the United States, N.W. Of the River Ohio Which by a Late Act of Congress Are Directed to Be Sold." Engraved by William Barker. Published by Matthew Carey, No. 118 Market Street [Philadelphia], 1785. University of Virginia Library Special Collections.

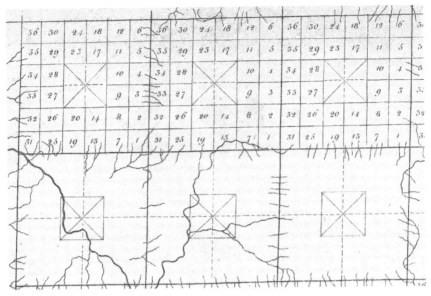

Detail of Map 2.

else. (This is why, for instance, in 2008 Sarah Palin could claim that Alaska is a "microcosm" of the United States: whereas no one could imagine a Russian politician claiming that, say, Tver—much less Omsk Oblast—is a "microcosm" of the Russian Federation.) And perhaps just as important, such a symbolic geography implies that representativeness and typicality are very good things.[14] In this ideal vision, America's democratic social space was to be "a universal and everywhere similar medium in which rights and opportunities were identical."[15] No particular place is automatically assumed to be more important than any other place.

One cannot get much further from America's relentlessly equalizing grid than Russia's series of concentric circles radiating out from a single focal point. But more important than this obvious contrast is what it suggests about how meaning inheres (or does not inhere) in geographic space. In the Russian map, what happens—in semiotic terms—as you move away from the center of the circle? I would argue that meaning is diluted, coherence fades, and entropy prevails (at least until you leave the provinces and approach the *borderlands*, whereupon a new symbolic system sometimes takes shape). Thus Vladimir Kagansky's schematic account of Russian space starts in the ideal center and from there moves out to the borderlands, listing the attributes that supposedly decline as we move further along this continuum: fullness (*plotnost'*), saturatedness (*nasyshchennost' elementami*), variety, unity, complexity ("the richness of forms and symbols"), connectedness, clarity and solidity of structure.[16] According to Kagansky, centers function as a kind of condensing force, places that work to concentrate meaning. As we will see, this understanding of symbolic geography has proven powerfully tenacious in Russian culture, underlying many texts well into and even beyond the Soviet period and often shaping the way space is imagined outside of Russia too.

A center is supposed to provide the ordering power necessary for meaningfulness and coherence. This implied function helps explain why a Russian historian would write (in 1901), "in order to understand any of Russia's peripheral regions, one . . . has to start by understanding this seed that gave rise to the Russian strength and vitality, which then spread outward to the borderlands."[17] Compare here Jules Michelet writing on Paris in his *Tableau de la France*: Paris, as "summary and symbol of the country," is "the center [that] knows itself and knows all the rest"; only here can the provinces "see themselves" and thus learn to "love and admire themselves in a superior form."[18] (Thus the multi-tome *Les Français peints par eux-mêmes*, a supposedly exhaustive account of French life in 1841–42, could devote two-thirds of its volumes to Paris, a city that contained less than 3% of the French population: the capital brings together and *stands for* all of France.)[19] Or as Victor Hugo said of the benighted Bretons, "like all provincials . . . they understand nothing of Brittany."[20]

In such a symbolic system, the capital can even pretend to *contain everything*.[21] Paris, Fonvizin writes, is "not a city at all [but] must in truth be called an entire world," and in the Jardin des Plantes F. N. Glinka believes that he has looked upon "all of nature in reduced dimensions." Fonvizin waxes slightly ironic when it comes to Parisian self-importance ("The residents of Paris consider their city to be the capital of the world and the world to be their provinces. They consider Bourgogne, for example, a near province and Russia a far one."). Still, neither writer really challenges the symbolic geography that underlies this vision: "it seemed to me that I stood at the focus of the universe," Glinka marvels.[22] In statements like these Russians are echoing French writers' own descriptions of Paris as the "encyclopedic and universal city," the same idea that is quite vividly expressed today on the monumental façade of Paris's Musée de l'Homme: "Choses rares ou choses belles ici savamment assemblées instruisent l'oeil à regarder comme jamais encore vues toutes choses qui sont au monde."[23] The intensely centripetal force of this sort of capital can tend to reduce everything else in the world to the status of a colonial holding.[24]

There are, of course, significant differences in how the French and Russian capitals function in each nation's geographic imaginary. But a key similarity is clear: for Chekhov's Lyzhin (in "On Official Business") as for Michelet and Hugo, only the center promises to *make sense* of everyplace else. Even today, educated Russians outside the capitals echo the belief that provincials must look through the capitals' lens in order to perceive anything, including *provintsiia* itself, with real clarity. The capital, they affirm, serves as "mirror" for the entire nation, reflecting "the true face of society" and thereby linking provincials to "the Unity of history."[25] And only the capital can lay claim to *representativeness*: by "creating the appearance of unity," the capital "takes upon itself the role of complete spokesman for all national and state interests and opinions."[26]

Moscow, Petersburg, and the Illusory Center

But where exactly is the center of Russia supposed to be? Ever since the early eighteenth century, when Peter I transferred the seat of imperial power from Moscow to Petersburg, both cities have been recognized as capitals (*stolitsy*), and in effect both have functioned as "centers."[27] In Yuri Lotman's terms, Moscow is the kind of capital that is "isomorphous with the state": such a city can "personify [the state], *be it* in some ideal sense" (in the way that "Rome the city is also Rome the world," for example).[28] Petersburg, by contrast, is located "eccentrically to its earth, beyond its boundaries," and "'at the edge' of the [nation's] cultural space."[29] A historical latecomer in a geographically peripheral location, Petersburg is more associated with innovation than tradition, and situated near regions that were long noted for being ethnically un-Russian. As Gogol writes in an 1836 description of Petersburg, "whoever has been to the Russian capital has been to *the edge of the earth*."[30]

Nonetheless, Petersburg is fully capable of functioning as a center. In fact Gogol's own provincials attest over and over that Petersburg is literally *nothing* if it is not a focal point; and as we read in the prologue to Andrei Bely's eponymous novel, "if Petersburg is not the capital, then there is no Petersburg. It only appears to exist."[31] Strangely, something similar holds true for Moscow, geographic middle *par excellence*: under certain circumstances, Moscow too can be deprived of its "center-ness." This is the strange idea—the idea of a "portable," fugitive, fundamentally illusory center—that Ilf and Petrov are playing with in Ostap Bender's scheme for moving the Soviet capital from Moscow to a nowhere town called Vasiuki: but only after changing the name of Vasiuki to Moscow, and that of Moscow to Vasiuki.[32]

As such examples suggest, one effect of focusing on *provintsiia* is to downplay the Moscow-vs.-Petersburg opposition that has been endlessly rehearsed: images of *provintsiia* bring into focus the fact that in many literary contexts, the two cities play virtually identical roles, in spite of obvious differences in what each "stands for" (tradition vs. modernity, east vs. west, feminine vs. masculine, etc.). In *Three Sisters*, when Chekhov's Prozorovs stand on their provincial porch and repeat "to Moscow! to Moscow!" what they are doing is virtually identical to what Gogol's provincials are doing in *The Inspector General* when they direct their gaze longingly toward Petersburg: they are dreaming of the capital's *signifying* power. For

Chekhov's characters as for Gogol's, the capital—any capital—is a quasi-magical and patently unreal ideal, toward which provincials look in the desperate hope that their insignificant lives will take on meaning when subjected to the center's ordering Logos.

Clearly the doubling of real-life capitals has done little to disrupt Russian culture's powerful center/periphery binary; indeed, having two competing "centers" may have rendered the capital/province opposition all the more powerful. Consider again the words of Chekhov's Lyzhin: "our homeland, the real Russia, is *Moscow and Petersburg*, but here is just the provinces, the colonies." Such a claim would seem to imply that part of what both Moscow and Petersburg have served to do is undermine the significance of everything that lies outside them. Or rather, perhaps it is the overdetermined insignificance of *provintsiia* that allows the capital—whichever capital—to take on such significance: like "black" people in America whose blackness has served to render others "white," the meaninglessness of *provintsiia* might actually make possible the meaningfulness of the capital.[33]

If *provintsiia* serves to embody Russians' anxious sense that life is elsewhere, this anxiety may well trace its origins to Peter's ex-nihilo, westernizing city, a place that Lotman describes as always "[presupposing] an external, non-Petersburg observer," "someone looking at it from the outside" (because it "does not have its own point of view on itself"). "Both Westerners and Slavophiles are equally the creation of Petersburg culture," Lotman asserts; both movements arose from the Petersburg-imposed necessity of creating for oneself a point of view from which to see "Russia."[34] Point of view was imagined as a geographic location. For Westernizers, it was an imaginary West (as Mikhail Shchedrin put it, "spiritually we lived in France"); for Slavophiles, it was "a similarly conventionalized idea of ancient Russia . . . from which to observe the real world of post-Petrine, Europeanized civilization."[35]

If we see both Westernism and Slavophilia as functions of Petersburg's strange relationship to the rest of Russia, we might then see *provintsiia* in the same way. Much as Lotman's Westerners and Slavophiles needed an external point of view from which to look at their own country, so provincials needed to believe, in order to convince themselves of their own existence, that they were *being seen* by someone somewhere else. Thus to some degree we can understand *provintsiia*, too, as an epiphenomenon of Petersburg, a side-effect of what Lotman describes as the "sharp increase in value-making" that resulted from the capital's sudden transfer: once the "center" reveals itself to be portable and therefore illusory, "what exists . . . and is 'our own' is negatively valued, while what is yet to come into existence in the future and is 'someone else's' is highly valued."[36] As Mikhail Epstein writes, Russian culture was "drawn to and striving toward the center, longing for the center and envying it, but it preferred nonetheless to locate this center outside itself rather than within itself—preferred not to make it its own, but rather to live in a state of painful alienation from the center, remote, neglected, isolated."[37]

Lotman's historical analysis of the capital helps us make sense of Epstein's suggestive but ahistorical diagnosis of "provincial" alienation, his claim that "a province is located, as it were, not in itself . . . Its own center has been taken out of itself and transferred to some other space or time." Lotman lends credence to Epstein's seemingly off-the-cuff claim that at certain historical moments, both Moscow and Petersburg have been figured as *provincial* "in relationship to an imperial power that was always [both] elusive and transcendental."[38] In fact, I would modify Epstein's statement only slightly so as to attribute Russia's sense of its own provincialism less to the nature of the autocratic state than to the educated elites' strained relationship to European culture: the idea of Europe—an idea that Petersburg aims to embody, though it can do so only imperfectly, self-consciously, and theatrically—is the "elusive and transcendental" entity in relationship to which Russia experiences its own provinciality.[39]

Provinces, Colonies, Borderlands, "N"

When Chekhov's bureaucrat assumes that everywhere outside of Moscow and Petersburg is "just the provinces, the colonies," his conflation of the two categories reveals how the Russian empire's geographically contiguous space could blur distinctions between what Europeans confidently designated "provinces" and "colonies." In the nineteenth century, Russians were still facing a series of conceptual and terminological dilemmas: "Was a colony [*koloniia*] a territory that was wrongly seized and exploited or simply an outlying area removed from and subordinate to 'the metropole'? Could colonies be possessed overland or did they have to be held overseas? Was a borderland more a matter of geographical location or of ethnocultural diversity?"[40] According to how one answered such questions, certain regions could be classified as colonies, provinces, borderlands, a combination, or perhaps none of the above.

While the act of colonizing was a reassuring sign of Russia's Europeanness, "it was not clear in every instance whether [Russians] had colonized their own country or someone else's."[41] (Hence Kliuchevsky's oft-cited assertion that "the history of Russia is the history of a country that colonizes itself" and debates as to whether or not Russian literature can or should be studied as a postcolonial phenomenon: both examples suggest that the Russian case might illuminate the uneasy relationship between provinces and colonies that has obtained in many times and places.)[42] As formerly peripheral spaces became assimilated into the idea of Russia proper, differentiating between native regions (provinces?) and foreign acquisitions (colonies?) proved difficult. The steppe, for example, was seen

by eighteenth-century Russians as being "at once different enough to demand
exploration, . . . un-Russian enough to be conquered and appropriated, . . . [but]
not, for all that, defined as a region wholly distinct from Russia."[43] Some regions
started out as being seen as exotic Others and ended up being re-imagined as repositories of pure Russianness (for example Siberia and, as I discuss in chapter 4,
to some degree the Ukraine).

But in the end "colonies" imply a degree of *exoticism*: even if they are geographically contiguous to the nation, colonial holdings are in some sense "far away."
And being provincial is not the same as being peripheral. A peripheral place can
be peripheral in one way (say, economically) but central in another (say, politically or religiously), whereas a provincial place is never central to anything. At
the same time, the meaning of *provintsiia* can rely as much on proximity as on
distance. A place can be provincialized by way of a certain nearness to something
else, something more important. In *The Cherry Orchard*, for example, Chekhov
chronicles the process by which the orchard, formerly the center of its own universe, is transformed into nothing more than a piece of land "only twenty versts
from town" with "the railroad close by."[44] The advent of the railway line renders
a formerly remote location no longer its own place, but rather one that is close
(enough) to another, more central place.

Provinces are Russian "core" places as opposed to exotic ones, and virtually all
nineteenth-century definitions of "interior" or "native" Russia assumed that the
(shifting) boundaries of this core were located at a "considerable remove from the
international boundaries of the empire."[45] (As the mayor exclaims of his remote
province in Gogol's *Inspector General*, "why, you could gallop for three years from
this place and not reach a border!")[46] Notwithstanding ongoing modifications to
the center's imagined borders, as Gorizontov writes,

> "interior Russia" was indeed interior. . . . Within the immense and diverse Russian
> empire, "interior Russia" was widely perceived as a place apart, a homogenous and
> self-contained place whose defining characteristics appeared *timeless and unchang-
> ing*. Regardless of how the edges of the interior were defined, . . . the most palpable
> effect of leaving the interior remained the experience of contrast. The interior was *a
> world of homogeneity, monotonality, uniformity.*[47]

By contrast, Gorizontov continues, "the regions beyond" the provincial interior,
including what we can designate colonial spaces, were "lands of difference."

If a colony is characterized in part by the colonizers' ability to imagine "its
future . . . as the exact opposite of its present" (as Russian and American statesmen imagined the future of the "empty" steppes and prairies, for example, before
these areas were incorporated into the idea of Russia/America itself),[48] a province

represents something completely different. *Provintsiia* evokes stasis, immutability, a permanent "backwardness" that is *not* in the process of being transformed into something else. As a "nucleus of typicality," a contemporary Russian geographer explains, the provinces are the symbolic repository of meaning that is timeless and static; they are "eternal and indestructible."[49]

Given such a geographic imaginary, once you find yourself in a nonexotic, non-borderland Russian space outside of the capitals, the physical location of the "center"—the capital—matters little; what is important is simply capital *vs.* province, the opposition itself. This helps explain why the existence of non- and semi-Russian places within the empire—places like Siberia, the Ukraine, the Caucasus, even the steppes—did little to undermine the dualistic province/capital opposition that prevails in literary representation. These ambiguous spaces could on occasion provide writers with material for the kind of attention to local detail and typicality that distinguishes regionalist writing in other traditions. But in the cultural imaginary overall, the empire's various borderlands, frontiers, and "colonies" were most often seen as being *opposed to* "Russia," with the result that the presence of all these less-than-Russian spaces within the territorially unified empire perhaps even intensified the tendency to collapse the heterogeneous regions of European or "central" Russia into the idea of "the provinces" (even as geographic definitions of European or central Russia remained open, of course, to adjustments).

The existence of exotic (but accessible) outer regions did not prevent people from seeing Russia proper as being divided between the capital(s) and the provinces, with the provinces conceived of simply as the not-capital, a mass of grimly uniform places in opposition to which the capitals took on their meaning. Hence literature's recurring "Town of N" (*gorod N*, perhaps better translated as "Town X" since in Russian the letter *N*, from the Latin *nomen* [name], functions as a placeholder much as *X* does in English). N is not just an anonymous place (*gorod kak gorod*, a town like any other, as Bazarov says of its instantiation in *Fathers and Sons*), but a place characterized exclusively by its overdetermined anonymity, marked by its namelessness.

Provinces, Countryside, Gentry Estate

In this book I use *provintsiia* and its cognates not loosely, not universally, and not ahistorically, but instead in the fairly specific sense that Russians began using them in the early nineteenth century. This approach is the only way to make sense of the way the idea has been deployed in Russian literary discourse. If, for example, we were to assume that in nineteenth-century Russia *provintsial'nyi* meant precisely what provincial and province mean in the subtitle of George Eliot's *Middlemarch* ("A Study of Provincial Life") or in Honoré de Balzac's "Scènes de la

vie de province," we would fail to appreciate crucial resonances of Russian usage.
And if we were to accept one scholar's casual assertion that "in almost any country
with a more or less broad territory there exists *provintsiia*," or if we were to use
the word *provintsiia* in reference to a Russian historical period (say, Kievan Rus)
when the category did not exist, or if we were to accept another scholar's assumption of a meaningful link between the Russian idea of *provintsiia* and the etymology of the Latin noun *provincia* (which some claim derived from *pro* and *vincere*
and thus referred to lands conquered by Rome)[50]—in other words, if we were to
use the term loosely—we would again risk distorting rather than illuminating the
Russian discourse about *provintsiia* and *provintsial'nost'*.

The noun *provintsiia* entered Russian from Polish with Peter the Great's reforms, when it was used to designate a large administrative and territorial unit of
the empire. Between 1768 and 1775 another round of reforms did away with the
term, replacing it with *guberniia*.[51] Once *provintsiia* lost its concrete administrative meaning (a meaning that now attached to *guberniia*), it gradually came to
refer simply to places outside of Petersburg and Moscow. Forms of both words co-
existed and shared overlapping connotations throughout much of the nineteenth
century, but thanks to a lack of clear geographic referent, it was *provintsiia* that
became more "semantically mobile" than *guberniia* and as such came to serve as a
more strictly qualitative judgment.[52] The idea of *provintsiia* persisted as a "phantom" category, as Liudmila Zaionts has described it, taking on rich cultural meaning and accumulating associations as an "open lexical form."[53] By the turn of the
twentieth century, dictionary entries tended to define *provintsiia* first as what it
was *not* (for example, "all of the country except the capital and a few large cities"),
and second as "an area with little culture."[54] Most of the connotations the term
accumulated over the course of the nineteenth century were negative, a fact that
would later be brought home by anxious-sounding Soviet-era assertions that in
a socialist country the word was no longer needed. In 1933 *Literaturnaia gazeta*
informs readers that "there is no longer any '*provintsiia*,' backward and dark,"
and in 1937 *Pravda* confirms it: "the gloomy word '*provintsiia*' has lost its right to
residence in our country."[55]

What exactly are we talking about when we talk about *provintsiia* in the nineteenth century, the period with which this book is concerned? First of all, *provintsiia* in this discourse is rarely linked with nature in any consistent way. The label
"provincial" does not refer to rural life, and only sometimes does it refer to the
life of the gentry estate (as I will discuss below). Rural life is the village (*derevnia*,
derevenskii), whereas the adjective *provintsial'nyi* (or *gubernskii*) generally refers
to provincial cities and towns, and sometimes to gentry estates that fall short of an
acceptable level of civilization. Peasants, then, are never provincials, and peasant
culture is not provincial culture. Peasants are not trying and failing to follow the

mode of the capital: they are simply not implicated in the semiotic system that has been described as "fashion, this great metropolitan idea . . . this engine that never stops, and makes the provinces feel old and ugly and jealous—and seduces them forever and a day."[56] What marks provincials—but not peasants—is a fatal lack of ease and naturalness. Peasants are not speaking bad French, and they are not boasting of their decidedly local high society. They are associated with a folk *authenticity*, and it is precisely authenticity to which the provincial sphere has no legitimate claim. Of course, the words "authentic" and "inauthentic" are virtually indefinable; or rather, they are definable chiefly against each other, in a Saussurean sense. And just as we know a thing is authentic only because it is not inauthentic, we know the provinces are provincial because we know that they are not something else, not the capital.

Derevnia (the village or countryside) may be sleepy, slow-moving, and isolated, but as we will see, *derevnia* is not lethally derivative, and its boredom is not the deadly sort associated with *provintsiia*—which helps explain why in expressions like *zaglokhnut' v provintsii* (to stifle or waste away in the provinces) the word *provintsiia* cannot be replaced with *derevnia*.[57] Only *provintsiia* is consistently linked with vocabulary like slime and swamp (*tina, boloto*), what Herzen labels in *My Past and Thoughts* "the slough of provincial life."[58] And as far as I know, there are no instances of *Derevnia N*—"Village N"—in Russian literature: villages, it seems, are associated with local specificity, and are unlikely to imply the same degree of monotonous interchangeability as provincial towns.[59] Thus at the end of Dostoevsky's *Demons*, throughout which the provincial capital that is the book's main setting has never been named, local peasants list the individual villages surrounding the city (are you going to Khatovo, to Spasov, to Usteevo, they ask?) as they try to help a pathetic nobleman wandering lost in the countryside.[60]

The distinction (provinces vs. village/countryside) could be made quite precisely by the time of Mikhail Zagoskin's "Three Suitors (Provincial [*Provintsial'nye*] Sketches)," a *povest'* (long tale) published in 1835: "Have you ever lived in the provinces [*v provintsiii*]? Not in the countryside [or in a village, *v derevne*], not in a tiny country hamlet [*v malen'kom uezdnom gorodke*], but in a provincial city [*v gubernskom gorode*], among people who speak with pride and almost always in French of their high society."[61] To be sure, despite Zagoskin's implication of a clear taxonomy, usage was not consistent at this time. In O. M. Somov's *A Novel in Two Letters* (*Roman v dvukh pis'makh*, 1832), for instance, the words *sel'skii, derevenskii, uezdnyi, oblastnoi*, and *provintsial'nyi* (adjectives denoting roughly village, rural, district, region, and province) are used virtually without distinction. In Gogol's writings *provintsiia* and its cognates occur infrequently, but *guberniia* and *gubernskii* recur countless times and carry the same semantic weight as *provintsiia* and *provintsial'nyi*; the same goes for Shchedrin, in whose *Provincial Sketches*

(*Gubernskie ocherki*, 1856–57) and *History of a Town* (*Istoriia odnogo goroda*, 1869–70) forms of *guberniia* predominate, largely because this word was the basis of official titles (*gubernskii gorod, gubernskoe pravlenie*, etc.).

The distinction between *derevnia* and *provintsiia* did not stop some writers from trying to finesse the relationship between peasant culture and estate culture (or to put it differently, between pastoral and provinciality) so as to draw on peasant authenticity for their own purposes. In *War and Peace* and *Anna Karenina*, for instance, Tolstoy implies a mysteriously close accord between the peasantry and the traditional gentry, seeming to suggest that whatever essence they supposedly have in common is the basis of an "organic" Russian culture. In large part by allying *usad'ba* (estate) life—the Rostovs and Levins of the world—with peasant authenticity and permanence, Tolstoy is able to make the noblest of his rural heroes absolutely nonprovincial no matter where they are. Dostoevsky too would have us believe that peasant virtue can cure provincial inauthenticity, but for him as for most other writers, peasant culture proved most useful in literary art as an *unexamined* ideal (and while his depictions of provincial derivativeness are all too persuasive, Dostoevsky rarely writes about peasant life as a convincingly real phenomenon). Such examples suggest that the *narod* (the common people)—or better, a fantasy of the *narod*—was far easier to incorporate into a positive idea of the nation than was *provintsiia*.[62] The (imaginary) common people are always organic and unified, whereas what is provincial, as we will see, is emphatically *not* organic and *not* unified, but rather messy, fragmented, and in-between.

What, then, of the gentry estate? Estates, regardless of their location, can be either deeply provincial (in the sense of culturally isolated and marked by inept imitation) or not provincial at all.[63] Obviously the estates in Gogol's *Dead Souls*, where "culture" exists only as random fragments of some far-off civilization, are the epitome of provinciality, occupying the same symbolic space as the nearby town. But in *Fathers and Sons* and *Anna Karenina*, while the Kirsanovs' and Levin's estates are not lavish establishments, they do exactly what such places are supposed to do: they produce their own version of elite culture—convincingly effortless and "natural"—which basically mirrors (or sometimes complements) the culture of the capital. In literary representation, such successfully achieved estates can allow the gentry to partake of rural life's "authenticity" even while providing them with a space for (high) cultural freedom, creativity, and a bit of useful labor—pursuits that are not opposed to the state's values, but which benefit from being somewhat sheltered from officialdom and state interference.

And in real life, too, estates that lived up to the standard of what has been called *stolichnost'*[64]—literally, "capital-ness"—could be experienced as oases of genuine culture in a provincial wasteland. A huge, lavish estate like the Sheremetevs', complete with its own opera company, was clearly not provincial, because it could successfully and self-confidently reproduce the culture of the capital. In Prince Ivan Dolgorukov's memoir of his travels in the early decades of the nineteenth century, the prince's relief is palpable whenever he arrives at a well-ordered gentry home, complete with park, music, and library. By contrast, what horrified him (and many others) was what they saw as the stunted and distorted culture of provincial towns: Torzhok after Petersburg, Dolgorukov writes, was "like a dark night after a bright fine day."[65] As these examples suggest, noblemen in the countryside—as semi-official agents of an "imperial government [that] wished to project its vision of civilization far out from the two capitals"—were often eager to cultivate a life more closely allied with the capitals than with surrounding places, thereby helping to "advance the cause of imperial civilization" in the provinces.[66]

Rural nobles had good reason to serve as outposts of imperial culture: in doing so, they "reinforced their attachment to the capital's reserves of wealth and status and hedged against the prospect that residence in the countryside could erode their symbolic elevation above the rest of Russian society."[67] Resources permitting, their residences reflected this attachment, as well as a clear aspiration to the status of what one historian of Britain calls, in a description of the "country house" and its role in the British cultural imaginary, "the image of true civilization and social cultivation" outside the capitals.[68] Ideally Russian estates, like British ones, were to serve as the mirror, not the obverse, of the capital: both were supposed to bring together everything good the world had to offer.[69] (The durability of this idea of capital/estate equivalency is suggested by the title of the popular turn-of-the-century journal *Stolitsa i usad'ba* [*Capital and estate*]—certainly not *Stolitsa i provintsiia*.)[70] A successful estate, rather than appearing as a provincial appendage of some far-off important place that made the rules and set the tone, could represent itself as the center of its own universe. In the poetry of Afanasy Fet, for instance, we "see the entire world from the manor house window,"[71] with the result that the estate stands as a place capable, in theory, of unifying the whole world's high culture—much as capitals claimed to do.

The fully achieved estate was supposed to appear always independent, always self-sufficient, both economically and semiotically.[72] Even for fairly modest landowners, the (appearance of) self-sufficiency was important—not only because it underwrote the fantasy of timeless universality that attached to the estate myth, but also because it helped position the estate as directly opposed to provincials' neverending efforts to copy and catch up. Above all, the successful estate was to exemplify what Fet, in his narrative poem "Two Lindens" (1856), calls "taste in the manner of the capital" (*stolichnyi vkus*)—that is, precisely the opposite of provincial taste.[73] In Fet's poem these words describe a manor house where good taste is sure to find comfortable, unstrained, even automatic expression, a place that promises to serve as that "image of true civilization and social cultivation" outside the capitals.

And yet, as we will see, it is precisely the *aspiration* to high culture that leaves the Russian estate vulnerable to degenerating into inauthenticity and incoherence: if the goal of an ordered, sophisticated, and culturally coherent microcosm could not be achieved, the space could quickly dissolve into semiotic disarray and second-rate imitation—in other words, provinciality.

The Provinces as a Literary Trope

The subject of this book is not life as it was lived by real people in Russia's real provinces; it is, rather, the *image* of the provinces (historically shaped but aesthetically and ideologically transformed) as it finds expression in mainstream Russian literary culture. The point of view of this literary culture is almost always situated in the capitals, no matter which Mikhailovskoe, Rome, or Baden-Baden a particular writer may have inhabited at a particular moment: Gogol in Rome writing about the always-anonymous Russian town, Tolstoy in Iasnaia Poliana writing about the heartland's agricultural estates, Dostoevsky in Petersburg writing about Skotoprigonevsk: all these writers are *central*—and thus in some sense *stolichnye,* allied with the capitals—by virtue of their relationship to the literary field of their day.

Since my goals are not those of a historian, I pay only glancing attention to the provinces' self-representation in, for example, the regional press (chapter 8). To the limited extent I use a historian's methodology, it is to reflect on the material and cultural circumstances that encouraged Russian authors to develop a certain set of images. In the end my argument concerns the curious symbolic weight that provincial places have been made to bear in Russian high culture; above all, I focus on the center's gaze—never neutral, and often grotesquely deforming—on the nonexotic near-periphery it defines as "the provinces."

One can and should conceive of a thousand correctives to the image of *provintsiia* originating in the capitals, given that writers and statesmen who identified with the center (even if they often did not originate there) invented the idea of a negative "provinciality" more or less for their own ideological purposes. As I discuss in chapters 2, 4, and 8, beginning with the reigns of Peter and especially Catherine, the autocracy aimed to make the provinces into a passive object of knowledge, dispatching geographers, journalists, ethnographers, statesmen, and military strategists to study various regions. Provincials' attempts to correct the resulting misrepresentations have been going on for nearly two centuries, and recent historiography has drawn attention to the importance of regional histories and historiography, even insisting, in Susan Smith-Peter's words, that "Russian history increasingly seems to be a history of regions."[74] Clearly, *historical* discourses, from nineteenth-century regional journalism to contemporary historiography, often attend respectfully to the realities and particularities of provincial places.

But it seems that once you start dealing with self-consciously literary texts—especially prose fiction that aspires to be high art—a positive version of localness becomes harder to sustain. Although historians have concluded that Imperial Russia was never a rigidly centralized state lacking variety and prohibiting initiative from below, literature tends to reproduce—or perhaps better, it helps to create and reinforce—an image of Russia that we recognize from the old state-vs.-society paradigm of Russian history. In literary texts, the local (i.e., the non-capital, because capitals are never "local") tends to be not only homogeneous and predictable but also static and stagnant, always in need of stimulus from the outside. The contrast between historical record and literary representation suggests that the trope of *provintsiia* was to some degree living its own life, oblivious to what was actually happening in real-life provincial places.

Part of the reason for this contrast is institutional: in order to be recognized as art, a text has to inscribe itself into a larger and agreed-upon discourse, an intellectual and aesthetic history analogous to a History in Pyotr Chaadaev's sense, or in Pierre's Bourdieu's terms, a field—and to do so in Russia, it must pass through if not originate in the capitals, from which authoritative art discourse emanates.[75] This is so not only because these cities have always been home to most of the country's journals, publishing houses, reviewers, universities, salons, censorship authorities, rich patrons, theaters, and so on, but also because of the symbolic geography we see reflected in Chekhov's "On Official Business": if significance is diluted as you move away from the center, it becomes especially difficult to combine localness with high-art status. Thus for someone like Nabokov, a devotee of art's very *highness*, the most "boring" literature of all is regionalism, because writing that aims to highlight the particularities of local lives and cultures cannot, for him, be inscribed in a discourse that would make it recognizable as Great Art.[76] (An analogy for women's writing, if somewhat imperfect, would be that it must be authorized by men: hence the many female texts preceded by forewords penned by male writers.)

I should note, though, one important aside when it comes to literature: the system I have been describing—the relationship between certain geographic spaces and a certain hierarchy of literary value—does not necessarily work the same way when it comes to genres other than prose fiction.[77] Lyric poetry, for instance, can foreground a supposedly unmediated communion between poet and nature, because even though in reality all genres involve forms of mediation, some genres allow for the repression or masking of such mediation more than others do. In the dramatic canon, too, what is deemed high and canonical is often not what is central or *stolichnyi* (which may help explain why Ostrovsky's plays remain unassailably canonical despite being associated with a provincial town *topos*). But prose fiction in general and novels in particular are so undeniably implicated in such systems (like publishing practices, forms of payment, serialization) that they do not have the option of pretending these systems do not exist. In order not to be marked as provincial, it seems novels often cultivate a *point of view* that is un-impeachably "central."

This may help explain why the status of prose as high art seems to depend much more on a strong association with the center/capital and its point of view than does the status of poetry or drama. The novel's more obvious reliance on the capital as a cultural "processing center" may also stem from the fact that novels must work to transcend what is manifestly trivial and mundane about their content ("daily life"). Or perhaps it goes back to the fact that the novel developed along with print capitalism and its mechanisms of distribution: from its inception the genre tended to rely more than other genres did on a kind of concentration—of money, power, and significance—in an urban center.[78] And if a novel is aiming to fulfill the realist injunction to depict the social *whole*, then that whole seems best visible in, or at least from, the center. As one of Dostoevsky's characters puts it in *Crime and Punishment*, "All these new ideas, reforms, and theories—it's all reached us out in the provinces, but to see everything and see it clearly, one must be in Petersburg."[79]

Or at least this would seem to be the case in the Russian tradition. Here it is worth recalling that the demand for "centrality" is not present in all literary traditions. In German-speaking lands, for instance, there was no single capital city throughout much of the period when novels were the dominant genre, and a text like Goethe's *Wilhelm Meister* does not seem to require the vantage point of such a center. In England, too, despite London's economic hegemony, neither Jane Austen nor George Eliot had much use for the capital, whether as setting or as point of view.[80] And in America the majority of writers who have been deemed "great," from Emerson through Philip Roth, have also been identified as regionalists.[81] In fact, by arguing for the determinative and often deforming power of the *provintsiia* trope, I am also arguing that in Russia the very idea of high culture—especially in narrative art—has developed a particularly strong association with the center (and that the geographic elusiveness of this center has only served to intensify its appeal). This association helps to explain why *provintsiia* took on such resonance in precisely the period when Russians' aspirations to what one might call "great culture status" were first being explicitly articulated.

Literature begins to imbue the provinces with intense symbolic import in the early decades of the nineteenth century—but it does so by insisting on their blankness and emptiness, by depicting provincial places as a featureless void. Indeed in many texts, the Russian provinces are not merely drab, philistine, or behind the times, as are, say, Balzac's provinces in the French tradition. Rather, *provintsiia* stands as the poisonous embodiment of cultural and psychic lack, a non-place where banality threatens to intensify into evil. In 1837 Vladimir Odoevsky writes that life in the provinces is a "bestial dream" (*zhivotnyi son*) in which "the interior of [one's] own soul becomes a hell";[82] by the time we get to Fyodor Sologub's *Petty Demon* (1907), the nameless town where the novel is set is "in the grip of alienation from the sky."[83] The "barbarity and ineradicable sorrow"[84] that Sologub attributes to his anonymous provincial city are already discernible in Gogol's working notes to *Dead Souls*—the text that definitively consolidates *provintsiia*'s role in Russia's cultural imaginary—in his insistence that the Town of N must embody "the highest degree of Emptiness" ("the reader must be struck by the dead insensibility of life" in the provinces, he says).[85] Such is the vision of the provinces we see recurring through Turgenev, Dostoevsky, Shchedrin, Chekhov, Sologub, and even beyond.

The trope of *provintsiia* and the provinces-vs.-capital binary proved so powerful that even those authors who contested it (including, as we will see, Tolstoy, Leskov, a number of women and regionalist writers, and sometimes Chekhov) were nonetheless obliged to engage with all-too-familiar images of stagnant, homogeneous provincial places. As a result, the very symbolic geography these writers aimed to critique often seems to hover just below the surface in their works. And according to the set of images they inherited, *provintsiia* never changes. Indeed, it is imagined as being fundamentally *ahistorical*: hence Bakhtin's description of provincial places as event-less, mired in a "viscous and sticky time that drags itself slowly through space."[86] In fact, even though Russian society underwent truly radical transformations in the years this book treats (roughly 1830 to 1900), *provintsiia* continued to be depicted in almost identical terms, as if changes as momentous as the end of serfdom, the rise of a market economy, revolutions in transportation and literacy, the gentry's decline, etc., were powerless to affect Russia's provincial core.

On Regionalism and Its Absence

The *provintsiia* trope is related to regionalism's weak presence in Russian literature—a surprising feature of the canon when we consider European Russia's vastness and the heterogeneity of its local subcultures. Historical factors, many having to do with the nature of the state, worked to discourage the development of literary regionalism in Russia. Here a comparison with America is helpful. In the American tradition, literary regionalism's importance reflects the politics of a country deeply divided by slavery; thus, "the South was the first 'region' in America."[87] There was, of course, no comparable political divide in imperial Russia, nor could there have been in an autocracy that aimed to have its subjects do without "politics" altogether. And as many historians have argued, the intensely centralized nature of the Russian state encouraged elites to look toward the center, toward the capital(s), rather than attempting to base either their power or their self-conception on local affiliations. And as I noted above, noblemen who could afford to live permanently in the capitals rather than on their estates very often chose to do so, opting to stay close to the central bureaucracy that was their main source of power and status.

While middling landowners seem to have felt closely tied to their localities (as recent historiography has emphasized), the richest and most sophisticated members of the Russian landowning class were often absentee landlords who treated their multiple estates as sources of income rather than as their true homes or "native" places (unlike, say, English gentry or American planters, whose political influence and identity depended on close associations with specific places outside the capitals).[88] As Peter Kolchin puts it, wealthy Russian noblemen "did not consider themselves representatives of *particular localities* so much as servitors in the government bureaucracy. Despite Catherine II's highly touted provincial reforms, noblemen on the whole continued to lack any kind of . . . *local* political identification," identifying instead with the autocracy (which was of course based in the capital).[89]

Russian high culture's insistence on the blankness of a homogeneous, timeless, and unchanging *provintsiia* becomes even more striking when we compare it to literary traditions in which "*what* happens depends a lot on *where* it happens" (in Franco Moretti's words).[90] In Jane Austen's novels, for example, narrative complications generally arise in certain English counties, and these narrative complications then meet their (matrimonial) resolutions in certain other counties. Furthermore, English Gothic novels are virtually never set in the regions where Austen's narratives unfold[91]—a sign that Britain's and even England's internal borders, those that divide regions, are meaningful for the narrative structure of English prose. In France, too, Balzac's enormous *Human Comedy* develops a whole anatomy of the country's very different, highly individualized provinces. While Lucien Chardon (in *Lost Illusions*, 1837–43) is as desperate to escape the provinces as any Russian hero has ever been, Chardon's cheerless provincial hometown is a real place (Angoulême), and Balzac describes this real place in great historical and social detail. Even the imaginary Yonville of *Madame Bovary*, which one might take to be the epitome of provincial anonymity, is located in a very real region of France (in fact, a subregion, Normandy's drab "pays de Caux"), and the particularities of this dismal locale are important to Flaubert's story. And of course the pattern is even more pervasive in the American tradition: we have learned to expect entirely different things of a story set in Mississippi than from a story set in Maine. In fact, to a large degree American prose fiction (and particularly American realism) developed in response to the pressures and contradictions of regionalist perspectives.

There are, of course, exceptions to the schematic picture I have just drawn. There are European texts depicting provincial locations characterized chiefly by a placeless provinciality (*Madame Bovary* is usually cited as the classic example, though as I have noted, this is not an entirely accurate characterization); there are American writers whose work turns on America's cultural provincialism rather than its specific regional identities (Henry James). On the Russian side, at times the nineteenth-century image of Moscow as both provincial (compared to Petersburg) and central to genuine Russian identity could serve to complicate the province/capital opposition, as could certain peripheral places (e.g., Siberia or the steppes) that not only were gradually assimilated into Russia proper but, as I noted above, could even be reimagined as quintessentially Russian.

Nonetheless, even a text like Sergei Aksakov's 1856 *Family Chronicle*, which might seem to belie the claim that regionalism is absent from Russian literature, in the end does little to challenge the prevailing image of *provintsiia* as more or less homogeneous. Aksakov's story is set in "Russia," but in a region far enough to the east that in his time (and certainly in his characters' time, the eighteenth century) it would likely have been considered not quite "provincial" at all, but instead a border region. This detail helps explain why *Family Chronicle*'s setting merits such precision and sustained attention, why it escapes being labeled as simply and anonymously "provincial." Similarly, even when Russian writers were "[filling] their geography with symbolic content" in the aftermath of 1812, this content was not usually pressed into the service of exploring or elaborating on regional particularity.[92] Thus while *War and Peace* makes quite explicit the symbolic content of the nation's real physical space—specific rivers crossed, plains surveyed, cities taken and abandoned, etc.—in the end Tolstoy uses geographic and topographic specificity to emphasize national unity. Likewise Dostoevsky, in a *Diary of a Writer* entry entitled "A Regional New Word" (*Oblastnoe novoe slovo*, 1876, addressed in chapter 9), acknowledges the regions' desire to "virtually emancipate themselves from the capitals" and "to say their own word," but he insists that regional uniqueness will always be less important than Russian unity: the particularities of regions will matter only because they will reveal that "in each [individual] place throughout Russia, all of Russia exists."[93]

According to the view that has generally predominated in Russian literary discourse, particular places can be worthy of representation only when a provincial part can stand in for the Russian whole—and indeed, writers of Russian regionalist literature tend to be canonized only when their local objects of interest can be seen in a synecdochic relationship to something larger, which is usually the nation. Writers who are not clearly situated within the capitals' literary discourse—including women and regionalists, as I discuss in chapters 7 and 8—often risk being seen as second-rate, or as mere sources for others to draw on. Thus, as we will see, Melnikov and Aksakov are typically mined for ethnographic "data," much as Nikolai Leskov is mined for "authenticity" and "Russian soul." In short, the provinces are thought to have (raw) material to contribute, but especially when it comes to literature, the aggregating, interpreting, and redisseminating of this material must be done in and by a center.

In place of regionalism, Russian literature gives us the trope of *provintsiia* and provincial *equivalence*, an idea reiterated over and over from Herzen through Chekhov and beyond. As Vladimir Sollogub writes in *Tarantas*, "All our provincial towns look the same. If you've seen one, you've seen them all." What is true of the built environment holds for the topography as well: "everything the same, the same, the same."[94] Indeed in *Dead Souls*, almost no trait is attributed to the Town of N that is not also attributed to "all provincial towns," and when Chichikov imagines that a runaway serf has ended up in "*some* Vesegonsk or another" (*kakoi-nibud' Vesegonsk*), he manages to name the place (a real town in the Tver region) while depriving this name of its power to denote specificity (cf. when a character in *Uncle Vanya* speaks disparagingly of life "in *some* Kharkov or Kursk").[95] Likewise the (imaginary) setting of *Brothers Karamazov* has a name (Skotoprigonevsk), but it is no more specifically characterized than *Demons'* Town of N; each place is exhausted by its averageness. Skotoprigonevsk's location is vague and its toponyms are along the lines of "Big Street" and "Market Square": compare this to the astonishing level of topographic specificity we find in *Crime and Punishment*'s Petersburg.[96]

In fact, if English writers spent much of the nineteenth century imagining a detailed picture of the British Isles (what Edward Said calls "a picture of England—socially, politically, morally charted and differentiated in immensely fine detail"—in which the nation's space was "surveyed, evaluated, made known"),[97] this is precisely what Russian literature by and large was *not* doing: it was not much engaged in imagining European Russia's regions in their distinctiveness and particularity. Whereas in Austen's *Mansfield Park* we have the gritty specificity of Portsmouth (its shipping economy, its naval jargon, etc.), in *Dead Souls* we have the anonymous Town of N, a place defined by what it lacks and what it is not. One result of this pattern is that in semiotic terms, the difference between something that happens in Ryazan and something that happens in Tver is likely to be minimal, simply because the differences between Russia's regions are dwarfed by the difference between capital and province—a distinction so fundamental and with such determinative power that the provinces tend to collapse, semiotically, into the "not-capital."

It is worth noting that what we might take to be a surreal insistence on the homogeneity of Russian provincial towns (Sollogub's "the same, the same, the same") at times reflects a certain material reality—the striking architectural and institutional uniformity that was the result of autocratic interventions. Beginning in Peter's reign and intensifying under Catherine, the central state issued a series of urban planning decrees intended to regularize the appearance of Russian cities. Every town center, depending on its place in a clearly established hierarchy, was required to contain the same combination of public buildings.[98] With rules aimed at standardizing everything from the number of rooms in a vice-governor's house to the angle at which structures should face the street and the number of windows each should possess, the autocracy sought to ensure that provincial cities were—or rather, looked—rational, orderly, regular, symmetrical, and permanent.[99] Of course, as often as not, these plans were not realized. When Nikolai I visited Nizhnii Novgorod in 1834, for instance, he was horrified to find that the city, with its houses jutting out into the streets at irregular intervals, did not look at all the way he thought a city should look.[100] But in theory a deviation from the plan constituted a failure. And so much effort did the state devote to regulating building exteriors that a significant portion of provincial police resources went to enforcing façade laws, all in an attempt to achieve an approximation of urban grandeur, or *paradnost'*.[101]

The ultimate goal of such interventions, as Smith-Peter explains, was to render the empire's population "more legible to the center": since the autocracy "prized order and legibility across space," it aimed to "reproduce a series of [identical] institutions, buildings, and social groups across the empire."[102] Again, as scholars have noted, the effort was often futile.[103] But the state persisted. Under Catherine all Russian cities were even ranked by law, and all cities were supposed to model themselves on cities the next level up. Thus a city like Tver became a model provincial city by looking like Petersburg, and other smaller cities were expected to pattern their replanning efforts after Tver's example. The ideal was explicitly European: provincial cities were supposed to try to look like Petersburg, which looked, or aimed to look, like Europe: we see as much when, for instance, Dolgorukov describes an architectural ensemble at the center of Poltava as a pathetic attempt to "make a miniature Petersburg."[104]

Backwardness, Modernity, and Imitation

To be provincial is to be in some sense behind, and you can only be behind if you inhabit a social world that believes in progress, fashion, the march of enlightenment, etc. In fact, as the expression "provincial backwardness" (*provintsial'naia otstalost'*) suggests, these two categories have long been closely linked: they took shape at roughly the same time in the eighteenth century, when Russian elites were embracing progress and capital-H History as ideals.[105] The story of Russia's anxiety about provinciality is the story of its desire to be modern and Western (two terms that have often been taken to mean the same thing). However, provinciality did not carry precisely the same meaning in eighteenth-century Russian culture as it came to do in the nineteenth.

Eighteenth-century belles lettres often represented the countryside—or more precisely, the landowner (*pomeshchik, dvorianin*)—as dreadfully retrograde, worthy of ridicule, and in desperate need of reform.[106] Indeed, after the nobility was "emancipated" from obligatory state service (a change that is usually dated to 1762, though the process began earlier), the at-loose-ends nobleman could be figured as a "problem" (much as "the peasant" and "the woman" would be in the nineteenth century), and thus he became an object of particular fascination. Clearly eighteenth-century writers took a keen interest in exposing the brutishness of rural gentry life: we recall Kantemir's hunting-obsessed noblemen, Novikov's corrupt judges, Radishchev's serf-masters, and Fonvizin's illiterate landowners.[107] But generally the setting of their exposés was an estate or village, not a town or provincial city. And again, the main target was less a place than it was the benighted rural nobleman himself, a figure in whom all that was supposedly rotten and archaic could be conveniently encapsulated and offered up for remediation.[108] For instance in a text like Novikov's 1772 "Letter of a Local Landowner to his Son" ("Pis'mo uezdnogo dvorianina k ego synu"), the crude, cruel landowner's low level of culture seems practically to cry out for the interventions of the modernizing state.[109]

While there is some connection between these satirical depictions of rural nobility and the later images of *provintsiia* that are the subject of this book, the tropes differ in fundamental ways: perhaps most importantly, while the landowners of eighteenth-century literature are certainly behind the times, a key point of that era's literature is that they need only follow the lead of the center in order to move ahead, toward modernization and enlightenment. In another entry in Novikov's epistolary series, for instance, a rural judge demands that his nephew abandon his studies in the capital and return home to join the family business of cheating petitioners.[110] But the young man simply refuses: by ascending the ladder of culture and civilization, he has effectively emancipated himself from rural ignorance. Similarly, in Fonvizin's *The Minor* (first staged in 1782), positive characters with strong connections to Moscow and Petersburg (e.g., Pravdin, whose name associates him with truth) point unmistakably toward the future enlightenment of Russia's primitive outback.

But in later representations of *provintsiia*, as we will see, such a clear path out of provincial backwardness is rarely available. This is so because in the nineteenth-century literary imagination, the provinces are not *simply* behind: they are stuck in a kind of jumbled-up a-chronology, not even located along the same timeline as the capitals and the West. Time in this version of *provintsiia* is time as Turgenev imagines it in *Fathers and Sons'* quintessentially provincial Town of N, a place that burns to the ground twice every decade and must be rebuilt from scratch ("it is a well-known fact that our provincial towns burn down every five years," Turgenev says).[111] Under such circumstances there is little possibility of any straight line of historical development; there is, rather, a confused relationship to nearly all normative periodizations, a hodgepodge temporality characterized by spasmodic and abortive attempts at forward movement and up-to-date "culture." Thus Melnikov's provincial merchant's living room will display a stuffed parrot alongside a bust of Voltaire, and a small-town intellectual like Kukshina in *Fathers and Sons* will throw together embryology and James Fenimore Cooper in one breathless exclamation.[112]

Indeed Turgenev insists elsewhere that even the most sophisticated and Europeanized Russians will remain provincial. In *Smoke*, for instance, Russian expatriates in Baden may be well-educated, well-off, and well-informed, but they utterly fail to become "modern" in any coherent or convincing way. Rather, the harder these characters try to "catch up"—with the result that their conversations in *Smoke* jump directly from the Aeginetan marbles to peasant communes and Harriet Beecher Stowe[113]—the more disordered their relationship to progress and history. In other words, nineteenth-century provincials are not straightforwardly behind the times in the way that Fonvizin's or Novikov's are; rather, they stand in a strangely oblique relationship to the timeline itself.

If such characters are constantly at pains to demonstrate their own up-to-dateness, it is because they sense the link between being nonprovincial and being modern. As a phenomenon of modernity, provinciality is bound up not only with modern forms of government (like centralized control and bureaucratization), but also with modern forms of consumption, economic exchange, entertainment, artistic trends, etc. As new forms of communication and circulation allow ideas and fashions to impose themselves on outlying areas, capitals consolidate what French sociologist (and provincial) Gabriel Tarde called their "imperious fascination . . . over a vast territory": Paris "reigns royally, orientally, over the provinces," according to Tarde, precisely because "every day, by telegraph or train, it sends into all of France its ideas, its wishes, its conversations, its ready-made revolutions, its ready-made clothing and furniture."[114]

In nineteenth-century Russia we see the same link Tarde describes between print culture, new forms of consumption, and provincial imitation. As early as Somov's *A Novel in Two Letters* (1831), a narrator from the capital not only disparages the locals' clothing, accents, and mannerisms, but declares that these people had been doomed to "ugly imitation" from the moment they adopted fashions "being spread about the provinces by Moscow journals."[115] In *Dead Souls*, the Pleasant Ladies of N know to pay close attention to the dress styles made available to them in the form of journal illustrations and sewing patterns from the capitals.

Clearly, being provincial means one is trying (and usually failing) to keep up with some external standard; it means being subject to judgment from the outside, and internalizing that judgment as part of your identity (again, in a way that peasants are not and do not). And imitation on the periphery is desperately serious because attaining to fashionability is no trivial concern: as Pascale Casanova writes, and as Tarde understood quite clearly, fashion constitutes "one of the main routes of access to modernity."[116] Indeed one might extend Casanova's remark on provincial writers—"to be decreed 'modern' is one of the most difficult forms of recognition for writers outside the center"—to provincials in general.[117]

Ideals imposed or borrowed from outside are often imperfectly understood; hence the strenuous effort with which provincials are obliged to approach fashion. And since fashion is a phenomenon based on the dissemination and imitation of *changing* patterns, provincials also sense that conforming to the capital's ready-made but never-constant models demands constant vigilance. But this effort and vigilance must be concealed—because the successful deployment of fashion requires that copying be denied and obscured (in today's language, being fashionable is supposed to look like "being yourself"). As a result, fashion and manners become ideal ways of exposing and shaming provinciality, because in *provintsiia* the labor involved in reproducing models imported from the capital can never be rendered sufficiently invisible: and as Bourdieu writes, the only legitimate relation to culture is "[that] which least bears the visible marks of its genesis."[118] Such a relation is unavailable to provincials, who are therefore denied "the privilege of indifference to their own manner," the kind of indifference that can be represented, as we will see in the case of Pushkin's Tatiana, as having no manner at all.[119] Hence the provincial's—and perhaps the Russian's—insuperable problem: imitation is unavoidable, but imitation requires effort, and effort precludes naturalness, and naturalness is essential to authenticity.

Illegibility and Mismeasuring

The state wants regularity and symmetry, unmistakable evidence that Enlightenment values are working to structure the unstructured life of the provincial outback—but literary representation instead highlights the provinces' disorder, filth, and incoherence. Literature dwells on the provinces' pervasive *un*intelligibility, as when Shchedrin describes the (imaginary) town of Glupov as "more a disordered pile of huts than a city," with "no clear central point," "streets running all over crookedly here and there," "houses spread out any which way."[120] Almost any description of a provincial place will register filth and chaos (mud and dust, decrepit buildings, sidewalks full of holes); the words *griaz'* and *boloto*, dirt and swamp, recur constantly. *Provintsiia* is a "mire of triviality" (*tina melochei*) where one is liable to "drown" in filth, as Shchedrin writes in his *Provincial Sketches* (1856–57).[121] Insisting, as many do, on the provinces' power to rot and defile, Shchedrin continues, "Oh provinces, you corrupt people!" (*o provintsiia, ty rasstlevaesh' liudei!*).[122] Here he echoes Herzen's words of a generation earlier from *Who Is to Blame?*: "Nothing on earth can rot [*portit*] a man like life in the provinces."[123]

Literature represents provincial attempts at culture as jumbled, inappropriate, mongrelized. When a character like Turgenev's Kukshina speaks of George Sand, German chemists, and Ralph Waldo Emerson in one breathless paragraph, her ideas signal the same *radical indiscriminateness* that characterizes the physical objects on Manilov's estate in *Dead Souls*, where a ramshackle "Temple for Solitary Meditation" is surrounded by peasants' log huts.[124] This is the disorienting ad hoc quality Dolgorukov is reacting to when he describes everything in Poltava as "not suited to the place, poor, low, and as the French say, *mesquin*."[125] As readers we react similarly when faced with, say, the mystifying street signs in *Dead Souls'* Town of N ("Foreigner Vasilii Fedorov," "Here Is The Establishment"), as well as myriad other examples of semiotic chaos that confront us in the provinces.

Sometimes literature gives us a version of provincial culture characterized by painful meagerness and constraint (as in Turgenev's "Hamlet of Shchigrov"), sometimes a culture steeped in excess and vulgarity (as in Chekhov's stories about provincial new money). But in all cases provincial society and taste are as discordant as the built environment, a fact highlighted in frequent descriptions of balls and other social gatherings that aim to be upscale but are in fact notable only for the varieties of confusion manifest in the party-goers' social status, manners, and dress. "My God, who wasn't there?" asks the dismayed Prince Dolgorukov after a banquet.[126] Culture in the provinces is always marked by a sense that ideas and objects have been appropriated without any understanding of their meanings or relationships. When Sollogub's *Tarantas* reproduces the menu from a grubby inn (a list of dishes rendered incomprehensible by francophone pretensions), or when Herzen's *Who Is to Blame?* describes how schoolchildren in a small-town gymnasium are made to chant in garbled "Celtic-Slavonic" or "Franco-ecclesiastical dialect,"[127] both are highlighting the fact that culture in provincial places is deformed by its struggle to imitate cultural models that are incommensurate with the locals' own history and abilities.

Indeed a key feature of *provintsiia* in literature would seem to be precisely the dissonance between grandiose claims and shabby realities. As we see in the ever-present tension between the state's imperfectly imposed ideals and the provincial town's messy, intractable facts, in *provintsiia* the disparity between intention and practice is hard to conceal—and such disparities command the rapt gaze of the artist, especially the novelist. *Provintsiia* allows artists to highlight and examine these incongruities, whether they reside in jarring juxtaposition (like an arbor next to log huts) or within one strange object (like the elaborately pointless "beaded pocket-case for holding a toothpick" given to Manilov by his wife). This juxtaposition of (pompous) ambition and abject (but heroically unacknowledged) failure to fulfill such ambition underlies, for instance, the passage in *Dead Souls* when Gogol tells us that the motley ball-goers all appear to be saying, "No, this is not the provinces, this is the capital, this is Paris itself!"[128]

In a practical sense, provincial incongruities stem from a critical absence of scale—a deficiency born of the fact that real life in the provinces affords few opportunities for developing standards of comparison (as we will see in chapter 5). In the paradigmatic European novel of a young provincial's education/ disillusionment in the capital, Balzac's *Lost Illusions*, the point is made explicitly: "In the provinces there is no question of choice or comparison," Balzac writes, whereas in Paris, "one learns, *one compares*."[129] The idea that the ability to draw subtle comparisons is a necessary (but not, one assumes, sufficient) corrective to provincialism recalls T. S. Eliot's essay "What is a Classic?" in which he declares, "By 'provincial' I mean here something more than I find in the dictionary definitions. . . . I mean also a distortion of values, the exclusion of some, the exaggeration of others, which springs, not from lack of wide geographical perambulation, but from *applying standards acquired within a limited area, to the whole of human experience.*" The result is a sensibility that "confounds the contingent with the essential, the ephemeral with the permanent."[130]

For Eliot provincialism is not necessarily geographically conditioned, but for him as for Balzac (and for Goncharov, Belinsky, and certain other Russians, as we will see), it springs from an inability to weigh one idea against another. In the absence of comparison, Eliot emphasizes, there can be no standards, no correct proportion: "Without the constant application of the classical *measure*, we tend to become provincial."[131] He assumes that there exists a clear set of standards that can offer salvation from provinciality, which for him is another word for cultural distortion ("the decay of a common belief and a common culture") that results from isolation, whether geographic or temporal. (Beyond that the most precise definition Eliot can offer of the provincial is that it is the opposite of the classical, and the classical is that without which "we tend to become provincial"—as I have noted elsewhere, attempts to define what is "provincial" almost always focus on what it is not.)[132]

If you are located on some sort of periphery (whether of geography, class, or "civilization") and are worried about provincialism, you are likely be focused on standards and measurements. For Eliot—that English writer and British subject from St. Louis, Missouri—such standards are embodied by Virgil, whom he identifies as the ultimate nonprovincial, "the classic of all Europe." Virgil is "both Roman and European," never beholden to "some *purely local . . .* code of manners."[133] As this statement makes clear, for Eliot as for a Russian critic like

Belinsky, the goal is universality. And not surprisingly, what universality really means is a version of Europeanness: as Belinsky put it in 1843, only "educated Europeans" possess the ability to be simultaneously "national" and "universal."[134] This equation of Europeanness with universality was what Dostoevsky would contest so bitterly, and it is what scholars of postcolonialism are still contesting today. But for traditions that had a shot at leaving provinciality behind and joining the club of European Civilization, a set of identifiable standards was to be welcomed.

Standards and measures here mean something very different from the provincial's nervous sidelong glance toward a dominant culture that demands slavish emulation. Rather, Eliot's definition of the measuring that can save a culture from provinciality implies a confident, virtually unconscious awareness that one has access to a wide but defined range of aesthetic and intellectual choices, and an implicit understanding that these choices all signify differently. This is the "maturity of mind" that Eliot says "needs history, and the consciousness of history"; and "with [this] maturity of mind," he claims, are "associated maturity of manners and absence of provinciality."[135] By contrast, the provincial's version of comparing—always asking, am I getting it right?—helps explain why artistic originality and innovation rarely reach full flower in provincial places (though they may *originate* there in some sense). If you are straining to conform to an external standard that seems to exist chiefly to pass judgment on you, you are unlikely to do much that is *intentionally* new or strange;[136] or rather, you are unlikely to be able to master newness and strangeness and turn them to your advantage.

This, as I will argue, is what is so remarkable about Gogol, and by extension about much of the Russian canon: Russian writers learned to make conscious and highly sophisticated use of the disproportions that attend provinciality. Gogol's world, in particular, is marked by the same distortions of scale and the same unnaturalness that afflict provincials, who are forever mis-measuring and forever trying too hard. But even as the Gogolian world does exactly what Eliot accuses provincials of doing—"[confounding] the contingent with the essential, the ephemeral with the permanent"—Gogol himself is never provincial in Eliot's terms. Or perhaps more accurately, Gogol's work and the tradition it helped to nurture remind us that views like Eliot's are by no means the last word on the phenomenon of provinciality—and as such they invite us to reconsider what it might mean to be provincial.

Although Russian literature has often depicted provinciality as the tastelessness or philistinism or backwardness of provincial Others, things provincial have always implied hard questions about the nation as a whole—which helps explain why the provinces, in all their overdetermined tedium, exercise such fascination over Russian writers. In a tradition that has constantly compared itself to a Western European standard, provinciality represents a far more serious threat to a positive view of the nation than it does elsewhere. In France, for instance, once you make it to Paris, you may fail or be disillusioned (witness Balzac's *Lost Illusions*), but at least you stand a chance of freeing yourself from provincial taint. Even more important, Paris itself will forever remain as the true, the undeniably central metropolis—the capital of the nineteenth century, in Walter Benjamin's formulation, and a very real standard to which one may aspire and which one may perhaps attain.[137] But in Russia, as we will see, the capital can be far more elusive.

And in any case, even making it to Moscow or Petersburg is no guarantee of transcending one's provinciality, because the Russian capitals, always trying to catch up to and imitate the West, may prove to be no less provincial than the provinces in comparison to the real center—that is, Europe. Given this anxiety—the worry that the relationship between capital and province might recapitulate the relationship between Western Europe and Russia—*provintsiia* assumes its role in Russia's cultural imaginary less because of its own intrinsic qualities than because of Russia's conception of itself as a whole. The provinces can provoke horror and revulsion not because they are different from the capitals, but because they might be the *same*—peripheral, backward, imitative, and inauthentic.

· CHAPTER TWO ·

Before the Provinces: Pastoral and Anti-Pastoral in Pushkin's Countryside

Однако вкус был, на манер столичный,
Во всём фасаде сохранён отличный.

And yet the capital's fine taste
Was clear throughout the manor's face.

—A. Fet, 1856

Pushkin's provinces are simply not provincial in the sense that later writers' are. And while his vision of Russian space was to resonate powerfully with certain writers (such as Tolstoy and Aksakov) who resisted the capital/provinces binary, in a book about peripheral places, Pushkin must be shifted a bit toward the margins. Among his most famous settings—most notably the Larins' countryside home in *Eugene Onegin*—are cozy estates and villages, places that are limited and behind the times but also culturally coherent and authentic, often presented with warm humor. Such places have nothing to do with the overdetermined emptiness that will characterize *Dead Souls'* Town of N. For my purposes, Pushkin's vision of the provinces—the *Onegin* version—serves mostly to emphasize the inventedness of the *provintsiia* trope that we see elsewhere. Indeed much of the present chapter focuses on spaces that could *later* be marked, in works by other writers, as provincial in the new sense of derivative, culturally barren, and homogeneous. These are qualities we will see foreshadowed in Pushkin's work only very occasionally: instead, in Pushkin's world, provincial places are more likely to be the site of a homey and reassuringly authentic Russianness, frequently tinged with affectionate irony.

Rarely does Pushkin turn his attention to the provincial capital (*gubernskii gorod*), a setting that for later writers will often serve as a prime locus of negative provinciality. And his representation of the imperial borderlands, as I explain below, is outside this study's purview: for my purposes, texts like the Southern poems are noteworthy mostly for the illuminating contrast they present with the *provintsiia* trope, since the exoticness of the Southern poems' settings helps make visible the dull nativeness of the provinces' decidedly *non*-exotic *near*-periphery. The main settings of Pushkin's provincial geography are countryside and village (*derevnia*), gentry estate, district town (*uezdnyi gorod*), and the steppes. This chapter analyzes how these places figure in *Eugene Onegin* (1825–32), "A History of the Village of Goriukhino" (1830), and *The Captain's Daughter* (1836).

As it appears in *Eugene Onegin*, the village or countryside is the repository of an intact, authentic culture that is at once local and emphatically Russian. *Derevnia* is also the setting of the parodic (and unfinished) story "History of the Village of Goriukhino"; in fact, on an imaginary map of Russia we might locate Goriukhino not far from the Larins' estate.[1] But Goriukhino is altogether lacking in the meaningfulness, order, and authenticity embodied in Tatiana's estate-world. Instead, Goriukhino's comical incoherence—both spatial and temporal—and its messy, meager culture begin to anticipate what *provintsiia* will signify for other writers in decades to come. *The Captain's Daughter*, in contrast to these texts, is set in the liminal environment of the steppe, a space that was, in Pushkin's day, symbolically situated somewhere between exotic foreignness and familiar Russianness. In fact *The Captain's Daughter* is about the process of transforming the wild steppes into the familiar provinces—the ongoing cultural work of imagining this territory as an integral part of "European" Russia.[2] And the liminal space of the steppe, as we will see, was where Russians confronted most dramatically the conceptual challenge posed by a *contiguous* empire.

In contrast to the steppe—an almost-but-not-quite-Russian space that elites tended to experience neither as homeland nor as colorful periphery—the empire's borderlands were clearly marked as exotic (and thus in the Romantic period they provided Russian writers with material that was thought to merit attention to local detail). As such they are not addressed here. Even though Pushkin famously honed his poetic talents in a version of the "Orient" (an East that in his case was actually the South, the setting of the "Southern Poems"), his treatment of such places has little to do with this book's topic, precisely because these places are not "the provinces." In works such as *The Fountain of Bakhchisarai*, *The Prisoner of the Caucasus*, and *Journey to Erezrum*, the emphatically non-Russian nature of the geographic setting is key. In some of these works the imperial periphery is represented as forbidding and masculine (*The Prisoner of the Caucasus*); in others, it is yielding and feminine, with borders vulnerable to the depredations of Orientalized outsiders (*The Fountain of Bakhchisarai*). But in any case, when reading these texts we always know ourselves to be somewhere other than "Russia proper."[3]

A great deal of sophisticated scholarship has explored how the metaphorical East provided a space where the nineteenth-century (male) poet could go to shake off ennui, experience awe upon seeing dramatic landscapes, indulge in passions proscribed at home, reflect on what might be lost by those who become civilized, and generally enjoy being "free" (because what happens in the Caucasus stays in the Caucasus).[4] This body of scholarship has done much to illuminate the relationship between Pushkin's poetics and Russian empire, but it has had far less to say about the more native geography that this chapter aims to illuminate.

Eugene Onegin: Province as Idyll, Culture as Nature

The Larin family's home and its surroundings epitomize a certain literary version of Russian rural life—*derevnia* as pastoral or idyll. As I explain in chapter 1, *derevnia*—like *glush'*, a word evoking a remote but sometimes cozy rural spot—usually signifies not *provintsiia* as the word will be understood for most of the nineteenth century (and beyond), but rather the countryside, the village, even the estate (indeed at times vocabulary like *derevnia* and *glush'* can facilitate a convenient blurring of such categories).[5] This version of *derevnia* may evoke isolation and drowsiness, but not, as will be clear in *Eugene Onegin*, the shamefully subordinate forms of cultural derivativeness that would later be so strongly associated with *provintsiia*.

Instead *Onegin* draws on a recurring topos of Russian Sentimentalism and Romanticism, movements that in the late eighteenth and early nineteenth centuries produced a number of paeans to small-town and small-estate ways. In writers ranging from Andrei Bolotov (along with others who "retreated" to their estates in search of a contemplative life) to Nikolai Polevoi (who wrote romanticized descriptions of village life as a model of social harmony), we note a departure from the earlier eighteenth century's straightforward vilification of rural backwardness, of the kind seen in writers like Novikov and Fonvizin.[6] The roots of these newly positive depictions of nonurban Russia are likely traceable to the Sentimental and Romantic ideas exemplified in a text like Karamzin's (Rousseauistic) *Poor Liza*. It is also worth noting, though, that the new focus on rural patriarchal virtues may have been encouraged by the Russian gentry's real-life desire to construct for itself a more positive and autonomous group identity: hence various efforts to represent their abodes as the "real" Russia.[7] In any case, this essentially positive vision of the Russian provinces—on which *Onegin* draws—is neither riddled with vices (à la

Novikov) nor ridiculously gauche and incoherent (as in the later trope that is this book's main topic). Instead we might characterize Pushkin's *provintsiia* as charmingly patriarchal.

Certainly at the Larins' estate we know ourselves to be in a markedly authentic and Russian place. While there is little in *Onegin* to indicate precisely where the family property is located, Nabokov places it "two hundred miles W of Moscow." Of course its geographic location is of minimal significance: the important thing is that this section of *Onegin* is essentially a pastoral, related to the classical pastoral but set in an explicitly Russian version of the countryside. (Nabokov concedes as much: even after having located the setting "between parallels 56 and 57," he allows that it is also "encroaching here and there upon Arcadia.")[8] Since the aim of pastorals and idylls is to "[oppose] simple to complicated life, to the advantage of the former,"[9] the countryside always takes on meaning in opposition to a larger "outside" world: thus *Onegin* does not open in the village (just as Goncharov's *Oblomov* will not open in Oblomovka), but in the metropole, in a chapter showcasing Petersburg's worldliness. And Eugene's sophistication derives above all from his close attention to the capital's ever-changing fashions. Artifice and foreignness, theatricality and keeping up—these are the influences that shape Eugene's pastimes, his intellectual life, his friendships, his love affairs, his meals, his toilette. Only after seeing the thoroughly modern Petersburg dandy in his element do we travel with him to the countryside.[10] As a result, even when we are in Tatiana's *derevnia*, we remain aware of the capital and the gaze it trains on outsiders—thereby bearing out Raymond Williams' point that only city people can write idylls.

Literature generally represents places like the Larins' home as always already lost (like Oblomovka) or in the process of disappearing, simply because such places cannot be represented by those who still live there.[11] Everything in Tatiana's environment, from her nanny's folk culture to the peasant girls' songs to Mme. Larina's taste for eighteenth-century novels, is vaguely associated with a past that has been lost to more up-to-date Russians in Pushkin's time. In place of development, change, and fashion, the idyllic chronotope emphasizes what is iterative and cyclical: in Bakhtin's analysis, "idyllic life and its events are inseparable from . . . [a little] corner of the world where the fathers and grandfathers lived and where one's children and their children will live."[12] These are apt descriptions of country life as it is depicted in *Onegin*, which emphasizes the continuity of rural ways. Here even houseguests conform to eternal types (fatty, fop, rogue, glutton), and the mazurka is still danced with a vigor that the capitals long ago rejected in favor of refined attenuation. *Derevnia* is above all a place "unaltered by that tyrant, fashion" (6:115); it is the locus of a supposedly eternal folk culture that is precisely the opposite of ever-changing fashions. Thus if the provincial ball in *Dead Souls* will showcase the inept copying of the capital's taste, in *Onegin* it preserves the *real* mazurka: one version of the provinces is where culture is degraded, the other where it is preserved.

A self-sufficient world, with its own intact and relatively rich culture, the Larins' *derevnia* is *authentic*. It is therefore unselfconscious, and Pushkin's narrator invites us to be highly conscious of this unselfconsciousness. In fact the sections devoted to the Larins' country life (especially chapters three and five) are primarily a celebration of this authenticity—a "simple Russian family" (6:51) eating simple Russian food, following simple Russian folkways (name day parties, fortune-telling, etc.). The countryside serves as an archive of Russianness, and it offers those in the capitals the possibility of "return": Tania's mother, originally a coquette from Moscow, has long ago forgotten her spoken French and given herself over to the local ways preserved in *derevnia*.

In literature this "authentic" version of estate life is very often construed as a remembered phenomenon, whether explicitly (the adult Oblomov lies on his couch in Petersburg and dreams of his long-ago childhood in Oblomovka) or implicitly (the Larins' way of life feels as marked by past-ness as do the reading habits of Larina-*mère*, who favors eighteenth-century sentimental fiction). Certainly the typical life trajectory of a well-off nobleman—early years on a country estate followed by education and work in the capitals, where the provincial arrives "always in the role of pupil"—encouraged a strong association between estate, childhood, and memory.[13] And it is important to note that such an association held only for *derevnia* life, not for provincial cities.

Of course Tania herself, despite her taste for French novels, is all Russian all the time; even her love for winter, we are told, is attributable to her "Russian soul" (6:98). Our belief in the Larins' paradigmatic Russianness requires us to accept the premise that there exists an implicit unity between the traditional gentry and the peasantry, that they share a similar "folk" culture. Compared to, say, a landowner like *Dead Souls'* Manilov or a Town of N dweller like Stepan Trofimovich in Dostoevsky's *Demons*—both of whom are entirely cut off from local, peasant culture—the Larins are meant to have a great deal in common with the common people. Tatiana's instinctive love for the countryside around her family's home reinforces this message, particularly in the long, fond good-bye preceding her departure (6:151ff). Indeed her love of nature is perhaps the most important mark of her Russianness, just as Eugene's indifference to it marks him as a troublesome outsider.[14]

Yet even as Pushkin insists that Tatiana is nothing if not Russian, we sense that her authenticity and naturalness are not entirely uncomplicated. A prime locus of her Russianness, for instance, is her family's *English* garden (*angliiskii sad*, the usual term for the "natural" landscape design that by Catherine's day had begun to replace the French formal style).[15] By Pushkin's time these gardens had come to reflect something of the dilemma faced by a generation of nobles torn between the imported aesthetic that shaped their tastes and the Romantic age's imperative to "be Russian."[16] The Europeanized Russian nobleman was unlikely to feel at home in rural Russia, where life on his estate often felt anything but natural (a phenomenon I discuss in chapter 1): thus gardens on grand estates were walled enclaves, off-limits to most serfs and deliberately isolated from the surrounding countryside, full of objects and structures (e.g., gothic ruins) that were "in the Russian context . . . doubly foreign."[17] The English garden in Russia, especially in its grander manifestations, was quite obviously nature in quotation marks.

Onegin does not reflect this reality.[18] Not only does Pushkin emphasize the Larin garden's coziness and intimate scale (for example, diminutives like mostik, luzhok, and lesok—little bridge, little pond, little forest—make it clear that this is not the vast, impressive park of a grandee, 6:71),[19] he draws no distinction between this space and the surrounding countryside. There is no hint of any barrier between the family's little angliiskii sad and the "peaceful valleys," "familiar forests," and "cheerful nature" with which Tatiana communes. Thus Onegin finesses the problem of (un)naturalness, allowing the "native virtues" exemplified by Tatiana and her (English) garden to stand as simply natural—as the pastoral mode requires. Of course, sustaining a pastoral vision requires that labor be either aestheticized or hidden:[20] Pushkin suggests as much in Onegin by informing us that the Larins' serf girls are required to sing as they pick berries, lest it occur to them to eat the fruits of their labors (a rule that implies "a certain unpastoral paranoia" on the part of the landowner).[21] This moment undermines Onegin's fantasy of derevnia as an unproblematically capacious category, not only encompassing gentry estate, garden, village, farmland, and uncultivated countryside, but also magically eliding the economic divisions among these categories.

A somewhat less idealized version of rural reality does make itself felt here and there in Onegin. Lensky's grave—which at first conforms adequately to pastoral convention (babbling brook, ploughman, shady nook)—soon gives way to a much less Romantic reality (dead wreath, weeds, and a bedraggled shepherd plaiting bast shoes [6:142]). And in the excised chapter detailing "Onegin's Journey," a stanza picturing Russian rural life stands in marked contrast to those describing more exotic locales. Here Pushkin gives us a pointedly anti-pastoral description of the village: broken gate, grey sky, cabbage soup, balalaika, and drunken peasants (6:200–201). Strikingly similar images, including threshing floors and drunken peasants dancing, recur in Lermontov's oft-quoted 1841 lyric "Rodina" (Motherland), which describes the poet's response to a peasant village: both Pushkin and Lermontov are probing the contrast between Russian reality and idyllic fantasy.

"Onegin's Journey" suggests anxieties—largely repressed in the work as a whole, as we have seen—that are almost inevitably present beneath the surface of Russian pastoral. This is the same tension Pushkin hints at, but does not fully develop, in his punning epigraph to chapter two, where Horace's Latin "O rus!" (roughly, "Oh countryside!"; footnoted in some Russian editions as "O derevnia!") is translated as "O Rus'!" (i.e., Oh Russia!, 6:31). And indeed it is the same dissonance that would be experienced by any sophisticated landowner returning to rural Russia, whether from state service or the capitals or abroad, with visions of settling down to a pastoral life.[22] The most basic requirement for conceiving of pastoral—*distance* from the countryside, as noted above—creates problems for the "returning" Russian landowner: the reality he faces is unlikely to be compatible with the pastoral ideal. Thus it is in such fleeting moments of failed pastoral that we can discern in *Onegin*—but just barely, and just maybe—a hint of what would later become the *provintsiia* of Gogol's estates in *Dead Souls*. Such passages hint at Russian pastoral's capacity to "veer easily into the realm of the squalid and the mundane, or even into the realm of nightmare."[23]

Since Tatiana, effortless and "natural," stands for the authenticity of *derevnia*, we might expect Eugene to embody a kind of provincialism, given the manifestly derivative nature of his thought and taste. Indeed, upon uncovering Eugene's "sources" (Byron, Napoleon, etc.), Tatiana wonders if he is nothing but "an imitation, a trivial phantom, a Muscovite in Childe Harold's cloak" (6:146–49)—questions that are never answered. But even if the answer is yes, there is no blaming geography. If Eugene's thinking is derivative, this lack of originality is attributable not to the provinces, but to his light-weight (Petersburg) education and his lazy tendency to "make others' thoughts his own" (6:23). If Eugene is bored in the countryside, this is not because the countryside is boring: he was equally bored in the city (6:28).

In the end Eugene's life on his estate has nothing in common with the cultural incoherence and attenuation of Gogolian *provintsiia*. Instead everything about him testifies to a thoroughly portable cultural *stolichnost'* ("capitalness"): where Eugene is, there is the capital—for better or worse. Just as the Larins' version of *derevnia* is inextricably linked with the peasant culture of the village, so is Eugene's linked with that of the capital. Because *stolichnost'* is portable in *Onegin*, the text is able to imagine a prosperous, sophisticated nobleman's estate serving as "the image of true civilization and social cultivation" in the provinces (as British country houses were supposed to do),[24] or as what Pushkin called the nobleman's "study" (his *kabinet* [8:52], an "ideal locus of intellectual, spiritual, and artistic development").[25] Such an estate could convincingly represent itself as the self-sufficient center of its own universe—"a closed model of the world," with "its own space and time, its own system of values, its own 'etiquette' and norms of behavior," as one critic describes the ideal Russian *usad'ba*. Here the whole world can be "seen from the manor house window" (to quote again a description of Afanasy Fet's poetry); the estate is both center and commanding point of view.[26]

And in such a scenario the estate is the mirror, not the antithesis, of the capital: both claim to bring together everything good the world had to offer, creating an environment where good taste can find comfortable, unstrained, even automatic expression. We see this possibility manifested in the serene tastefulness and dignity of Eugene's manor house, which was built in accordance with a stable canon of taste that was both "simple" (an elusive quality, as I will discuss) and entirely Russian, down to the portraits of tsars on the walls:

> Почтенный замок был построен,
> Как замки строиться должны:
> Отменно прочен и спокоен
> Во вкусе умной старины.
> В гостиной штофные обои,
> Царей портреты на стенах . . .
> (6:31)

> The ancient manse had been erected
> For placid comfort—and to last;
> And all its solid form reflected
> The sense and taste of ages past.
> Throughout the house the ceilings towered;
> From walls ancestral portraits glowered . . .[27]

Pushkin's description here recalls Fet's 1856 *poema* "Two Lindens," in which the severe façade of a patriarchal manor house exemplifies "the taste of the capital."[28] This self-confident air of *comme il faut* could not be further removed from the cultural mishmash and insecurity that mark the estates of provincial imitators like Gogol's Manilov. Eugene may be affected (indeed by chapter eight, Petersburg's high society asks mockingly what role he'll play today—perhaps "Childe Harold, or a Quaker?" [6:168]), but he appears to be supremely secure in all his affectations—and without *anxious* imitation, there is no *provintsial'nost'*. Nabokov suggests as much in his commentary on *Onegin* when he quotes Edward Bulwer-Lytton's 1828 novel *Pelham*, in which one Lady Frances admonishes her son, "Whatever is *evidently* borrowed becomes vulgar," whereas "*original* affectation is sometimes good *ton*."[29]

What we might call Eugene's masterful affectation has something in common with the truly complicated "simplicity" that Tatiana achieves in Petersburg high society. At the Larin family's modest country estate, it is not difficult to convince us that Tatiana is effortlessness incarnate: firmly embedded in folkways and nature, making no attempt to conform to standards borrowed from the capital, at home she is predictably authentic. What is striking, though, is that she remains just as authentic after having reached the pinnacle of Petersburg's social world—a point that the text makes most insistently by lauding her naturalness and "simplicity" at a ball. Of course, the way one behaves at a ball is anything but natural: to comport oneself correctly—"naturally"—in this environment is the result of intense acculturation, requiring knowledge of myriad subtle conventions (which is why in later texts, the small-town ball would become an ideal showcase for displaying provincial ineptitude: already by 1840 Herzen would write, "the provincial ball has been described a thousand times").[30]

Tatiana's exemplary behavior reflects the same values as the Onegin stanza, combining formal intricacy with the appearance of ease and naturalness—a combination much admired by the social world that *Onegin* portrays. When Tatiana is reintroduced to us in Petersburg high society, she is first identified only as "a lady" entering a ballroom, seen through the eyes of the admiring crowd.

Она была неторопливa,
Не холодна, не говорлива,
Без взора наглого для всех,
Без притязаний на успех,
Без этих маленьких ужимок,
Без подражательных затей . . .
Все тихо, просто было в ней,
Она казалась верный снимок
Du comme il faut . . .) . . . (6:171)

She isn't hurried or obtrusive,
Is neither cold nor yet effusive;
She casts no brazen glance around
And makes no effort to astound
Or uses those sorts of affectation
And artifice that ladies share—
But shows a simple, quiet air.
She seems the very illustration
Du comme il faut . . .[31]

By praising his heroine's lack of "manner" in the voice of the crowd of socialites who observe her, Pushkin pays tribute to her "natural" grace while implicitly acknowledging its artfulness, thereby hinting that naturalness is an illusion sustainable only by those who can erase all traces of the effort that mastery costs.

Furthermore, in this passage where we might expect a description of Tatiana, we encounter instead a series of negations: the lady is *un*hurried, *not* cold, *not* chatty, *without* an arrogant demeanor, *without* pretension or ambition, *without* any little affected gestures, *without* imitative artifice. What, then, is she? She is "quiet" and "simple," apparently—but even these two terms suggest absence rather than presence. Finally, we are told that she is the epitome of a French expression—*comme il faut*—that the poet finds untranslatable. We already know that Tatiana's mysterious naturalness is closely linked with her Russianness, yet here we are told it can be described only in an untranslatable *French* expression. In the next stanza we find a similar reluctance to attribute positive qualities to the heroine, and another refusal to translate into Russian a word used to describe her:

Никто б не мог ее прекрасной
Назвать; но с головы до ног
Никто бы в ней найти не мог
Того, что модой самовластной
В высоком лондонском кругу
Зовется *vulgar*. . . . (6:172)

One couldn't label her a beauty;
But neither did her form contain,
From head to toe, the slightest strain
Of what, with fashion's sense of duty,
The London social sets decry
As *vulgar*. . . .[32]

No one could call her beautiful, Pushkin tells us, but "no one could find in her any trace of what London high society's autocratic fashion would call *vulgar*." Pushkin gives us "vulgar" in English, allowing it to stand as another untranslatable evocation (along with *comme il faut*) of Tatiana's *je ne sais quoi*.

In such passages we are again put on notice that Tatiana's simplicity is in fact strangely complicated. Her essence—authentic and Russian—remains impervious to any form of dilution or adulteration, even in the most Europeanized and "artificial" domains of Russia's highest society. And here we see the degree to which Tatiana's character reflects the aesthetic values of *Onegin* itself: even when she is described in foreign vocabulary (*comme il faut*), Tatiana is native; even when she imitates markedly conventional Sentimentalist fiction (her first letter to Eugene), she is sincere; even when walking in her English garden, she is Russian. By happily acknowledging Tatiana's acts of cultural adaptation and thus the complicated, hybrid nature of her (Russian) selfhood, Pushkin signals his own comfort with the many self-conscious and self-confident acts of literary borrowing, imitation, and bricolage that permeate *Eugene Onegin*—a text that is anything but anxious when it comes to its own mastery of cultural codes, *and thus anything but provincial.*

Pushkin's heroine too, whether in the countryside or at a high society ball, is the opposite of provincial, at least in the sense that this descriptor would come to be understood in the next decade or so. The qualities Tatiana lacks—artifice, affectation, imitativeness—are precisely those signs of effort that Russian writers would soon be using to signal their characters' provinciality. These are the signs of *trying*—and when it comes to manifesting the correct relationship to culture (whether culture in the sense of the highbrow or merely the conventions of polite society), to be seen as trying at all is to be trying too hard. If the marks of your labor remain visible, even getting it exactly right gets you nowhere. For instance, in Lermontov's *A Hero of Our Time*, Pechorin's déclassé rival Grushnitsky manages to look ridiculous—to look as if he is quite obviously making an effort—while wearing an ordinary greatcoat. But Pechorin's taste is so impeccable (or rather, so unimpeachable are the Petersburg credentials that underwrite this taste) that he looks "natural" even when decked out as an "ethnic" native: "on horseback in Circassian costume I look more like a Kabardian than many Kabardians themselves."[33] With these words Lermontov winks at us to confirm that Pechorin's naturalness is not *really* effortless (Pechorin does not claim to *be* more natural, but rather to *look* more natural—that is, "more like a Kabardian"),[34] but his act is authoritative enough to make Grushnitsky's unnaturalness that much more visible.

Like Pechorin, and quite unlike poor Grushnitsky, Tatiana attains to what her social world deems the only legitimate relation to culture, a relation that "least bears the visible marks of its genesis." The truly cultured individual will never reveal anything "studied" in his or her taste, instead "[manifesting] by ease and naturalness that true culture is nature." Thus Tania attains to what will always be out of reach for a provincial—"indifference to [her] own manner," an indifference that can be depicted as having no manner at all.[35]

"A History of the Village of Goriukhino": Life Outside of "Public Time"

"The district town has no history": Pushkin makes this declaration in his working notes to the unfinished manuscript titled "A History of the Village of Goriukhino" (8:719).[36] The parodic "Goriukhino" represents an attempt to write the history of a history-less place, and as such it comments on the comically strange shape, or non-shape, of (provincial) Russia's past, with its randomness and supposedly nonteleological character. The "Goriukhino" fragment consists of some dozen pages Pushkin attributes to an uneducated landowner named Belkin, who might be described as the ultimate provincial.[37] Belkin is provincial in a way that Tatiana Larina is not: the Larins' estate draws on a rich local culture while maintaining a healthy connection to the "outside world" (Tatiana's reading, Eugene's library), whereas Belkin's isolated manor house is effectively cut off from anything we might call culture (no journals, no books besides a primer and a composition manual, no interlocutors, no correspondents). Belkin's interaction with the larger world has been limited to three months at a Moscow boarding school followed by a brief stint in the army. And the cultural resources available to him in Goriukhino are decidedly meager, so meager that an "extremity" of boredom drives him to "sew some pages together" so as to "to fill them with anything whatsoever" (8:129, 131). He attempts and abandons various genres (epic, tragedy, ballad, essays, tales) before settling on history.

But history, too, proves difficult. Belkin finds that its highest ranges ("universal" and "national" history) have already been exhausted by scholarship, and writing the history of the provincial capital (*gubernskii gorod*) would require too much research. Moving further down the hierarchy, he considers writing "a history of our district town [or county seat, *uezdnyi gorod*]," only to learn that "the one significant event recorded in [the town's] annals was a terrible conflagration that destroyed its marketplace and courthouse ten years ago." Finally he settles on writing a history of his little village (*selo*) Goriukhino, thanks to some household records he uncovers in the attic. This pile of calendars and account books, long buried in a basket of trash, seems to Belkin an "inexhaustible store of economical, statistical, meteorological, and other scholarly observations" promising to disclose the "full history of my ancestral estate for almost a full century, given in the strictest chronological order" (8:132–33). On the basis of these sources, Belkin ends up producing an impossibly incoherent text, characterized by an "agglutinative character and amorphous shape,"[38] full of hilariously adventitious observations. We learn, for instance, that the elder Terentii ("who lived around 1767") could write with both hands as well as with his foot, that a "half-witted girl" used to tend swine near the swamp, and that "the male inhabitants of Goriukhino are mostly of medium height" (8:134–36): "Goriukhino" is funny precisely because it bears the marks of its author's "total lack of discrimination between significant and trivial events."[39]

Perhaps this is a history of a place that has no history. But what do we mean by history if we say, as Chaadaev said of Russia itself, that a place has none? Judging from the case of Goriukhino, it seems that the unstructured time and space of *provintsiia* cannot be assimilated to what J. G. A. Pocock defines as "public time": "History—in all but a few, rather esoteric, senses of the term—is public time. That is, it is time experienced by the individual as public being, conscious of a framework of public institutions in and through which events, processes and changes happened to the society of which he perceives himself to be part."[40] Provincial places are often characterized precisely by being cut off from public time. Goriukhino is a village, but in this sense it corresponds to the Bakhtinian chronotope of the provincial city or town (*gorod*), which we might see as a thoroughly degraded version of pastoral. Bakhtin's provincial town is defined by the absence of "advancing historical movement"; what it can accommodate are not "events," Bakhtin writes, but "only 'doings' that constantly repeat themselves."[41] Deep *provintsiia*'s spatial isolation results in a kind of temporal stasis: provincial time is stagnant and repetitive (rather than dynamic and progressing) because provincial space is cut off from other spaces.

Geographic insularity creates a temporal disjunction, depriving events of meaning by depriving them of connections to larger systems, because any individual occurrence becomes "intelligible" only once it is seen in relationship to the great "plot" of which it is a part: "the significance of all . . . stories depends in part on seeing their narrative relationship to expanding circles of plots within plots."[42] In the oft-quoted words of Hayden White, only "the form of a story" (key to which is the demonstration of causality) can guarantee the truth value of a historical narrative.[43] In place of "the form of a story," Pushkin's aspiring historian gives us a welter of details, from dun-brown cows and snippets of folk laments to notes on mushrooms. Declaring himself incapable of ordering information, "linking component parts," or "stringing together fictitious events," Belkin instead "writes down separate thoughts, with no connection or order, just as they presented themselves" (8:131–32). The result:

> May 4. Snow. Trishka thrashed for rudeness.
>
> 6. The dun cow has died, Senka thrashed for drunkenness.
>
> 8. Clear skies.
>
> 9. Rain and snow. Trishka thrashed on account of the weather.
>
> 11. Clear skies. Fresh snow on the ground. Killed three rabbits. (8:134)

"Trishka thrashed on account of the weather": the source implies a causal relationship where there should be none, and Belkin follows its lead, implying linkages where they cannot be "uncovered." What scholars have called the "unique realia" (!) of life in Goriukhino—the often baffling facts of everyday provincial existence—seem to resist the causal linkages necessary for creating a plot.[44] In other words, the pervasive triviality of provincial life is funny because it resists narrativization, overcoming efforts to impose order on it.

Historical narrative is always mediating between two poles: "On the one hand there are all the occurrences of the world . . . in their concrete particularity," whereas "on the other is an ideally theoretical understanding of those occurrences that would treat each as nothing other than a replicable instance of a systematically interconnected set of generalizations."[45] "Goriukhino"—the Russian provinces—is "all the occurrences of the world in their concrete particularity." The European historians from whom Russians took their cues in Pushkin's time assumed that their task was to establish the linkages among all these elements, to uncover the relationships capable of revealing history's progressive nature—in Guizot's words, "to link together facts so diversified . . . into one great historical unity."[46] And while Russians tended to judge their past by comparing it with that of European nations, Russia's history defied the paradigm of orderly development. Besides centuries of "regression" (e.g., the period of Mongol-Tatar rule), it offered striking evidence for the importance of accident and randomness, thanks to the concentration of power at the very top of the social hierarchy. (Voltaire, for one, declared that if Peter the Great had died in the midst of his labors, "the vastest empire in the world [would have fallen] back into the chaos from which it had barely emerged.")[47] To Pushkin and his contemporaries, their nation's history appeared erratic, marked by ruptures and diversions, and thus ever at risk of sinking into mere contingency. In Yuri Lotman's words, Russia's past was characterized by an "inconsequentiality" that rendered it "'inorganic,' illusory, or nonexistent" (*"neorganichnymi," prizrachnymi, nesushchestvuiushchimi*)—words that could also be enlisted to describe the culture of *provintsiia* as it appears in literature.[48]

The Captain's Daughter: Turning the Steppes into the Provinces

Lotman's characterization of Russian history notwithstanding, in *The Captain's Daughter* Pushkin draws on a famously chaotic episode in this history to write a famously tidy narrative. *The Captain's Daughter* treats the mass upheaval known as the Pugachev rebellion, a Cossack-led uprising that convulsed the western reaches of Imperial Russia in 1773–75.[49] The Russian empire had worked throughout the eighteenth century to "assimilate" the Eurasian steppes, but at the time of the rebellion, the region still had many of the hallmarks of a frontier. When Pushkin was writing his historical novel in the 1830s, one could probably have described the area around Orenburg (where most of the action takes place) as the eastern edge of "European Russia," with Asia perhaps just over the horizon; during the 1770s, when the story is set, the area's status as "Russian" was far less secure.

The novel opens on a gentry estate in Simbirsk *guberniia*, several hundred miles west of the open steppe around Orenburg and Ufa. When we meet the young protagonist and narrator Grinev, he is in the act of cutting up a map—a map, he says, "[that] had been obtained for me from Moscow and had been hanging on the wall of my room without being the slightest use to anyone." Given the map's uselessness, the boy opts to make it into a kite; thus his "study of geography" stops with "fixing a bast tail to the Cape of Good Hope" (8:280).[50] It seems Moscow may produce and disseminate as many maps as it likes, but that does not guarantee that anyone will look at them: the capitals are very far away from Simbirsk *guberniia*. And as the sociologist Michael Biggs writes, "we should not underestimate the difference of rulership in a mapless world."[51]

Here it is useful to compare the opening of another novel, roughly contemporaneous with *The Captain's Daughter*, that also meditates on relationships between geography and power. Near the beginning of Jane Austen's *Mansfield Park*, the children of an English baronet mock their déclassé cousin for her ignorance of crucial matters. "Only think," one child says, "my cousin cannot put the map of Europe together—or my cousin cannot tell the principal rivers of Russia—or she never heard of Asia Minor . . . ! Did you ever hear anything so stupid?"[52] The father of these children, Sir Thomas Bertram, derives his income not from his Mansfield Park estate but from his Caribbean plantations: geographic knowledge stands here as a sign of the mastery and control that English colonialists aimed to exercise over their "holdings" in various parts of the globe. In Austen's world even children understand the Foucauldian relationship between knowledge and power, especially when it comes to things like *mapping* Asia Minor and "the principal rivers of Russia."

But in the place where *The Captain's Daughter* begins—the Grinevs' remote estate—it is not hard to see why a map of the world would be judged irrelevant. In Bakhtin's terms, the estate chronotope is a world of isolated and ahistorical domesticity, as is signaled to us in *The Captain's Daughter* by the fact that the "action" opens with jam-making (a scene we might just as easily envision at the Larins' rural home). An estate typically provides the setting for a "family novel" or a "provincial novel," genres that have their roots in the idyll and thus in folkloric temporality.[53] Such narrative forms privilege the clan (the family as it stretches across time, over generations), fostering a circle-of-life view of the world and imagining places where "the cyclical repetition of the life process [is] of crucial importance."[54] In other words, this is not a chronotope that deals with "the central, *unrepeatable* events of biography and history."[55]

But Grinev is soon posted as an officer to a remote fort on the steppes, whereupon he leaves behind the "estate world" of the book's opening passage and enters the "unrepeatable events of biography and history." On his way east across the steppes, he meets a mysterious Cossack: this Cossack will later turn out to be Pugachev himself, the rebel leader and pretender who claims to be the true tsar.

When the rebellion breaks out, Grinev, who has since fallen in love with Masha, the daughter of the fort's commander, is able to save his fiancée thanks to his previous relationship with Pugachev; after the rebels are vanquished, revelations about Grinev's interaction with the arch-traitor call into question his loyalty as a Russian subject. In the end Grinev is saved from prison when his betrothed—now the orphaned daughter of a war hero—appeals directly to Catherine the Great, convincing her that there was nothing treasonous in Grinev's dealings with Pugachev.

By initiating its hero into historical time, *The Captain's Daughter* reflects on the process by which the Russian state was establishing control over the steppes, how it was bringing this liminal and problematic geographic region (problematic from the state's point of view, that is) into the "correct" relationship with both history and power. Places that have History in Pocock's sense (i.e., where time is "experienced by the individual as public being, conscious of a framework of public institutions in and through which events, processes and changes happened to the society of which he perceives himself to be part") are places that are on the map. But as Pushkin's Grinev learns, the steppes in the 1770s were only *in the process* of being mapped—that is, being physically and intellectually appropriated—by the Russian state. Beginning in the reign of Peter and continuing through the nineteenth century, Russians were engaged in the projects of data-collecting, resource-identifying, place-naming, ethnicity-categorizing, and land-mapping that were deemed necessary to modern forms of rule. Proceeding in the name of utility and military security, they did more or less what other European powers did when attempting to bring territory under control.

Thus Catherine issued clear instructions to the servitors she dispatched to remote parts: "You must proceed to learn about the province that has been entrusted to you . . . and for this purpose, you are to obtain reliable map[s] of sufficient detail."[56] Imperial officials were supposed to be able to *place on the map* all "regiments, towns, settlements, villages, outlying farms, seasonal work camps, monasteries, hermitages, manufactures, and any places of human habitation, as well as rivers, lakes, marshes, woods, farmland, steppes, roads, and *the location of [all] . . . borders.*"[57] But despite Catherine's list of items that were to be mapped, the steppe was also supposed to be *empty*, and for a long time Russian officials insisted on this emptiness even though they knew the land was populated by hundreds of thousands of nomadic people and by growing numbers of Russian settlers. As Willard Sunderland puts it, in the eighteenth century "the steppe was claimed by geographical science and promptly turned into a void": no matter who might actually live there, Russian elites generally persisted in seeing the steppe as "an alien and empty frontier."[58] And an "empty" space, in the mind of the modern state, is a transformable space—indeed, it is a space in need of transformation. Consider, for example, the orgy of re-naming that took place under Catherine: New Serbia became New Russia, the Iaik River became the Ural River, Turco-Tatar names were replaced with Hellenic ones, etc.[59]

None of this is surprising, given the fact that from Peter's time on, the autocracy's goal had been to "turn . . . formless emptiness into formed space" (beginning with the city of Petersburg itself, which rose dramatically from nonbeing into being).[60] In the eyes of the autocracy, as Sunderland writes, "the old steppe was Asian and stateless," while the new one was to be "state-determined and claimed for European civilization."[61] But at the time of the Pugachev rebellion, the question of where Russia actually *was* had no obvious answer:[62] given the empire's constant expansion, it took a great deal of effort (surveying and resurveying, mapping and remapping) to make borders appear as "natural and permanent" as the state wanted them to.[63] The century following Catherine's—Pushkin's century— was characterized by an "obsession with borders," a preoccupation that went along with "the birth and spread of the *clearly marked territorial limit* as a 'peripheral organ' . . . of the sovereign state, equipped with symbols of majesty and guarded by policemen, soldiers, and customs officials."[64]

Yet as we see in *The Captain's Daughter*, on the steppe there is nothing easy about what geographers call the territorialization of rule, the "symbolic fusion of political authority and geographical area." This process has produced the maps that teach us to see the earth's surface as crisscrossed by distinct borders, with lines dividing land (and even sea) into unambiguous state territories, and blocks of different colors "implying that [each] interior is a homogeneous space, traversed evenly by state sovereignty."[65] But such a way of imagining space is the end result of a long conceptual and technological process—a process that was difficult enough in Europe, and that proved even more challenging in the great flat expanse of the southern Eurasian landmass, where people encountered very few "natural" frontiers and where nomadism had long been the rule. Given what one nineteenth-century traveler called the steppe's "exhausting uniformity,"[66] where were the *borders* supposed to be? And without borders, where was the modern state itself?[67]

Characters in *The Captain's Daughter* repeatedly confront such problems, in part because much of the text is devoted to covering ground. After Grinev leaves his home estate to take up the military posting his father has arranged for him, he makes his way first to Simbirsk, then to Orenburg, and finally to Fort Belogorsk—a fictional outpost "forty versts from Orenburg" that the protagonist anticipates will be "a godforsaken [*glukhuiu*] fort on the edge of the Kirgiz-Kaisakh steppes" (8:293–94).[68] During the fighting he moves around even more (e.g., to Belogorsk; to the village of Berda, where Pugachev has his headquarters; to Tatar hamlets, Kazan, and various destroyed villages).

The landscape Grinev traverses is always an unmarked "dreary wilderness" "[extending] in every direction," "crosscut with ridges and ravines," usually "covered with snow." In this environment even natural topographic features fail to establish boundaries: Grinev finds that things look exactly the same on one side of the Iaik River's "monotonous banks" as they do on the other. When he is told they are approaching Belogorsk, Grinev still sees nothing: "where *is* the fort?" he asks. There is no impressive boundary setting off this supposed outpost of state power—which is actually nothing more than a "small village surrounded by a palisade"—from the empty space all around. Once settled, Grinev looks out his window and sees "a melancholy steppe [stretching] out before [him]," where the ragged edge of civilization—a few huts, some chickens, an old woman gathering her pigs—bleeds imperceptibly into an undifferentiated flatland (8:294–96).

The landscape in *The Captain's Daughter* is above all *illegible*: if one goal of the modernizing state was to make space legible, this landscape was going to present difficulties. When a storm appears, for example, sky merges with land, leaving nothing distinguishable in the "darkness and whirling snow": "everything disappeared . . . darkness everywhere" (8:287). Utterly disoriented, Grinev "[looks] in all directions hoping to see some sign of human habitation or roadway, but [*cannot*] *discern anything*" (8:288). Pushkin was not alone in suggesting that the steppe's unrelieved horizontality threatened to disable the systems of scale and contrast that we rely on for the distinctions necessary for making meaning. As the French traveler Leroy-Beaulieu wrote in the 1890s, the Eurasian landmass offers "hardly any *juxtaposition*"—and in a landscape where everything blurs together, signs become unreadable.[69]

The land is not the only thing that is unreadable: the people of the steppes are equally hard to figure out. When Grinev first arrives at Belogorsk, the only "ethnics" initially present are a few Bashkirs and the Cossack soldiers themselves (who turn out to be more "ethnic" than anybody had anticipated). Only gradually does the bewildering diversity of the population become evident: Grinev explains that the region is in fact "inhabited by a number of *half*-wild peoples [note the *half*-] who had only recently accepted the Russian Emperors' suzerainty. Because of their frequent revolts, their ways unaccustomed to law and civilized life, and their instability and cruelty, the government could keep them under control only by maintaining constant surveillance over them" (8:313). Soon the list of ethnic designations lengthens, though these peoples are never clearly differentiated: Kirgiz, Tatars, Kalmyks, and unspecified "half-savage peoples" appear along with the Bashkirs and—most threatening and destabilizing of all—those "shifty" Cossacks, who are "not to be relied on" (8:314, 316).[70]

The Cossacks are the most threatening precisely because they are the closest thing to "Russians" around: they are the internal other. In the eyes of the state, the Cossacks' duty—their reason for being, in effect—was to guard the borders of the Russian empire. But Grinev tells us that "these Iaik Cossacks, whose duty it was to guard the peace and safety of the region, had themselves for some time been restless subjects, posing a threat to the government" (8:313).[71] The Cossacks are imperial border guards who turn on the empire, "half-literate" people who write imperial manifestos (8:317), Orthodox Christians who team up with heathens, semi-Russians (or maybe semi-Ukrainians?) who dress in Kirgiz robes (8:347). Their instability is mirrored in characters like the neither/nor "baptized Kalmyk," who is willing to follow Russian orders and torture a captured Bashkir (8:313), only to end up being killed himself by a Cossack who has defected to the rebels: nearly everyone's position, it seems, is potentially fluid among these "half-savage" and "semi-barbarian" peoples.[72]

The Cossacks and various "others" in *The Captain's Daughter*, all of whom are liable to melt back into the unmapped and unreadable landscape at any moment, suggest that this part of Russia might not have borders at all. The best the Russian empire has been able to do here is to write its bloody history on the rebels' bodies (the old Bashkir prisoner whose ears, nose, and tongue were cut off as punishment for another uprising thirty years earlier; Pugachev's lieutenant with his slit nostrils and branded cheeks; the laboring convicts with faces "disfigured by the executioners' tongs" [8:338]: but despite these marks their loyalties remain unstable, and the land itself, it seems, remains *un*marked.

Franco Moretti has pointed out that historical novels set along internal borders—those that divide states *within*—are often about treason, or near-treason: an internal borderland is where the son of Gogol's Cossack hero Taras Bulba takes up with the Polish enemy, where *Waverly*'s hero gets mixed up with the Jacobites, and where Balzac's Marquis de Montauran in *The Royalists* (*Les Chouans*) makes a last stand against the French revolutionary state.[73] *The Captain's Daughter*, too, has to do with near-treason and with what we might call the elasticity of state loyalty, and if Pushkin's tale is set along any border at all, it is probably an internal one. But in a sense what is notable about *The Captain's Daughter* is that the borders in this text are so hard to locate. How is one supposed to be loyal to a state that is so hard to find on the map?

From its epigraphs to its closing lines, Pushkin's text returns again and again to questions of honor and dishonor, paternity and paternal blessings, ranks and regiments, legitimate and illegitimate hierarchies. It is a text that wants all these lines to be clear (family lines, lines of command, lines on the map). But Grinev's story implies that out on the steppe, even an upstanding Russian nobleman risks getting mixed up with a traitor like Pugachev—a figure who first appears out of a blinding snowstorm in an unnamed "remote place, in the middle of the steppe, far away from any habitation" (8:277). Fighting against those you deem to be half-savage and semi-barbarian peoples does not offer the same pay-off, one might say, as fighting against a more clearly defined enemy: as Savelich tells Grinev, "it'd be something else if you were marching against Turks and or Swedes, but here one's even ashamed to say who you're fighting with!" (8:344). And Grinev recognizes that the landscape itself favors the rebels in a "tedious and petty war against brigands and savages," who are always "disappearing" and "reemerging" into and out of the steppe (8:363).

At the end of *The Captain's Daughter*, the "pacification" of the rebels is represented more as the dying down of a storm than as a military victory—and it is certainly not represented as the definitive claiming of a clearly demarcated territory. In fact the story ends not with Pugachev's defeat but with Grinev's reintegration into the structures of imperial power: Catherine II, in response to Masha's appeal, exonerates him. Masha, having made her way to the imperial court from Simbirsk, delivers her petition to Catherine in the gardens of Tsarskoe Selo: and significantly, we are told that she never even sees the capital itself (she returns to Simbirsk "without as much as taking one curious look at Petersburg"). There is no need for Masha to go to the capital, since this is a story about the capital's effort to extend its own power and authority over far-off places. And at the very end of *The Captain's Daughter*, the state does seem to be making some progress in this regard, as evidenced by the framed letter "in Catherine's own hand" that is still displayed at the family estate in Simbirsk Guberniia, where Grinev's descendants "thrive to this day." (8:374)

The Captain's Daughter does not focus on a decisive moment of conquest or surrender. Nor does it represent one definitive claiming of "foreign" territory for (or as) Russia; indeed, the action takes place in territory that is nominally Russian already. The process of "domesticating" the Eurasian steppelands was intermittent and irregular, a somewhat undramatic process that anticipates the undramatic and "boring" kind of space the steppes would later become. Once the state consolidated power over this region, the steppes would go from being dangerous and foreign to being dull and Russian—in other words, to being *provincial*. In Pushkin's time you could travel more or less south from Orenburg and get to the (metaphorical) "east," but already by the 1830s the steppes were not an exotic, capital-R Romantic periphery.[74] Then again, they were certainly not the Russian heartland either. This was an environment that was fairly hard to exoticize, but where it was fairly easy to feel alienated: liminal and uncomfortable, yes; foreign and exotic, not really.

As we have seen, Pushkin's version of rural Russia is most often positive, pastoral, and gently comical—quite unlike what we find in the slightly later *provintsiia* trope that is this book's main focus. But Belkin's garbled "history" in "Goriukhino" points to one link between Pushkin's generally benign (if condescending) image and the darker ones that predominate a bit later. Witness the fact that Lotman's characterization of Russian history—inorganic, illusory, nonexistent—draws on the same vocabulary that writers of the 1830s and 1840s enlist when describing *provintsiia*: in the provinces as in Russian history, things happen and artifacts turn up without rhyme or reason (thus we read of a painting hanging in a provincial landowner's manor house in *Dead Souls*, "there was no way of knowing how or why [it] had gotten there").[75] The parallel hints at links between *provintsiia* and Russia's putative ahistoricity—the comically shapeless "non-history" that Pushkin highlights in "Goriukhino," where the only available version of the past is ridiculously inconsequential, and the equally chaotic conditions confronted by Catherine's armies in the featureless landscape of *The Captain's Daughter*.

The chaos and eclecticism of life in a place like Goriukhino—or Russia—can serve to expose the weaknesses of theoretical programs or all-explanatory metanarratives like those that claim to discern history's "universal laws." Provincial settings, besides being funny (recall the elder Terentii, capable of writing with both hands as well as with his foot), highlight the inapplicability of (European) theories to (Russian) realities, particularly when it comes to history and temporality. In the decades after Pushkin's death, many literary texts would fixate on the provinces as a way of examining Russians' relationship to historical time. And as we will see in subsequent chapters, the provinces as they are represented in such texts are often not simply "behind"; rather, they exist in a strange and ambiguous temporality, in which ideas have no roots in real history and real places.

And finally, in Pushkin's work we see the beginning of the processes that would soon allow formerly exotic places like the steppes to accommodate *provincials* like Belkin—"ordinary" Russians who understand that the places where they live are far away from what counts, but are nonetheless quite clearly within Russia proper. In the texts addressed in the following chapter, Russia's open spaces are no longer associated with what is liminal and uncanny; instead, they have been assimilated to a version of "merely provincial" culture that is unmistakably Russian. This culture is typically characterized by repetition, imitation, and distortion; over and over, we are told that it is *boring*. No longer a site of adventure or danger, and only sometimes a site of humor, the little steppe town will become a *gorod N* (Town of N), a *gorod kak gorod* (a town like any other)—just another component of what Herzen's memoirs call "the land of silence and dumbness."[76] But as boring as it is said to be, this version of *provintsiia* becomes a locus of great aesthetic productivity because in these texts we begin to see the provinces imagined in the bizarrely paradoxical terms that will prove so artistically fruitful for the rest of the century.

· CHAPTER THREE ·

Inventing Provincial Backwardness, or "Everything is Barbarous and Horrid" (Herzen, Sollogub, and Others)

Elle avait de beaux yeux pour des yeux de province.
— Jean-Baptiste-Louis Gresset, 1747

Torzhok after Petersburg is like a dark night after a bright fine day.
— Ivan Mikhailovich Dolgorukov, 1810

"The provincial ball has been described a thousand times": by 1840, when Alexander Herzen writes "Notes of a Young Man" (sketches based on his experience in exile in the Russian provinces), he feels obliged to assume that his reader already knows what to expect from any description of "provincial" mores.[1] The same assumption will be implicit in his 1846 novel *Who Is to Blame?*, which has its origins in the sketches. Here Herzen claims there is no need to specify the location of the town where the action takes place (it "resembles all the others"),[2] though he nonetheless enters into a fairly detailed account of daily life in the unnamed *gubernskii gorod*. From the 1830s through the 1850s, many writers followed this pattern: they rehearsed what they themselves repeatedly acknowledged to be clichés of provincial life, trotting out the same topoi even as they insisted that everybody already knew all about what they were describing, even to the point that insisting on the banality of the trope became part of the trope itself—and they did this despite the fact that this way of conceiving *provintsiia* was in fact quite new.

The current chapter considers not only how a new image of the Russian provinces took shape in literary texts, but also how these texts insisted that the image was *old*: by the 1830s, not only is it assumed that the provinces epitomize all that is grimly familiar, it is further assumed that such has always been the case, and that everyone has always known it. In the texts analyzed here, the supposedly timeless, ahistorical nature of *provintsiia* becomes both a stereotype and a preoccupation. And in a slightly later period, this is the image of *provintsiia* that will come to serve as a static non-modernity against which other forms of time and historicalness take on value.

In order to understand the novelty of the conception, consider what came before: before the idea of provincial stasis and anonymity took hold, Russian writings about places outside Petersburg and Moscow assumed neither temporal stasis nor an undifferentiated wasteland characterized by repetition, imitation, and distortion. It was once possible to see *provintsiia* as a series of diverse and particular places, and to do so in a variety of ways. A 1769 poem by Mikhail Chulkov, for example, lists Russian cities according to the products for which each was famous. A few of these associations still make sense to us today (e.g., metalwork from Tula), but most are now opaque references requiring explanation (candles from Vologda, soap from Shuia, etc.).[3] Chulkov might well have been baffled by Vladimir Sollogub's assertion that in the provinces "everything's the same, the same, the same,"[4] or by Anton Chekhov's later claim that a traveler might easily mistake "Sumy for Gadyach, or Ekaterinburg for Tula."[5]

By the second third of the nineteenth century, thanks to a shift traceable in part to the Catherine-era policies discussed in the introduction (e.g., legislation aimed at standardizing provincial architecture and urban planning), even an ancient city with a distinctive and well-documented past—a clear identity based in history—could be reduced to just another *gubernskii gorod*. Take Vladimir: once a capital in its own right, undeniably "a center of political and symbolic power," under Catherine it became merely one of the empire's many administrative towns.[6] After being designated a provincial capital (*gubernskii gorod*) in the autocracy's reformed administrative structure, the town was rebuilt to reflect its new status: streets were laid out on a grid that replaced the crooked medieval pattern, for instance, and only those merchants who could afford to build houses conforming to new architectural guidelines were permitted to reside on the main avenue. Vladimir was on its way to becoming not a place that was famous for its cherries (as it had been) or its glorious medieval past (which the current autocracy preferred to ignore), but rather what Turgenev's Bazarov would later call "a town like any other," *gorod kak gorod*. By 1836 a visiting Moscow nobleman would direct his attention mostly toward the town's unfashionable ways ("they still wear wide sleeves . . . retired men parade in their old uniforms . . . few speak French").[7]

A few years later in Sollogub's *Tarantas* (1840–45), a tourist seeking information about local history is told that there are no books about Vladimir: the Vladimir bookseller offers him a book about Tsargrad instead, clearly assuming that the difference between two provincial towns is negligible.[8] Finally, in his memoirs Herzen takes Sollogub's non-description of not-Vladimir as a way of explaining why Vladimir requires no description: in recounting his experience there as an internal exile, Herzen assumes that readers already know exactly what this provincial town looks like, since the inn has already been "faithfully described in Sollogub's *Tarantas*."[9] In Herzen's account as in others', nothing about Vladimir is particular to Vladimir; the place is merely another iteration of the provincial town—"the land of silence and dumbness," as he calls it in his memoirs, above all preoccupied with conforming to directives received from Petersburg's Ministry of Home Affairs, most of which seek to impose ever stricter forms of standardization on provincial life.[10] By the time Herzen takes the town as a model for the mind-numbing *gubernskii gorod* of *Who Is to Blame?* he says explicitly that "there is no need to specify the time and place with chronological or geographic accuracy": the town where the novel is set "resembles all the rest."[11]

I am not arguing, however, that literature's new insistence on provincial sameness and dullness is simply a result of Catherinian policies, a "reflection" of changes in historical circumstances. Rather, this image of *provintsiia* takes on significance because it meets a larger need: insisting on the monotony of provincial places allows Russians to think about the consequences of centrality and peripherality more generally, and thus (eventually) about modernity and non-modernity—all crucial issues at a time when educated elites are increasingly worried about their relationship to European ways of measuring both time and space. *Provintsiia* starts to be experienced as banal and monotonous because it is perceived as *backward*; as a scholar of British India puts it, "an overwhelming sense of the banality of one's life is a damning marker of economic and ideological subordination."[12] Russian writers tend to depict provincial backwardness as a permanent condition, not even in the process of "modernizing": to be in the provinces is to be static, *stuck*. Again we see a parallel with colonial and postcolonial literature: in representations of the British imperial periphery, for example, "being able to *move* contains the potential to thwart the pervasive banality of the local space that imprisons its dwellers through the misfortune of their birth." Much as in Russian depictions of the provincial town, stasis itself comes to be associated with "impoverished natives" and their lack of freedom.[13]

While the texts analyzed in this chapter span the years between approximately 1820 and 1845, most are from the 1830s and 1840s, the period when a newly anonymized, homogenized, and static image of *provintsiia*—an image that was to persist in literature up to our own time—was taking definitive shape. Since this book's larger topic is *provintsiia* as trope, I focus mostly on prose fiction. But I also refer to memoirs by Herzen and Ivan Dolgorukov, whose nonfiction writings are valuable for understanding the evolution of certain now-familiar ideas. Dolgorukov's travel accounts are particularly notable because they represent, in a sense, a road not taken: these texts attend to the specificities of life in real and diverse provincial places, and as such they reveal what might have gone into the development of a Russian version of literary regionalism—a development that never happened. In prose fiction what proved to be far more productive than the realities of regional difference was the fantasy of provincial equivalence—in Sollogub's words, "everything the same, the same, the same."

The idea of sameness underlies virtually every (post-Dolgorukov) text analyzed in this chapter, in addition to others that will be addressed only briefly. Orest Somov's *A Novel in Two Letters*, Vladimir Odoevsky's "The Sprite," Vladimir Dal's *The Unlucky One*, Aleksei Pleshcheev's *Everyday Scenes*, Sollogub's "Serezha," *The Apothecary's Wife*, and *Tarantas*, and finally Herzen's "Notes of a Young Man" and *Who Is to Blame?*—all depend on a certain shared idea of *provintsial'nost'*. And in them we see developed not only the character of the anxiously aspiring province-dweller, preoccupied with fashion, taste, and up-to-dateness, but also a more disturbing, far darker vision: the provinces are starting to appear not merely as unfashionable or sleepy or behind the times, but as a place of immurement and blight—"this backwater . . . this prison, this exile, this confinement," says Sollogub—a "desert" where "unbearable melancholy" reigns alongside cultural incoherence and dead materiality.[14] While these texts are less well-known than Gogol's works (which occupy the next chapter), in them we begin to see the possibility of imagining the provinces in terms that are bizarrely paradoxical and thus, it seems, aesthetically productive. In the 1830s and 1840s literature begins to represent *provintsiia* as a place at once forbiddingly unknown and familiar to the point of banality, at once a barren void and the domain of an oppressively dense materiality.

Dolgorukov and the Road Not Taken

"I would have gone to Paris, since I like sensation, uproar, theater, luxury, et cetera, et cetera, and where is there more of all that than in France? But he who has neither estate nor money lives as God decrees": thus does Prince Ivan Mikhailovich Dolgorukov (1764–1823) explain his eccentric decision to travel within Russia for pleasure. The prince took a number of such trips (in 1810, 1813, and 1817), which resulted in a series of lively travel narratives focused on the specificities of various—clearly differentiated—provincial places.[15] His decidedly domestic voyages were undertaken "without any goal, just to travel";[16] clearly, Dolgorukov would have laughed at the character in *Tarantas* who declares "travel" to be impossible inside Russia (in Russia, says Sollogub's stolid landowner, one merely "drives to one's destination").[17] Yet Dolgorukov himself, though he served as governor of Vladimir *guberniia* from 1802 to 1812, claimed never to have seen an actual "provincial town" until he was twenty-seven years old: "I had known Tver and Novgorod for a long time, but the former of these could be called an outpost of Moscow, and the other of Petersburg. Volodomir [Vladimir] is the real provinces."[18] Here, then, is an example of a well-educated and sophisticated Muscovite—a courtier, poet, and playwright—who decided that provincial places were worth seeing. In Russia's far-flung cities and towns, Dolgorukov always sought, and often found, material for historical and aesthetic contemplation, as well as the distinctive qualities that served to differentiate these places from one another.

Describing dozens of Russian towns and villages, Dolgorukov certainly speaks as a *stolichnyi* (capital) sophisticate who directs his assessing gaze toward the local sights, but he does not dwell on the obvious opposition between *stolitsa* and non-*stolitsa*. Instead he judges each place on its own merits, noting which towns have interesting churches and historical landmarks, where the views are more and less picturesque, etc. While some towns prove inconsequential, each is allowed to be inconsequential in its own way.[19] Not once does he invoke any formulation along the lines of "a town like any other"—the sort of truism without which it would soon be almost impossible to write about provincial places.

Nor does Dolgorukov automatically assume that culture, daily life, or polite society outside the Russian capitals will be painfully second-rate. He acknowledges when efforts are strained (one local ball evokes first laughter, then pity),[20] but he also praises the polite society of Kharkov, for example, for its delicacy and good taste (combining the "sweet simplicity [of a small town] with the gentle fastidiousness of a large city").[21] Even the balls he attends in places like Saraisk and Nizhnii Novgorod are decidedly not ridiculous, whereas by the 1840s, Herzen and others will assume their readers share the belief that such events will inevitably showcase provincials' comical failure to meet a standard set by the capitals. Dolgorukov, by contrast, assumes that he himself will be judged by local norms: his memoirs recall his careful efforts to learn "all the customs of provincial [*provintsial'noi*] life" when he arrives for state service in Vladimir.[22] He is simply not very interested in seizing opportunities to indict locals for falling short of some external *stolichnyi* paradigm. Even when recounting how the provincial governor's wife in Tver insists on adhering to tedious protocol in order to maintain a grand appearance,[23] the prince does not take this as an opportunity to indict the provincial governor's wife (*gubernatorsha*) for pretension or social striving, as would surely be the case in a later text. (Indeed, a reader of Russian fiction of the 1830s and 1840s would have little trouble predicting more or less what was likely to follow the words "the wife of the provincial governor of Tver.")

However, even in Dolgorukov's naïve descriptions—naïve in the sense that they are relatively unmarked by the conventions that would soon begin to shape literary depictions of provincial life—we see signs of what is to come. In a Tula *gimnazium*, Dolgorukov expresses astonished distaste at the teacher's garbled French, which the schoolmaster defends as "today's taste and beauty of style."[24] And in a tiny schoolhouse amidst the "empty fields" outside Kursk, he watches as a drunken teacher requires pupils to memorize lines from the torn-out pages of a long-outdated court calendar:[25] here the visitor from the capitals experiences *provintsiia* as wasteland, a place so remote that "culture" can reach it only in the form of meaningless debris, which is then recycled (memorized, imitated) despite its meaninglessness.

When Dolgorukov finds himself repulsed by some bewildering instance of cultural abjection or meanness, it almost always stems from the "Europeanizing" pretension that would later be thought to epitomize *provintsial'nost'*, even if he is not (yet) judging it in precisely these terms. And when we look at *provintsiia* through the eyes of the worldly prince, not only do we see the "raw material" that fed the *provintsiia* trope, we also begin to understand why this trope, with its insistence on the absurdity and deformation occasioned by acts of copying, was to prove useful for diagnosing what would later be seen as the ills afflicting *all* of Russian culture. In the decades to come, it would always be in the act of *imitating* that cultural inadequacies would be exposed.

One should remember that this was not generally the case in the eighteenth century: according to that era's neoclassical literary standard, imitation was not in itself problematic. If, in the eighteenth century, "you rigorously applied the normative requirements for writing an ode or an epic . . . you were making literature": and therefore, thanks to this "conception of literature [as] so abstract and yet so normative that it could be used to certify texts as literature," copying did not automatically signal degradation.[26] Thus eighteenth-century Russians who aspired to high culture (not only in the literary realm but in other realms too, such as estate design) did not find imitation especially worrisome. Copying becomes a problem at the same moment in the early nineteenth century (the age of Romanticism) when originality and national distinctiveness become cultural problems as well—at the same time, not coincidentally when the idea of provinciality began to preoccupy Russian writers.

Dolgorukov's consternation is more often provoked by provincial towns than by estates. He tends to experience the latter as oases of ease and culture: arriving at a "large manor house with a balcony and a rotunda," he exclaims, "how cheerful to meet such comforts [*pokoi*] after a storm on a dark night!" But of a provincial town he can only note glumly, "Torzhok after Petersburg is like a dark night after a bright fine day."²⁷ For Dolgorukov, an estate can serve as true culture's mirror and emissary in the provinces, an image of order and *comme il faut*. The town is more likely to appear as the opposite; for him as for later writers of prose fiction, it was in towns that the provinces' disturbing motleyness—*pestrota*—was most clearly on display. In the provinces townspeople of varying backgrounds and classes tended to mix more freely than in the capitals, and this looseness of social boundaries struck outsiders, including Dolgorukov, as distasteful, improper, and vaguely promiscuous. In Dolgorukov's memoirs we get a glimpse of the phenomenon when the prince recalls bringing his young bride (brought up in Petersburg's elite Smolny Institute) to visit her native village, which she had not seen since early childhood. Both are shocked and, it seems, somewhat repelled by the strange crowd that comes out to meet "the daughter from the capital." "My God, who was not there?" the suddenly fastidious prince exclaims, listing the mishmash of guests, "all sorts of riff-raff," from district judges to scriveners.²⁸

Though Dolgorukov rarely thinks in terms of a strict provinces-capital binary, he is well aware of the role played by a particular hierarchy of imitation in Russian life, a system that dictates who copies whom. "Moscow is the model for all cities!" he writes, "Whatever you see there is what they want to imitate everyplace, whether appropriately or not; and Moscow, in its place, looks toward the City of Peter [*grad Petrova*]."²⁹ He describes how the governor of Poltava, with ample resources at his disposal, has attempted to make of his city "a small-scale Petersburg"; but resources notwithstanding, the end result of these top-down improvements is something "incongruous with the place, poor, low, and as the French say, *mesquin*."³⁰ The adjective *mesquin* (shabby, petty) points forward to what provincial culture will signify in so many later texts—something trivial and second-rate, falling short of a grandeur to which it too obviously aspires. All this is evident in Dolgorukov's description of the architectural ensemble "in the newest taste" that has recently and awkwardly been "stitched onto" the edge of Poltava, a collection of fancy buildings and one trompe-l'oeil painting on a large wooden panel. The painted panel stands in for a structure that has not yet been built, as if to acknowledge the façade laws governing provincial cities even while conceding that the standard being imposed by the far-off capital had proven impossible to meet.³¹

Dolgorukov senses that when it comes to grandeur, context is everything—which is why imitation proves risky out on the steppes. In the center of Poltava's new square stands a new monument to Peter the Great, which is, in Dolgorukov's judgment, an adequately impressive piece of work. But the monument's position—its "unfortunate location" on the edge of a town on the edge of a steppe, "a bare, unpopulated steppe that assaults the gaze without relief," an "enormous and unwooded expanse"—this position somehow renders a satisfactory monument incongruous,

even vaguely ridiculous. Outside another provincial town Dolgorukov reacts similarly when coming upon a bustling marketplace "in the middle of an open field,"
where he is struck by the juxtaposition of "empty field" and commerce; "imagine
that someone sliced off Il'inka [a busy shopping street] from Moscow . . . and stuck
it here," he writes.[32]

In Dolgorukov's usage the adjective *stepnoi* carries a sharply negative tinge, and
the noun *step'* is likely to be preceded not just by modifiers like "empty," "vast," and
"wild," but also by words like "terrible."[33] For him this landscape is characterized
strictly by lack (*no* woods, no towns, no fields, no bushes);[34] it actively resists being civilized and tends to obliterate even the memory of civilization. Dolgorukov
writes, "Anyone like me, who has never been anyplace but Moscow and Petersburg
or other such cities . . . and is traveling a long road through the steppe," will certainly "cry out" once he finally reaches a town, "'Thanks be to God! There still exist
for me life and people!'"[35] Here Dolgorukov's account echoes those of many others
who found the Russian landscape not only monotonous (with its "exhausting uniformity," "desolate wastes," etc.), but an impediment to culture of any kind.[36] Pyotr
Chaadaev, in his famous remarks on Russians' exclusion from capital-H History,
seems at times to blame the landscape—the barren steppe where "all resemble
travelers . . . leaving no traces"—for its role in draining meaning from human
beings' civilizing labor.[37] In the words of the historian Kostomarov, Russia's "excessive geographic space" posed a threat to the human spirit.[38] One passably grand
statue is not enough to bring "civilization" to such a setting.

Ryleev and Zagoskin: The Provinces Take Shape

Around the time Dolgorukov was publishing his memoirs, Mikhail Zagoskin and
Kondratii Ryleev both wrote fictional works featuring characters who are labeled
"provincials" (in literature "the figure of the *provintsial* predates the image of
provintsiia"),[39] but in the end neither author is particularly concerned with the
provinces as such. Zagoskin's 1817 comedy *Mr. Bogotonov, or a Provincial in the
Capital* (*Gospodin Bogotonov, ili provintsial v stolitse*)—based loosely on Molière's
Le bourgeois gentilhomme (1670)—is perhaps the first title of a Russian literary
work to feature any form of the word *provintsiia*. But while Bogotonov is "a provincial," it is not clear that he is meant to be a *representative* provincial. The words
provintsiia and *provintsial'nyi* do not appear in the play, and the play does not really call attention to the *stolitsa*-vs.-*provintsiia* divide; in fact the most important
opposition at work in Zagoskin's comedy is not capitals vs. provinces, but simply
enlightenment vs. ignorance, or perhaps good morals vs. bad.[40] Zagoskin makes
his character a *pomeshchik* (landowner) who has abandoned his rural estate for
Petersburg not because the playwright wants to make a point about the provinces,

but because in a Russian comedy, someone from outside the capital must be called upon to play a role that in Molière can be filled by a (Parisian) bourgeois.

In other words, Zagoskin uses a geographic overlay to make points (about social climbing and the virtues of knowing one's place) that Molière can make without recourse to geography, since everyone in *Le bourgeois gentilhomme* is thoroughly Parisian. Molière's main character, Jourdain, is a crude but rich cloth merchant who, as a bourgeois aspiring to join the aristocracy, makes inept attempts at the gentlemanly arts. In France there is no need for such a character to originate in the provinces; the oxymoron of the French title (it is not possible to be a "bourgeois gentleman") does the job of setting up the conflict. Jourdain allows himself to be swindled by a cunning nobleman whose status he idolizes; Bogotonov, like Jourdain, is being fleeced by a high-ranking nobleman in need of cash. But in Zagoskin's version, the swindler-aristocrat is heavily marked as *stolichnyi*: not only is he both from and of Petersburg, he has just come from frittering away his own money in Paris.

Clearly, geography signifies in the Russian play in a way it does not in the French.[41] Thus while there is nothing in Zagoskin's play that is really *about* the provinces or provinciality, it does point toward a kind of semi-latent geographic symbolism, a series of images that are in a sense waiting to be filled with content.[42] A similar dynamic is discernible in Ryleev's feuilleton entries of 1821, which appeared under the title "A Provincial [*provintsial*] in Petersburg." Ryleev adopts the point of view of someone visiting Petersburg from a "little district town" in a "steppe *guberniia*,"[43] though he too has little interest in the provinces or provincialism as they would later come to be understood. His aim is simply to say something about "human nature," with the *provintsial* standing in for a more or less generic outsider.[44] Commenting on this newcomer's experiences in the capital serves as a way of making quasi-universal points (e.g., "people are easily bamboozled" and "women like expensive hats"), as Ryleev's narrator makes explicit ("people are always people, in all times and places!").[45]

And yet, here as in Zagoskin's comedy, the provinces-capital divide is in effect waiting to be activated. It is present, for example, in the fact that Petersburg is where newcomers encounter consumer goods and novelties unheard of back home, like the Parisian hats that the provincial's wife insists on buying (as always, Paris is where the best stuff comes from), or the whole range of kaleidoscopes— German, French, English—that he discovers in a shop on Nevsky Avenue. When the saleswoman asks, "is it true you've never seen [kaleidoscopes] before?" Ryleev's *provintsial* responds, "Where would we have seen them, miss? We live in the boondocks [*v glushi*], far from the capital. No such rarities ever make it out there to us."[46] Here we begin to perceive the link between being provincial and failing to be modern, which will be more fully developed in the next decade.

If Ryleev's feuilleton and Zagoskin's *Mr. Bogotonov* use the figure of the provincial to help make points that are not chiefly about place, by the time Zagoskin writes his 1835 prose narrative "Three Suitors (Provincial [*Provintsial'nye*] Sketches)," he is clearly drawing our attention to the provinces and provinciality as (negative) phenomena in their own right.[47] No longer are these labels overlaid on top of other categories as a form of shorthand or convenience, and neither can such terms be understood as neutrally geographic. In "Three Suitors," provinciality has come to evoke something that is simultaneously more negative and more significant than in earlier texts. Note the full version of a passage cited partially in this book's first chapter, in which Zagoskin opens "Three Suitors" by calling our attention to specifics of vocabulary meant to signal that the provinces themselves have become an object of scrutiny:

> Have you ever lived in the provinces [*v provintsii*]? Not in the countryside [*v derevne*], not in a little district town [*v uezdnom gorode*], but in a provincial town [*v gubernskom gorode*]—among people who speak with pride, and almost always in French, about their high society, about their sense of good and bad taste, even about the different circles into which their society [*obshchestvo*] is divided. If you . . . want to know, even in a superficial way, what a provincial town really is [*chto takoe provintsial'nyi gorod*]—not twenty years ago, but now, in our time—then listen.[48]

This passage, in addition to drawing a distinction between the *provintsiia* and the countryside or village, also assumes an equivalence between the adjectives *gubernskii* and *provintsial'nyi*—thereby confirming that at this time the two words were being used almost interchangeably (with the exception that *gubernskii* was required for official state designations—e.g., *gubernskii gorod* for "provincial capital," *gubernskii sekretar'* for "provincial secretary," etc.).[49]

Such clear vocabulary distinctions were by no means observed in all texts of this period, or of any period; for example, as I noted in chapter 1, Somov's 1832 *Novel in Two Letters* uses the adjectives *sel'skii*, *derevenskii*, *uezdnyi*, *oblastnoi*, and *provintsial'nyi* more or less indiscriminately. Nonetheless, the precision we find in the opening lines of "Three Suitors" puts us on notice that Zagoskin is depicting what he expects his readers to recognize as a distinct phenomenon, even if the vocabulary used to designate the phenomenon is unstable. In fact the instability of the vocabulary reminds us that understanding what the provinces mean in literary texts is not a matter of tracking certain words, but rather of attending to a recurring topos.

"Everything the Same, the Same, the Same"

"All our provincial towns are the same. If you've seen one, you've seen them all"[50]—such is the verdict of Sollogub's traveler in *Tarantas*. In fact, Sollogub seems to devote nearly as much space (page after page) to insisting on the sameness of "all provincial towns" as Dolgorukov devoted to their various distinguishing features: in the span of two decades, it had become not only possible but virtually obligatory to dwell on such places' absolute equivalence. While Dolgorukov rarely measured provincial places against the capitals, these later texts tend to remind us, early and often, that they are looking at the provinces from the far-off center. Almost every work addressed here opens with an explicit reminder of the provinces-capital divide ("The district town of S. is one of the saddest little towns in Russia," "In an imaginary provincial town," etc.),[51] a framing gesture ensuring that whatever comes after is marked as provincial before it is allowed to be anything else. Thus in prose fiction of the 1830s and 1840s, the capital is immediately established, and steadily maintained, as the standard against which everything and everyone will be judged. *Stolitsa* is becoming necessary as *point of view*, and when seen from the far-off center, everything in the provinces looks identical. (This point of view will remain typical of Russian novels for decades: when a character in *Crime and Punishment* asserts that "to see everything and see it clearly, one must be in Petersburg," we know exactly what he is talking about.)[52]

We are warned not to expect novelty: Aleksei Pleshcheev opens his novel *Everyday Scenes* (1852) by noting that "the physiognomy of the town of Bobrov was among the most ordinary, with 'everything as it was supposed to be,'"[53] just as Herzen's provincial town in *Who Is to Blame?* is introduced by a row of government offices "painted the usual yellow color."[54] Often we encounter long lists of nouns—and often the same nouns from one text to another—serving to underscore predictability and tedium. In *Tarantas*, the list includes "public offices, the Assembly of the Nobility, an apothecary, a river, a town square, a shopping arcade, two or three street lamps, and the governor's house."[55] In *Everyday Scenes*, we read about "public offices painted a dull yellow, the governor's house with Venetian windows and a balcony, a club where people played cards on Saturdays and danced on Thursdays," all "there as everywhere."[56] Such passages enumerate the attributes of *provintsiia* in ways meant to imply that we might easily have drawn up the same lists ourselves. "Always the same stationmasters, the same post coaches," Sollogub writes in "Serezha," concluding with a list of conveyances—*dormeuse, calèche, diligence*—that one will "always" encounter on the streets.[57]

If the capitals stand for constant change and movement—"life in the capital is like a torrent, carrying everything away with itself," says a character in *Tarantas*—the provinces stand for pure stasis: "flat on the left . . . flat on the right . . . everywhere just the same."[58] Time here is as monotonous as space, and space is almost lethal in its monotony:

> The surroundings are dead; land, land, land, so much land that your eye tires of looking at it; the road is wretched . . . carts are pulled along . . . the peasants curse—and that's it. And there—either the caretaker is drunk, or cockroaches crawl along the

ceiling, or the soup smells of tallow candles . . . how can a decent person occupy himself with such filth? And most desolate of all is that over this whole vast space there reigns some sort of horrible uniformity that exhausts you and won't let you rest. . . . There's nothing new, nothing unexpected. Everything the same, the same . . . and tomorrow will be as it is now. Here is the station, there again is the same station, and there yet again is the same station; here is the village elder who begs for vodka, and there again to eternity are all the village elders who beg for vodka.[59]

The provinces are frozen in time, outside of history ("nothing new, nothing unexpected"); like the colonial peripheries of European empires, they are experienced as static and meaningless because they are believed to be "left out, existing on the margins of events that powerful people represent as central to what matters in the world."[60] Thus in an epilogue of sorts attached to the end of *The Apothecary's Wife*, a year has passed since the story's events, but we are told that nothing has changed here because nothing *can* change here, except perhaps the buildings might become even more decrepit and the sidewalks even more impassable.[61] The people are as predictable as the built environment: from one town to the next, says Sollogub, "local society is even more alike than are the buildings"; from one estate to the next, says Herzen, you meet identical people with different last names.[62]

In such places nothing happens just once; everything is iterative. "As it was last year, so it is this year, and so it will be next year. Just as once you met a fat merchant in a magnificent caftan," accompanied by his wife with blackened teeth, so will you meet him again. "And you will keep on meeting him"—same caftan, same black teeth—until you may wish to "lock yourself up in a room" and withdraw from life itself.[63] Herzen's inescapable merchant and his wife with her inescapably black teeth—such images point toward what we will encounter in Gogol's provincial abyss of repetition and stasis.

Even as the provinces are depicted as nauseatingly repetitive and familiar, constant assertions of their always-already-known-ness are accompanied by descriptions of the people who live there as exotics and even freaks, rare specimens of the barely human. In *Tarantas* Sollogub notes that the Russian peasant might be compared to "a savage from the Aleutian Islands"; for Zagoskin, provincial social structures call to mind India's caste system.[64] In Herzen's memoir of his 1830s exile in "the slough of provincial life,"[65] we encounter a whole catalogue of bureaucrats so spiritually deformed that they are virtually monstrous—the kind of people who in *Who Is to Blame?* will make a show of killing a rabbit under a bell jar "in the name of science."[66] The governor of Perm *guberniia* is "a peculiar sort of beast that is met with in the forest, in the wild, a beast that ought to have been studied," and ladies in Vyatka flock around the visiting tsarevich "like savages around a traveler."[67] "Notes of a Young Man" likens provincials to the Japanese and (most inexplicably) to "albinos";[68] *Who Is to Blame?* looks even further afield for images to convey provincial alienness, comparing the inhabitants of a tiny district town to "the wild men of Australia" ("as if they too had gone unrecognized, placed outside the law by mankind").[69]

As a way of pleading with readers not to reject what he has "uncovered" in the far-off provinces, Herzen even dedicates the "Notes" to two French naval explorers; the grotesqueries of Russian provincial life are worthy of our attention, Herzen suggests, just as the intrepid naval explorers did not disdain even those islands "whose only inhabitants were loathsome slugs and a few strange-beaked birds."[70] In this strange parallel (provincials = loathsome slugs) we note that a geographic space described as provincial and thus unambiguously Russian can at times play a role similar to that of colonies and imperial peripheries in other literary traditions: *provintsiia* for Herzen is a space that must be penetrated by explorers from the metropole before it will yield the sorts of "discoveries" that might make it somewhat interesting. But this "interestingness" will always be the fleeting product of metropolitan eyes and wit; at any moment, *provintsiia* is likely to revert to being banal and static, and always all too familiar.

Imitation, Unnaturalness, Constraint

Provincials crave anything that makes its way to them from the capitals—whether consumer goods, journals, gossip, or people—with almost equal intensity. Hence these texts' insistence on the provincial person's devouring gaze, greedily directed toward everything *stolichnyi*. In *The Apothecary's Wife*, an avidly curious "provincial dandy" serves as a kind of chorus, tracking the main character (a baron from Petersburg) in order to remark on his waistcoat, his carriage, and his stationery, asking questions about the provenance and cost of his fashionable belongings, and complaining that it is impossible to procure or even to imagine such goods in a small town.[71] The passion for any sort of intelligence believed to originate in the capitals leaves provincials vulnerable to deception (a fact that will be key to the plots of *Dead Souls*, *The Inspector General*, and *Demons*); thus, in *A Novel in Two Letters*, the visiting Petersburg aristocrat invents ridiculous dance moves ("pas de chamois, pas de gazelle, pas de Bedouin," he calls them) and convinces the "little local dandies" that such is the latest style.[72] When the provincial dandy in *The Apothecary's Wife* smells a perfumed letter sent from Petersburg, he reacts ecstatically ("oh the fragrance! . . . One knows immediately it's from the capital!").[73] This young man's clothing reveals "clear signs of a provincial dandy," but he has not given up trying. Rather, his failures induce him to try harder; he begs the baron, for example, to make available his fashionable jacket for copying.[74]

But when the aspiring fop inquires as to whether a certain look is currently being worn in Petersburg, the baron's cool response is, "I don't know, to tell the truth."

People dress as they wish"—which is, of course, untrue.[75] In reality no one, in any place, who aspires to stylishness can dress "as he wishes"; there is no "fashion" without imitation and assiduous *following*. When Herzen asserts that in Italy, unlike in Russia, everyone simply "dresses as he pleases" ("in Europe people get dressed, but we [Russians] dress up"; "our own clothing is alien to us"), he is imagining a European naturalness only to highlight what he sees as Russian unnaturalness.[76] Somov's fastidious narrator (in *A Novel in Two Letters*) concedes that there is really nothing wrong with the way one pretty *provintsialochka* (little provincial maiden) is dressed, but nonetheless he finds himself put off, reminded of a "fashionable Parisian doll."[77] Only those in the world's various centers have perfected the delicate balance of conformity and deviance that is essential to appearing "effortless" in the deployment of what we know as fashion.

Provincials know that to be provincial is to be behind; by 1821, Ryleev's visitor to the capital senses that he will always be trying to catch up. And as I discuss in chapter 1, you can only be behind if your world believes in things like progress, fashion, and the march of enlightenment (whereas, as we will see in chapter 8, literary regionalism imagines static "folk" worlds that are immune to fashion's seductions). Thanks to modern technologies of communication, reproduction, and dissemination, the capital can begin to impose on the rest of the country "every day, by telegraph or train, . . . its ideas, its wishes, its conversations, its ready-made revolutions, its ready-made clothing and furniture."[78] And in modernizing Russia as in Tarde's France, attaining to fashionability becomes a serious matter indeed, since fashion constitutes "one of the main routes of access to modernity."[79]

All fashion is copying, but fashion in the provinces is copying that is obvious and arduous: no provincial would even pretend to be free to dress "as he [or she] wishes." Somov's gentry maidens in their steppe town are condemned to "pitiful, ugly imitation of the misbegotten fashion plates spread throughout the provinces by Moscow journals"; in *Who Is to Blame?* "provincial lady aristocrats" speak strictly in clichés lifted from sentimental literature (e.g., "feminine hearts," "tender feelings of the soul").[80] Maintaining the correct *ton* in the provinces, Somov says, is possible only for those living on a few of the very grandest estates (places that are not really *in* the provinces, as I discuss elsewhere).[81] For the rest, mimicry results in a conspicuous lack of naturalness, as Somov and Sollogub note in their repeated references to provincial affectation (as Somov puts it, "all those pretty pretensions to artfulness, grace, with, and so on").[82]

The provincial ball is the best venue for showcasing failures of taste because a highly choreographed social ritual, one that is supposed to come off as effortlessly graceful, will inevitably highlight acts of imitation, almost always appearing, in Herzen's words, "stupid, awkward, exceedingly poor and motley"; awkwardness is simply unavoidable, he says, "in a little town under such rare circumstances."[83] Over and over writers focus on balls in the provinces even as they insist that everyone already knows all about them: in *A Novel in Two Letters*, a detailed description of such an event immediately follows the words, "don't expect from me a detailed description of a village ball: just read the fifth chapter of *Onegin*" (though Pushkin's Larins are not provincial in the way this word comes to be used by the 1830s).[84] Despite such demurrals, as a setting for literature the provincial ball proves irresistible: it allows writers to expose not only failures of taste, but also the excruciating effortfulness that comes to be associated with the provinces, where "everything is done with such pretensions, so *unnaturally*," that it seems no authentic life is within reach.[85]

Once provincials are seen to be expending effort, they are immediately marked not only as unnatural (the opposite of Tatiana Larina, whose perfect naturalness and "simplicity" are discussed in the previous chapter) but also as *unfree*. Thus among the chief signs of provinciality are watchfulness and anxious servility, as we see here in Somov, who asserts that "pathetic imitation" has the effect of

> depriving [provincials] of their freedom of movement, subjugating the young ladies
> to a sort of mincing ceremoniousness and evoking melancholy in the experienced
> observer, who in the capitals has become used to triumphs of taste and subtlety. Add
> to this the forced and unwilling quality of conversation that is poor in thought or
> even wit, the statue-like expressions on the faces, the frozen or the vacantly wan-
> dering gaze, the unvarying and unpleasant grimaces, the constrained gait . . . woe,
> woe is our brother who finds himself at a ball or a party among the rural gentry,
> especially where there is dancing! It is no festivity, but rather sheer torture, and the
> ultimate abasement for provincial maidens![86]

Deprivation, subjugation, force, unwillingness, abasement—the vocabulary here underscores the extraordinary degree to which provincials are thought to be constrained. At the same time, Somov's description of the baron—"the *experienced* observer, who in the capitals has become used to triumphs of taste and subtlety"—directs our attention to the kind of expertise that is absent in the provinces because it can only be developed by way of ample opportunities for comparison—opportunities that are available only in the metropole (a process Goncharov highlights in *An Ordinary Story*, the topic of chapter 5).

"Everything is Barbarous and Horrid"

Inexperience, isolation, and copying generate the spectacular failures of taste—especially the inept *mixing* of styles and registers—that mark the provincial milieu. Sollogub writes in "Serezha," for example, that "in our enlightened time everyone knows what architecture is"—with the exception of those in the para-digmatic provincial town of Zubtsovo, where the concept "means nothing." See, for example, Sollogub's description of the grotesquely overgrown mansion of a local landowner, who has spent decades building on additions, ornaments, and flourishes:

> Some sort of undefined, indefinite heap of roofs, corners, chimneys, planks, and windows. For a long time the traveler can't imagine what it is: is it an unfinished ship, or some other sort of phenomenon, or a monument to Noah's Ark; then fi-nally he begins to suspect that it is perhaps a house. He gets closer—yes, it really is a house. But what a house, what an original house among houses! The façade is indented at the corner, like the legs of a dancing instructor in third position. On the walls, sometimes with upholstered panels, little windows are sprinkled around in apparent competition with each other, first bumping into each other, then with-drawing to a respectable distance. To this façade on all sides had been added little houses, outbuildings, and wings with the same romantic disorder.[87]

The same kind of meaningless flourishes are added onto the interior of an inn in *Tarantas*, where "the ceiling is painted with various little flowers, peaches, and Cupids," and everything is marred by "pretensions to filthy foppery."[88] The inn's menu, too, is so distorted by francophone affectation (and garden-variety mis-spellings) that it is incomprehensible: diners can choose, for example, between *sup lipotazh* (*soupe le potage*, i.e., "soup the soup") or *kuritsa s rys'iu* ("chicken with lynx [*rys'*]"—no doubt intended as chicken with rice [*ris*]).[89] In *Who Is to Blame?*, the all-pervading pretension in a small town leads to cultural deformation, with "titu-lar counselors behaving like Roman senators"[90] and schoolchildren made to line up and chant in garbled French (a "Celtic-Slavonic" or "Franco-ecclesiastical dialect"). What Herzen emphasizes above all is the resulting incoherence: motley uniforms, strange frock coats, confused gossip; a church that combines Byzantine, classical, and Gothic elements; and carriages of every conceivable shape and size, including one that resembles "a pumpkin from which one quarter has been sliced off."[91]

Carriage, church, manor house, inn, menu—all underscore the indiscriminate nature of provincial taste, a chaos that results from ignorance of what things and words might actually *mean*. This is the version of provinciality that will later be highlighted—and indicted for its failings, both aesthetic and moral—in characters like *Fathers and Sons'* shallow, babbling *provintsialka* Kukshina. What Turgenev's *nigilistka* (female nihilist) has in common with Sollogub's menu and manor house is a "culture" that is overflowing with importations and thus disordered to the point of unintelligibility. If in some texts provinciality signifies chiefly meagerness (as in Turgenev's "Hamlet of Shchigrov" or Shchedrin's *The Golovlyov Family*), here it is marked by the promiscuous mixing of incompatible elements, what Somov calls provincials' "incongruous dandyism of attire, the motleyness of their bad taste."[92]

Incoherence can be worse than meagerness, worse than mere poverty or cultural scarcity. Herzen muses that "in small, patriarchal German towns" one might live a life that is simple and "limited" but also "pure" and "moral," unlike in *provintsiia*. And Sollogub's poor apothecary's wife (*aptekarsha*), who has been forced to move from her wholesome German hamlet to the Russian provinces, recalls that back home she was poor, but her father's house was full of books and peace, both expressions of a cultural order that infused life with meaning: "everything in the little town [breathed] intellectual activity and youthful spiritual revelry."[93] In her Russian "Town of S." she finds "the same poverty but without poetry, the same cares but without consolations, the same spiritual loneliness but without hope": "Everything is barbarous and horrid."[94] Sollogub makes the same point in the Slavophilic dream scene toward the end of *Tarantas*, in which the narrator imagines the utopian future of a town that is currently characterized by filth, lack, and brokenness.

> The streets were not standing like sad wastes [*pustyniami*] but instead teemed with movement and people. Nowhere were there fences in place of houses, no houses with mournful exteriors, broken windows, or ragged house serfs at the gates. There were no ruins, tottering walls, or filthy shops.[95]

What is not there in the future is, of course, exactly what *is* there now—rags and dirt. As Herzen puts it in "Notes of a Young Man," the locals live "up to their necks in filth."[96] Filth, swamp, slime, dust (*griaz', boloto, tina, pyl'*)—such words recur constantly in descriptions of the provinces, suggesting not only degradation but also the kind of messy category confusion and disorder associated with *provintsial'nost'*. If dirt is "matter out of place," then the provinces are where nothing can ever be where it should be.[97]

Unredeemed Materiality and Feminine Detail

If Sollogub's Town of S. is indeed "barbarous and horrid," as the *aptekarsha* would have it, perhaps this is so because S. hints at the provinces' unredeemed materiality, all of that horrifying *stuff* that will crowd Gogol's towns and estates. Consider the opening passage of Sollogub's tale:

> The district Town of S. is one of the saddest little towns in Russia. Both sides of its one dirty street are lined with submissively stooped little houses, dark gray-ish

brown, practically covered over and half weighed down by boards, little houses that rather resemble beggars in their rags, pitifully beseeching passersby. Two or three churches—lofty luxury of the Russian people—are sharply distinguished from the dark background. And an old wooden bazaar, repository of nails, flour, and lard, gazes sadly at itself in an enormous puddle that never dries out. From two or three low little houses, the drunken faces of clerical workers are peeking out. On the left a tavern shows itself with the inevitable fir tree; behind it, the jail with its lattice fence; and on the right, tacked onto the dilapidated gable is a black board with the inscription "*Apteka*, Apotheke."[98]

Here as in so many texts, *provintsiia* is characterized by a density that is *merely* physical—nails, flour, lard, rags, boards. The street is almost—but not quite—devoid of life (we briefly glimpse a few drunken faces); for the most part things have replaced people as what we need to know about the town. Gogol's lists will go much further in this direction (refusing, for instance, to differentiate between the animate and the inanimate: "a string of pretzels, a woman in a red kerchief, a crate of soap, a few pounds of bitter almonds, shot for small arms, half-cotton cloth, and two salesclerks"),[99] but already in the writers considered here, we see the beginnings of this persistent association: the provinces are linked to a noticeably thick version of materiality. Things here are just things, and they strike us as repellent not so much due to their own qualities (because what after all is wrong with pellets or pretzels?), but rather due to their quantity (which suggests grotesque accumulation) and their apparent resistance to being made meaningful.

Tarantas sums up provincial "culture" with yet another list (samovar, grinding mill, thresher, cold fish soup, meat pies), concluding that provincials need only "cabbage soup and a bathhouse, a storage cellar, a tarantas, and rural rot."[100] "Serezha" gives us "the same pastries, fish, cookies, cutlets . . . your hard rolls, your morocco boots, your cabbage soup so thick it can barely be poured from the bowl."[101] These recurring catalogues of mundane nouns suggest not only predictability but also a certain equivalence, even interchangeability, thanks to their flat one-after-another iterativeness.[102] Enumerated for us in ways that conspicuously refuse order, related by little besides contiguity, invested with no significance capable of drawing our attention away from their materiality—one might understand the material culture of *provintsiia* (if one can even call it culture: it looks more like debris) as the opposite of Mandelshtam's Acmeist yearning for a "Hellenized" world, where every object would be a "utensil," filled with purpose and meaning:

Hellenism is a baking dish, a pair of tongs, an earthenware jug with milk; it is domestic utensils, crockery, the body's whole ambience . . . any personal possession

that joins part of the external world to a man . . . Hellenism means consciously
surrounding man with utensils [*utvar'*] instead of with indifferent objects; the metamorphosis of these objects into the utensil; the humanization of the surrounding
world; the environment heated with the most delicate teleological warmth.[103]

By contrast, in the version of *provintsiia* under consideration here, almost every
object strikes us as "indifferent," and we find nothing that might "unite the external world to humanity."

One passage in *Tarantas* takes the listing technique to an extreme: the carriage (*tarantas*) that is itself described in quite minute detail is also stuffed with an
implausibly large quantity of objects, all of them tallied up in a paragraph full of
nouns. A partial census would include boxes and containers of all kinds, an enormous featherbed, seven feather pillows in cotton cases, meat pies, anise vodka,
roast fowls wrapped in paper, cheesecakes, ham, bread and rolls, a tea service,
rum, glasses, a milk pitcher, clothing, children's books and toys, gifts for the landowner's wife, lamps, kitchen vessels, and finally "three monstrously large trunks,"
each stuffed with still more "rubbish" and tied up with ropes.[104] (By contrast, the
young *stolichnyi* dandy who aspires to sophistication carries almost nothing: one
thinks of the strenuous minimalism of our own time's fashionable pretensions.)

Given *provintsiia*'s association with this sort of petty detail and miscellany, the
provincial might be described as a kind of anti-sublime. The sublime is meant
to strike us with a combination of grandeur and *uniformity*, and to do so at one
stroke. Details will always resist being perceived as a unified whole; the detail
"acts as a brake on perception," slowing us down and threatening to mire us in
what is ordinary and low—and, especially in the case of provincial details, what
is feminine.[105] Clearly, if we were to locate such binaries as masculine/feminine,
high/low, abstract/concrete, unitary/fragmentary, form/formlessness, sublime/not-
sublime, etc., each on the same continuum as capitals/provinces, the provinces
would always occupy the same pole as would the fragmentary, the feminine, and
so on.[106] Take Sollogub's tarantas, symbol and repository of things provincial: by
filling the vehicle with bits of "rubbish" (*khlam*) virtually all of which is domestic
in nature, the text brings together the provinces, petty detail, and femininity.

The tarantas thereby enacts what Naomi Schor calls "the unchallenged association of women and the particular"—an association which in turn has its roots
in the enduring link between femininity and an often degraded version of the
material world (as opposed to the spiritual world, the domain of masculinity).[107]
Indeed the terms in which critics have denigrated *provintsiia* and women's writing (and sometimes regionalist writing too, as I discuss in chapters 7 and 8) prove
to be strikingly similar: female writers, not only in Russia, are supposedly guilty
of an unseemly preoccupation with detail, of producing "'pointless' or 'plotless'

narratives stuffed with strange minutiae," texts that are "obsessed with things we do not understand, perhaps even grotesque."[108] And like the female body, the space of the tarantas/*provintsiia* seems to be infinitely subdividable, always subject to being even more chopped up into even more little nooks, which can then be filled with even more bits of domestic trash.

Writers often insist on the insignificance of such details by invoking the word *meloch'*—(a feminine noun meaning trifles, trivialities), which recurs in descriptions of specifically provincial places. See, for example, Odoevsky's story "The Sprite" (1837), which is about what happens to a man who leaves the capital to go live on his estate:

> The more a man attends to his material needs—the more highly he values his domestic (*domashnie*) affairs and domestic (*domashnie*) woes, other people's opinions, their attitudes and behavior toward him, his own trivial (*melochnye*) pleasures, in a word, all the trifles (*meloch'*) of life—then the more he is unhappy. These trifles (*melochi*) become for him the whole of existence . . . and since such trifles (*melochi*) are innumerable, his soul is subject to innumerable irritations . . . and the interior of his own soul becomes for him a hell.[109]

Odoevsky's character comes to share the exclusively corporeal preoccupations of his stolid neighbors, whose thoughts never waver from dogs, lunch, and the other "innumerable trivialities" that occupy them in the absence of higher concerns.

In the provinces, the narrator informs us, one encounters the same human vices and weaknesses as one does in the capitals but in forms both more powerful and more petty, simply because provincials lack the loftier distractions that might prevent them from spending "every minute of their existence in an entirely debased state." In a place where all concerns are material, a degrading power accrues to minutiae, and life becomes a "bestial dream" (*zhivotnyi son*).[110] Just so Herzen identifies the "bestial desires" (*zhivotnye zhelaniia*) and pervasive triviality of provincial life—the indolence, the "food that would kill anyone accustomed to a European diet," etc.[111] In the absence of all "theoretical interests," a few people may preserve vestiges of an intellectual life, but even they are stunted by "provincial stagnation."[112]

Herzen's "Notes of a Young Man" and *Who Is to Blame?* rehearse virtually every provincial cliché, from filth and vulgar clothing to bureaucracy and bad French, in order to drive home the point that the provinces deaden mind and soul, leaving intact only the body and its wholly predictable demands. But when Herzen dwells on this kind of base corporeality, he does something that most other writers considered here do not: he conceives of the provinces as a *milieu* in the sense of an environment that shapes character. This is especially evident in *Who Is to Blame?*,

a text that is preoccupied with the human losses—the failures of development—
occasioned by provincial culture. The point is made bluntly and repeatedly:
"Nothing on earth can ruin a man like life in the provinces."[113]

   Herzen's understanding of environment is much closer to Balzac's than to, say,
Sollogub's (or for that matter to that of Gogol, whose characters cannot be shaped
by milieu because they are hardly "characters" at all). Thus Herzen concedes that
one sometimes encounters provincials who would have been better—would have
been *human*—had they not been stunted or dissipated by the conditions under
which they lived: "One met with people who had at first possessed some kernel
of a human soul, some sort of possibility—but they had fallen fast asleep in this
pitiful, narrow life."[114] This is a possibility for which most of the writers treated
here do not allow, and one that mitigates the moral fault of Herzen's provincials
("Poor people! . . . are they to blame that with their mother's milk they imbibed
inhuman ideas, that they were deformed by their upbringing, that all their higher
needs were stifled?").[115]

You Can't Get There from Here

Despite Herzen's understanding of place as milieu, there is a certain placelessness to his conception of *provintsiia*. In *Who Is to Blame?* he explains that "there
is no need to specify the [setting's] time and place with chronological or geographic accuracy,"[116] not even a need to distinguish much between, say, a tiny
district town (*uezdnyi gorod*) and a larger one (*gubernskii gorod*). If a landowner
from some "RR" were to arrive in some "NN," he says, those in NN would immediately recognize Mr. RR as one of their own.[117] Even more tellingly, for Herzen
Moscow itself can stand in for *provintsiia*: life there is dirty and coarse, rigid and
unchanging, with a "deep-seated hostility to anything new." Much as Goncharov's
aging Oblomov will recreate Oblomovka on the outskirts of Petersburg, Herzen's
crude landowner Negrov manages to inhabit Moscow in what is described as a
thoroughly provincial manner, recreating the life he once lived on his estate—"an
endless succession of days and nights, monotonous, empty, and dull."[118]

   If, for Herzen, Moscow can be provincial, perhaps this is because he perceives
that all of Russia might be provincial. This is a point he makes explicitly in *My
Past and Thoughts* ("We look on Europeans and on Europe just as provincials
[*provintsialy*] look upon those who live in the capital, with deference and a feeling of inferiority"), and one that will be developed by later writers.[119] Herzen's
provincializing of Moscow calls to mind Mikhail Epstein's claim that both of
Russia's capitals have at times been figured as provincial "in relationship to an
imperial power that is always [both] elusive and transcendental."[120] One might
say that Russia's provinces, too, are elusive (if not transcendental): like the capitals

in Epstein's formulation, the provinces often seem to occupy no fixed location; indeed they are sometimes placeless to the point of nonbeing. Herzen suggests as much when he writes about the paradigmatic town he calls Malinov (described in detail in "Notes of a Young Man" and later taken as the basis of NN in *Who Is to Blame?*). Even in travel accounts encompassing everything on earth, Herzen claims, you will not find Malinov, because it "lies outside the circle of the world."[121]

Herzen's Malinov does not exist—but nonexistence does not keep it from being "the worst city in the world," since "it's impossible to imagine anything worse for a town than total nonexistence [*nesushchestvovanie*]."[122] Elsewhere Herzen says the same of a very real city, the *gubernskii gorod* of Perm in the Urals: "Perm is a strange thing. . . . Perm is government offices + a few houses + a few families," but it is "not a center, not a focus"; it is instead "the decided absence of all life."[123] Other writers echo Herzen's negation: having a name and an administrative function and even a history does not, it seems, guarantee existence once one is located in *provintsiia*. Throughout the nineteenth century, Perm—a city with quite a distinctive location and history—is variously described as a "deathly emptiness," an "empty place" without meaning or reason to exist, characterized by "utter silence all around": "nothing but carrion!" (and it is described in such terms even as writers call attention to its grubby materiality—muddy streets, drunken merchants, etc.).[124] Such passages—in which provincial places waver on the edge of nonbeing—call to mind the worlds of *Dead Souls* and *The Inspector General*, characterized as they are by "emptiness, eventlessness, and nonbeing [*nebytie*]."[125]

In a footnote to "Notes of a Young Man" (the same note in which he draws a parallel between provincials and "loathsome slugs"), Herzen again gestures toward the idea of the provinces' nonexistence, this time by linking his representative provincial town ("outside of the circle of the world") to another work, Dal's 1839 tale *The Unlucky One* (in Russian *Bedovik*, from *beda*, misfortune or disaster), which turns out to be the source for the invented toponym Malinov. Herzen writes that before he himself reached Malinov, only one other traveler had preceded him: "and he brought back from there an example of a tailless ape, which he called in Latin 'Bedovik.' [This ape] almost disappeared between Petersburg and Moscow."[126] Herzen then cites the issue of *Notes of the Fatherland* in which Dal's story appeared.[127]

The Unlucky One is about a typical "little man" of the period, a clerk named Evsei Stakheevich Lirov whose haplessness and forbearance recall Gogol's Akaky Akakievich in "The Overcoat." But unlike Akaky Akakievich, Lirov lives in the provinces, in a stagnant, petty town (Malinov) that is precisely as we have learned such a town must be: people there fill their time with pointless and repetitive visits, conversation is limited to gossip and weather, and a rigid decorum governs social relations ("In a narrow circle, thoughts become narrow as well").[128] While

Akaky Akakievich's fatally audacious act is the purchase of a new coat, Lirov's is an ill-conceived decision to go to the capital.

The idea of leaving Malinov seizes Lirov when he is mocked by a passerby ("with such strange habits why bother serving in the provinces? . . . You might as well go to the capital, give people a good look at you!"). But we sense immediately that the capital will prove both elusive and illusory:

> He repeated to himself: to the capital! And a new thought flashed like lightening in his tangled head. "To the capital" he thought, "To the capital . . . no, there's definitely no place in the capital for such an eccentric or unlucky type [*chudak, bedovik*] . . . but what if I were just to go there and find myself a place? If I were to be lucky, if I were to find myself a really powerful patron . . . after all I'm my own master . . . well, what if?"[129]

The rest of the narrative consists of Lirov's protracted and ultimately unsuccessful attempt to make his way from the provinces to either Moscow or Petersburg. His first goal is Moscow; the possibility of Petersburg is initially too daring to occur to him ("The thought of Moscow alone was already spinning his head . . . and now the two capitals [were] like two fairytale visions").[130] Unable to decide on a destination ("Moscow or Petersburg—it's all the same to me"),[131] swept back and forth by indecision, misfortune, and bad counsel, Lirov repeatedly changes direction. In the end, as the chapter titles indicate, he is not permitted to reach either city:

> Ch. 1: Evsei Stakheevich decides to go to the capital (. . .)
> Ch. 4: Evsei Stakheevich sets out for Petersburg
> Ch. 5: Evsei Stakheevich sets out for Moscow
> Ch. 6: Evsei Stakheevich sets out for Petersburg
> Ch. 7: Evsei Stakheevich really sets out for Petersburg
> Ch. 8: Evsei Stakheevich sets out for Moscow
> Ch. 9: Evsei Stakheevich arrives somewhere
> Ch. 10: Evsei Stakheevich, in expectation of further blessings, sits in one place (. . .)
> Ch. 12: Evsei Stakheevich has enjoyed his trip and has returned

Approaching Moscow, the clerk makes it as far as the village of Chernaia griaz; approaching Petersburg, he gets as close as Chudovo, but no further. His time is spent repeatedly passing through Tver, Novgorod, Valdai, Torzhok, etc., often only half aware of where he is.[132]

> Had he ever thought, when he was sitting home in Malinov, idly tracing his finger back and forth on the map between Moscow and Petersburg, that he'd be fated to

wander between those two points not just with his finger but in actuality . . . for weeks in succession, here and there, in the end reaching neither?[133]

While his servant berates him for time spent "racing senselessly back and forth between Petersburg and Moscow," "never setting eyes on either,"[134] Dal's little provincial man covers and re-covers the same ground, seemingly trapped in a kind of feedback loop, all the time dreaming of the glorious capitals that he will never see. The story ends with his return to Malinov.

If in Herzen the provincial town verges on nonexistence, in Dal it is the capitals that seem to occupy the threshold of reality, or at least reality as it exists for provincials. Lirov can dream of the capital all he wants (either capital, since both are "the same to him"), but the narrative is structured to suggest that in *The Unlucky One* the capital—not unlike Petersburg in *The Inspector General*, or Moscow in *Three Sisters*—is an unreachable place for a provincial, because it stands for a strictly unrealizable ideal. Thus Lirov is "fated," as Dal says, to vacillate back and forth between two points, neither of which is attainable from where he begins. Here as in many works of literature, capitals and provinces would seem to be in a relationship of mutual nonexistence, or perhaps occupying different ontological levels: you can't get there from here.

"The Highest Degree of Emptiness"

The works treated here make it clear that the *provintsiia* trope did not originate with Gogol, whose work is the subject of the next chapter. But it was Gogol's art that was to make *provintsiia* speak so powerfully and enigmatically to "Russianness" in a larger sense, and it was thanks to his radically original reworking of the trope— his ability to associate *provintsiia* with a range of meanings it had not previously evoked—that the image became such an enduring one. One might say that Gogol activated certain contradictions that were more or less latent in the idea of *provintsiia* as it appears in the texts addressed in the present chapter.

We have seen how literature insists on *provintsiia*'s materiality (nails, flour, lard)—and yet, at the same time, literature's provincial places are *empty*. *Provintsiia* is crammed full of material things, and yet barren—the "sad wastes" of *Tarantas*, the "empty" life of Herzen's landowners, etc. We expect as much on the steppe ("no matter where you go or what you do you get nowhere"),[135] but it is striking to read the same insistence on the emptiness of provincial towns and estates, which are in fact crowded with disparate artifacts of human activity. Here too Herzen sees "the same emptiness everywhere," "an absolute and multifaceted emptiness," emptiness so profound that one cannot understand "why these people got out of bed, why they moved, what they lived for."[136]

Dead Souls will take this paradox—the idea that in the provinces, emptiness coexists with a surfeit of *merely physical* objects—to surreal extremes, dwelling on provincial materiality (the interiors of Korobochka's and Pliushkin's houses, the Pleasant Ladies' obsession with fabric) while also insisting that the defining feature of *gorod N* is what it describes as a desolate void.[137] In the writers surveyed in this chapter, the paradox is registered only as a vague contradiction, one that it is implicitly acknowledged but not addressed or exploited. For Gogol, however, it will become the basis of a new and unsettling artistic vision—"a sense of boundless superfluity that is soon revealed as utter emptiness"—as well as a powerful way of imagining Russian national identity. It is left to Gogol to explore—or perhaps better, to invent—the relationship between "the desolation of the gigantic country and its hidden inner dynamics," between Russia's apparent brokenness and its sublime promise.[138]

· CHAPTER FOUR ·

"This is Paris Itself!":
Gogol in the Town of N

Art has the provinces in its blood. Art is provincial in principle,
preserving for itself a naïve, external, astonished and envious look.

—Andrei Sinyavsky, 1976

Wandering these backwaters, I've seen such dreary things that it was hard
for me to believe there somewhere exists magnificent Moscow, art, *et cetera*.
And yet it seems to me that genuine art and thought can in fact only appear
in such a backwater.

—Andrei Platonov, 1927

Pronouncements like Platonov's and Sinyavsky's are made possible by Nikolai
Gogol, in whose work the provincial backwater becomes not just a recurring image but a governing trope of Russian literature. Sinyavsky and
Platonov both connect their vision of the provinces to the fictional world that
Gogol created: it is in a study of Gogol that Sinyavsky argues for art's essentially
provincial nature, and Platonov describes his experience in the Tambov region
as a "crushing dream" of immersion in a "Gogolian province."[1] In Gogol's imagination the category of *provintsiia* accrues meanings well beyond narrowness,
distortion, and deathly stasis, tipping over into something more mysterious and
darkly resonant than what we have seen in the writers addressed so far. Thanks to
Gogol the provinces became symbolically central to Russian identity, a touchstone
without which it would be difficult to imagine works as diverse as Dostoevsky's
Demons, Shchedrin's *The Golovlyov Family*, Chekhov's "Ward No. Six," Sologub's
Petty Demon, and Dobychin's *The Town of N*. Even for writers who were to depart

from Gogol's symbolic geography in various ways, his work established the centrality of the trope itself, and engagement with the trope was unavoidable. After *Dead Souls* and *The Inspector General*, the Russian provincial town would always risk being characterized by the adjective "Gogolian."

The "Gogolian province" is epitomized by *Dead Souls'* Town of N, a place defined almost wholly by absence and lack. In his working notes to the novel's first chapter, Gogol conjures up his provincial city in the following terms: "The idea of the city. The highest degree of Emptiness. Empty talk. . . . How the emptiness and impotent idleness of life are replaced by a turbid and meaningless death [*mutnoiu, nichego ne govoriashcheiu smert'iu*]." A bit later he continues, "The reader must be struck by the dead insensibility of life" in the provincial town.[2] "The highest degree of Emptiness," "the dead insensibility of life": this is a somewhat more mystifying vision of *provintsiia* than what we have seen in other texts of the 1830s and 1840s. Sollogub and Herzen may describe *provintsiia* as being plagued by bad taste, motley culture, repetition, and status anxiety, but they are less likely to go so far as to equate provincial life with "turbid and meaningless death."

Gogol's provinces are not just philistine, not just behind the times, but seem instead to represent an unfillable cultural and psychic void. This chapter examines the historically shaped (but aesthetically transformed) meanings of "the provinces" that inform Gogol's thought, particularly in *Dead Souls*, *The Inspector General*, and *Selected Passages from Correspondence with Friends*—texts that span much of his career but share almost identical concerns when it comes to *provintsiia* and its meanings. (Indeed, there is little "development" in this particular set of ideas, which is why I do not address Gogol's works in strictly chronological order.) *Provintsiia* here takes on a function it is not consistently called upon to fulfill in the works of other authors I have considered. In Gogol's works the concept very clearly serves as a way of raising questions about Russian identity more broadly. We begin to understand why provinciality is more deeply worrisome in Gogol's Russia than elsewhere: Gogol capitalizes on the painful fact that in Russia, the provinciality of the provinces can be seen to reflect the provinciality and perhaps even the "inauthenticity" of the nation as a whole.

An Aside on Ukraine

As I discuss in chapter 1 of this book, the provinces are provincial because they are not something else; they are defined by what they lack. One thing the Russian provinces are not, at least for Gogol, is Ukrainian. Before discussing the significance of Russian *provintsiia* in Gogol's work, we would do well to examine, even if briefly, how he conceived of the relationship between Russia and (the) Ukraine, as well as the vocabulary he used to write about them. While somewhat tangential to this chapter's main argument, a clarification is essential—particularly since it has been argued that for Gogol, Ukrainian national or folk identity represented a standard of organic culture against which Russia, an imperial power thought to be plagued by a fundamental lack of *narodnost'* (national identity), could be judged and found lacking.[3]

The status of both Ukrainianness and Russianness is, I would argue, unstable in Gogol's oeuvre, a fact that should not be surprising given the complexity of the Russia-Ukraine relationship both in his time and ours. Gogol was born and raised in Ukraine's Poltava region, and his life spanned a period when Ukraine was almost universally seen as an integral part of the Russian empire, when it was unproblematically referred to as "Little Russia" (*Malorossiia*, a term that "Great Russian" nationalists still use on occasion but that Ukrainians now find offensive). His family had the kind of mixed background that was not at all unusual for the Ukrainian gentry: their heritage was partly Polish; they usually spoke Russian at home but at times they spoke Ukrainian; they corresponded in Russian but read in Russian, Ukrainian, and Polish; Gogol's father wrote comedies in Ukrainian, but Gogol himself wrote only in Russian. The family did not experience their Ukrainianness as being in conflict with their status as loyal subjects and at times servitors of the Russian empire—much as Ivan Dolgorukov (whose travel writing is analyzed in chapter 3) waxes poetic about Mazeppa, Khmelnitsky, and water-melons as he approaches Ukraine, even as he expects the educated state servitors there to be "cosmopolitans" with whom he has a "shared language," people who serve "the same empire [*derzhava*]."[4]

In Gogol's day, "Great" Russians (or those who identified with an imperial version of Russian culture, including some Ukrainian elites) could choose to see "Little" Russian identity as simply, and benignly, a variant of Russianness, or even as a quaint version of the Ur-Slavic soul. Thus Faddei Bulgarin could interpret *Evenings on a Farm near Dikanka* as a reflection of the national (i.e., Russian) spirit, thanks to the fact that Ukrainians had supposedly preserved a pure form of Slavicness.[5] As Bulgarin's interpretation suggests, at times it seems to have been possible to locate (or imagine) a purer version of "Russianness" on the margins of the empire, in a place that was not in reality straightforwardly Russian, than it was to locate this sort of national purity in the (Russian) provinces. Certain other liminal or outlying regions also proved capable of accommodating the national imaginary in this way: in Aksakov's *Family Chronicle* and Turgenev's *King Lear of the Steppe*, for example, the steppes—in reality an ethnically mixed space where Russians were relative latecomers—are depicted as repositories of Russianness, much as Siberia would be treated in later texts. (And here we note a parallel with British literary history, in which, as Katie Trumpener has shown, the "Celtic fringe" was not only incorporated into "English" literature but also reimagined as central to that "English" tradition.)[6]

It made perfect sense that when Gogol wanted to make a name for himself, he set off for the Russian imperial capital of St. Petersburg: this was where you went to make a career, any career. His departure did not suggest a renunciation of Ukrainianness; rather, it signaled ambition.[7] Though the analogy is imperfect, think of an Indian writer today who chooses to write in English: because the English language is backed by an empire (or by multiple empires), it promises a more direct pathway to membership in "Great Literature" (always a concern for Gogol, who was nothing if not ambitious) than would a more "minor" language. It was in Petersburg that Gogol became famous as a Russian writer—but he did so by making canny use of his "Little Russian" identity. As soon as he arrived in the imperial capital he recognized that things Ukrainian happened to be in vogue, and he immediately wrote to his mother back home, asking her to send him anecdotes, vocabulary, folklore—whatever might be useful for capitalizing on the trend. The result was his first successful publication, a story cycle set in a "Little Russian" village, written in Russian but full of folksy Ukrainianisms and bits of local color. (Indeed the tales' attention to what is emphatically local calls to mind Russian Romantics' interest in the *realia* of imperial borderlands: *Dikanka* glosses unfamiliar regional vocabulary, just as Pushkin did in his notes to *Prisoner of the Caucasus*.)

For the rest of his life—including in his most famous texts, which are set not in Ukraine but in Russia—Gogol's perspective was informed by his Ukrainian origins. But exactly *how* these origins shaped his views of Russian culture, empire, and language—none of this is at all straightforward. Some of his Russian contemporaries took offense at works like *Dead Souls*, *The Inspector General*, and "The Overcoat," in which they discerned an anti-Russian bias that they attributed to his Ukrainianness; others read his work as a sincere if anguished paean to the "Russian soul." Both readings are plausible, and each satisfies a constituency; in fact, "the Gogol wars," which started in his time, are still going on today. One version of the fight pits Gogol against his more uncompromisingly Ukrainian contemporary Taras Shevchenko, who not only wrote in Ukrainian at a time when the tsarist authorities had forbidden it, but even suffered exile for his impassioned defense of Ukrainian language and culture. In this reading—Gogol as the anti-Shevchenko—Gogol becomes a sell-out to the imperial overlords.[8] But on the other side, there are ongoing attempts to represent Gogol as a passionate Ukrainian nationalist, even as rabidly anti-Russian. In this interpretation, Gogol becomes a sort of fifth-column presence in the literature of the Russian empire, subverting imperial culture from within (and here the analogy would be Kafka, a Czech Jew writing in and thereby "infiltrating" German).

For my purposes, it is sufficient to note that the rural Ukraine of Gogol's early tales (in particular the folksy stories collected in *Dikanka* and *Mirgorod*) has little in common with the barren *provintsiia* of "Great" Russia as it is represented in the texts I consider here. And even if one believes that Gogol saw Ukraine as symbolically opposed to Russia proper (in which case the symbolic fullness of Ukraine might be seen as a condition of the symbolic emptiness of Russia), the opposition seems only to have encouraged him to collapse the diverse regions of Russia into the category of "the provinces," thereby freighting this ill-defined category with even more significance than it carries in the work of his contemporaries. The Russian provinces—their slippery meaning, their suggestive emptiness—are virtually an obsession for Gogol, who returns to them again and again, often in an interrogative mode, asking questions that will never be answered.

Places, Named and Ranked

Where exactly are Gogol's provinces located? *Dead Souls* is set in a *gubernskii gorod*, the capital of a *guberniia* (administrative region). *The Inspector General* is set in a smaller "district town" (perhaps the very rough equivalent of an American county seat), designated by *gorod* and *gorodok* (sometimes modified by *uezdnyi* and *malen'kii*, "district" and "small") as well as by *v glushi* and *v derevne* (roughly, in the countryside). Gogol uses vocabulary similar to that found in Zagoskin's 1835 "Three Suitors" (see chapter 3), but unlike Zagoskin, who attempts to distinguish among such terms, Gogol collapses them into the same conceptual category.[9] And indeed, as I have discussed elsewhere, the terminology used to refer to provincial places in the 1830s and 1840s was not consistent. As noted in the previous chapter, this fluidity is especially apparent in the almost interchangeable use of *provintsial'nyi* and *gubernskii*. Gogol uses *guberniia* constantly and forms of *provintsiia* rarely: In *Dead Souls* the adjective *provintsial'nyi* never occurs (though the construction *v nashikh provintsiiakh* is used twice, 6:18, 577),[10] while forms of *guberniia* and *gubernskii* appear over and over. In *The Inspector General* various forms of *provintsiia* recur alongside the occasional *guberniia*, as when stage notes describe the mayor's wife as a *provintsial'naia koketka* ("provincial coquette," 4:9) and Khlestakov disparages yokels as *provintsial'nye gusi* ("provincial geese," 4:61).[11]

While these lexical distinctions carry little meaning in Gogol's work, what does signify is the provincials' acute awareness of the fact that Russian towns were ranked by law. Under Catherine, as I discuss in this book's introductory chapter, every city was assigned a place in an official hierarchy, and every town center, depending on its place in the hierarchy, was supposed to contain the same combination of public buildings.[12] Such regulations reflected not only an Enlightenment desire for symmetry and the state's determination to manifest its power in the provinces, but also the imperative to look like Petersburg, which in turn looked, or aimed to look, like Europe: ideally, every Russian city was to model itself on cities the next level up.

Just as Gogol's bureaucrats in the Petersburg tales are ever aware of the Table of Ranks that determines their possibilities in life, so everyone in the world of *Dead Souls* is implicitly aware of this spatial hierarchy, and as a result, there is nothing in this world that does not aspire to be something else, something on the next level "up."[13] The young son of the landowner Manilov ("Themistoclius," a name suggesting acute cultural confusion) has already internalized the system. To the question "which is the finest city in France?" little Themistoclius answers, Paris; and then to the questions "What is our finest city?" and "What's another fine city?" he answers readily, St. Petersburg and Moscow (6:30). As a *gubernskii gorod*, N itself functions as a kind of capital in relationship to the smaller towns lower down in the hierarchy (such as, for example, the "poor little district town" with its "rural tedium" (*bednyi uezdnyi gorodishka, uezdnaia skuka*) that is mentioned in passing; 6:110). And for the governor's ball, everyone from miles around (from the local district towns, villages, and estates) converges on N, thus reinforcing its place as a *gubernskii gorod* (provincial capital) in the ranking system (provinces → capitals → Europe) that structures provincial lives.

And where exactly is N? The town is introduced and described in the very first lines of *Dead Souls*, but of course it will never be named. The nameless backwater is then reduced almost to placelessness as well when the narrator describes it as "not far from both capitals" (6:206): one glance at a map reveals that it is impossible to be simultaneously "not far" from Petersburg and Moscow, two cities that are four hundred miles apart. Perhaps the most intelligible geographic message we can take away from this statement is a confirmation that N is located within European Russia, maybe somewhere in between Moscow and Petersburg; that is, it is *not* located in Ukraine or on the steppes or in any of the other border regions. "Not far from Petersburg and Moscow," then, actually evokes both "no place" and "in the very middle of the undifferentiated space that is (European) Russia." In *The Inspector General*, too, we are never told where the play is set, though the mayor scoffs at another character's surmise that the central authorities may be trying to sniff out traitors "in a little district town": "What is this, the borderlands or something? From here you could gallop three years and not get to a border" (4:12). Again, we do not know exactly where we are, but we know we are far from any border—that is, we are in the heart of European Russia.

Given the extreme homogeneity Gogol attributes to provincial places, is this not all we need to know? We are not invited to think about exactly where these works might be set, considering the uniformity and repetition that characterize

Gogol's provincial world. In *Dead Souls* many passages suggest that any provincial town can stand in for any other, and the city of N is above all just like all other provincial cities. In fact, almost no trait is attributed to it that is not also attributed to "all provincial cities." Chichikov's room at the inn is familiar (*izvestnogo roda*), the inn itself is also familiar (again *izvestnogo roda*, and *kak byvaiut gostinitsy v gubernskikh gorodakh*), the town's architecture is familiar (*izvestnoi*), the men in the town are "like they are everywhere, of two types" (i.e., fat and thin), the paint on the buildings is "that eternal yellow color"—the examples could easily be multiplied (6:8, 14).

In a paragraph describing the inn's common room, forms of the construction *to zhe* (the same) recur six times, summed up with the words, "in a word, everything the same as everywhere" (*slovom, vse to zhe, chto i vezde*, 6:9). The outlying landscape is described with a similar emphasis on familiarity and sameness: the landscape unfolds "as always with us" (*po nashemu obychaiu*); a few peasants are said to be yawning "as usual" (*po obyknoveniiu*); and finally, the narrator sums it all up with "in a word, the familiar sights" (*slovom, vidy izvestnye*, 6:21–22). Such uniformity suggests that even a provincial place about which one knows nothing is in effect always already known, since the provincial admits of no real variation, no individuality.

However, this seemingly implausible degree of uniformity points to social and historical realities of which Gogol was well aware. As I have explained in the introduction, Russia's provincial towns generally *did* look the same, a regularity that was the intentional result of urban planning practices that had been in effect since the time of Peter and especially Catherine. The autocratic state sought to ensure that Russian cities appeared orderly and rational, characterized by a symmetry meant to convey stability and *paradnost'* (grandeur), rational, orderly, regular, symmetrical, and permanent, with an emphasis on façades and *paradnost'* (grandeur).[14] Hence the real-life standardization Gogol describes in his essay "On Present-Day Architecture," published in the 1835 collection *Arabesques*, which notes that provincial cities feature avenues "so regular, so straight, so monotonous, that having crossed a street, one feels such boredom that one lacks all desire to look at another one" (8:61–62).

Dead Souls' Town of N exemplifies what "On Present-Day Architecture" describes as "the latest architecture of our European cities," whose deadening repetition made Gogol long for something—anything—*exceptional*: the essay calls for "majestic and colossal" buildings, "looming monuments," structures "so awful in their enormousness" that "the mind freezes before them in shock" (8:62, 66–67). Elsewhere in *Arabesques* (in an essay on teaching geography to children), Gogol suggests that when it comes to places of such numbing uniformity as N, there is literally *nothing to say*:

Let the pupil learn what Rome is, and Paris, and Petersburg. . . . *Everything that is common to all cities should be excluded from the description* of each individual one. In many of our geography textbooks it is still common to note in descriptions of every provincial town [*gubernskogo goroda*] that there is a gymnasium, a church. . . . But why? It is sufficient to tell the pupil from the start that we have gymnasiums in every provincial town, and churches too. But the Kremlin, the Vatican, the Palais Royale, Falconet's monument to Peter, the Kiev Monastery of the Caves, and the Court of King's Bench—these are unique in all the world. (8:104, emphasis mine)

"Only what distinguishes a city from the mass of other cities" is worthy of attention, and whatever repeats itself, whatever is *not singular*, should be ignored altogether (8:104). But if we apply these standards to *Dead Souls'* provincial setting, what, then, could there possibly be to say about the place?

A few years after *Dead Souls*, as we will see in the following chapter, Ivan Goncharov's *An Ordinary Story* (1846) will approach the problem of ordinariness and repetition by insisting that ordinariness and repetition are defining traits of urban modernity, and as such are to be embraced. In fact Goncharov represents the tendency to value what is singular and extraordinary as a specifically *provincial* delusion, one that can be dispelled by moving to the capital and submitting to its discipline. But Gogol's solution to the problem of N's ordinariness is to exaggerate this ordinariness to the point of absurdity, making the town's lack of defining features its defining feature.

Making the Provinces Visible

The provinces, it seems, are hard to see: and Gogol's work reveals an almost obsessive attention not just to *provintsiia* itself but to the process by which it might be made legible. He was not alone in this preoccupation. Just as his 1828 arrival in Petersburg had coincided fortuitously with a moment of "Great Russian" enthusiasm for all things "Little Russian," so his writings about *provintsiia* in the 1830s and 1840s dovetailed with, and were likely encouraged by, a period of intense official engagement with the question of how best to study the provinces (see chapter 1 for more on these state efforts). Beginning in Peter's time and intensifying in the decades following the Pugachev rebellion, the autocracy had turned its gaze outward, dispatching to Russia's various regions not just military forces, but also researchers who were charged with transforming these far-off places into objects of knowledge.[15] Such efforts took on even more urgency in the 1830s and 1840s, as the need for economic modernization motivated the central autocracy to create "provincial statistical committees" and other tools for learning about provincial places.

The goal of all these efforts was to "make the local visible to the center":[16] thus Gogol's imaginative excursions into the Russian provinces formed part of a trend among elites in the capitals. In trying to collect economic, agricultural, civic, meteorological, and legal data under nearly impossible conditions, the information-seeking bureaucrats, like Gogol, were inspired by the belief that knowledge of provincial life was essential to helping Russia understand itself. In the words of the civil servant Konstantin Arsenev, commenting on information-gathering efforts in the same year that *Dead Souls* was published, "knowledge of one's homeland . . . in view of our general striving for *narodnost'* . . . ought to be required of every statesman, civil servant, soldier, estate owner, industrialist, merchant, and, in general, every educated patriot."[17] The provincial statistical committees had much work to do, or at least much work to appear to do, if they were to fulfill Petersburg's order to "discover and catalogue the Russian people."[18]

The bureaucrat-researchers being dispatched to provincial cities were liable to meet a reception nearly as bizarre as Khlestakov's in *The Inspector General* or Chichikov's in *Dead Souls*, since their diligent efforts to compile statistical pictures of various places and institutions were met by equally diligent efforts to thwart them. Herzen's account of the absurdity and grotesquery he encountered during his internal exile in the 1830s resonates strongly with Gogol's imaginary provincial world, giving us a sense of how Gogol's fanciful thinking was to some degree a response to contemporary concerns. Herzen's description of compiling (and inventing) statistical data in a Vyatka government office might have been excerpted from *Dead Souls*:

> The Ministry of Home Affairs [Internal Affairs] had at that time a craze for statistics: it had given orders for committees to be formed everywhere, and had issued programs which could hardly have been carried out even in Belgium or Switzerland; at the same time there were to be all sorts of elaborate tables with maxima and minima, with averages and various deductions from the totals for periods of ten years (made up of evidence which had not been collected a year before!), with moral remarks and meteorological observations. Not a farthing was assigned for the expenses of the committees and the collection of evidence; all this was to be done from love of statistics.[19]

Herzen obligingly invented data, "[drawing] up summaries of the tables with eloquent remarks introducing foreign words, quotations, and striking deductions." Predictably, since no extra resources were allocated for this work, the "facts" that were collected were at times as Gogolian as the process by which they were compiled. For instance, Herzen recalls reading a statistical report from "the unimportant town of Kay" that included the following entry:

"Drowned—2. Causes of drowning not known—2, and in the column of 'total' was set out the figure 4."[20]

By Herzen's account, his fellow bureaucrats in Vyatka were relieved to accede to his superior (because *stolichnyi*) knowledge; his problematic status as a political exile, he writes, counted for nothing compared to the cachet associated with everything from the capital. His expertise was valued because the work of studying *provintsiia* was not meant to be undertaken by provincials on their own: provincials were not deemed capable of making sense even of themselves. Implicit in the state's project was the assumption that only the capital could interpret the mass of raw data to be unearthed in the provinces (as will become even clearer in chapter 8). For instance, when the Vyatka bureaucrats received instructions from Petersburg that the tsarevich's visit required "an exhibition of the district's various natural products and handicrafts . . . arranged according to the three natural kingdoms," the locals were thrown into a panic by the need to establish categories of "animal, vegetable, and mineral" ("where to put honey, for instance?")—and Herzen saved the day. As a representative of the capital's intellectual authority, he was called upon not just to invent facts, but also to bestow order on the chaos of *provintsiia*, an order that provincials themselves could neither perceive nor invent.

Gogol spent far less time in provincial Russia than Herzen did, and there is little to refute S. A. Vengerov's assertion "Gogol knew absolutely nothing of real Russian life": such is the title of a 1911 article charging that the author of *Dead Souls*, a text so often taken by nineteenth-century readers as an exposé of hard realities, had spent less than two weeks in the Russian countryside, and most of that inside a moving carriage.[21] But because Gogol shared with his contemporaries the belief that you have to know the provinces if you want to know Russia, and you have to know Russia if you want to be a true patriot, he devoted a great deal of time to reading and thinking about such places, as evidenced not only by his own published works but also by various book reviews, notes, unfinished projects, etc., which span decades. As early as 1830 he was writing a geography textbook for children; in the late 1840s he composed for himself a long, detailed summary of an eighteenth-century travelogue about the Russian provinces; at the end of his life he was working on what he projected would be "a living geography of Russia" (9:277–415, 642).

Gogol's texts often seem less concerned with the provinces themselves than with the act of *looking at* the provinces. At one point in the essay "On Present-Day Architecture," he remarks that tall buildings ("huge, colossal towers") are essential in a capital city—because how else will the capital be able to keep watch over the surrounding areas (*dlia nabliudeniia nad okrestnostiami*)? The capital needs to be able "to see at least a verst and a half in all directions," he asserts, so as always to be "surveying the provinces [*obozrevaia provintsii*], foreseeing everything in advance" (8:62). The probing gaze the center directs toward the periphery, and the periphery's reaction to this gaze: this relationship structures not just "On Present-Day Architecture," but a whole series of Gogol's texts.

The Inspector General (1836), for example, returns again and again to the behavior of provincials who suddenly become aware that the capital has turned its eyes upon them, an awareness that leaves them feeling both gratified and deeply anxious. Petty malefactors in the anonymous provincial city fear the accusatory and unmasking gaze of Petersburg, but they long for it as well—because, it seems, their inconsequential lives might become *meaningful* when seen through the capital's powerful lens. Gogol's provincials dream of the capital not only because of its associations with power and material rewards, but also because of its ability to confer *significance*. One character sums up this view of the capital's signifying power when he begs Khlestakov to inform Petersburg that *he exists*: "In Petersburg tell all the various bigwigs . . . that in such-and-such a town there lives Peter Ivanovich Bobchinksy" (the provincial place—"such-and-such a town"— goes unnamed even by its own inhabitants; 4:67). Thus in *The Inspector General* the capital looks (occasionally, and unpredictably) at the provinces in order to inspect, indict and control; the provinces look back in order to imitate, to see themselves reflected in the eyes of the powers-that-be (thereby confirming that they actually exist), and to formulate alibis as needed.

A similar preoccupation with looking and studying is evident in the last work Gogol published in his lifetime, *Selected Passages from Correspondence with Friends* (1847). *Selected Passages* is a bizarre mix of religious homily and reactionary diatribe posing as a series of personal letters. These letters imagine the provinces as the object of the capital's gaze and as a field of inquiry, a blank space yet to be filled in on Russia's conceptual map. Like the provincial statistical committees, this text quite clearly takes part in the effort to "make the local visible to the center."[22] Gogol counsels his readers to approach provincial Russia "as a new land, hitherto unknown to you," with the explicit goal of collecting information about provincial life. He returns again and again to the idea that "we"—that is, presumably, we residents of the capitals—know nothing of Russia: "Great is the ignorance of Russia within Russia, since everyone lives in foreign journals and newspapers, not in his own land" (8:303, 308). Gogol includes himself among the ignorant—"I know absolutely nothing of what is inside [Russia]," he laments (8:311; thus he more or less pleads guilty in advance to the charge Vengerov would later level against him).

The solution lies in the assiduous compiling of data: "In the same way that a Russian traveler arriving in some celebrated European city hurries to see all the antiquities and famous sights, in exactly the same way, and with even greater curiosity, after you have arrived in the chief town of a [Russian] district or province, strive to get to know the sights. They are not in architectural works or antiquities but in people" (8:303). Again and again Gogol insists upon the need to gather information directly from the provincial source, as when he addresses the wife of a provincial governor who must become acquainted with the town where her husband is posted: "In the brief time you have spent in the town of K__ you have come to know Russia better than in all your previous life" (8:311). One chapter of *Selected Passages* bears the title "It is Necessary to Travel around Russia" (*Nuzhno proezdit'sia po Rossii*, 8:301), an exhortation that is constantly repeated over the course of the letter and throughout *Selected Passages* as a whole. Gogol urges his audience to travel around the country with the goal of bringing back intelligence that will reveal "Russia in its true aspect" (*v istinnom vide [Rossiia]*, 8:302). Having previously suggested (in *Dead Souls*) that people in the provinces are all more or less the same, conforming to a few basic types, here he seems to try to convince himself that if one looks hard enough, essential truths will be revealed.

But looking at provincial Russia will not be easy. For one thing, if you are from one of the capitals, then convincing yourself that the locals are anything like you is going to require a heroic act of imagination. A striking example of the elite outsider's alienation in *provintsiia* occurs in the letter "The Russian Landowner" (*Russkoi pomeshchik*). (Note, too, the typical and suggestive Gogolian pleonasm of the title, for in this context what could the *pomeshchik* possibly be if not *russkoi*?) In this letter's opening line, Gogol assumes that the first challenge facing the Russian *pomeshchik* recently arrived in the countryside is, in effect, to believe himself to be a Russian *pomeshchik*. Rather bizarrely, he asserts that "the most important thing is that you have arrived in the countryside and that you *set yourself to being a pomeshchik*" (*Glavnoe to, chto ty priekhal v derevniu i polozhil sebe nepremenno byt' pomeshchikom*, 8:321, emphasis mine). Here the relationship to what should be one's native place is represented as anything but natural: one cannot imagine, say, an English baronet arriving at his ancestral home and having to convince himself that he really is an English baronet who really does live and belong in this particular place. (The same holds true for the provincial governor and his wife: Gogol urges them to *try* to think of the provincial city in which they have just arrived as their "native town," thereby conceding that it may be a rough go.)

Advice like this suggests that being a member of the Russian landowning class was one thing, but for the richest and most sophisticated landowners, actually living on one's provincial estate and fulfilling the duties of a *pomeshchik*, and feeling oneself to be at home while doing so, was a different thing altogether. In fact it was a challenge that seems here to require a degree of grim determination. *Selected Passages'* advice to the *russkoi pomeshchik* reflects the historical situation of the landowning class as I outlined it in this book's first chapter: the ties binding wealthy Russian noblemen to their provincial estates were often weak (compared to those that bound European nobles or American planters to theirs), and Russia's most cultured noblemen were unlikely to view provincial regions as their "native" places. As Peter Kolchin writes, the wealthiest Russian noblemen, far from feeling at home on their estates, "typically felt trapped or isolated" when they were there.[23] Thus in *Selected Passages*, when Gogol assumes that a highbrow nobleman who lands in the provinces will feel deracinated, even bewildered, this assumption reflects certain realities.

To the provincial governor's wife who is facing this challenge, Gogol offers the following helpful advice: look at your whole provincial town as a doctor looks at an infirmary (*kak lekar' gliadit na lazaret*), and try to "convince yourself that all the sick people in the infirmary are in fact your kinsmen . . . then everything will change before you: you will be reconciled with people and will be at war only with their illnesses" (8:310). The image of provincial city as sick ward is repeated and developed a few pages later, when Gogol urges the governor's wife to lay out all the town's problems for the bishop: "Show him your entire infirmary [*lazaret*] and display before him all the illnesses of your patients. . . . Inform him constantly of all the fits, symptoms, and manifestations of the illness" (8:316). Here we recall the improbable images used by Sollogub and Zagoskin to emphasize provincial alienness (albinos, "Aleutian savages," "wild men of Australia"). Clearly, in Gogol's day members of educated society in the capitals were becoming accustomed to reading about the "animal instinct and self-debasement by which the life of the provincial outback was distinguished" (in the words of a memoirist writing about the Decembrists' experience in exile), or what Herzen calls "the slough of provincial life."[24]

The provinces could be depicted both as horror show and as repository of true Russianness, their inhabitants both as freaks and as representative Russian types. In keeping with this tendency, *Selected Passages* represents the life of the provincial city as a collection of symptoms so horrific that an outsider must work to convince herself that the city's inhabitants have anything to do with her at all, that they are in fact her "kinsmen" (*vashi rodnye i blizkie k vashemu serdtsu liudi*, 8:310); the town is so loathsome that she must be counseled on how not to avert her eyes. Compare Herzen's description of an infamous Vyatka official as "a peculiar sort of beast that is met with in the forest, in the wild, a beast that *ought to have been studied*." Gogol shares Herzen's assumption: even if what one sees in *provintsiia* is repellent, one is morally obligated to look, with the goal of putting together an ethnography of the *lazaret* that is provincial Russia.

"Such is the Nature of the Provincial City"

When we first see *Dead Souls'* Town of N in the novel's opening paragraphs, we are made to feel nearly as disoriented as *Selected Passages'* bewildered addressees who have recently been deposited in the provinces (the landowner who must convince himself that his estate is in fact his home or the governor's wife who can only understand her town as a pest-house). *Dead Souls'* setting consists of a few structures (the Administrative Office, a sentry box, some cabstands) scattered randomly throughout a bleakly unintelligible pseudo-public space: the effect is one of overwhelming cultural incoherence (6:141). About half the novel recounts events that take place in the town itself; the rest of the narrative traces the movements of the hero, Chichikov, through five outlying provincial estates. All these estates are close to N, and we see all the landowners but one in town as well as in their homes: clearly, in *Dead Souls* provincial estate and provincial city occupy the same symbolic space. If, as I have noted before, the estate can be either provincial or cosmopolitan, the estates in *Dead Souls* are as unambiguously provincial as the town; in both these places, even the latest modes will partake of their setting's essential provinciality.

The governor's ball represents a crescendo of provinciality, a climax that occurs at the moment when all the townspeople deny their provinciality most vigorously: we are told that everything and everyone at the ball seems to be saying, "No, this is not the provinces, this is the capital, this is Paris itself!" (*net, eto ne guberniia, eto stolitsa, eto sam Parizh!*, 6:163). But here all efforts to be unprovincial are doomed. These people are provincial in their essence, and this essence will inevitably expose itself. At the very moment when everyone in N can agree that "this is not the provinces," there will appear, say, a strange hat that violates every rule of fashion. There is no getting around it: "This is unavoidable, such is the nature of the provincial city: somewhere it will inevitably reveal itself" (*no uzh bez etogo nel'zia, takovo svoistvo gubernskogo goroda: gde-nibud' on nepremenno oborvetsia*, 6:163–64).

Like the Town of N, each landowner's home contains a few vestigial and fragmentary bits of imported "culture," seemingly the flotsam and jetsam of a distant civilization. Manilov's garden, for instance, reveals inept attempts at English landscape design: a ramshackle arbor, dubbed the "Temple for Solitary Meditation," is surrounded by peasants' log huts. And inside his house, what is described as "an exceedingly elegant candlestick of darkened bronze, with the three Graces of antiquity and an elegant mother-of-pearl escutcheon" stands alongside another candlestick, one that is broken, ugly, home-made, jerry-built (6:22, 25). Here as elsewhere, Gogol uses incongruity and juxtaposition—the Three Graces alongside tallow-covered rags—to convey the incoherent and derivative nature of what passes for culture in the provinces.

Similarly, the prints that adorn the landowners' walls are a sort of cultural detritus washed up on the provincial shore. They depict everything from watermelons and a boar's head (at Pliushkin's house) to Greek military leaders (at Sobakevich's), and none of them seems to bear a coherent relationship to its current location (6:95, 115). As the narrator says of one such picture, "there was no way of knowing how or why [it] had gotten there" (6:95). The estates' furnishings attest to both the meagerness and the illegibility of provincial culture. The same goes for the vulgar painting of decidedly unknown provenance that has somehow ended up on the wall of the town inn: the narrator speculates that this image of "a nymph with breasts so large that the reader has probably never seen the like" was "brought back to us in Russia" by "one of our grandees, art lovers who buy [such things] in Italy on the advice of their couriers" (6:9).

Passages that highlight such incoherence draw attention to the threat of meaninglessness that haunts a syncretic culture like that of nineteenth-century Russia, a culture that borrowed freely and conspicuously. In Manilov's estate and Sobakevich's paintings, we see Gogol's aesthetically self-conscious version of what we saw in Sollogub's grotesque provincial mansion (in "Serezha," a house resulting from decades of random accretion) and Herzen's provincial church (in *Who Is to Blame?*, a structure combining Byzantine, classical, and Gothic elements). In each case, the authors highlight objects and styles that have been shorn of context and promiscuously mixed together, thus signaling a fear that Russian culture had not yet done the work of imbuing these objects with significance.

Of course, Russia's cultural syncretism was a source of great creativity and strength for artists, as Monika Greenleaf and many others have noted.[25] But this syncretism and cultural borrowing also generated anxiety—a fact that helps explain not only Russian literature's preoccupation with *provintsiia* and *provintsial'nost'*, but also Gogol's frequent hints that in Russia, provinciality cannot be confined to the provinces. In *Dead Souls* and *The Inspector General*, in which characters insist tirelessly on the essential and absolute difference between capitals and provinces, such assertions are often cast in doubt by the works as a whole, both of which open up the possibility that there is in fact *no* genuine standard of *stolichnost'* against which the provincial might be judged.

For instance, Khlestakov and the townspeople in *The Inspector General* expatiate at length on the wonders of the capital that are lacking in the provincial town, but in the end what Khlestakov tells the locals about the capital is what they themselves already "know." He simply responds to their image of Petersburg, an image that is quite capable of accommodating the idea of, say, a 700-ruble melon. Khlestakov tells stories of being "taken for" an important official in Petersburg, and the mayor's wife is duly impressed (4:48): in a world where being "taken for" a VIP is just as good as being one, a belief in the capital's essential superiority is merely what we might call these characters' foundational mirage, the delusion that generates all their other delusions. There is nothing to suggest that this conviction has any more basis in reality than does Khlestakov's fantastic melon.

Thus Petersburg and the very idea of *stolichnost'*, along with the absolute standard that this idea implies, begin to resemble floating signifiers. Khlestakov's ecstatic riff to the postmaster suggests as much: "Of course there aren't many people here [in this little town], but why should there be? After all it's not the capital [*ved' eto ne stolitsa*]. Am I right—after all, it's not the capital? . . . After all only in the capital is there real *bon ton*, none of your provincial boors . . ." (4:60–61). *Ved' eto ne stolitsa*: just as forms of the word "province" (*guberniia*) recur constantly in *Dead Souls* and *Selected Passages*, in *The Inspector General* "capital" and "Petersburg" are so often repeated that they stop sounding like geographic labels and start sounding more like talismanic invocations. Petersburg is a quasi-magical animating idea behind both Khlestakov and the townspeople's response to him: it is a "conferring power," "seat of authority, ground of judgment." And yet in the end it is an *empty* idea, functioning only as "a powerful absence in the play."[26]

When the writers who were Gogol's contemporaries mock provincial failures of taste, they typically do so because provincials *are* failing (their dance moves are ridiculous, their fashions are behind the times, etc.). But Gogol's indictment of provinciality is somewhat different: his Town of N can never be anything but an attempt to be something else, *even when it gets everything right*; the townspeople's attempts at fashion will remain fruitless *even when they are successful*. The narrator concedes, for example, that the ladies of N really do rival those of Petersburg and Moscow when it comes to observing proprieties and following fashions: "When it came to such things as knowing how to behave, how to maintain good tone and conform to etiquette, as well as a great number of the most subtle proprieties and especially how to observe the dictates of fashion down to the tiniest details—in all this they surpassed even the ladies of Petersburg and Moscow" (6:158). But in the end it makes no difference; they can do nothing but try to catch up, and even their most perfect efforts will be marked by the fact that they are efforts. Similarly, when the narrator insists twice in the space of five lines that the dandies of N do everything—shave, flirt, speak French—"just like they do in Petersburg" (6:14), the reference to the capital only draws attention to the fact that some fundamental problem has not been solved.

Dead Souls at times implies and at times states explicitly that there is *no* difference between province and capital, no matter how much the characters and even the narrator may insist that there is. The narrator concedes, for example, that there is no difference between the provincial landowner Korobochka and her imaginary "aristocratic sister" in the capital, who yawns over novels and attends witty social gatherings (6:58). And he allows that the bear-like landowner Sobakevich, seemingly the incarnation of Russian provinciality, would have been no different had he been born in Petersburg. Sobakevich would be just the same, Chichikov muses, even if he had received a modish education and lived in the social whirl

(6:106). And finally, in the novel's last chapter, the author (by this point seemingly distinct from the narrator, and possessing greater authority) reflects significantly that one feels the same melancholy upon entering *any* town, "even if it's a capital" (*khot' dazhe v stolitsu*, 6:241). Once again we are reminded of the narrator's claim that N is "not far from both capitals": geographically this remains baffling, but conceptually it becomes suggestive in yet another way, hinting as it does that the differences between Russian province and Russian capital are not as essential as many think, or perhaps even that both are equally "provincial."[27]

Despite the characters' intermittent insistence on the absolute difference between capital and province, the capital, too, is implicated in provinciality; or put another way, even if the provinces cannot believe themselves to be as good as the capital, the capital can be as bad as the provinces. As a result, in Gogol's world, actually going to the capital represents no solution, any more than it would for Chekhov's three sisters a few generations later. In his major works, rather than sharing his characters' belief in an absolute difference between province and capital and in the capital's incontestable primacy, Gogol comes close to imagining a world without *any* cultural or geographic locus of authenticity.[28] The meanings of province and capital begin to run together, a blurring of conceptual boundaries hinting that more is at stake in these texts than merely the provinciality of provincials. In fact, the characterization of N in the working notes to *Dead Souls* ("the dead insensibility of life") recalls the image of the capital that emerges in his other texts.

The similarities between Gogolian province and Gogolian capital are especially evident in the Petersburg tales, with their repeated evocations of empty, death-in-life existences; both Petersburg and provinces, it seems, can stand as "locus of the negative" and "capital of illusion."[29] The parallel is underscored by the essay "Petersburg Notes of 1836," in which Gogol represents the capitals much as he did the provinces in *Dead Souls*—as a place possessing virtually nothing that is native (*malo korennoi natsional'nosti*) but much that is alien and unassimilated (*mnogo inostrannogo smesheniia, eshche ne slivshegosia v plotnuiu massu*). He likens the city to an inn full of transients where everyone mindlessly apes European ways, a place so un-native as to be "something resembling a European-American colony." When Gogol writes that "it's hard to grasp a general impression of Petersburg," he might as well be writing again about the difficulty of describing the provinces, which, as we have seen, resist being figured out (8:177–80). Despite what is supposed to be the provinces' paradigmatic ordinariness, Gogol often hints at something indecipherable behind the seeming familiarity (hence the questions and non-answers that recur in *Dead Souls*: what does it mean when a Russian coachman scratches his head? "God knows—you won't be able to guess. It means a great many different things when the Russian folk scratch the backs of their heads"; 6:215).

Provinces and capitals—seemingly opposed to each other and even appearing to derive their significance from this opposition—are ultimately the same: this is what renders Gogol's vision especially complex, even paradoxical. Gogol insists on what Mikhail Epstein calls, in a passage cited in this book's introduction, the "alienation from itself" that is a structural characteristic of the provinces. Here it is worth again calling attention to Epstein's diagnosis: "A province is located, as it were, not in itself; it is alien not in regard to someone or something else, but to itself, inasmuch as its own center has been taken out of itself and transferred to some other space or time." Provincials are forever yearning for something that is somewhere else, "not here, not at this place, but 'there.'"[30] While other authors of the era write about alienation and cultural incoherence in the provinces, Gogol refuses to confine such alienation to a geographical location, and he goes much farther in exploring its consequences; in effect, his representations of the provincial world amount to *theorizing* provinciality.

Things and Thingness

Much of this implicit theorizing occurs in Gogol's treatment of *things*. *Dead Souls* is full of ostentatiously physical objects characterized by a "'sticking-out' thingness," with one detail after another "underlined and outlined by its absurdity."[31] Sometimes, as we have seen, an accumulation of pointedly unrelated items serves to draw our attention to an incoherent and dross-like "culture." Often such objects are marked as feminine in some way, as "superfluous" details in narrative so often are. See, for example, the Pleasant Ladies' conversation, which touches on flounces, stripes, checks, "sprigs and spots, spots and sprigs," armholes, bodices and busks, farthingales, and cotton batting before culminating in an ecstatic paean to "little festoons."[32]

Some of Gogol's lists read as critiques of a contemporary culture that he saw as marked by proliferating detail, what he called "broken-up trivia," "atoms" and "component parts," pettiness and dispersion (8:74, 66, 107). (Hence his intermittent interest throughout his life in the overpowering force of the sublime, which promised an antidote to multiplicity and triviality.)[33] Some of these lists pointedly refuse to differentiate between animate and inanimate objects (as in a passage from "The Carriage" cited in the previous chapter, which inserts a peasant woman in between pretzels and a bar of soap),[34] thereby evoking the questions raised by *Dead Souls'* paradoxical title and the premise of its plot (how can a soul be dead? can a scrap of paper have value? and are these characters even alive?). In almost all these passages, we sense an intensified version of what we saw in texts by Gogol's contemporaries, many of whom tended to associate the provinces with an especially dense version of materiality (see chapter 3). In such cases it is not necessarily the attributes of the objects themselves that leave us queasy (though at times it is); rather, we are often repelled—and fascinated—simply by the objects' profusion, a copiousness that hints at uncontrolled and grotesque accretion.

Certain objects in *Dead Souls* seem to possess what we might call a hyperbolically trivial quality. In the Pleasant Lady's drawing room, for example, we encounter a pillow "with a knight embroidered on it in worsted, the way things always are on canvas: the nose came out as a ladder, and the lips as a rectangle"—an object that is not exactly confusing or out of place (an embroidered pillow is not inappropriate in a drawing room), but is nonetheless vaguely puzzling. First we are struck by the way Gogol zooms in on it, inexplicably separating it out from whatever its surroundings might be and insisting on its physical presence. Then, however, we are struck by the pointedly inconsequential nature of the object itself, much as we are with the "tiny beaded pocket-case for holding a toothpick" that Manilov's wife has made for him (6:26). Both are obviously products of human labor (almost all of the physical objects highlighted in *Dead Souls* are man-made) and represent efforts that would have been better directed elsewhere; both make demands on our attention that feel unreasonable or unwarranted.

Knight pillow and toothpick case both embody a kind of a mismeasuring, a mismatching of effort with outcome that generates dissonance between grandiose claims (implicit or explicit) and sordid or meager realities. Such dissonance arises often in *Dead Souls*, and we have seen forms of it in other writers as well (as when the menu at a provincial inn in *Tarantas* advertises *sup lipotazh—soupe le potage*, i.e., "soup the soup"—or when schoolchildren in *Who Is to Blame?* speak "Celtic-Slavonic" or "Franco-ecclesiastical dialect").[35] What is notable in Gogol's text is that the incongruence can reside within one object: pillow and toothpick holder invite us to feel wonder or disgust at the labored, precious aestheticization of a trifle, the seriousness of effort devoted to something so insignificant. Such passages touch on one reason behind the *provintsiia* trope's resonance and staying power: besides being a way for Russians to think about being cultural latecomers, lingering on these objects can make palpable the vaguely nauseating contrast between the world we live in and the world we might aspire to (often with the nausea arising less from the lowliness of our reality than from the unworthiness of our aspirations).[36]

Belinsky writes that in *Dead Souls*, "life is encapsulated and dissected into tiny trivialities, and *these trivialities are then endowed with general significance.*" The book's pathos derives from this tension, he continues, from the contrast between the vaguely sordid "social forms of Russian life" and this life's "deep substantial source."[37] All of this suggests that these objects have something to teach us about why provinciality becomes a common way of talking about problems of taste, as well as why taste is so important. Such questions will be explored in the next

chapter in connection with Belinsky and Goncharov, both of whom recurred often to issues of proportion and disproportion, measuring and mismeasuring—
issues that are, I will argue, intimately connected to provinciality.

"Art is Provincial in Principle"

Gogol's own language is marked by the same kind of unnaturalness and distortion that afflict the provincials of *Dead Souls*—but his work makes masterful *use*
of such disproportions. If Gogol himself were provincial in the way his characters
are—always asking, am I getting it right?—it is unlikely that he would have been
able to master these disproportions and make use of them as he did. Perhaps this
helps explain why artistic originality and innovation tend not to reach full flower
in provincial places: if you are straining to conform to an external standard that
seems to exist chiefly to pass judgment on you, you are unlikely to do much that
is *intentionally* new or strange.[38] Or rather, you are unlikely to be able to master
newness and strangeness and turn them to your advantage as Gogol did.

  Gogol's deliberate strangeness may help us understand why his writings, even
as they established the provincial wasteland as one of Russian literature's recurring tropes, also opened the way to the eventual revaluation of provincialism.
Sinyavsky, for example, asserts that Gogol's genius arose precisely from his provinciality. He writes that Gogol was far too "provincial" (*provintsialen*) to strive
for anything like the naturalness and ease of a poet like Pushkin, who "whispered
verses in his cradle" because poetry was his "native language." Instead Gogol
created prose that was constantly "aware of its own formation," perpetually and
often awkwardly self-conscious (*eto rech', besprestanno pamiatuiushchaia o svoem
oformlenii, preispolnennaia soznaniia sobstvennogo sloga*), with its artistry arising
out of this very awkwardness and self-consciousness.[39]

  If Sinyavsky can assert that "art is provincial in principle," or if Platonov can
say that "genuine art and thought can in fact only appear in . . . a backwater,"[40]
then in Russia the "provincial" has come to mean something different than it does
for someone like T. S. Eliot, for whom, as I discuss in chapter 1 of this book, "the
provincial point of view" is quite simply inimical to high cultural achievement.
Because disproportions are the stuff that provinciality is made of, mismeasuring
and the absence or misapplication of *standards* are provinciality's most telling
marks. In "What is a Classic?" Eliot defines provinciality as a sensibility that "confounds the contingent with the essential, the ephemeral with the permanent."[41] But
Gogol built an entire oeuvre on "confounding the contingent with the essential, the
ephemeral with the permanent," managing to make conscious and highly sophisticated use of the disproportions that attend provinciality while being in no way
provincial himself.[42] In doing so, he created resources on which later Russians were

able to draw; a French writer, it seems, would be unlikely to echo Sinyavsky's assertion that art is "provincial in principle, preserving for itself a naïve, external, astonished and envious look."[43] Gogol made claims like Sinyavsky's possible; he is the exhilarating exception to the rules as the central authorities wish to define them.

When Turgenev's provincial intellectual Kukshina in *Fathers and Sons* comes out with a jumble of disjointed cultural allusions, we know exactly where the author and we ourselves stand in relation to this material: its provinciality serves to confirm our sophistication. But in a book like *Dead Souls*, our pleasure must derive from very different sources, because here we can never quite define our relationship to the provincial dissonances that are put on display, both in the objects the text depicts and in the language it uses to depict them. If we are not allowed to feel complacently unimplicated in Gogolian provinciality—if we are not granted permission to regard it with the self-satisfied eye of the aesthete—this is largely because the author refuses to clarify his own stance toward his material. As we have seen, the myriad physical details that pack *Dead Souls* are laid out with a "flat miscellaneousness" that defies hierarchies of judgment and significance.[44] Not only are we presented with the kind of incoherence that, as I have noted, so often characterizes provincial culture, we are also denied any standard, any point of view, from which we might judge its incongruities. Gogol's refusal to clarify his stance toward the bizarre world he creates causes the dissonance of *provintsiia* to become *our* problem, an indictment of *our* failures, aesthetic, intellectual and moral.

· CHAPTER FIVE ·

"I Do Beg of You, Wait, and Compare!": Goncharov, Belinsky, and Provincial Taste

> For what is culture if not the measuring, accumulation,
> and preservation of that which is valued?
> —Dmitry Merezhkovsky, 1909

Ivan Goncharov's 1846 novel *An Ordinary Story* focuses explicitly on the relationship between the capital and the provinces and what this relationship means for Russia's future. Goncharov's contemporary Vissarion Belinsky read *An Ordinary Story* as "a blow against romanticism, dreaminess, sentimentalism, and provincialism . . . what benefits this work will bring to society!"[1] The same year, in his essay "A Look at Russian Literature in 1847," Belinsky again enlists Goncharov in the struggle against what he sees as a specifically *provincial* backwardness. Like Goncharov—and unlike, say, Gogol—Belinsky associates the right kind of literature and literary culture with a fairly straightforward version of historical progress; when he writes that *An Ordinary Story* is fighting the good fight against "romanticism, dreaminess, sentimentalism, and provincialism," he is aligning provincialism with a list of outdated values that must be repudiated in the name of Russia's future. But in other contexts too—contexts having nothing to do with a novel that juxtaposes province and capital, as Goncharov's does—Belinsky's cultural critique recurs to the same vocabulary, at times repeating *provintsiia* and its cognates so obsessively that the terms become baffling, almost mysterious: what exactly do these words mean? Such is the case in "Something about Nothing," Belinsky's 1835 article devoted to Russia's nascent literary culture, where forms of the word *provintsiia* recur fifty-five times (!), often italicized, and often in contexts where one would expect another term altogether (2:7–50).[2]

This chapter considers first Goncharov's *An Ordinary Story* and then works by Belinsky in order to analyze what provinciality and the provinces signify for these writers, both of whom are concerned with how Russia might work to develop a coherent (literary) culture. Both pay close attention to the processes by which one goes from being provincial to being not provincial, an attention reflecting their shared belief that readers and other consumers of culture need to be *trained*. While both focus on acquirable tools and skills, they are interested not in static canons of taste but in how exactly Russians might articulate standards of judgment that can be disseminated, learned, and revised as necessary—and they see such standards as key to becoming nonprovincial. Their underlying assumption is always that readers' capacity for discernment—the ability to distinguish good from bad, or bad from worse—is something that will either be learned or not learned, either fostered or impeded, depending on conditions. As Bourdieu puts it in his charmless but precise way, "the ideology of charisma regards taste in legitimate culture as a gift of nature, [but] scientific observation shows that cultural needs are the product of upbringing and education."[3]

For Goncharov and Belinsky, thinking about *provintsiia* and not-*provintsiia* is a way of thinking about the particular conditions that might allow Russian producers and consumers of culture to stop being old-fashioned—to learn to be "in step with the age," in Goncharov's words, or in Belinsky's, to become attuned to what is "living, *modern* and true" in art (10:311, emphasis mine). In classic novels of education and becoming modern—the paradigmatic example of which is probably Balzac's *Lost Illusions,* on which Goncharov may or may not have drawn while writing *An Ordinary Story*[4]—one leaves the provinces and goes to the city to join modern life with the goal of becoming rich and famous. Whether or not one succeeds in becoming rich and famous, one is almost certain to become modern, thanks simply to the *scale* of life in the metropolis. As *Lost Illusions* tells us, in Paris "the scale of everything" forces Lucien Chardon (also known by his aspirational name, Lucien de Rubempré) to repudiate his "provincial ideas of life"; his perceptions are transformed once "the horizon widened, [and] society took on new *proportions*."[5] The same holds true for Goncharov and Belinsky: to a great degree they, too, believe that becoming nonprovincial and thus modern depends on having access to a sufficient *quantity* of cultural artifacts and ideas.

Scale allows for comparing and choosing: "In the provinces there is no question of choice or comparison," Balzac writes, whereas in Paris, "one learns, one *compares*."[6] With changes in scale (the "new proportions" to which Balzac refers) come changes in judgment, a fact reflected in an old Parisian's sage advice to a newcomer—"I do beg of you, wait, and compare!"[7] The result is a new level of discernment: *Lost Illusions* devotes long passages to the myriad subtle distinctions that life in the capital will require Lucien to master. The account of Lucien's introduction to fashionable society, for instance, is structured entirely around his realization that he must learn to discriminate; words like "compare," "different," "distinctions," and "subtle perception" recur over and over.[8] This is what interests Goncharov and Belinsky—the incremental process by which provincials can lose their provinciality, and the circumstances under which such a transformation becomes possible.

Taste and Calculation in *An Ordinary Story*

In *An Ordinary Story*, a young man leaves the provinces (the past) and comes to the capital (the present and the future), where he receives an arduous and necessary initiation into modernity: a familiar plot. But perhaps somewhat less familiar is Goncharov's suggestion that to become modern is to become *ordinary*, to join the crowd. The callow protagonist arrives in Petersburg convinced of his own exceptionalness; by the end of the novel, he has adopted the view of his uncle (and mentor), whose position might be summed up by the snide rhetorical question he poses to his provincial relative: "Why should one person openly deviate from the established order?"[9] Or as the mentor puts it when dismissing his protégé's favorite literary characters, "These are exceptions, and *exceptions are almost always bad*" (1:324, emphasis mine). We might initially find this to be a rather mystifying statement—because what's necessarily bad about exceptions?—until we understand the link that Goncharov's novel is establishing between standardization, large scale, and modernity, all of which, it seems, are achievable only in the capital.

Starting with his work's title, Goncharov calls our attention to the importance of ordinariness (and as I will discuss below, we note here a sharp departure from Gogol's insistence that only what is exceptional deserves representation—a departure that signals the growing ascendancy of self-consciously realist writing, since realism privileges the ordinary). *Obyknovennaia istoriia* is sometimes rendered as *An Ordinary Story* and sometimes as *A Common Story*; less common translations have been *The Usual Story* and even *The Same Old Story*. The Russian *obyknovennyi* resonates with the English adjectives "ordinary" and "usual" (what is repeated and therefore expected, even banal), but also with "common" (what is shared, what unites us, or what "we all" know and do). And Goncharov's novel might itself be described as ordinary in the sense that it is full of easily recognizable devices: obvious parallelisms and oppositions, repeating episodes, perfunctory characterization, a markedly symmetrical structure (two parts of roughly equal length, plus epilogue)—everything would seem to encourage us to read the tale of the two Aduevs, uncle and nephew, as quite a familiar sort of work indeed.

An Ordinary Story is also short and tightly schematic, structured almost as a parable or a fairy tale. The plot is skeletal: a young man, Alexander Fyodorovich Aduev, leaves his pastoral estate—which the book calls *provintsiia*—to pursue glory in Petersburg. A well-off and somewhat gifted youth (the "somewhat" will prove important) with capital-R Romantic convictions, Alexander believes he is destined for an extraordinary life. In Petersburg he seeks the patronage of his uncle Pyotr Ivanovich Aduev, who has already achieved worldly success (money, status, refinement, a proper marriage) in a thoroughly ordinary way: he has worked hard, invested his time and money wisely, made pragmatic choices, and developed the necessary connections. Having decided to live rationally, he treats his wife respectfully but coldly (treatment that will eventually destroy her well-being). The elder Aduev has cultivated a realist's view of life (realist in the sense of Kissinger, not Stendhal), always assessing conditions and prospects with a cold eye before taking any action. The plot, such as it is, traces the incremental, episodic process by which Alexander comes to understand—with his uncle's rather cruel and gloating assistance—that he is not in fact extraordinary, and that his best option is to conform to the ways of the world (stop writing mediocre poetry, abandon dreams of romantic passion, pursue an established career, marry for money). At the very end, to some degree, Alexander Fyodorovich and Pyotr Ivanovich switch places: as Alexander is finally becoming "realistic," Pyotr decides to abandon his prestigious career so as to take his dying wife abroad for a cure.

Unlike most of his contemporaries, Goncharov uses *provintsiia* to refer to a version of country life—the more or less self-sufficient microcosm of a middling-gentry estate. In fact in *An Ordinary Story*, the word *derevnia*—countryside or village—is occasionally substituted for *provintsiia*, as when the young Alexander explains his decision to come to Petersburg ("I was sick of being in the countryside [*v derevne*]—everything was the same," 1:207). Here "the provinces" most often designates a rural place with its own qualities and its own name (Alexander's estate is called Grachi), not an anonymous *gubernskii gorod N* with an imitative, second-rate culture. But the difference between *gubernskii gorod* and *derevnia* is of degree, not kind, in Goncharov's text: both occupy the semiotic space of *provintsiia*. When Alexander, just arrived in Petersburg, recalls the provincial capital (*gubernskii gorod*) where he once attended school, the town is subsumed into his memories of *provintsiia* generally, both forming part of a cozy premodern world ("he recalled his provincial town [*gubernskii gorod*], where every encounter, no matter with whom, was somehow interesting: if Ivan Ivanych was going to see Pyotr Petrovich, everyone in town would know why," 1:203).

In *An Ordinary Story* the difference between village and provincial town is nothing compared to the difference between provinces and capital, the binary that structures the narrative as a whole. Thus when Goncharov's Petersburgers occasionally employ "*provintsiia!*" as an epithet or insult (as when the elder Aduev wishes to dismiss an idea as old-fashioned and absurd), it matters little whether they are referring to the village or to a small city (1:303). Life in both these places is depicted as being everything life in Petersburg is not: provincial social relations are stable, based on traditional patriarchal mores; the landscape is pastoral and lovely; mealtime is all-important. Time is cyclical, structured around agricultural rhythms and the liturgical calendar; everyone knows each other and his permanent place in a clear hierarchical system. Nothing ever changes. Progress is not a value.

The capital, predictably, is the opposite: when Alexander first steps out onto the streets where people run madly past each other without exchanging greetings, Petersburg strikes him as mere "turmoil" (1:203), a city of strangers where one must learn to be "alone in the crowd" (1:207).[10] Pyotr Aduev enjoins his nephew to see in this crush "the modern, educated, thinking, working [or acting, *deistvuiushshuiu*] mass" (1:421); and once Alexander accustoms himself a bit to Petersburg, he recognizes "the rationally active crowd" (1:209). These thoroughly urban creatures ("those in the countryside won't reach this point for a long time," says Pyotr) represent the only way forward, the only way to be "in step with one's age [*vek*]." Being in step with one's age—being *modern*—is this text's great imperative, as Alexander finally comes to understand at the end of the book: "What's to be done, *ma tante*? . . . Such is the nature of the age. I'm proceeding in step with the age: one mustn't lag behind!" (1:467). When the aunt questions whether one is in fact obligated to follow the imperative of one's time in all things, her husband answers with a resounding yes. The goal is *progress*: "Where there is reason, cause, experience, and gradual movement, there is progress," because under such circumstances, all are "[striving] toward perfection and the common good" (1:422).

So important is progress that the elder Aduev urges his nephew not just to leave the past behind, but to forget it altogether (he himself cannot remember his own brother's wife, Alexander's mother, and that, he believes, is as it should be; 1:196). The provinces are for cultivating memories, but the capital is for forgetting; forgetting is a necessary condition of joining your fate with that of your cohort in order to be in step with your age (1:218). In *An Ordinary Story*, the metropolis is the only place where one can escape the vertical, hierarchical relationships that structure provincial life, replacing them with the up-to-date horizontal bonds that unite one's "generation." We will see a similar conviction in the work of certain women writers a generation or so later: cohorts, not families, are what move progress, and cohorts take shape in the capital. Hence Pyotr Aduev's praise for "today's youth," whose "mental activity and energy" are unburdened by the "old language . . . of solicitudes and sufferings" (1:423).

In the capital, everything is measurable and quantifiable, and knowledge takes the form of numbers: "To be incapable of counting [or calculating, *rasschityvat'*] is to be incapable of thinking," says the elder Aduev; "in plain Russian, he who does not calculate [*ne rasschityvaet*] is called a fool" (1:233). Everyone in Petersburg quantifies and calculates. Alexander's job, for instance, is to count other people's money, although money is not the only thing that is counted in the capital: "in our positive age, and especially here in Petersburg . . . *everything* is regulated, not just fashions but even passions and business affairs and pleasures, *everything is weighed, checked, appraised*" (1:387, emphasis mine). Pyotr Aduev is introduced to us by the quantity of horses and servants he possesses (three each) and by an estimate of his age ("between thirty-five and forty"): the only reason we do not get the exact number is that he himself conceals it, "not out of petty vanity, but due to some sort of deliberate calculation (*raschet*), as if he were intending to insure his own life at a higher rate" (1:193).

Such passages makes explicit the close relationship between Petersburg's mania for quantifying and the money economy that rules its way of life, a relationship with which Pyotr Aduev is quite comfortable. As he explains to his nephew, "in our time, money is the touchstone," the test of everything (1:329). To lose time is to lose money (Pyotr is always aware of the clock); talent, too, is "capital." When Alexander asks incredulously, "you measure [talent] in money too?" the answer is yes, of course—"he who writes better makes more money" (1:233). In *An Ordinary Story* one can easily list such instances of "valuation," the various processes by which everything from time, talent, and love to poems, eating, pleasure, vanity, and friendship can be assigned money value (hence the repetition of the word *raschet*). Uncle Aduev insists that one must always "calculate" in romance, for instance, and above all in marriage (1:233). Such calculation does not mean simply adding up one's fiancée's rubles (which Pyotr describes as acting *s raschetom*): that would be venal, he explains (1:244). Rather, choosing a wife must be done with calculation in a broader sense (*po raschetu*), as part of the process of assessing one's options (*rasschityvat'*) while "choosing among women" (1:243). After all, as Pyotr Ivanovich has already explained, in the capital "*everything* is weighed, checked, appraised."

As Aduev's words suggest, the capital's economy requires people to choose among many similar but not quite identical options (this wife, or that one? this sort of waistcoat, or that one?)—choices that are neither necessary nor possible in the provinces, where people are, in Goncharov's representation, minimally engaged with the money economy. On the younger Aduev's estate, nature's abundance translates into material abundance when it comes to things that are homemade and homegrown (linen, honey, "raspberries from our own garden"), but not when it comes to things that must be purchased with money (which is always scarce; 1:199; 1:183).[11] Goncharov's provincials locate value in what is thought to be unique and therefore in possession of an irreducible essence (*our* bees' honey, *our* estate's raspberries, the daughter of *this particular* neighboring landowner). But Petersburgers have embraced money's power to do away with essences, dissolving things into abstractions so as to be able to turn them into different things (since "the moment of exchange of a material commodity into money universalizes and abstracts qualitative physical difference and specific history").[12] The capital's money economy can abolish any object's "qualitative physical difference and specific history"—all that is local, material, fixed, and specific—by rendering it liquid and exchangeable.

In the capital, large, impersonal systems—not just the money economy but also bureaucracies, factories, newspapers—make possible a *magnitude* of production, reproduction, and knowledge that strikes Alexander, just arrived from the provinces, as radically different from anything he has ever seen. Watching a government office full of bureaucrats passing papers around, Alexander notes the parallel with his uncle's factory, where one man shapes a lump of clay, another fires it, a third gilds it, etc. Bureaucrats and factory hands work according to an intensified division of labor, and they work ceaselessly, without rest, "as if there were no people involved at all, just wheels and springs" (1:226–27). Such conditions do not exist in the provinces, at least not in Alexander's experience.

The result of these systems is not only quantity, but also order and regularity—many instances of the same thing, or many instances of almost the same thing. It is this combination—scale, repetition, regularity, slight variation—that allows Pyotr Aduev and other adepts of the capital's "knowledge economy" to recognize *patterns*. Whereas the naïve provincial Alexander thinks in terms of what is singular and never-again, his uncle thinks in terms of what has happened many times before and will therefore, probably, happen again. Alexander, disappointed in romance, cries, "the heart loves once!" His uncle corrects him—no, the heart loves over and over, and love stories have been more or less the same since Adam and Eve, "with slight variations" (1:299, 239). When speaking of his nephew's successive romantic interests, the elder Aduev repeatedly substitutes one young lady's name for another (Maria, Sofia, Nadezhda, Iulia, etc.), even as Alexander continues to insist on the uniqueness and unrepeatability of each.

Clearly, Pyotr Aduev understands that the proportions of life in the capital both permit and require this sort of pattern recognition, a skill that occasionally even allows him to predict outcomes. When he reads the manuscript of a story that Alexander has written, Pyotr is able to guess the ending: "They read for two evenings. After reading the second evening, Pyotr Ivanych—to his wife's amazement—foretold what the continuation of the story would be. 'How do you know?' she asked. 'Simple! The idea isn't new—it's been written about a thousand times'" (1:338). Similarly, when Pyotr submits his nephew's manuscript to a journal under his own name rather than Alexander's, not only does the journal's experienced editor know immediately that Pyotr cannot be the author, he also correctly diagnoses the cultural pathology of the actual author—Alexander—whom he has never met ("The author must be a young man. He's not stupid, but somehow angry at the whole world. . . . Probably he's been disappointed," 1:341). Modern people—people in the capital—do not need to be particularly attentive to what is unique or extraordinary; what counts for them is ordinariness and repetition, because ordinariness and repetition create the patterns that make available new forms of insight.

A person who cannot master the skills of recognizing, calculating, and predicting might as well "sit at home in the village," Pyotr says: in the capital it behooves everyone to "constantly think and recall what you did yesterday and what you're doing today in order to know what you have to do tomorrow; you must live by *ceaselessly gauging* yourself and what you're doing [*s bespreryvnoi poverkoi sebia i svoikh zaniatii*]" (1:249, emphasis mine). Only by way of this tireless measuring of everything against everything and everyone against everyone will you have a chance of achieving anything at all (1:249). In Petersburg, comparisons are both necessary and unavoidable: Alexander cannot help but see "the multitudes of talented people among whom he can play no role," with the result that "every new phenomenon in the world of science or art" makes him painfully aware of what he has not accomplished, highlighting "comparisons that are not to his advantage" (1:445). Only when he returns (temporarily) to the provinces is he isolated enough to indulge in the fantasy of his own exceptionalness—"*here* . . . he is the best, the cleverest of all! Here he is the idol of all, for several versts around!" (1:445).

An Ordinary Story suggests that all forms of isolation—a narrow circle of acquaintances, a limited exposure to arts or fashions, a circumscribed education or range of reading—will result not just in naïveté, but in bad judgment and an inability to evolve, even in the capital. People who socialize narrowly cannot distinguish a genuinely intelligent person from a fake ("Tafaeva receives very few guests," Pyotr tells Alexander, "so *in her narrow circle* Surkov is able to pass himself off as a lion and a clever fellow," 1:348). When Alexander retreats into "his own special world," refusing all contact with others and "chatting only with his own 'I'" ("alone with only oneself . . . a person sees himself as if in a mirror; only then does he learn to believe in human greatness and worthiness"), his aesthetic judgment becomes worse than ever even as his confidence in his views intensifies (hence his complacent recollection of a line in *Woe from Wit*: "why hold others' views so sacred?" 1:267). Only breadth of exposure improves judgment. Alexander arrives in Petersburg with an unfashionable jacket (unfashionable even though, as he objects, it was made by the finest tailor in his home province: "he works for the governor!"); two years later, the narrator asks, "who would've recognized our provincial in this young man with his elegant manners and foppish suit?" (1:230).

We have seen how Gogol, in *Arabesques* and elsewhere, insists that only "that which cannot be categorized as ordinary" is worthy of attention. For him, whatever repeats itself, whatever is not singular, should be ignored altogether; thus of geography textbooks he writes, "Let the pupil learn what Rome is, and Paris, and Petersburg. . . . Everything that is common to all cities should be excluded from the description of each individual one." Our attention must be directed only to those few phenomena that are "unique in all the world," he says.[13] Gogol's solution to the ordinariness of the Russian provincial city is to exaggerate its predictability to the point of near-surrealism (as he describes *Dead Souls'* Town of N, "everything the same as everywhere").[14] But Goncharov approaches the problem of ordinariness and repetition by insisting that ordinariness and repetition are defining traits of urban modernity, and as such they are to be embraced. Indeed, as we have seen, he represents the tendency to value what is singular and extraordinary as a specifically *provincial* delusion, one that can be dispelled by moving to the capital and submitting to modernity's discipline—a discipline that relies on large scale and constant repetition.

Exposure to "others' views"—the more the better, it seems—is the way forward. And therefore, scale is everything. Only by considering a wide range of options does one develop the sense of discrimination that fosters good judgment, in everything from manners and fashions to people and paintings. Alexander's taste in literature improves thanks to his editorial experience at a journal, where he "helps with choosing, translating, and correcting articles by other people" (1:234). And Pyotr Ivanovych's keen discernment is clearly attributable to the fact that "he reads, in two languages, everything important that's published in all fields of human knowledge; he loves art and has a fine collection of paintings of the Flemish school" (1:218). Hence his ability to assess correctly Alexander's stories and poems (verdict: not great)—he has read many other stories and poems against which he can measure them.

Here we have an entirely nonmystical account of how one develops what we call "good taste." There is nothing magical or inborn about it; rather, this ability is simply another product of the calculating and comparing made possible (and necessary) by life in the capital. As we watch Alexander go from being unstylish to being stylish, what we might once have taken to be the seemingly instinctive, *innate* grace of the *honnête homme* (the "harmonious individual," the "person of general culture and varied interests"—the anti-provincial, as it were)[15] is revealed to be merely another acquired competency. Alexander himself, when still a newcomer in Petersburg, thinks he sees in one of his romantic rivals ("the count") a perfection of manner that is truly effortless—an *inexplicable* "simplicity, elegance, and . . . gentleness in his manner," an ability to converse "without the least effort or pretension" and always "with tact" (1:272). Yet even the count's flawless deportment soon reveals itself to be the product of long acquaintance-ship and exposure. Speaking of literature, he makes "casual and accurate re-marks about contemporary Russian and French luminaries," revealing that he is "friendly with first-class writers," both Russian and French; "about some of them he spoke with respect, about others, with a light touch of caricature" (1:272). In other words, the count has had a lot of practice.

Alexander's provincial home is full of *singular* memories, evoked by singular places and singular artifacts (the very pond in which he played as a child, the very lilac bushes where he first kissed Sonia, the very linden trees planted by his father, etc.): in *An Ordinary Story*, *provintsiia* sustains the fantasy of uniqueness (1:446). (And in this Goncharov differs sharply from his contemporaries, for whom *provin-tsiia* often signifies nothing but sterile repetition—"everything the same the same, the same," as Sollogub says—or motleyness and disorder, as in Gogol's provincial interiors.)[16] But the capital forces Alexander to acknowledge that he is merely one man among many similar men. Knowing that his nephew must accept this hard truth, Pyotr Aduev works to inculcate in the young provincial the fact of his own ordinariness, repeatedly reminding him that each man is "neither an angel nor a demon, but *a person like all people*" (1:217). When Alexander accuses his uncle of making him hate himself ("you showed me I was worse than others"), Pyotr coolly reminds him that in reality he is "neither worse nor better than others" (1:420). Only at the very end of the book, as Alexander prepares to return to the capital for good after a sojourn in the provinces, can he articulate the lesson that Petersburg has taught him: "It's no scatterbrain who's coming to you this time, no dreamer or dis-appointed man or provincial [*provintsial*], but just a person, *one among many such people* in Petersburg—as I long ago should've been" (1:449, emphasis mine). This wistful acknowledgment signals Alexander's transformation into a *modern* person.

An Ordinary Story comments on what it might mean to believe in a straight-forward version of progress (history is moving forward), one that is clearly keyed to geography (the way to move forward with history is to leave the provinces, which are stagnant and *behind*, and go to the capital, which is dynamic and *ahead*). Yet it is important to recognize that this position is not necessarily shared by Goncharov himself: indeed, the overall trajectory of *An Ordinary Story* com-plicates such a position, both in the main characters' less-than-happy fates and in the figure of the elder Aduev's wife, who represents a sort of untaken middle path (one that might have turned out to be more propitious than either side of the stark binary represented by Alexander and Pyotr). In other words, *An Ordinary Story* is commenting on Pyotr Aduev's enthusiastic embrace of a certain version of urban modernity, but not necessarily endorsing it.[17]

Clearly, what the provinces represent for Goncharov is not always what they represent for his contemporaries. In Gogol, for instance, the provinces cannot really be described as behind the times; rather, Gogol's provinces are a mishmash of objects and styles and words that seem to occupy *no* (single, identifiable) time. The same holds true in certain of Turgenev's works, as we will see in the following chapter. In this sense Gogol's and Turgenev's versions of *provintsiia*, quite unlike Goncharov's, raise the possibility that Russia might be permanently outside of the authoritative chronology implied by European history. According to the protagonists of *An Ordinary Story*, the provinces are quite simply lagging behind—which is why one must abandon them in order to join history's march forward, "[striving] toward perfection and the common good" (1:422).

Belinsky and the Overcoming of Provincialism

In the world of *An Ordinary Story*, the work of moving forward—"striving toward perfection and the common good"—must be done incrementally and collectively. Belinsky concurs, and he expresses an even stronger confidence in art's and criticism's ability to move society ahead. In answer to the question "What is criticism?" he writes, "criticism is ceaselessly moving, it proceeds forward, it gathers new material, new data for science" (11:123). Like Pyotr Aduev, who urges his nephew to get in step with the times, Belinsky tells his readers that a correct relationship to the present moment is a defining feature of legitimate criticism (criticism should "always be truthful in its relationship to its own time"), as is the ability to contribute to progress ("it must be a step forward, a discovery of the new, a widening of the limits of knowledge," 11:123). Here the vocabulary of dilation (widening the limits) recalls Goncharov's emphasis, in *An Ordinary Story*, on the expansive and expanding dimensions of urban life, which affords unprecedented opportunities for comparison, assessment, discernment, and (therefore) progress. The more you are exposed to—the more you see and know—the finer your judgment will be, and the better equipped you will be to move forward.

Like Goncharov, Belinsky sees transformative power in the sheer amplitude of cultural options made available by urban modernity. This is what Balzac calls "the scale of everything" in Paris—the innumerable choices that present themselves to newly arrived provincials, transforming their views simply by revealing society's true dimensions. Inhabitants of the metropolis are constantly making distinctions, comparing one thing against another, *deciding*; hence the Parisian's advice to a just-arrived provincial, cited above ("wait, and compare!").[18] Belinsky, too, believed that opportunities for comparing form the foundation of aesthetic and cultural discernment: "The worthiness of things is always revealed and assessed most truly through comparisons," he writes, "Yes—comparison is the best system and the best form of criticism of what is beautiful" (1:130). These words appear in an 1835 review of a now-forgotten historical novel, but over the years Belinsky returned again and again to the idea that aesthetic worth can be judged chiefly by way of juxtaposing one thing against another: "comparison is my favorite principle: things are understood best of all by means of comparison" (1:367).[19] Thus he calls for the wide dissemination of numerous examples of good literature: more opportunities for comparison will lead to better judgment ("anyone who has read and understood even one novel by Walter Scott or Cooper will be in a position to truly assess the value" of mediocre efforts like *Dmitry Samozvanets*, he says; 1:130).[20]

In reviewing *An Ordinary Story*, Belinsky echoes Goncharov's own preoccupation with measuring and juxtaposing, repeatedly weighing one thing (one text, one character, one talent) against another in an effort to speak precisely and defensibly about literary merit. Assessing the character of Alexander Aduev, for example, Belinsky writes that the protagonist shows "not talent but half-talent"; assessing Goncharov himself, "his talent is not first-rate, but it is strong, remarkable"; assessing *An Ordinary Story* overall, he ranks it against other contemporary novels such as Herzen's *Who Is to Blame?* (10:326, 327). Over and over Belinsky urges us to appraise dispassionately so as to understand clearly, as when he accuses readers of misjudging the character of Pyotr Aduev by viewing him in terms of crude extremes rather than as a complex combination of cold egotist and honest, noble person. Echoing the words of Aduev himself, Belinsky writes, "a man is neither a devil nor an angel" (10:341, 342).

Like Goncharov, Belinsky knows that in the provinces, opportunities for this kind of nuanced assessment are rare. Small town life, he writes, does not encourage subtle gradations in relationships: if you know a person, he is either an enemy or a dear friend—"there are virtually no intermediary [*srednikh*] relationships" (10:328). Provincials are not stupid, they just have no way of knowing that their way of life is not the pattern for life everywhere, since they have not had enough opportunities to compare (10:329). And here we begin to see why Belinsky shares with Goncharov not only a focus on judging and juxtaposing, but also a striking preoccupation with *provintsiia* and *provintsial'nost'*—striking, that is, for a literary critic whose work would seem to have little to do with questions of place.

Many of Belinsky's writings hint that "provincialism"—not a word he ever really defines—poses a threat to Russian cultural development.[21] This anxiety finds most conspicuous expression in an 1835 essay with the suggestive title "Something about Nothing": this is where, while surveying the current state of Russian literature, Belinsky invokes *provintsiia* and its cognates fifty-five times. Although these words seem to carry similar implications for him as they do for Goncharov, in "Something about Nothing" *provintsiia* and *provintsial'nost'* are far less geographically conditioned than in *An Ordinary Story*. Simply put, Goncharov locates provinciality in the provinces (Alexander Aduev escapes provinciality by leaving his countryside estate and submitting to the capital's discipline), but this is not the case with Belinsky, as we will see.

In "Something about Nothing," forms of *provintsiia* recur most frequently—sixteen times—in the description of *Library for Reading*, a new journal that had begun appearing in 1834 and was enjoying unprecedented success, thanks largely to the entrepreneurial efforts of its semi-scrupulous editor, Osip Senkovsky (2:17–22). Much scholarship has been devoted to the reaction the *Library* provoked among Russia's tiny community of highbrow readers and writers, many of whom were infuriated by its combination of marketplace success, scandalous editorial practices, and erratic quality. In "Something about Nothing," Belinsky actually develops one of the more cogent analyses of the new publication (i.e., his essay is not just another diatribe accusing cultural parvenus of degrading the purity of art). Still, his vocabulary is puzzling: what exactly does he mean when he calls the *Library* "provincial"? Over and over, and often in italics, Belinsky deploys *provintsial'nyi* as though the word possessed explanatory power:

> I ask you not to forget that my main argument about the *Library* consists of the fact that this is a *provincial* journal, that it is published for the *provinces*, and that it is strong due only to the *provinces*. So I will now move on to a detailed account of the signs of its exclusive provincialism. (2:21; all italics in original)

In a passage promising to explain why *Library for Reading* was enjoying such success, a long lead-up would seem to be preparing us for a major revelation—but again, the only explanation turns out to be that the journal is "provincial":

> It seems to me that I have identified the reason for this success that runs so counter to common sense and coherence [*prochnogo*], for this strength that carries within itself the germ of death and that is so constant, so unweakening. I am not representing my discovery as anything new, since it may be shared by many; I am not representing my discovery as a weapon that's bound to be fatal to the journal under consideration here, because the truth is not a strong enough weapon where there exists no literary public opinion [*net literaturnogo-obshchestvennogo mneniia*]. The *Library* is a *provincial* journal: that is the reason for its strength. (2:17)

A few pages later he makes the same point with the same vocabulary and the same italics: "The secret of the ongoing success of the *Library* consists in the fact that this journal is above all a *provincial* journal" (2:19). And again, at the end of the article, by way of conclusion: "The *Library* is a *provincial* journal, and in this is contained the secret of its power, its strength, and its credit with the public" (2:41).

Of course, if Belinsky were talking about readers who lived in the provinces, the term's meaning would be clear. But in "Something about Nothing" only once does a form of *provintsiia* refer to geography (Belinsky pictures the delight of a gentry family receiving an issue of the new journal *Library for Reading*, which will be read cover to cover since there is nothing else to read—"Isn't it true that such a journal is a treasure for the provinces?" 2:20). Elsewhere he is careful to put us on notice that by "provincial" he is not referring only to people outside of Petersburg and Moscow: "the inhabitants of both the provinces and the capitals" share the same needs and desires when it comes to journalism, he says; "there are so many readers like this [i.e., provincial readers] even in the capitals" (2:20–21). Similarly, when he calls for the translation of more and better contemporary European literature, he laments that even the "foreign literature" section of *Library for Reading* is "entirely saturated with provincialism," characterized by "provincial wit, provincial amusement" (2:32).

Other members of the literary establishment joined Belinsky in using "provincial" as a kind of slur, but for them, the word denoted people who actually lived outside the capitals. In an 1834 issue of *The Telescope*, for instance, an anonymous writer attributes the success of low-brow literature to "provincials'" belief that a little reading after dinner encourages digestion ("in Russia [nowadays], a writer achieves glory in the hinterlands [*v glushi*], on the steppe, in Saratov").[22] Nadezhdin concurred: the *Library for Reading* was for people in the provinces.[23] Gogol's analysis of the *Library* (in his article "On the Development of Periodical Literature in 1834 and 1835") attributes the "provincial" tone of Russian journals to the fact that poor and elderly readers "in the provinces" need a little something to read, just as they need to shave twice a week.[24] In fact, letters pretending to be from "offended provincials" (often signed "from Tver," a toponym that could stand for a paradigmatic provincial town) were a journalistic trope of the day.[25] For example, when Pushkin was editor of *The Contemporary*, he wrote and published a "letter to the editor" in the voice of a naïve reader from Tver, purporting to express the opinions of "humble provincials."[26]

In an era of burgeoning print culture, expressions of contempt for provincials suggest an effort to locate in the provinces a problem that in fact had little to do with geography: literary elites were losing the power to control taste, which would now have to be shaped and guided rather than prescribed. By the 1830s a tiny percentage of educated Russians had attained to a kind of Europeanness in and through high culture, only to see their values compromised by the advent of writers and readers who happily produced and consumed fare their betters saw as second-rate. Thus Pushkin mocked the "provincial politeness" of journalists struggling to emulate high-society etiquette, much as Pyotr Vyazemsky, in a review of Gogol's *Inspector General*, complained that "provincial" upstarts were lowering standards of taste.[27] Calling bad readers "provincial" was an attempt to quarantine them, cordoning them off from the rest of cultural life.

Though Belinsky, too, relies heavily on the word "provincial," his response to Russia's changing literary scene differed sharply from those cited above, as is suggested by the fact that he refused to apply this label only to those living outside the capitals. Unlike, say, Vyazemsky, who might have preferred that provincial arrivistes be excluded from literary discourse altogether (hence the quarantining efforts), Belinsky embraces the role of pedagogue, and he advocates for developing rules that can be *learned*. The goal is to help people go from being provincial to being not provincial, which is perhaps why he does not often use the word "taste" (*vkus*). "Taste" tends to suggest a nonacquirable, probably inborn, and possibly aristocratic "je-ne-sais-quoi," recalling the values of salon culture rather than those of an upstart proto-*intelligent* like Belinsky, for whom the pedagogical mission of criticism was of overriding importance.

Belinsky's didactic intentions are unmistakable in "Something about Nothing," in which he worries less about how *Library for Reading* might offend the sensibilities of the educated few and more about how its lack of coherent standards threatens to prevent unsophisticated people from assimilating the conventions they needed to know in order to become competent readers. Belinsky believed it was criticism's job to serve society as teacher and "guide" (*guverner*), "speaking high truth in simple language" (as he puts it in an article of 1836; 11:125). Given the weighty responsibility Belinsky assigned to criticism, the worst thing about *Library for Reading* was its complacent renunciation of what he (and others) saw as the basic canons of aesthetic integrity. The *Library* was promulgating an idea of criticism that threatened to remove it altogether from the realm of shared guidelines. As Senkovsky put it, "My idea of impartial criticism is when, with a clear conscience, I tell those who wish to hear me what personal impression a given book has made upon me [. . .] Consequently, there can be no room for argument after one has read a critique."[28]

Belinsky recognizes that such "personal criticism" might well obviate the utility of criticism altogether. For all "theories, systems, laws, and conditions" of aesthetic judgment, he writes, the *Library* substitutes "personal impressions."

> We're told . . . that what's still left is personal impressions, and that the critic can lay them out. That's all fine, although the personal impressions an educated person receives from a work of art must certainly be in agreement with one theory or another, with one system or another, or at the very least with some law of the beautiful, because even leaving aside theories and systems, these days we know of many laws that might be derived from the very essence of a creative work [*sushchnosti tvorchestva*]. (2:38)

Belinsky was convinced that passing off "personal impressions" as criticism was a self-serving abdication on the part of the *Library*'s editors, one that would be especially disastrous given the burgeoning numbers of unsophisticated readers whose level of literary culture he deemed dangerously low. Hence his insistence, in "Something about Nothing" and elsewhere, on the need for a "systematic" collection of "aesthetic laws," a set of more or less agreed-upon guidelines (2:49).[29]

Virtually all Russian readers, Belinsky says, would be "reduced to a state of extreme distress and confusion if you were to read them a poem and demand their opinion of it without telling them the author's name" (2:20). They rely on a version of Foucault's author function, trusting that "the names printed at the bottom of the poems and articles in the *Library* will free them from any danger," eliminating the possibility that their own "ignorance in matters of art" might be exposed (2:21). An author's name serves to "vouch for [a work's] worthiness, and in the provinces such a warrantee is more than sufficient" (2:20). And Belinsky recognizes that the ability to judge is a longed-for and legitimate marker of cultivation: "Inhabitants of both the provinces and the capitals don't just want to read, but also to judge what they've read; they want to distinguish themselves by way of their good taste, to shine with sophistication, to astonish others with their opinions [or judgments, *suzhdeniiami*]" (2:21).

The desire for confidence in one's opinions, along with the fear of getting it wrong, explains "provincial" readers' habitual "respect for the authorities," an unquestioning deference that leaves their taste dogmatic and rigid, incapable of adapting to aesthetic change and slow to accept innovation (2:19). Indeed it seems that for Belinsky, one way we can know that a standard is good—that it is legitimately authoritative—is that it can change, that it can evolve of its own accord in response to changing circumstances. Referring to a series of markedly outdated or otherwise superseded authors and texts, Belinsky writes, "The provinces cannot imagine that the eminent Mr. Ushakov has now been definitely discharged from the ranks of the eminent. Who could doubt the worthiness of stories by Monsieurs Panaev, Kalashnikov, and Masal'skii? Yes, in this sense, the *Library* is a provincial journal!" (2:21).

Provincials' deference to authority makes them easy targets for manipulation—which again suggests why Belinsky sees such danger in journalism's abdication of critical responsibility. In a sense provincial readers are like the bumbling but dangerous revolutionaries in Dostoevsky's *Demons*, isolated in their far-off Town of N. These provincials are vulnerable to manipulation precisely because they are always seeking validation from some distant authority; they are ever ready to change their minds "at the first hint from our progressive corners in the capital."[30] In the same way that Dostoevsky's provincial terrorists cannot act unless they believe their actions to be line with some far-away "central" intelligence, so

Belinsky's provincial readers prefer their opinions prevalidated: one result of being provincial, it seems, is a constant readiness to take orders from someplace else.

Incoherent journalism cannot help Russia's new readers develop aesthetic
principles that are coherent, flexible, and capable of evolving in response to new
conditions and works of art. In fact *Library for Reading* does the opposite, thanks
to its extreme motleyness and inconsistency (what Belinsky calls its propensity for
"speaking in several different languages at the same time" [2:19]), its willingness
to serve as what Nadezhdin called "a storage room for all the wares produced by
writers."[31] Gogol echoes these concerns in "On the Development of Periodical
Literature," charging that *Library for Reading* exhibits *"neither positive nor negative
taste—there is none at all."*[32] The *Library's* main defining feature would seem to be
this lack of defining features, this radical unevenness. Gogol quotes the editors incredulously: "At the *Library for Reading*," they declare, "we do not leave any story
in its original form, we rework every one. Sometimes we make one out of two,
sometimes out of three, and the piece is significantly improved by our revisions!"[33]
Without proper standards of judgment, one cannot make proper distinctions, and
the resulting aesthetic failure is marked above all by indiscriminate combining—
"what a mix," Belinsky says of the *Library*, "a motley, heterogeneous miscellany"
(2:19).[34]

Radical unevenness and indiscriminate mixing are signs of provinciality. As
we have seen in previous chapters, literary texts often associate *provintsiia* with
incongruous combinations, juxtapositions of ideas and objects that have been appropriated without any understanding of their meanings or relationships. *Library
for Reading* exhibits the same kind of ostentatious heterogeneity—which explains
not only why it struck such a nerve with educated Russians who were worried
about their tradition's development, but also why Belinsky enlists the vocabulary
of provincialism to talk about its aesthetic failures.

Clearly Russia's literati were provoked by *Library for Reading's* syncretism,
which pointed toward the syncretism of emerging print culture generally. But in
the 1830s there was something else about the *Library* that was just as arresting: the
journal attested to a new *magnitude* of cultural production and consumption. Its
readership was, by contemporary standards, shockingly large, with an oft-cited if
not quite verifiable subscription rate of 5,000 (Gogol called it "an elephant among
the petty quadrupeds").[35] Responses to the *Library* typically rehearsed these numbers in a tone "[bordering] on the hysterical," offering "hyperbolic accounts of the
fortunes to be made in Russian letters" and of the supposedly inevitable degradation that would accompany increasing numbers of texts.[36] In the opinion of the
literary establishment, quantity was unlikely to be compatible with quality.

Again, Belinsky's response was different: for him, the solution to problems
that might be created by circulating texts on a large scale could only come from

circulating even more texts on an even larger scale. In effect he is anticipating the conditions of Petersburg life as Goncharov describes them in *An Ordinary Story*—a density of culture, an abundance of examples and counter-examples that will allow for choices, comparisons, fine nuances, and degrees of calibration (why this poem instead of that one? why this waistcoat and not that other one?). The conditions of the modern metropolis—which in Belinsky's view need not be confined to the actual metropolis—will make it possible for Russian culture to leave provinciality behind.

"This Perfect Proportion"

For Belinsky as for Goncharov, provinciality springs from an inability to weigh one idea against another. And here again we recall T. S. Eliot's "What is a Classic?," which argues that in the absence of comparison, there can be no standards, no correct proportion—and "without the constant application of the classical *measure*, we tend to become provincial."[37] In fact, much like Belinsky in "Something about Nothing" and Goncharov in *An Ordinary Story*, Eliot seems obsessed with measuring and gauging, ever mindful of the need to "preserve the classical standard, and to measure every individual work of literature by it." For artists who originate in cultures that worry about being on a periphery, standards can serve as a safeguard against provinciality, which as Eliot writes is not a question of geography, but rather "a distortion of values, the exclusion of some, the exaggeration of others, which springs, not from lack of wide geographical perambulation, but from applying standards acquired within a limited area, to the whole of human experience."[38]

For Belinsky as for Eliot, the ultimate goal is a kind of universality. Belinsky aims to cultivate readers' aesthetic sensibility (what he terms *chuvstvo iziashchego*, literally a "sense of the elegant") not for its own sake, but because this sensibility is an essential "condition of human worthiness" (*uslovie chelovecheskogo dostoinstva*) that can help an individual transcend what one might call a provincialism of the soul—in Belinsky's words, those "personal hopes and personal interests" that limit our capacity for clear judgment (2:47). Only those who develop such a sensibility—which one might also term, in deliberately prosaic language, a "skill set"—are capable of "rising to the level of universal [*mirovykh*] ideas, of understanding nature . . . in its unity" (2:47). If we are unable to rise to the level of the universal, we are left with a conception of life (and an aesthetic) that is impoverished in its *provinciality*, provinciality in the sense of a sadly limited and blinkered "localness": "what remains is only the banal 'common sense' that is necessary for the domestic side of life, for the trivial calculations of egoism," Belinsky writes (2:47).[39]

The topic of the next chapter is Turgenev, whose work Eliot saw as exemplifying the sense of measure—"this perfect proportion, this vigilant but never

theoretic intelligence, this austere art of omission"[40]—that is necessary (if not sufficient) for producing "classic" works of literature, those that "in the end [prove]
most satisfying to the civilized mind."[41] The Russian critic Dmitry Merezhkovsky
concurred with Eliot's judgment: Merezhkovsky deemed Turgenev "a genius of
measure [*genii mery*], and consequently, a genius of culture. *For what is culture
if not the measuring* [*izmerenie*], accumulation, and preservation of that which is
valued?"[42] The measuring of what is valued: this is what Goncharov's young provincial Aduev is learning to do in the capital, thereby laying the groundwork, in
a sense, for a writer like Turgenev, the "genius of measure" whom Merezhkovsky
also deems to be Russia's first "genius of Western Europe."[43]

· CHAPTER SIX ·

Back Home: The Provincial Lives of Turgenev's Cosmopolitans

Let us imagine a man who lives in Akron, Ohio, and teaches the
history of the Italian Renaissance. It is dreadful to think what he
has to reconcile.

—Saul Bellow, 1957

For us . . . the real present was not in our own countries. It was the
time lived by others, by the English, the French, the Germans. It was
the time of New York, Paris, London. We had to go and look for it
and bring it back home.

—Octavio Paz, 1990

Ivan Turgenev is a supremely cosmopolitan writer. It is difficult to imagine anyone more worldly—less provincial—than this multilingual aristocrat who spent
decades of his life abroad, moving easily across borders and involving himself
in contemporary European intellectual life, ever aware of European civilization
and "progress" as standards that had to be acknowledged, whether they were to be
embraced or rejected. Merezhkovsky called Turgenev "the first Russian writer to be
discovered by Europe," the writer in whom the West "first sensed that Russia is also
Europe."[1] Indeed Turgenev was so worldly that in Russia he was at times mocked
as a rootless and effete Euro-aristocrat, forever running off to Baden-Baden in a
fit of pique (hence a series of anecdotes in the style of Kharms, all ending with the
words "Turgenev took fright and that very night ran off to Baden-Baden").[2] But
Turgenev's peculiar version of worldliness was not straightforwardly Eurocentric,
and the symbolic geography of his work, which is almost always more complex
than a simple capital-centric model, reflects his ambivalence.

In fact his oeuvre forms a crucial part of the provincial trope, with its focus on the relationship between *provintsiia* and the problem, or the hope, of a specifically Russian temporality. When Turgenev is writing about Russian space, he often seems to be thinking just as much about Russian *time*, often posing or implying the question, "Is Russia 'behind'?" Analyzing spatial relationships in his texts (between centers and peripheries, for instance) requires us to think about how these relationships condition ways of thinking about historical time (what counts as ahead and what counts as behind, for example). In Turgenev's view, it seems, Russia is not "modern," but it is not simply "backward," either. Hence his focus on the gentry estate: estates were places where Russian elites could work to rethink their relationship to historical time, moving beyond the assumption that centers (capitals) are ahead and peripheries (provinces) are behind. Turgenev's interest in different versions of the gentry estate and their different temporal modes signals his awareness that even to articulate the problem in such terms (modern vs. backward) risks tacitly accepting what Arjun Appadurai calls "Eurochronology"—an assumption that "the West" will always provide the standard units for measuring progress and time, and thus the normative version of modernity.[3]

Despite his thoroughgoing cosmopolitanism, Turgenev does not stake out the position of a (proto-modernist) *déraciné*, the kind of cosmopolitan intellectual who tends to think art is best when it is most "universal," and that what is most universal happens in the center.[4] On occasion Turgenev's texts indict provincial cultural failings, and at times they enact a *stolitsa/provintsiia* binary in a way that would seem to correspond to Pascale Casanova's center/periphery schema (see chapter 1): such is the case in "Hamlet of Shchigrov" (1848), *A Provincial Lady* (1850), and *Diary of a Superfluous Man* (1850), for instance. But in his major novels—*Nest of the Gentry* (1859), *Fathers and Sons* (1862), *Smoke* (1867), *Rudin* (1856), and *Virgin Soil* (1877)—categories like "ahead" and "behind" rarely carry the same straightforward meanings that they do in other European traditions. Similarly, for Turgenev, simply making it to the capital—whether literally or symbolically—will not solve Russians' problems, nor will a worldly education guarantee their assimilation into European culture (with European culture understood to be cosmopolitan, modern, and "universal"). Indeed, for many of Turgenev's characters, a Europeanizing education lies at the root of the most grievously damaging forms of provincialism.

Countryside and Provinces, Mimesis and *Imitatio*

If we think of geographic space in Turgenev, what might come to mind first is not the *stolitsa/provintsiia* binary, but simply rural Russia, especially as it appears in *A Hunter's Notes*: forests and fields, gentry estates, tiny villages, and long passages of nature description that students must be induced to read. These sketches (which appeared in *The Contemporary* between 1847 and 1851 and in a separate edition in 1852) rarely reproduce the standard capitals-vs.-provinces opposition that was already structuring so many literary texts by this time, and they certainly do not represent the provinces as a series of interchangeably blank spaces defined solely by their opposition to the capitals. Rather, *A Hunter's Notes* often attends to decidedly local details, and even insists on their localness—noting almost pedantically, for instance, that a sketch's setting is the *eastern* part of Orel Province, not the western part.[5] The sketches are saturated with specific, and specifically located, natural phenomena.[6]

If, as Michel Jeanneret writes, artistic representation encompasses both *imitatio* ("the operation of *rewriting* which legitimizes all classical literature," "art as an autonomous mechanism") and mimesis ("art as a reflection of the world"), then most of *The Hunter's Notes*—those parts that focus on countryside and nature—fall clearly on the side of mimesis.[7] But at the same time Turgenev was lavishing attention on the flora and fauna of a particular Russian subregion, he was also writing works that reproduced the familiar capitals/provinces binary, works shaped by a pointedly Gogolian worldview—and these texts tend much more toward the practices of rewriting that characterize *imitatio*. It seems that as soon as Turgenev writes about *provintsiia* and *provintsial'nost'* (rather than about, say, the eastern part of Orel *guberniia*), we enter *imitatio*'s "operation of rewriting": in other words, the provinces appear as a trope.

I have in mind here the play *A Provincial Lady* (*Provintsialka*), the novella *Diary of a Superfluous Man*, and the sketch "Hamlet of Shchigrov," a story that was collected in *A Hunter's Notes* but has little in common with the volume's dominant focus on peasants and nature. In *Diary of a Superfluous Man* Gogol's influence is felt everywhere in the anonymous district (*uezdnyi*) town of O__, which meets all the criteria of a Gogolian provincial backwater (an "amazingly filthy town square," soul-crushing boredom, and outlandishly bad taste, 4:175). Turgenev's narrator even echoes the by now familiar claim that there is no need to describe the ineptly staged ball, since "everything about it was just as it usually is," right down to the "provincial lions with their convulsively distorted faces" (4:194).

A Provincial Lady, too, openly reprises Gogolian themes: one might even read it as a rewriting of *The Inspector General* with the focus squarely on the mayor's conniving wife and daughter, or as a reimagining of the ninth chapter of *Dead Souls* from the point of view of the Pleasant Lady and the Lady Pleasant in All Respects. In Turgenev's text as in Gogol's, the provincial's main task (beyond trying to escape the provinces) is to keep an eye trained on all things *stolichnye*; as Turgenev's heroine puts it, "we poor small-town dwellers [*uezdnye zhiteli*]—we do not forget . . . we forget nothing" (2:408).[8] In fact *A Provincial Lady* is so

dependent on the essentialized difference between *stolitsa* and *provintsiia* that
there is little to say about the action (the wife of a small-town landowner plots to
charm a visiting Petersburg count into finding her husband a job in the capital)
that is not already said by the title. The *provintsialka*'s husband objects to leaving
his estate—"My place is here! I'm master here!"—but his attachment to *his own*
place, so inconsequential it is never named, cannot overcome the centripetal pull
exerted by the capital.

In Gogol's world, so complete is the symbiosis between provincial characters
and provincial settings that it would be difficult to describe these characters (whose
interior lives are mostly unavailable to us) as "products" of their milieu. Even the
just-arrived outsiders Chichikov and Khlestakov are of a piece with the provincial environment; they adapt immediately to its ways, and these ways make no demands on them that they are not prepared to fulfill. While Gogol's *reader* may feel
profoundly alienated by these texts' estates and Towns of N, his characters are right
at home. Not so in Turgenev's world: in *Diary of a Superfluous Man*, the provincial
setting serves to highlight, if not cause, the narrator's alienation, what he famously
calls his superfluousness (*lishnost'*)—the only trait, he claims, that distinguishes
him from other people. As a result, even as we recognize in *Diary of a Superfluous
Man* another iteration of the Gogolian provincial town (*imitatio ad nauseam*), in
fact the town signifies somewhat differently: here the distorted culture of *provintsiia* and the alienation it produces in the narrator serve as the beginning of an
explanation for social and moral pathologies, most notably the narrator's debilitat-
ing self-consciousness, his unnaturalness, his "agonizing strain." And this strain, he
insists, is not just the appearance of artificiality, but *actual* artificiality: "I did not
just seem to be so, I really did become unnatural and strained" (4:173).

Turgenev is raising the possibility that for provincials, a comfortably authentic,
"natural" relationship to culture might be forever out of reach. Here we recall
Lotman's classic analysis of the post-Petrine nobility: ideas and behaviors that
were neutral in Europe "took on value" once transferred to Russia, Lotman explains, thereby *accentuating* (rather than replacing) "the non-European aspects of
daily life." "A Russian was not supposed to become a foreigner," Lotman continues,
"he was merely supposed to act like one"—but only sometimes, and only while
remaining carefully aware of which codes he was deploying at a given moment.[9]
In such a context, "natural" behavior can be as marked as "unnatural" behavior
(see: Tatiana Larina); you can *act* natural, but you cannot *be* natural. Remaining
unconscious of one's relationship to one's own culture was a luxury that educated
Russians could rarely afford.

The same poisonous inauthenticity we saw in *Diary of a Superfluous Man* is
the subject of "Hamlet of Shchigrov." The story points forward to many of the
concerns that will animate Turgenev's later novels, including not just the *skuka*

(oppressive boredom) of provincial life, but also a strangely disordered relationship to culture and to historical time, a disorder that threatens to empty provincial lives of meaning. "Hamlet of Shchigrov" is set on a remote steppe estate at a gathering of markedly local characters—"our steppe brothers," in the words of one guest, who conform to dismal provincial types (3:253). When one guest describes himself as someone who "[passes] here for a wit," the quip confirms what has been implicit in the opening passage: "here" is provincial in its constant awareness of an external standard to which it aspires but which it fails to attain (thus the host's wines are imported from Moscow, the guests' suits are made by a Moscow tailor, etc.). If, as was explained in this book's introductory chapter, a few estates managed to become *stolichnye* by successfully reproducing or reflecting the capital's culture, this one clearly does not: in "Hamlet of Shchigrov," estates are provincial.

Having established that there is a center toward which this periphery is always looking, the narrator recounts his conversation with a small landowner, a widower identifying himself only as "Hamlet," who tells the story of his life—a life he insists is absolutely typical for men of his time and class. As the stranger puts it in the last lines of his monologue, "as an unoriginal [*neoriginal'nyi*] person I do not deserve a name of my own. . . . If you really want to give me some title, then call me . . . call me Hamlet of the Shchigrov District. There are many such Hamlets in every district" (3:273). He is at once a provincial Everyman and a thoroughly ersatz specimen.

Here as in *Diary of a Superfluous Man*, we are invited to draw a connection between a certain cultural pathology—never clearly defined, but closely related to *neoriginal'nost'*—and a certain place. The role of milieu is highlighted in Hamlet's description of the isolated estate where he once lived with his wife, rendered with an abundance of detail (a fact to which the storyteller draws our attention—"note in what detail I'm describing it," he says; 3:167). If Gogol's detailed descriptions of provincial places are characterized by a stifling material thickness, Turgenev's specifics in "Hamlet" serve mainly to underline the meagerness of this life: a few knickknacks from Catherine's time, busts of Goethe and Schiller, awkwardly drawn portraits on the wall. The same phrases of Beethoven are played again and again on an out-of-tune piano, over which hangs "a well-known portrait of a blond maiden with a dove on her breast and her eyes raised up" (3:167). Withered garlands, yellowing albums, clichéd images—the manor house is clearly meant to encapsulate the thinness, derivativeness and stasis of what passes for culture in the deep provinces.

What happens to such artifacts of high culture when they end up not merely on a provincial estate, but out on the steppe, the vast Southern Eurasian flatlands? Russian elites from Radishchev, Chaadaev, and Sollogub to Gorky, Berdiaev, and Trotsky tended to see the steppe not just as empty, but as *irremediably* empty, a space that actively resisted being "filled up" with culture; they worried about the steppe's capacity to "swallow up," disperse or dilute the achievements of civilization. Where culture is spread so thin, artifacts risk losing their connections with each other. No energizing encounters or webs of meaning seem possible, and thus no models for transformation or development; whatever has ended up out here is now inert, going nowhere. In "Hamlet of Shchigrov," the steppe estate's version of *provintsial'nost'* is paltriness and insufficiency, a few objects largely shorn of context but carefully, almost fetishistically, preserved and displayed. The bust of Goethe, the yellowed sheet music—these are clearly scarce goods, *defitsitnye produkty*.

Of course the steppe is far from *inherently* provincial, imitative, or stagnant—like any place or any person, it can be experienced as provincial in these ways only after it has been brought into contact with, and forced to submit to, another power, another discourse. Take, for instance, Turgenev's later tale *King Lear of the Steppe* (1870), in which Russia's vast open plain is represented as not having undergone "provincialization." Here as in Aksakov's *Family Chronicle*, the steppe is the dominion of a larger-than-life premodern hero—the nobleman Martyn Petrovich Kharlov, a virtual bogatyr who submits to no outside power at all. There are no busts of Goethe on Kharlov's steppe estate, no washed-up vestiges of European high culture: the manor house walls are decorated with whips, horse collars, and sabers—objects with their own meaning and use, entirely appropriate to their setting. We are not told the estate's precise location because all we need to know is that we are in Kharlov's sovereign domain, the domain of a brutally "authentic" steppe nobleman who looks out the window of his rude manor house and declares, "There it is, my kingdom! . . . It's all mine!" (8:166–67). Kharlov dresses like a Cossack and confidently devises an implausible family tree that places him and his clan not on any periphery, but at the originary center of all that matters to him, including history. We could hardly be further away from the etiolated "European" culture of the estate drawing room in "Hamlet of Shchigrov," a place "so stifling [one] could hardly breathe" (3:267).

And indeed, in "Hamlet of Shchigrov," Hamlet tells us that not long after his marriage, his wife wasted away and died—supposedly of consumption but in reality, it seems, of a specifically provincial form of ennui, a "hidden wound at the bottom of her soul" that was caused, "perhaps, by living so long in the countryside [*v derevne*]" (3:268). Clearly *derevnia* here signifies not the life of the countryside or village (peasant huts do not display busts of Goethe), but rather that of a steppe estate in its fully provincialized form. (See chapter 2 for an account of the historical and cultural process that transformed the steppe's meanings, thanks to which the steppe went from being exotic frontier to being boring *provintsiia* or *derevnia*.) And Hamlet's wife's "festering wound" that can be neither named nor cured is a literalization of what many texts describe as the deleterious and sometimes even lethal boredom of provincial life—as Turgenev puts it in *Smoke*, in the remote provinces "people vomit from boredom" (7:389).

The steppe manor house, with its petrified cultural dross, is the material manifestation of a particular relationship to culture, and much of "Hamlet" is devoted to establishing how such a relationship might have come about. To that end, we learn about Hamlet's upbringing and education, which took place on yet another isolated and uncultured estate (the third in the story, counting the one where Hamlet and the narrator meet). His mother hired a "French" tutor who was actually an incoherent jumble of European labels ("a German named Filipovich who came from the Nezhin Greeks": here as in many other texts, the steppe seems to attract failed and déclassé Europeans, just as it attracts busts of Goethe) before shipping him off to Moscow University. There he learned to parrot received ideas, repeating dreamy verses, meditating on "the beautiful," and joining a circle (*kruzhok*), which he identifies as the place where his own fatal "lack of originality" would become undeniable (a *kruzhok* is the end of all "authentic development," he says). In fact, the circle gives rise to the chief attributes we have learned to associate with *provintsiia*: "pretentions," "vulgarity and boredom," and constant, intrusive surveillance (3:262–63).

And even when Hamlet finally goes to study in Germany, he remains "the same unoriginal creature" he was at home. Rather than overcoming his provincialism, he further immerses himself in copying, pretension, banality, and ennui—reading philosophy alone, socializing only with "dimwits" from Russia's "grain-producing provinces," enjoying little contact with Germans or with any form of daily European life beyond a few "strained" conversations with the natives. So isolated is he that even a genuine "thirst for knowledge" leads him nowhere (3:263–64). One might expect an educated man to be well enough prepared to take advantage of Europe's richest intellectual environment, but Turgenev's hero instead lives out the tragedy of the autodidact—less Shakespeare's Hamlet than Hardy's Jude the Obscure, who can accumulate knowledge but for whom this accumulation will never cohere into an intelligible whole, simply because it bears no proper relationship to any life he has ever lived. In effect he brings the steppes with him to Europe—and on the steppes, ideas and art objects are forever deprived of the contexts that give them meaning. As a result, Turgenev's hero is afflicted with a version of the psychic wound he has diagnosed in his wife.

Hamlet's autobiographical monologue pivots on the repetition of a particular word: "originality" (*original'nost'*) and its cognates recur over and over in his self-analysis (twenty-two times in the course of a relatively short text). The word functions as an attempt to sum up the complex pathology of his own character: "I am literally perishing because in me there is absolutely nothing original." Everything he has ever done has been marked by this fatal absence of originality, he says; "I was born in imitation of another." What exactly is this crucial, elusive "originality," and how did it come about? While we might initially assume that we know what the word means, once we have heard it invoked time after time, it begins to feel slippery. The definitions offered by the speaker are too tautological to be of much help: what is missing in the unoriginal person, he says, is "something uniquely one's own, something individual, personal" (*svoego-to, osobennogo, sobstvennogo*); lacking this mysterious "something," a person is "just one more storage room full of clichés." "I'm no provincial [*provintsial*]," "I'm no steppe bumpkin [*stepniak*]," Hamlet declares, assuring us that he speaks French and German fluently and "purely," has spent three years abroad, "knows Goethe by heart," etc. (3:257–59).

These protestations signal to us what he later says outright: his lack of originality stems from his outsider—or perhaps better, *semi*-outsider—relationship to European culture, which for him is the only culture that counts. This is the same problem that finds material expression in his wife's manor house, where the décor represents a doomed attempt to transplant ideas and artifacts to a place where they can never signify as they are meant to. Hamlet's most passionately spoken utterances concern the utter *incompatibility* of Hegel, of all German philosophy, indeed of all "learning" (*nauka*) with "Russian life" and "our daily existence": his exposure to European culture has poisoned his experience of his homeland. So, he asks rhetorically, why bother learning about all these things—why not just stay in Russia? His answer is that staying at home would have been no solution either, since his native place would nonetheless have remained unintelligible. Staying in Russia would not have solved his problem any more than making it to Petersburg or Moscow would have helped Gogol's small-town bureaucrats or Chekhov's Prozorov sisters. The problem, Hamlet says, inheres in Russian life itself, which refuses to disclose its significance: "I would've been glad to take lessons from her—from Russian life, that is—but she just keeps mum, my little dove" (3:260).

One thinks again of Hardy's Jude, the gifted working-class man who makes his way to a university town: he tries to decipher the signs of the intellectual life surrounding him, tries to force them to yield up their meaning, but such meaning will never be available to people like him. And just as it does not matter how perfectly Gogol's provincial ladies manage to copy Petersburg fashions, neither does it matter how fluently Turgenev's Hamlet speaks French and German or how much Goethe he knows by heart. His provinciality is an irremediable condition, and he is forever precluded from what he calls "authentic development" (3:262). To occupy such a relationship to culture is to be a native of nowhere: this is what Mikhail Epstein calls the provinces' "alienation from themselves," leaving provincials forever yearning for something that is somewhere else, "not here, not at this place, but 'there.'"[10]

Fathers, Children, and Estates

The steppe estate that figures in "Hamlet of Shchigrov," with its vestigial and in-congruous culture, is by no means typical of all Turgenev's estates. Far from it: three estates figure in *Fathers and Sons*, and not one of them embodies this kind of *provintsial'nost'*. Bazarov's parents' home is isolated and poor (in a "far-off region," a boondocks [*zakholustia, glush'*, 7:109, 112] decisively set apart from the rest of the world in both space and time), but it is not strewn with washed-up fragments of a distant civilization. Rather, it is a space of quiet labor, where Bazarov learned to see the world as a workshop. Marino, the Kirsanovs' estate, is a slightly shabby version of the idyll ("not an area that could be called picturesque": as Arkady ap-proaches his childhood home he sees roofless huts, tattered peasants, trees resem-bling "beggars in rags"; 7:15). It is old-fashioned and perhaps even retrograde—the elder Kirsanovs' habits and tastes, like those of Pushkin's Larins, recall an earlier generation's, and patriarchal norms have not yet completely decayed—but it is not at all provincial: far from being imitative or culturally incoherent, Marino is self-sufficient and self-respecting. (In fact the narrative's dramatic effect requires that Marino represent not a brittle, syncretic culture but a relatively intact and coher-ent one, precisely so that Bazarov can come and break it open.)

Like the Larins' estate-world in *Eugene Onegin*, Marino is one of those settings where literature occasionally permits members of the Russian gentry to experi-ence their lives as "natural" (see my remarks above on Lotman's analysis of the post-Petrine nobility). But the status of the Kirsanovs' estate is not stable in the same way the Larins' is (and as I discuss in this book's introduction, for an estate to succeed in representing its way of life as "natural," "simple," and "timeless," the *appearance* of stability and permanence was required). Indeed Marino's status is quite precarious, not only because of the historical moment when the story takes place (immediately before the serfs' emancipation), but also because *Fathers and Sons* invites us to compare it to two very different estates, Bazarov's (described just above) and Anna Sergeevna Odintsova's.

Odintsova's estate resembles the Kirsanovs' in that it is by no means provincial. But it differs crucially from Marino in that it is *consciously* not provincial—and its nonprovinciality is due not to any vestigial patriarchal regime, but rather to the heroic, even despotic efforts of its mistress, a wealthy young widow who single-handedly staves off the entropic provincialism of country life. There is nothing natural about living at Odintsova's. We are told in passing that her estate is called Nikolskoe, and that is located "about forty versts from the town of ***," "on the slope of a bare hill" (7:73).[11] That is all we learn about its location, and that is all we need to learn: like each of the estates in *Fathers and Sons*, Nikolskoe is a world unto itself. And what is important about it is not its location, but the fact that the mistress's money, intellect, and iron will are keeping provincial disorder at bay by imposing strict discipline on every aspect of life. Anna Sergeevna Odintsova—like Tatiana as she glides into the ballroom at the end of *Eugene Onegin*—is defined above all by a "serenity" (variations of *spokoino*—peacefully—occur repeatedly in reference to her) that she herself has willed into being. Her bearing is "dignified"; her dress is "simple"; she speaks very little. Her gaze is "serene and intelligent— precisely serene, not pensive," with "serene" here signifying the appearance of effortlessness (an appearance she sustains by invisible force of will; 7:68–70).

Though Odintsova's house was built by a local (*gubernskii*) architect, there is absolutely nothing provincial about it: no awkward mixing of styles, nothing "frivolous or pointless," just a plain—but not too plain—house, with the usual columns, gables, and coat of arms. The furnishings are "rather elegant"—but not too elegant—in an entirely conventional, predictable, *comme-il-faut* manner: "in the usual formal way," "without any particular sort of taste" (7:76). What is meant here by the words "without any particular sort of taste" is certainly not bad taste; it is, rather, the opposite of a provincial's tastelessly visible striving. Odintsova's house encapsulates a kind of anti-aesthetic aesthetic that is available to those who have ample economic and cultural capital but no interest in taste as creative self-expression or as overt political statement.[12] It is about predictability, order, and efficiency: the sooner Odintsova's rooms are furnished, the sooner she can move on to learning the Latin names for plants, as is her plan.

"Order is needed in all things," she says: because only extreme regimentation can stave off what she repeatedly calls the boredom that would otherwise overcome anyone living in the countryside (*v derevne*). To that end, time at Odintsova's is subjected to a "measured, somewhat imperious punctuality," one that establishes what Jane Costlow calls "a model of absolute order."[13] So measured and controlled is the flow of time at her home that it is impossible, the narrator tells us, to sense its passage. Time here is cyclical in the sense that footmen serve dinner at precisely the same hour every day, but this cyclicity is far removed from that of the idyll, which is nature-based and essentially agricultural (needless to say, there is no talk of farming at Odintsova's dinner table). Life at Odintsova's is structured around habits that offend Bazarov's "democratic sensibility" (like servants in livery), and the mistress does not deny that yes, "in that sense [she is] perhaps an aristocrat"—but nonetheless there is nothing retrograde about this place, nothing backward looking (7:85).

Neither is there anything particularly modern: temporality here is unrelated to progress; rather, it is organized as a defense against the monotony and chaos assumed to be threatening on all sides. Odintsova understands that nothing "in the countryside" can be left to chance, lest provincial tedium and purposelessness overwhelm all of life. But she expresses no desire to inhabit progressive history, history in the sense of Pocock's "public time" (see chapter 2):[14] instead she uses her estate to make time orderly and meaningful on a small scale, creating a local temporality that allows for clear and deliberate ways of thinking. Odintsova is thus entirely free of the disabling anxiety that characterizes provincials, the apprehension that deforms those Turgenev characters who are always painfully aware they inhabit a periphery, a behind-the-times place that resists being dragged into real time.

In *Fathers and Sons*, the epicenter of provinciality is not the gentry estate, but instead an anonymous provincial city, another Town of N. Toward the middle of the novel, in the strangely unmotivated interlude when Bazarov and Arkady decide to go "take a look" at this N, they seem to be anticipating the possibility of a freak show. In this sense the town does not disappoint: the governor's nickname is "slops," guests at a ball speak in nonsensical "French" exclamations ("ah fichtrrre," "pst, pst, mon bibi," etc. [7:68]). The two young men learn that this "city like any other" (Bazarov's dismissive formulation) regularly burns to the ground and must be built anew ("it is a well-known fact that our provincial towns burn down every five years," 7:64, 62).

In town Turgenev's protagonists meet the *provintsialka* Avdotya Nikitishna Kukshina, a coarse woman, vaguely promiscuous and semi-educated in Europe, who is introduced to them as "an *émancipée*" (7:61). Kukshina serves as perhaps the most complete (and misogynistic) embodiment of predictably ugly provincial phenomena in all of Turgenev's oeuvre, perhaps in all of Russian literature. She longs to be known as a "progressive woman" (*peredovaia zhenshchina*, 7:61), a person who is decidedly modern, moving forward in step with History. But how is "progress" possible in a city that is regularly reduced to ashes and must be reconstructed from nothing? What does it mean to live in a house that has to be rebuilt twice every decade? It is difficult to imagine a more apt symbol of a failed attempt to join the linear, progressive temporality that Kukshina longs for, the kind of temporality that characterizes modernity's view of itself.

Her house, her clothing, her habits and facial expressions—all announce, even before she speaks, a repellently incoherent quality, one that is diametrically opposed to Odintsova's disciplined orderliness. Kukshina's material environment is marked by slightly unwholesome forms of hybridity and mixing, a failure to establish the boundaries necessary to keep things and ideas in their proper places: is that person with her a servant or a companion, and is this room a drawing room or a study? Why is she "half-reclining" and "a bit disheveled" in a silk dress, and why are there cigarette butts mixed in with her papers? Her piano is out of tune; her fingernails are "blunt"; she sings a mix of gypsy songs and romances.

Kukshina's ideas reflect the same kind of disorder as does her house, a disorder that dooms her to triviality: thanks to a "passion for chemistry," she has invented a resin "to make dolls' heads that won't break," and she has resolved to go to Heidelberg to meet the inventor of the Bunsen burner ("why of course!"). In one brief, breathless statement, Kukshina refers to George Sand, embryology, and Ralph Waldo Emerson (7:63–64). When her talk jumps from German chemists to Macaulay to James Fenimore Cooper, we are meant to understand that her culture is a jumble of imported ideas, materials that have no more organic relationship to their current location than did the busts of Schiller and Goethe stranded on the steppes in "Hamlet of Shchigrov." Kukshina is provincial not because her materials are outdated or meager (they are in fact quite up-to-the-minute and copious), but because they lack the coherence—the clear interrelationships—that would allow them to make sense. Indeed, her thoughts signal the same radical indiscriminateness as do the physical objects in *Dead Souls*.

Kukshina must be made a laughingstock not only because her ideas are derivative and incoherent, but also because she has failed to make her relationship to these ideas look effortless. This is perhaps the ultimate source of her provinciality: she is obviously trying, and her *effort* renders her fatally unnatural. If Odintsova is rigorously serene (as well as "simple," "intelligent," and "dignified"), Kukshina is the opposite: "She was forever tense. She spoke and moved in a very casual and yet awkward manner. . . . No matter what she did, she always seemed to be doing precisely what she did not want to be doing. *Everything she did appeared to be done on purpose, as children say, not simply, not naturally*" (7:63, emphasis mine). As we have seen before, to be provincial is to be an imitator in whose imitations the marks of labor remain shamefully visible—and Kukshina will never be able to "manifest by [her] ease and naturalness that true culture is nature." A provincial, like a parvenu, cannot attain to "the privilege of indifference to [her] own manner."[15]

Rudin and *Nest of the Gentry*: The Provinces and Historical Time

Odintsova creates her own version of time by ordering her own strictly delimited space, outside of which it is almost impossible to imagine her existing at all. By contrast, in *Rudin* (1856), the eponymous hero—one of Russian literature's paradigmatic "superfluous men," full of fancy talk but incapable of work or action—inhabits no space of his own. Rudin drifts around: born in the provinces (Tambov), educated in Moscow and then abroad, he has returned to Russia a rootless wanderer. When the book opens he is in effect already a stray; having just arrived at a sophisticated country estate, he demonstrates his unreliability (talking too much while saying too little) before leaving to drift around Russia and Europe until finally he dies.

Rudin's superfluousness is inseparable from his desultory movements through space, particularly in the novel's final chapter and epilogue. We learn of his years covering ground—Moscow, Simbirsk, Germany, various provincial towns, other unnamed places—seemingly in search of a livelihood (e.g., a vague project involving "making a river in __ Province navigable"; 5:315), but really for no clear reason; he has "gone around various places," as he puts it, "wandering around [*skitalsia*] not only physically but spiritually too" (5:311). When he encounters an old friend in yet another provincial town (the *gubernskii gorod S__*), Rudin can give no clear reason for being here rather than in some other place (his presence in the town is "quite by chance," he says; 5:310). It is impossible to tell exactly what motivates his movements, why he chooses one destination over another. When told—while traveling through "one of the remote provinces of Russia"—that no horses are going his way, his response is, "It doesn't matter. I'll go to Tambov" (5:309). No wonder those who know Rudin expect that "he'll end up dying in some Tsarevokokshaisk or Chukhloma" (5:302). Tsarevokokshaisk and Chukhloma are names that signify a kind of namelessness: they are real towns, but they stand in for unreal towns, towns where nothing of significance could possibly happen.

In the end, however, Rudin does *not* die in such a history-less or placeless place—at least not in editions of the text published after 1860, when Turgenev added a few crucial last lines. Early redactions of the novel conclude with Rudin wandering off from the town of S__, followed by the line, "And may the Lord help all homeless wanderers!" (or "pilgrims," *skiltal'tsam*; 5:322). But on the last page of the version we read today, the hero does not drift off to expire in some backwater; rather, he perishes dramatically, on a specific and highly meaningful date and spot. He dies, but he dies at the very epicenter of historical significance, on the barricades of the June Days uprising in Paris. A French sharpshooter kills him "on June 26, 1848, in Paris, when the rising of the 'national workshops' was already nearly defeated"; he falls while waving a sword and a red flag (5:322). This death is usually read as granting Rudin a degree of redemption, presumably not only because it demonstrates courage, but also because it incorporates his life into a larger and markedly *historical* narrative, one that implies a redeeming teleology.

Such an ending—of Rudin's life and of the novel—works to shift both hero and text decisively out of the zone of the provincial and closer perhaps to that of "public time" and even "world literature." In Rudin's last, long conversation with his friend Lezhnev, which takes place in Russia, we notice a distinct rhetorical heightening surrounding the topic of his peregrinations. Rudin's inconstancy is now presented not as a character flaw or even as a symptom of Russia's problems, but as a deep mystery ("solve this riddle for me!"), the solution to which may lie in the fact that "the love of truth burns more strongly in [him] . . . than in many others" (5:319–20). Lezhnev, recalling that Rudin has called himself a Wandering Jew, raises the possibility that his "eternal wanderings" serve somehow to "fulfill some higher purpose, the meaning of which remains unknown to [Rudin himself]" (5:321). If so, then maybe all this roaming around has been something akin to a pilgrimage, and Rudin is himself a pilgrim, like the hero of Leskov's "Enchanted Wanderer" (the *ocharovannyi strannik*, with *strannik* meaning both wanderer and pilgrim). Read in this light, Rudin's movements serve to call our attention to the potential for significance in all the seemingly insignificant spaces he has traversed—even places like Tsarevokokshaisk and Chukhloma.

Nest of the Gentry, too, raises the hopeful possibility that *provintsiia* might in the end not be divorced from historical time. Like *Rudin* and *Fathers and Sons*, the text opens with a return ("Fyodor Ivanovych Lavretsky has arrived," 6:11) and then goes on to consider the relationship between *provintsiia* and the nation's place in capital-H History. Rather than representing Russia's heartland as the periphery of some far-off and aspired-to center (like Kukshina's Town of N in *Fathers and Sons* or the steppe estate in "Hamlet of Shchigrov"), *Nest of the Gentry* explores the possibility—also present in *Fathers and Sons*, though less explicitly developed—that a gentry estate, or maybe even a provincial town, could be its own center, a "nest" rather than an appendage to a distant metropole it aims only to imitate. The homecoming it stages leads to no happy ending, but it does suggest that a version of progressive history might be possible in "deep" Russia.

The novel's geography encompasses a series of locations in the Russian provinces—the estates of Lavriki, Vasilevskoe, and Petrovskoe, and the town of O__—each of which is a place in its own right, its identity not determined by distance from or proximity to anyplace else. Nothing in the text allows us to determine exactly where these places are, though it is clear that the capitals are not only far away but also of no great importance (Lavretsky, we are told, does not even stop in Moscow or Petersburg on his way home from Paris): *Nest of the Gentry* is not reprising the *provintsiia/stolitsa* binary. But it does illustrate once again the pernicious effects of imposing European ideas on Russian youth. The novel's hero, Fyodor Ivanovich Lavretsky, is unfit for (Russian/real) life, as was his father before him, thanks to émigré tutors who have "sown confusion" in their young minds (6:41). Lavretsky *père* was educated by a "retired abbé and encyclopédist" who poured into his head "the undiluted wisdom of the eighteenth century," wisdom that failed to "mix with his blood or penetrate to his soul" (6:31). After living a while in London, he returned ("reeking of Great Britain," 6:38) to his estate to impose rational farming practices on his peasants. He then imposes on his son, who will be the novel's protagonist, a garbled "European" upbringing. Young Fyodor Ivanovich, raised alone on the steppes, is made to wake at four a.m. and "run around a pole" before writing French dithyrambs and shooting crossbows under the supervision of a Swedish lady and a young Swiss, all while dressed in Scottish garb (6:41): compare the childhood tutor of Turgenev's Hamlet, "a German named Filipovich who came from the Nezhin Greeks" (3:262–63).

The education of Lavretsky *fils* was perhaps meant to make him a citizen of the world, but he ends up as isolated as any provincial who has been deformed by an idiosyncratic body of knowledge haphazardly transmitted. The results of "capricious education" and "artificial isolation" are what a reader of "Hamlet of Shchigrov" would expect: Fyodor Ivanovich Lavretsky is awkward, "some sort of queer pedant": "any professor would have envied him some of what he knew, but at the same time he did not know many things that any schoolboy had learned long ago" (6:43–44). Despite a lucid mind (and "a healthy air of the steppes" attributable, it seems, to his peasant mother; 6:26), despite having read widely and thought deeply, Lavretsky is an eccentric. Moreover, he is tormented by this fact, and feels as painfully self-conscious as any provincial: "Lavretsky was conscious that he was *not free*" (6:43).

What does it mean to be "not free" as a result of one's relationship to knowledge? Lavretsky's miseducation has enclosed him in an "enchanted circle" (6:43) where he is unable to link ideas together in patterns or juxtapose them in fruitful encounters—much in the same way the isolated artifacts of culture in "Hamlet of Shchigrov," adrift on the steppe and shorn of context, become inert and meaningless. Ultimately it is the discontinuity between what Lavretsky knows and what *others* know that leaves him paralyzed, always "[standing] in the same place, locked up and constrained within himself" (6:43). Knowing the wrong things, or even knowing too much, is as bad as knowing nothing, because the autodidact or the "outsider artist," brilliant though s/he may be, will always be "a culture of one," an exception that proves the rule.[16]

In short, to know the wrong things is to be in the wrong relationship to one's own place and time. This makes Lavretsky *provincial* in a way that Liza—the lovely and markedly Russian girl with whom he falls in love, a girl who has never left her home—clearly is not. More than once we are told that Liza "has no words of her own" (6:83–84), but her wordlessness, I would emphasize, is the opposite of provincial imitation or diffidence; rather, it is a sign that what she knows is too important to be articulated.[17] Her wordlessness is also the opposite of provincial garrulousness like Kukshina's: in *Nest of the Gentry*, it is not Liza but Varvara Pavlovna (Lavretsky's unfaithful wife) who never stops talking, and constant wit and chatter are key to her impersonation of a Frenchwoman (she styles herself "*une vraie française par l'esprit*").

Liza, like a peasant, cannot be provincial because she is simply not *modern* enough: and provinciality, as I have discussed elsewhere, is a decidedly modern phenomenon, tied up with imitation, fashion, and (incipient) consumer culture. Varvara Pavlovna, recently returned from Paris, incarnates what is most modern

and most shallow in the Russian apprehension of European culture—Europe as
the site of entertainment, consumer goods (she talks a lot about things like *savon
à la guimauve*) and a breathless, trivializing print culture. Her male counterpart is
Panshin, a visiting Petersburg bureaucrat whose smooth manners accord with his
glibly cosmopolitan opinions. Panshin declares complacently that "all nations are
in essence the same," and that Russia—"lacking inventiveness" and having "fallen
behind Europe"—has no choice but to "borrow willy-nilly" from the West (6:101).

Together Varvara Pavlovna and Panshin represent a modernity of debased
dilettantism that *Nest of the Gentry* locates not in the provinces, but rather in a
certain version of "Europe": the Europe of ever-changing fashions, middle-brow
theater, and the newest perfumes (like "Victoria's Essence," 6:125). The serious,
idea-freighted Europe aspired to in "Hamlet of Shchigrov" is present in *Nest of
the Gentry* only in the somewhat marginal figure of the German music teacher,
Lemm, who carries with him a thoroughly authentic high culture wherever he
wanders in search of a living. No matter how far he penetrates into the Russian
outback, Lemm's relationship to this version of European culture remains intact—
which is what allies him with Liza, who has her own version of an organic culture,
one capable of encompassing Bach, folktales, and saints' lives.

It is mainly Liza—a classic sweet young thing, what Russians call a *Turgenevskaia
devushka* (Turgenev girl), but with an extra infusion of Orthodox spirituality—
who provides the counterpoint to the text's various examples of cultural distortion.
Liza escaped Frenchification at the hands of a frivolous and cynical Parisian governess, Mlle. Moreau, and was shaped instead by her Russian (and very Orthodox)
peasant nanny, Agafia Vlaseevna. Mlle. Moreau's dismissive and leveling refrain
"tout ça c'est des bêtises"—"that's all nonsense!"—is directly countered by Agafia
Vlaseevna's luminous spirituality, which infuses all experience with depth and im-
prints on Liza's soul "the image of an ever-present, omniscient God" (6:112).

It is this version of Russia, the Liza version, to which the hero Lavretsky aspires to *return*. And we experience Russianness in this book not through Liza
(for whom it is simply the air she breathes, not an "experience" at all) but rather
through Lavretsky, who comes home after long expatriation. Passages of nature
description, for example, serve to call attention not simply to nature, but to a
markedly Russian version of nature—a Russianness that would of course not be
visible to one who had never left it. Naked steppe lands, peasant huts, and shim-
mering birches all present to Lavretsky (whose act of *looking* is repeatedly emphasized) a "Russian picture" (6:50). An entire chapter is devoted to his experience
of sensual and sensory immersion in this environment: for a whole day he sits at
the window, "plunged into a kind of peaceful stupor" as he listens to varieties of
near-silence. Here forms of the word silence (*tikho, tishina*) occur seven times in
one paragraph, where virtually the only sound is the buzzing of insects (6:64–65).

As Lavretsky immerses himself in this torpor, he imagines it as a charmed "circle" (*krug*) to which one must be resigned upon entering ("whoever steps inside—must submit!"). Having struggled to escape one "enchanted circle" (that of his deforming education; 6:43), he now sees an alternative in another closed circle: a version of Russia that approximates "the bottom of a river" (this phrase occurs twice), where one can be engulfed in an utterly "idle peace." There is no progress here, no history—all of that is happening elsewhere: "At that very moment in other places on earth, life was seething, hurrying, thundering along; here the same life was flowing on noiselessly, like water through marsh grasses." History does exist, in other words, only not here, not at the bottom of the river; here time stands still.[18] At this moment such a life suits Lavretsky, who has not been treated well by the modern, "outside" world. Not only does he submit, willingly if temporarily, to the "boredom," "idleness," and "dead silence" of this place, he finds himself thoroughly "enchanted" by it (6:64–65).

Lavretsky finds life in deep Russia to be not only "mysteriously pleasing . . . cheerful and wonderful," but also "unexpectedly strange and at the same time so long and so sweetly familiar" (6:84). The passage might have been devised to illustrate Benedict Anderson's argument about how "national identity" functions in modernity: "nationalness" must be experienced as a feeling that is at once "unexpectedly strange" and "sweetly familiar." This sensation is what is needed to underwrite the narratives of "identity" that become necessary once we are embedded in what Anderson calls the "secular, serial time" of modernity, the de-enchanted time that all moderns inhabit—the kind of time into which Lavretsky (like Oblomov and not a few other nineteenth-century Russian heroes) has been dragged against his will.[19]

But I would argue that in the end *Nest of the Gentry* is able to imagine a version of *provintsiia* that is not only native and authentic, but also productive and portable: the provincial estate as it is envisioned here will be carried into the future, even if Fyodor Lavretsky's generation will not be the one to do it. Liza, the Slavophile ideal, ends up immured in a convent "in one of the remote regions of Russia" (6:152), suffering a fate that suggests she is perhaps not such an ideal after all, and Lavretsky himself simply lives out his life honorably, accomplishing little. But in the book's epilogue, set eight years later, Lavretsky contemplates the younger generation now living on the estate—happy, active "young people" who were educated in the capitals but are entirely at home in *provintsiia*—and he thinks, "Enjoy yourselves, grow up, you forces of youth . . . life is ahead of you, and for you things will be easier: you won't have to seek your path as we have done, to struggle . . . in darkness; we had to work hard just to remain whole, and how many of us failed?—but for you there's work to do" (6:158).

This ending is of course characteristic of Turgenev in its careful moderation, its repudiation of two extremes. It rejects the glib argument for Europeanization offered earlier by Panshin (to modernize is to westernize, since "all nations are in essence the same"). But for all the book's Slavophilic undertones, the ending of *Nest of the Gentry* also questions the timeless, autarkic Orthodox ideal that would leave Liza stranded in a remote convent to atone for everyone's sins. In other words, the epilogue manages to foresee, if dimly, a generation for whom "provincial" Russian culture will be neither a cacophony of imported Europeanisms nor an authentic-but-atrophied "charmed circle." Rather, to adopt once again Anderson's terms, it will become part of a "narrative of identity" that can be enlisted to do the work of modern life.

Smoke and *Virgin Soil*: Expatriation and Itinerancy

Fyodor Lavretsky leaves Europe and returns to provincial Russia so that *Nest of the Gentry* can imagine a future Russian identity that would make it possible for Lavretsky's countrymen to join history on their own terms. The book can be read as a rejection of cosmopolitanism, or at least a rejection of the notion that "all nations are in essence the same." *Smoke*, a pointedly satirical novel of 1867, is set a world away from *Nest of the Gentry*'s Russian heartland, but it reveals a similar skepticism when it comes to the virtues of worldliness. *Smoke*'s setting is the international watering hole of Baden-Baden, a milieu that highlights what has often been represented as the Russian propensity for borrowing and mixing: a willingness, as Monika Greenleaf writes, to adapt ideas that were "sometimes up-to-the-minute but more often chronologically out of sync with European fashion," conflating these ideas and making use of them "*simultaneously*," regardless of their temporal or geographic origins.[20] We have already seen Turgenev's critique of this phenomenon in *Fathers and Sons* (Kukshina's Town of N, with its culture that keeps burning itself down), and in "Hamlet of Shchigrov" (the steppe estate's "culture" consisting of a few hollowed-out and fetishized artifacts).

In "Hamlet of Shchigrov," characters cast adrift in the flat calm of steppe time sit in silence; their provincial culture has no content, and therefore it has no words—there is only the sound of spoons striking against teacups. By contrast, the expatriated Russians in *Smoke* never stop talking. Their version of provinciality, like Kukshina's, is marked by excess and garrulousness, thanks precisely to their willingness to mix elements from wildly incompatible cultural and chronological registers. "One moment holding forth on the role of the Celts in history, the next transported into the ancient world," their expatiations range dizzyingly from one place and time to another (7:258). They speak in much the same way Kukshina does, and to the same effect. Over and over in *Smoke* again we encounter passages like the following, some of which continue for pages:

Voroshilov suddenly exploded, naming in a single breath, almost choking, Draper, Virchow, Mr. Shelgunov, Bichat, Helmholtz, Stahr, Štúr, Reumont, Johannes Müller the physiologist and Johannes Müller the historian, clearly confusing the two, Taine, Renan, Mr. Shchapov, then Thomas Nashe, Peele, and Greene. (7:266)

Both the self-styled radicals and the conservatives (the two Russian political camps at the spa) spew a mind-numbing and hilarious mélange of up-to-the-minute "ideas" ("the titles of just-published pamphlets and, in general, names, names, and more names," 7:258), almost silly enough to make Kukshina seem like a model of systematic thinking. Like hers, their discourse is macaronic to the point of incomprehensibility; page after page of *Smoke* features a jumble of languages, politics, social classes, fashions, music, and nationalities.

These people are in what they take to be a worldly setting (a spa town, which is at once everywhere, "Europe," and nowhere) engaged in what they take to be worldly conversations, but they remain unmistakably provincial. Once again Turgenev's Russians have brought their provinciality with them to Europe because their ideas are not rooted in a clear history or social reality. Thus they treat utterly disparate phenomena as if they were interchangeable, allowing themselves to pass without transition from the Aeginetan marbles to reflections on the peasant commune (7:258–59, 249). But at the same time they remain cognizant of their own tenuous grip on "Europe," and are therefore seized with "reverential tremors" in the face of anything French, ever prepared to concede "the overwhelming superiority of a clever foreigner" (7:270, 250).

And always in the background of their chatter is an awareness of the "deepest steppe" and its "blind darkness," out of which all Russians, Turgenev suggests, have only recently emerged. When the protagonist Litvinov receives a letter from his family estate outside Ryazan, his father's complaints (his grain is selling poorly and his coachman has been bewitched: the end of the world must be near) serve as a jarring reminder of the obscurity and torpor of darkest *provintsiia*, a place that seems to Litvinov to exist in an entirely different historical moment, or perhaps in no historical moment at all. Indeed life back home is so blatantly incommensurate with life in Litvinov's current location that reading his father's letter *here*—"in Baden of all places"—strikes him as positively "bizarre" (*chudno*), as if, he thinks, he had turned a corner and stepped into some long-ago time (7:278–79).

The ostensibly modern time that these Russians try to inhabit in Baden makes no more sense than the stagnant timelessness of the deep steppes. Like Kukshina in her provincial city that has to be rebuilt every five years with whatever materials are at hand, Turgenev's Russians in the European resort town do not have the luxury of living in a coherent or even a clearly identifiable historical moment, in which ideas would have roots in real history and real places. Though they talk constantly about "the future of Russia" (e.g., 7:266), they are no better positioned than is Kukshina (who so longs to be "progressive") to move *forward*. Reflecting on his compatriots who come to Baden to absorb the latest ideas, Litvinov thinks mournfully that soon enough "the wind will change, and the smoke will blow in another direction . . . smoke . . . smoke . . . smoke!" (7:399). Thus *Smoke* ends with neither forward movement nor unity, but with dispersal and a slow falling apart.

Likewise *Virgin Soil*, Turgenev's last novel, ends with dissolution and is set among deracinated seekers, though *Virgin Soil*'s seekers (the "populists" and "nihilists" of the 1870s) remain mostly in Russia. They are trying to drag their country into progressive time by way of capital-R Revolution, but instead they themselves end up melting away into trackless and timeless space. And because one of the book's goals is to imagine how Russia's vastness might be incorporated into a coherent and progressive vision of history, *Virgin Soil* incorporates settings that are virtually unmentioned in the rest of Turgenev's oeuvre, encompassing not only capitals and estates, a sizable provincial capital (*gubernskii gorod*), villages and countryside, but also a factory, railroads and roads, and even (in references at the novel's end), Perm and the Urals. As we follow a loosely affiliated group of revolutionaries who move around Russia in search of the common people (the *narod*, who occupy space in their own way), the novel invites us to think about what their fruitless search bodes for the nation's historical trajectory.

The geography of *Virgin Soil* is shaped by the itinerancy of these would-be revolutionaries. First we follow the hero Nezhdanov from Petersburg to the provinces, a trajectory quite typical for an 1870s populist (and directly opposed to that of the Balzacian hero, whose goal is to make it to Paris (*monter à Paris*). We track other characters as they move from Petersburg to various estates, and from town to town throughout Russia. Unlike in Dostoevsky's *Demons*, in which the wanderings of revolutionaries also figure prominently, in *Virgin Soil* there is little sense of any far-off mastermind who might be directing all this movement: Turgenev's radicals appear to be more or less adrift. The taciturn and unsophisticated nihilist Mashurina, for example, has left her impoverished family in Southern Russia for no ideological reason we can discern and has traveled to Petersburg, where she ends up being radicalized, somehow, in a process we do not witness (9:139).

Turgenev's revolutionaries believe that in order to "know" the common people, one must "go to" them, and this belief motivates their attempts to penetrate Russia's far-off places. But to go to the people, one character declares, is to enter a dangerous dark "forest": the *narod* is "just as obscure and dark [*glukh i temen*] to us as any woods!" (9:153). The adjective *glukh*, translated here as "obscure," also carries implications of voicelessness and deafness, impenetrability and occlusion; the emphasis is on the common people's imperviousness. The main character—Nezhdanov, a bastard son of the aristocracy who has thrown in his lot with the radicals—is charged with "getting close to the peasants," but he finds himself able to do nothing but "study" them. The "chasm" dividing them from himself is simply too wide to be breached (9:213–14).

The revolutionary politics of all the characters, with the exception perhaps of the preternaturally wise factory worker Solomin, seem to have been shaped at least as much by their experiences in Russia's capital city as by any coherent ideological agenda or far-reaching political network. In fact the novel's plot would be inconceivable without the metropolis, the capital's explicitly modern, urban space. Turgenev's innovation here—that is, what we do not see in his other novels—is not so much to incorporate the metropolis into the story (only the early chapters are set in Petersburg), but to reveal how characters who have been shaped by urban modernity are moving across and into Russia, changing the country as they penetrate far-off places (and in so doing helping to disrupt the provinces/capitals binary).

What happens to Nezhdanov, Mashurina, and their comrades in Petersburg is something that simply could not happen in another place: they *mix* with all different sorts of people. Nezhdanov the radical meets Sipiagin, the wealthy aristocrat, in a box at the theater—something that is possible only in a city large enough to provide the venues (theaters, cafés, train station waiting rooms) where truly disparate groups come together, and not always by choice. At first Nezhdanov is baffled to find himself chatting with "this aristocrat" ("How did we manage to come together? And what does he want from me?" 9:150), but the radicals are learning that their cause demands such physical spaces. As one of them declares sententiously, "we must establish ties with all levels of society, starting with the highest!" If Russia's revolutionaries intend "to act, to turn the world upside-down," he continues, "we must not live apart from that world . . . in our own narrow little circle" (9:154, 152). *Virgin Soil* suggests that such an "establishing of ties" might be possible, but probably only in a metropolis. Once outside of Petersburg (and nearly all the action transpires outside of Petersburg), opportunities for class mixing are rare.

In the provinces, unlike in the capital, the revolutionaries' activities tend to segregate and isolate them, putting them at risk of losing each other and melting away into Russia's untrackable spaces. The streets of the provincial town—empty "even on a Saturday evening," with only the taverns full of people, and all of them drunks—are lined by tumbledown shacks and the grim, dull façades of merchants' houses locked down for the night; the market square reeks, and the newly planted trees lining the main boulevard are already dying (9:192). The villages (*sela, dereven'ki, derevnia*, 9:338, 192, 301), too, are poverty-stricken, decayed, and above all *cut off* from contact with outsiders; again the only gathering places are taverns, which are full of raucous and violent peasants. Outside of Petersburg, *Virgin Soil* suggests, Russia is a series of nonoverlapping or even noncontiguous worlds where different sorts of people are unlikely to come together. Even the factory that features prominently in the narrative offers no space for inter-class communication, let alone revolutionary agitation; the radicals have no real contact with the factory hands and are left bemoaning the workers' intractability and passivity.

Virgin Soil concludes with dispersal and a kind of petering out, much as *Smoke* does, and much as *Rudin* would have if Turgenev had not added the final passage and had instead allowed the protagonist to drift off toward "some Tsarevokokshaisk or Chukhloma." By the last chapter of *Virgin Soil*, the cabal of would-be revolutionaries has been broken up, Nezhdanov has killed himself, and those who have escaped arrest seem to be wandering around Russia and Europe with no aims that make any sense to the reader. Like Dostoevsky's *Demons*, *Virgin Soil* ends without resolution or "wrapping up"; instead the characters simply scatter, melting away to parts unknown. A year and a half after this dispersal, in what amounts to a postscript, a minor character named Paklin meets Mashurina, by chance, on a bleak, insignificant Petersburg street. Mashurina, whom we last saw being sent off to Geneva to deliver a cryptic note in a language she could not read, is now traveling here and there on the passport of an Italian countess. When Paklin asks who "directs her movements," she gives no answer, and when he asks where she lives, she responds, "wherever I end up" (9:339).

The last words of *Virgin Soil* are spoken by Paklin as he watches Mashurina depart: "Nameless Russia!," he says—"*Bezymiannaia Rus'!*" (9:339). *Bezymiannaia* here might also be translated as anonymous, unknown: it suggests provincial places like Tsarevokokshaisk and Chukhloma, whose names stand in for namelessness. Here as elsewhere, Turgenev hints that such places will tend to resist attempts to enlist them in a grandly "historical" narrative. In *Fathers and Sons*, Kukshina's desire to graft European time onto provincial Russian reality results in a pandemonium both semiotic and chronological and a town that burns down every five years (7:62). The protagonist of *Smoke*, too, senses that Russia's "deep steppes" do not inhabit European temporality; likewise the main characters in "Hamlet of Shchigrov" and *Nest of the Gentry* are unable to integrate what they have learned from their ostensibly up-to-date European educations with how they must live in Russian places and times.

For Turgenev as for other Russian writers, a preoccupation with inorganicism and a focus on policing various forms of perceived authenticity (by, say, shaming a *provintsialka* like Kukshina) are responses to failed attempts at imposing a normative (European) chronology on Russia. Such failures are best highlighted in provincial places, which, as we have seen, often inhabit a disordered kind of time. And while a Balzacian provincial stands a chance of making it to Paris, thereby joining his life to progressive history, for Turgenev's Russians such a task can prove impossible. Hence the provinces' role in Turgenev's oeuvre: *provintsiia* highlights Russians' struggle join to modern time in a way that would not require them to burn down their own houses—their own cultures and histories—twice every decade.

CHAPTER SEVEN

Transcendence Deferred:
Women Writers in the Provinces

Man is by his very nature more universal than woman.
—Vissarion Belinsky, 1840

Transcendence is unevenly distributed and experienced.
—Claudia Rankine, 2015

By now the patterns literature has used to structure Russian space have become familiar: the extreme homogeneity and interchangeability of provincial places, their second-rate and second-hand culture, namelessness and placelessness, static and fundamentally ahistorical nature. Above all there is the endlessly rehearsed provinces-vs.-capitals opposition: the further one moves from the imaginary center—the metropole, wherever it might be—the more one finds that meaning is diluted, coherence fades, and entropy prevails. To be a provincial writer is to confront the challenges created by such a schema; to be a female provincial writer is to find those challenges compounded. And yet a number of women made successful careers writing in and about the provinces, including a group sometimes called the *provintsialki*—the provincial ladies—who were for several decades among Russia's more widely read authors. To some degree their writing complicates the familiar image of provincial places as blank and meaningless, but it also reveals that they were never allowed to forget about the symbolic and geographic systems that relegated them to marginality. As a result, their work often reveals an especially direct engagement with these systems.

Beginning in the 1830s, women writers developed a subgenre of prose fiction that Catriona Kelly has termed "the provincial tale"—generally a young woman's coming-of-age story set outside the capitals (whether in a small town or on a minor gentry estate) and often focusing on the various obstacles women must overcome if they are to lead lives that are to any degree satisfying. Sometimes characters in these tales manage to overcome obstacles (arranged marriages, controlling aunties, etc.) and forge their own way—hence what Kelly calls "the escape plot"— while others end up immured in provincial misery.[1] In some versions of the story, *provintsiia* itself is what women must escape (as in Nadezhda Khvoshchinskaia's *Boarding School Girl*); in other versions, female characters find it possible to live more or less free lives in provincial places. Sometimes the heroine is a manifestly exceptional person, superior to everything and everyone around her; sometimes she is an ordinary provincial lady.[2] But for virtually all these protagonists, means are modest, prospects are limited, impediments and coercion are everywhere: the provincial tale is largely about constraints.

Despite such constraints, the *provintsialki* do not always reprise the images of stagnant provincial life made familiar to us (and to readers in these women's era) by men's texts. At times women writers make a case for the virtues of *provintsiia*; indeed feminist critics have argued that some women writers sought in the provinces a version of Virginia Woolfe's room of one's own, a space of cultural productivity located at a welcome remove from the male-dominated literary culture of the capitals.[3] Of course the attempt to do so carried risks: the *provintsialki* worked in constant, anxious awareness of the powerful hierarchies (*stolitsa > provintsiia*, male > female) that could return at any moment to haunt their narratives, and some of their attempts to rethink the meaning of provincial places were more successful than others, both aesthetically and biographically. But the effort itself, which continued in (some) women's writing for several decades, was significant in that it sought alternative ways of imagining Russian space and Russian lives outside of the capitals.

The *provintsialki* were well-educated and had connections in the capitals (hence their ability to publish and eke out a living by writing), but in general they were forced by circumstances to live in the provinces. While some abhorred their environment's coarseness and intellectual poverty, others made their peace with provincial life, even embraced it.[4] What is most important for my purposes is that these writers typically refused to assign more semiotic weight to the metropoles than to other places, and they often actively figured themselves—or they were figured by readers and the literary establishment—as provincials, or as authors explicitly if not exclusively identified with provincial places and themes.

Provincial women were doubly marginal, as Irina Savkina has pointed out, and art making is different on the margins.[5] As a result, writing by women, like writing produced in and about *provintsiia*, inevitably raises questions about canonization and periodization—how we decide what is good and what is bad, what is up-to-date and what is behind the times—simply because the standards and timelines we have developed to make such assessments are grounded in certain kinds of work and not in others.[6] Just as accepted literary periodizations (the age of Romanticism, of Realism, etc.) tend to stigmatize female authors as "behind," so writing in and about places deemed provincial will often fail to reach an acceptable level of "modernity."[7] This stigma attaches persistently, for instance, to the "smaller" national literatures on Europe's periphery, where spatial decentering has often been experienced as temporal decentering. As Pascale Casanova writes, "To be decreed 'modern' is one of the most difficult forms of recognition for writers outside the center."[8]

It is also one of the most difficult forms of recognition for women writers, particularly in the nineteenth century. In Russia, critics at times "rejected women's entry into realist writing just when realism would become the main path for writers' professional aspirations in creating a specifically Russian national literature."[9] According to standards taking hold by the 1840s, in order to count as both realistic and modern, Russian literature needed to be publicly oriented and explicitly engagé—which meant it also had to be masculine. Certain earlier modes of writing had been fairly congenial to women (the "society tale," for instance, and the literature of "sensibility"), but once literature was supposed to be the work of professionals in the public sphere, women's contributions were less welcome.[10] In France and America, too, women were often systematically excluded from consideration as "serious" writers, since seriousness—like "realism"—tended to be defined against modes of writing in which women had already proven themselves highly productive.[11] In Belinsky's 1843 essay devoted to women writers (and especially to Elena Gan), he allows that in the past, when Russian literature served merely as light entertainment, work by women writers differed little from that written by men. But, he implies, once Russia began to approach a "European" level of culture—at which time literature would "serve as the mainspring of social life in every phase of its historical development"[12]—women would probably have less to contribute.

The genre of the provincial tale reflects women's need to negotiate this situation: stories about the limitations faced by provincial women could be read as a response to the oppression of women generally, thereby fulfilling the new injunction to produce socially engaged literature. And the provincial tale typically underlined precisely the kind of subjugation that women writers were expected to denounce—that is, the subjugation women and girls experienced within marriage and the family. As Kelly writes, "effective propaganda for the emancipation of women demanded that they be represented as unfree, yet capable of freedom."[13] The provincial tale allowed writers to dramatize this tension, staging conflicts between provincial women—unfree, but worthy of freedom—and the limitations imposed on them by a restrictive milieu.

The authors whose work I have taken as examples—Elena Gan (1814–42), Mariia Zhukova (1805–55), and Nadezhda Khvoshchinskaia (1824–89)—lived most of their lives in the provinces, and all were well known in their day. I focus on them in part for these reasons, but more importantly because they made explicit their interest in provincial places and themes, and were seen as provincials by readers. Critics spoke of them "as one speaks of one's poor provincial relatives"; even today, many articles about Zhukova originate in publications devoted to local and regional studies, and Gan's biographers often ignore her aristocratic lineage and sophisticated education to focus instead on her provincial origins.[14] Although they wrote at a time when readers had already formed an idea—not a positive one!—of what "the provinces" were, these women nonetheless chose to figure themselves as provincial authors—certainly to some degree *faute de mieux*, but also, perhaps, in an attempt to imagine how a positive authorial identity might also be something other than a *stolichnyi* one.

Elena Gan: The Female Genius in the Provincial Crowd

Elena Gan's work was praised in her lifetime, but her reputation was also well served by her premature death (in 1842 of tuberculosis, at the Lermontovian age of 28). The fact that she died Romantically young and in the provinces caused her biography to dovetail with what was seen as the message of her fiction: talent, especially women's talent, will go to waste in a Russian backwater. Witness Belinsky's reflection on her career: "Distance from the life of the capital is a great misfortune for both soul and talent: they either fade into apathy and idleness, or they take on a provincial style [*provintsial'noe napravlenie*]."[15] (And for Belinsky, as I have argued in chapter 5, the term "provincial" carries connotations that are somewhat complex, but always negative. Provincialism for him represents narrowness of culture—a fatal flaw in an artist, because it marks a failure to be in step with one's times.)

Gan's work often features heroines who are trapped in and oppressed by provincial life (its gossip, conformity, low levels of culture), but at the same time these women generally possess an innate refinement that will remain untouched by circumstances; despite degrading surroundings, they are anything but degraded (indeed they tend to wear their spiritual superiority on their sleeves). They are, however, persecuted. In "Society's Judgment" (1840), for instance, the provincial "crowd" (*tolpa*, a recurring word in women writers' descriptions of genteel local society) sees a gifted authoress as a monstrous "freak of nature."[16] Taken together, the titles of two of Gan's stories—"Society's Judgment" and "A Futile Gift" (1842)—would seem to encapsulate her portrait of provincial mores and their devastating effect on anyone, especially any woman, who is superior to those around her. As she writes in "The Ideal" (1837), "for a man with an elevated mind, life in the provinces is unbearable; but for a woman whose nature has placed her higher than the crowd, it is truly awful."[17]

But by showcasing such squandering of talents, Gan also highlights the possibility of female genius. In order to do so, she uses the provinces to stand in for what all of Russia—indeed, all the world—might be thought to inflict on Romantic geniuses and sensitive souls. In "The Ideal," nothing changes as the sensitive heroine moves with her military husband from town to town (from the "filthy streets of a Jewish settlement" to a garrison village "full of half-wild Ukrainians")—"today, tomorrow, and forever, always the same thing."[18] Gan's provincial environments can be read as an intensified version of *any* society's deadening banality, their coarseness serving to highlight the exceptionalness of her heroines. For Gan, as Kelly writes, "the social exile of the woman writer emerges as the distant equivalent of the political exile of the male writer, as celebrated by Russian Romanticism. To be marginal is a tragedy, but it is also a mark of social distinction."[19] And this kind of marginality, while it is perhaps especially visible in a provincial backwater, in the end is determined not by geography but rather by a character's unchangeable and mysterious inner essence.

"The Ideal" drives home the point with the character of Olga, the poetic—*highly* poetic—young girl who has been married off to a coarse army officer. The story's opening lines suggest it will adhere to a familiar template: it opens at a provincial ball, which, as Herzen wrote around this time, "has already been described a thousand times."[20] There are a few hints of *poshlost'* (excessive hair pomade, etc.), but provincial vulgarity or awkwardness is not the point. Rather, the setting serves mainly to highlight the lovely heroine—her "simplicity" and grace, her bearing at once "childlike" yet "noble, even a little proud"—as she enters the ballroom, looking around her "as the Christians once did when they faced wild beasts in the Roman colosseum."[21] The narrator's attention is fully absorbed by "this unusual woman," this "bright poetic soul . . . surrounded by a swarm of poisonous wasps."[22]

While the ball is indeed a painful social occasion, its painfulness has nothing to do with its provinciality; rather, the heroine's character is simply too elevated for any form of society. "A soul that longs for deep, true feeling," "a mind that sees the emptiness beneath propriety's masquerade"—such beings will never be reconciled with "that despot, society," but will be obliged to live "while holding burning coals in their hands."[23] Holding burning coals in one's hands is a problem that has no geographical solution: like Pushkin's Tatiana, Gan's Olga is no better off in Petersburg, where life proves to be as shallow as it is in the provinces (and where she is cruelly seduced by a heartless poet with "fiery black eyes").[24]

Olga's innate superiority makes her the target of incessant gossip from "the crowd," who resent her "cold indifference" to society's "petty envy and gossip, the plague of provincial towns" and sneer at her preference for solitude, her devotion to reading, and her "simplicity of dress" (in listing the qualities that most provoke her heroine's jealous peers, Gan checks off all the Tatiana boxes).[25] Much the same pattern repeats itself in "Society's Judgment," in which once again we learn that a woman's "slight deviation . . . from run-of-the-mill ordinariness" will be severely punished, no matter where she is (and daring to write stories, as this heroine does, is quite beyond the pale).[26] Gan's provinces are bad, but for the exceptional woman they are not necessarily worse than anyplace else.

And in one sense the provinces may be better: in more than one of Gan's stories, a far-off corner of the world allows girls the kind of unstructured but rigorous education that is generally denied them elsewhere, one that would be almost inconceivable in the capitals. In "The Ideal," Olga's mother, who herself has "read all of French philosophy," gives her daughter access to a large library ("from Plutarch to Genlis to Mme. de Stael"), cultivating in her "a sense of honor to the very highest degree" through the study of "great men's magnanimous deeds" in classical history. Thus Olga learns to "feel and act on the model of the ancients," adhering to such principles "in spite of all obstacles, just as the Roman did when he sacrificed himself to his own word." Here, Gan says, Cicero takes the place of Balzac: Olga's "perfect isolation" makes possible a kind of classicism—an orientation toward a "higher," ancient world—that would not be possible in a more worldly environment.[27]

Gan's female characters who grow up in this kind of rural isolation can be shaped by an intellectual life that has nothing provincial about it; indeed some of them receive a markedly classical education that aspires to *universality*, thereby removing it from any specific time or place. Although in "The Ideal" this upbringing occurs in an unnamed part of Crimea, in "Society's Judgment" the heroine receives a comparable education—the same emphasis on antique texts and virtues, with the same disastrous consequence once she enters "society"—in the Russian provinces, where "[her] mind and heart mature under the influence of the Golden Age."[28] In deep *provintsiia*, for Gan, it is sometimes possible to create an environment that "is nurtured not by the spirt of [one's] own time" but by that of the ancient world.[29] In such an intellectual environment, it might not really matter where you are: just as, say, Ralph Waldo Emerson, living in the civilizational backwater of Concord, Massachusetts, could will himself to believe that his own intellect placed him at the very center of world culture, so might a girl in the Russian countryside read Cicero and Mme. de Stael and imagine something along the same lines.

Absolute distance from the capital makes possible what any degree of proximity would preclude—that is, the ability to orient oneself toward an entirely different "center," far from the capital's worldliness in time as well as in space. Gan never suggests that the provinces are or could be home to a *social* life congenial to the elevated soul; in fact she rarely depicts a "society" that is anything other than degraded, no matter where it is located. Instead what an isolated place can provide is respite from all sociality and recourse to the universal. Whereas the ideal gentry estate, as we have seen, mirrors the contemporary culture of the capitals, Gan's imaginary *glush'* enclaves train their gaze on an ideal much further afield than Moscow or Petersburg, looking toward some far-off time and place embodying precisely those virtues that are not represented in any iteration (provincial or *stolichnyi*) of contemporary society. Such a gesture toward universality—the insistence on occupying a position that is effectively *above* any provinces-capitals binary—makes sense for those who are profoundly socially marginalized, including women.

Mariia Zhukova: A Provincial Life "Poor in Events, but Rich in Feelings"

Mariia Zhukova (1805–55) was also widely read in her day and was probably even more consistently associated with the provinces than was Gan. Born in Arzamas, she grew up there and in the nearby countryside before spending most of her adult life in Saratov, traveling occasionally and making a living by writing and copying paintings. She married young but lived separately from her husband.[30] Her depiction of provincial life is somewhat more sanguine than Gan's: *provintsiia* for Zhukova can be painfully constraining, especially for women, but it is also the locus of friendship, folk traditions, warm patriarchal social relations, and nature. In Zhukova's world, it is people in the capitals who are more likely to be superficial, their social relations shaped by conformity and deception, while provincials are capable of deep and sincere emotion.

Zhukova's early story "The Provincial Girl" ("Provintsialka," 1837—the first Russian text to use this form of the word in a title) might be read as a kind of manifesto, laying out a defense of why one might choose to write about *provintsiia* and provincials, and why one might do so in a way that does not simply recapitulate the already-familiar tropes. The story opens in an aristocratic Petersburg drawing room where characters are identified by their titles in French (la Comtesse de C***, etc.). The heroine Katia is entirely at home in this environment (she is at this point the worldly widow of a general), but she has never lost the appellation *provintsialka*—a word that seems to represent for her an honorific or an elective identity, a part she chooses to play in the *grand monde*. Katia's success in the capital's high society is only underscored by the fact that she is always called *provintsialka* ("*Mon cher*," asks one old aristocrat of another at a ball, "how could such a miraculous creature appear from the provinces?"),[31] a role that allows her to expatiate charmingly on the superiority of provincial life (thus her uncle teases her for believing that friendship is "higher, purer, and more perfect" in the provinces).[32]

Indeed the chief opposition at work throughout this story is less provinces-vs.-capitals than it is provinces-vs.-high society (*svet*), as when the uncle scolds, "O *provintsialki, provintsialki!* You look on everything in a strange way, you take offense at everything, always with prejudice against the upper classes [*protiv vysshego klassa*]!"[33] In such passages Zhukova describes life in the capitals not just in negative terms, but in precisely those negative terms that other writers use to describe the provinces—suggesting that she is not so much complicating the provinces-capitals binary as she is revaluing its two poles. Thus the capital is a "desert" (*pustynia*) where no sincerity and authenticity are possible ("Le grand monde est un bal masqué") and where people can only repeat received ideas, but the provinces are "real life":[34] "Oh, Uncle, it's dull living in this desert (*v etoi pustyne*)! . . . My provincial instincts seek emotion and thought, and real life is flying away from me!"[35]

In the tale's brief Petersburg prologue, Katia encounters the man (Mstislav) whom she loved and idolized in her innocent provincial youth, thus setting up a backstory that provides the plot. Briefly: Katia and Mstislav had fallen in love when he was stationed in her town in 1812; Mstislav abandoned Katia; Katia married the old general; Katia was widowed. In Petersburg Katia is reunited with Mstislav, who has been conveniently cut down to size; they marry and settle in the countryside: the end. The story seems to move past prologue only after it leaves the capital (via a perfunctory detour to Italy, necessary to the plot), whereupon it goes back to the provincial world that has shaped the heroine—"back," that is, in the sense that for any narrative that opens in the capitals, *provintsiia* represents a return (whether to childhood or to a mythic collective past, etc.).

In many narratives, *provintsiia* is accessible only in memory; it is long lost, effectively cut off from everyplace else (e.g., Goncharov's hero can see Oblomovka only in his dreams as he lies asleep in Petersburg). But Zhukova sets the main action of "The Provincial Girl" in an old-timey and idealized version of *provintsiia* while nonetheless allowing her characters to move freely between the provinces and other locations: her provinces are not stagnant places, cut off from other places and from historical events. In 1812 even Katia's quiet family circle is talking about Wellington, reading newspapers, figuring out maps: "Had some long-time inhabitant of Kaluga, Tambov, Penza or some district town [*uezdnyi gorod*]" seen these places, he would recognize the enlivening effects of the campaign (even in the provinces, "the private [*chastnost'*] has given way to the social [*obshchnost'*], as if some wizard had . . . transferred the isolated little town to some other place").[36] Indeed Zhukova's portrait of provincial social mores has little in common with what we have come to expect. There is none of the punishing gossip so often evoked in descriptions of provincial women's lives; at balls Katia is dressed taste-fully and "simply."[37] Though the locals worry that Katia's true worth will go unrec-ognized in the small town ("If only she were in Petersburg, walking down Nevsky! There they'd recognize her value!"), she lives happily with her father, an upright civil servant who exhibits a kind of solidity and self-confidence rarely ascribed to provincial characters.

However, Zhukova first introduces the reader to *provintsiia* with a sharp caveat—a kind of preemptive concession—by representing the district town through the eyes of a sophisticated capital-dweller who happens to be driving through: "It's true, the picture of a district town flatters neither the eyes nor the imagination." This "fine resident of Petersburg," looking out the windows of his carriage and experiencing "involuntary horror" at the sight of the dilapidated little houses, "is seized with cold at the thought—what if we ourselves were fated to pass a whole life in these tiny little houses?"[38] Zhukova's long description marshals many of the same details we have seen in texts that insist on the inert and grubby materiality of provincial places ("wooden houses covered with boards," etc.). But unlike those writers, Zhukova is not interested in making us believe that such physical details are the signs of a de-graded life; rather, her point is that we must look beyond them: "Would the passing [Petersburg] beauties believe it if you told them that in these little houses with their tiny windows . . . people live cheerfully, indeed often very happily, and that in this monotonous and quiet life there is love and poetry?"[39]

In other words, her celebration of provincial life transpires under the sign of "nonetheless": *provintsiia* can be defended, but only defensively ("the life of a dis-trict town is so insignificant . . . that I fear I may bore you").[40] Thus we read about the idyll of Katia's childhood only after being asked to overcome our "involuntary horror" at the appearance of a provincial town that "flatters neither the eyes nor the imagination."[41] Only if we manage to get past our disgust we will we appreciate the heroine's "little room" looking out on a "little garden" with "little birch trees" (*komnatka, sadik, berezki*), and beyond that churches, greenery, a path stretching toward open fields, and finally, beyond that, to Katia's mother's grave—all evoking in the heroine not melancholia but happy memories.[42] The panoramic view blurs the line between town and fields, home and nature, conflating provincial small-town domesticity with pastoral.

The dullness of provincial life is acknowledged: the town itself is much like the one in Zhukova's later story "Nadenka"—one of "our provincial towns," "like any other provincial town," with the same sense of iterativeness and predictability that we have learned to associated with such places.[43] "The Provincial Girl" imagines a traveler coming upon Katia's hometown: "Exhausted by monotony the traveler walks, his gaze seeking vainly for something new: everything is the same!"[44] But here the town is also, to a degree, revalued. Yes, in a place where nothing happens the years blend together, Zhukova admits, but boredom has its benefits: "in this monotonous picture there is life, charm, . . . the secret activity of nature, a whole world of insects buzzing among the flowers."[45]

Thanks to such eventlessness, provincials like Katia—especially women, who are the only real provincials, according to Zhukova's definition—*feel* more deeply than do others:

> If a provincial's days are poor in events, they are nonetheless rich in feelings; feeling is deeper and more religious where it is more concentrated, and if the inhabitant of the *grand monde* [*svetskii zhitel'*] can sometimes be accused of lightness of feeling, the provincial woman [*provintsialka*] sins by her excess and intensity of feeling . . . . I speak here of provincial women, because in district towns men are occupied with state service, the latest order, the governor's arrival, denunciations and replies . . . they have no time for feelings. . . . But Katia—ah! Katia was a true provincial! Her outer life was like one of those streams that are quiet and peaceful on the surface, while the water boils at the bottom.[46]

Zhukova claims that such a life is well suited to a particular kind of narrative, one that focuses on everyday reality and on the long stretches of time that intervene between life's rare moments of drama and intensity:

> Sometimes history [*istoriia*] appears to us as a unified whole, but only because history, not taking account of details, takes from the life of its hero only the main features, considering them only from one point of view . . . and omitting everything that bears no direct relation to the role that he plays in the chronicles.

But if one were to consider the details of this typical hero's life, she continues,

> seeing him in his private everyday life as we see our friends, he would appear to us far more trivial, often weak, inconstant—in a word, an ordinary person, not so different from others. The greatness in him would be lost in his everyday life precisely because [this greatness] appears rarely rather than always, at long intervals that are taken up with trifles; but history neglects this.[47]

Katia learns the same lesson when she reencounters the chastened Mstislav and recognizes him as just "a man like other men, with all the same trifling weaknesses." Like *provintsiia*, the thoroughly humbled, "realistic" version of one's original erotic desire is a commendably reasonable choice.

Zhukova seems to have found in *provintsiia*, always so strongly associated with the everyday and monotonous, a particularly good setting for driving home her key point: there are no heroes in the *real* world. When Zhukova writes that "the life of a provincial is like a path winding among the fields in the flat plains of Penza or Samara province," she is using *provintsiia*'s slow rhythms to "[resist] the eventfulness of a literary plot. . . . In Zhukova's aesthetics, a country walk best evokes the large, relatively flat expanse of a real lived life."[48] Indeed the story closes with a final defense of the everyday and its place in literature: "In each person's life there are minutes, hours, and years of truly poetic existence; they pass, and the person reenters the usual circle of life, utterly prosaic, attracting no attention."[49] This gesture serves to align not just Zhukova's narrative technique but also the provinces themselves with "real life."

Zhukova's later story "Nadenka" (1853) reprises many of the same themes as "The Provincial Girl." Once again in "Nadenka," the provinces are not cut off from the capitals but are closely tied to them, and characters seem to travel easily back and forth. *Provintsiia* is set against *svet* (high society), in comparison to which it is characterized by sincerity, simplicity, folk culture, patriarchal social relations, useful labor, and a rich inner life; the eponymous heroine finds happiness in "prayer, nature, and labor."[50] Again the line between provincial and pastoral (*derevnia*) is blurred, particularly in Nadenka's luxuriously overgrown garden (so unlike "those regal [*tsarstvennye*] gardens" in Petersburg, we are told), and in her little house "at the very edge of the town" on a street leading out to fields and woodlands.[51] In this social world the noun "provincial" (*provintsial, provintsialka*) can occasionally be deployed as a mild insult ("the young man dances well, he's from Petersburg, nothing like our provincial boys [*nash brat provintsial*]"; "oh those poor provincial girls, always putting on airs!"), but in such cases it tends to characterize the speaker more than it does the person being described.[52] And even those locals who aspire to high society (*svetskie*) ways—showing off their French, copying Moscow dress patterns, etc.—are not marked by any particular awkwardness or inauthenticity; the heroine's mother, for instance, speaks "pure Parisian French," if somewhat bookish and dated.[53]

As a proud, impoverished widow who misses the high status she enjoyed in the town when her husband was alive, Nadenka's mother desperately wants her daughter to make a prestigious match. The plot revolves around her attempts to marry Nadenka off to Lemetev, a fashionable young visitor from Petersburg ("*un jeune homme tout à fait distingué!*") whose talk of fancy balls, foreign authors, and Italian opera causes a stir in provincial society.[54] Lemetev is marked by what Savkina calls a kind of *superstolichnost'*, a deliberately highlighted "hyper-capitalness" that defines his character. "Coldly formal, somehow British, 'gentlemanly'" (with "gentlemanly" in English), he induces envy and anxiety in the townspeople. They conclude that his statue-like demeanor must point to "the mysteries of Petersburg *comme-il-faut*,"[55] but in fact we are given to understand that beyond this *superstolichnost'* there is virtually nothing to his character. Lemetev falls in love with Nadenka, but only slowly does he come round to the idea that he might marry a simple girl and live happily and within his means in the provinces, rather than finding a rich bride and living in the capital. Here as in "The Provincial Girl," sober, *realistic* choices make for a reasonably happy ending.

But "Nadenka" is distinguished from Zhukova's earlier story by its sustained attention to nature and its explicit focus on far-off steppe towns, whose very remoteness, the narrator contends, saves them from provincial taint. A long paean to such places opens the text:

> Think of me what you will, but I openly declare my passion for our provincial towns [*gubernskie goroda*], and not those that are close to the capitals, the ones that are covered with the dust of the big post road, the ones that could be taken for suburbs of the capital: no! I declare my passion for our towns far off on the wide steppe, like the towns scattered on the banks of the Volga, for instance. Yes, I love them, and I love them despite their sickly streets and their bad sidewalks, and their squares packed with little houses marked for demolition, despite even their dusty boulevards and their ever-sagging lime-trees. I love them for this broad steppe stretching out as far as the sea and embracing the town with its green waves, and for their light blue caressing sky, and for their dark warm nights, and for the broad Volga with her hilly banks and green flood-lands with their copses, bright lakes and poplar stands at the very foot of the hills. I love their little villages and dachas with their gardens and groves, stretching deep into the steppe and scattered over the spurs of the hills, and the rich fields where the golden grain ripens and the fragrant melons patches spread out, or the high sunflowers descending in tall ranks across the hillside, whose dark foliage recalls the vineyards of rich Burgundy.[56]

The passage continues in this vein, as do various others throughout the story, enumerating the steppe's insects and ducks, sunflowers and snails, deploying noticeably specific nature vocabulary (names of grasses, etc.), and emphasizing the openness and freedom of the steppe: certainly this landscape constitutes anything but a provincial blank.

Yet once again, such praise is expressed under the sign of "despite" ("Think of me what you will . . . I love them despite . . ."), with the result that the luxurious nature description ends up sounding vaguely compensatory (we may not have Burgundy's vineyards, but we do have sunflowers and snails!). The idea that a provincial life is worth living—that it is in fact *real* life—must always be defended. Nadenka's mother is bitterly disappointed that her daughter has no wish to escape *provintsiia*, which is as much as to say that there is nothing special about Nadenka: she is just an "awkward *provintsialka*," her mother thinks, with "no longing for anything better," "satisfied with her life in a backwater [*glush'*] and with her petty [*meschanskimi*] occupations."[57] In this her mother is correct: Nadenka is ordinary. But then so is Lemetev, the narrator tells us, despite his Petersburg credentials.[58] Once again, as in "The Provincial Girl," ordinariness is associated with the provinces and with *reality*—and both are thought to possess a degree of dignity worthy of serious representation. Zhukova's provincials know this: they may pay attention to dress patterns and gossip from the capitals, but their concerns are sincerely and deeply local, and they are not trying to escape.

Nadezhda Khvoshchinskaia: "What Kind of Life Is This?"

Not so for the heroine of Khvoshchinskaia's novella *The Boarding School Girl* (*Pansionerka*), for whom staying in the provinces would mean ending her life, certainly figuratively and perhaps literally as well. Khvoshchinskaia was of a later generation than the other writers considered in this chapter, and *The Boarding School Girl*, which was first published, and widely read, in *Notes of the Fatherland* in 1861, reflects historical shifts that were beginning to promise new opportunities for women who embraced "modernity." These opportunities were as yet more likely to be imagined than enacted, but in Khvoshchinskaia's novella they change the course of the heroine's fate. Indeed the author of *The Boarding School Girl* presents her *provintsialka* with a stark choice: escape or death.

Khvoshchinskaia herself lived virtually her whole life (1824–89) in the provinces (Ryazan) where she was part of a modest gentry family. Having been born two decades after Zhukova and a decade after Gan, she belonged to a generation that enjoyed more opportunities to make a living by writing. She was the oldest of three very literary sisters—occasionally referred to as "the Russian Brontes"—all of whom wrote and published. Khvoshchinskaia was well-enough educated (at home and very briefly in Moscow) to qualify as an intellectual; in fact provincial society seems to have deemed her too intellectual, judging from the fact that she married only toward the end of her life.[59] For decades she relied on her writing to support herself and other family members, making and maintaining the requisite literary connections in Petersburg and publishing stories in prominent journals (under the male pseudonym "V. Krestovskii"). Virtually all of her work is set in the provinces, and much of it explores female characters' attempts to negotiate the severe constraints placed on them by provincial mores and by their lack of economic autonomy.

The Boarding School Girl is built around a psychological battle between a very young provincial woman and a somewhat older man from the capital, a contest of wits with life-changing consequences (and a very common post-*Onegin* storyline, which more than one woman author rewrote in ways granting more agency to the heroine). Khvoshchinskaia explores the possibility and the consequences of overt female rebellion, mapping the "battle of the sexes" onto geography: in order to win, the heroine must escape the *gubernskii gorod* and make her way to the capital. Because she does escape, she wins; had she stayed in *provintsiia*, she would have lost. Only in Petersburg is the girl able to come out on top.

The title *The Boarding School Girl* refers to the status of the heroine, fifteen-year-old Lolenka, who is a day student in a school for (more or less) genteel girls in an anonymous *gorod N*. To be a *pansionerka* was not the same as being an *institutka*: state-sponsored *instituty* were more elite than private *pansiony*. Furthermore, day students like Lolenka were of even lower status than their fellow *pansionerki* who were boarders. Thus Khvoshchinskaia's heroine, as a member of a petty gentry family clinging to its technically and tenuously noble status, comes from a social stratum that is significantly overrepresented in nineteenth-century Russian fiction—overrepresented, I think, because of the remarkable self-consciousness, doubt, and observational acuity encouraged by unstable social status.

Khvoshchinskaia's *gorod N* is entirely familiar: once again we find stasis, pettiness, pervasive meanness, and extreme cultural poverty, all combined with strenuous aspirations to gentility; by 1861 the trope was so well established that a few words could suffice to evoke this version of the provinces. Unlike Zhukova's provincial towns, Khvoshchinskaia's seems to be entirely cut off from the rest of the world, tightly circumscribed, and minimally connected to the surrounding world of nature and agricultural labor. Within its confines, physical space is illegible; all we see are the ravines, puddles, ruts, and fences that chop up the landscape and reinforce the sense that there is simply *nowhere to go*.

Nor is there anything to do: Khvoshchinskaia's characters complain incessantly of a mysteriously powerful idleness. Forms of the word *skuchno* (dull, boring) recur constantly, climaxing in a passage that represents provincial *skuka* as being virtually apocalyptic, so intense it may presage "the end of the world":

"It's dull!" said Veretitsyn.
"But what's to be done? Wait a bit, it'll get more cheerful." [said Sofia]
"When?"
"Soon. When something reaches an extreme, that means it'll be over soon. Everyone's gotten so bored that they surely have to stop feeling that way soon. This is just before the end."
"Before the end of the world?"
"Of something . . ."[60]

We are struck by this bizarre insistence on the extremity of provincial boredom, a boredom that presents itself as both overdetermined and inescapable; clearly, these characters are not just complaining about an idle afternoon. Instead, like

characters in British colonial and postcolonial literature who find themselves
"stuck" on a periphery they experience as meaningless, Khvoshchinskaia's provincials are registering what a scholar of postcolonialism has called "the pervasive
banality of the local space that imprisons its dwellers." Believing themselves to be
"left out, existing on the margins" of all events that matter in the world, these post-
colonial subjects can imagine no forward movement in historical time, at least not
as long as they occupy a peripheral space.[61] Thus Khvoshchinskaia's provincials,
instead of imagining time, imagine the end of time.

In *The Boarding School Girl* most characters' movements are confined to an
unlovely garden, overgrown but fenced in and described as a "wasteland," where
they wander purposelessly, going nowhere.[62] Here, over the back fence, Lolenka
encounters the bitter young intellectual next door, Veretitsyn, who has been exiled
to the provinces for some vague and not-too-serious political offense (not serious
enough, that is, to make him interesting: Veretitsyn is a whiner who never stops
blaming his misery on circumstances beyond his control, even once he manages
to escape N). In a series of conversations, Veretitsyn deliberately convinces the innocent Lolenka that her life is empty, stupid and pointless (which in fact it is). He
also introduces her to Shakespeare, which stands in here for the life of the mind
generally.

Veretitsyn torments his young neighbor in large part to distract himself from
his own impossible love for the impossibly good Sofia, the text's paragon of self-
sacrificing femininity (about whom we learn little except that she is "perfect"). As
Veretitsyn pines away for Sofia, Lolenka pines away for Veretitsyn. Sofia in the end
allows herself to be married off to a rich landowner in order to please her mother;
Veretitsyn nevertheless loves only Sofia, pointlessly and from afar; Lolenka, initially heartbroken over Veretitsyn, opts out of love altogether, as we will see. As this
summary suggests, *The Boarding School Girl* aims to frustrate any desire we might
have to see the characters' desires met—at least their romantic ones. Veretitsyn and
Lolenka confront each other in a plot that inevitably makes us think (and perhaps
hope) that they might become lovers, but the *telos* in this book is emphatically *not*
family life: in fact if Lolenka wins this particular battle of the sexes, her prize will
not be the boy, but rather the right to be done with all boys.

Up to a certain point, Khvoshchinskaia's plot would seem to recapitulate a
pattern we know well from Pushkin, Lermontov, and other male writers: sweet
young girl encounters cynical older man who both enlightens and wounds her.
But the difference is that in this text the girl, rather than serving as a vehicle for
the male hero's development, keeps hold of the narrative, which comes to be about
her transformation and her life. Veretitsyn lacks the intellect and magnetism of an
Onegin or Pechorin: his ideas are ready-made, and he is full of self-pity. After he
has tutored Lolenka—condescendingly, sententiously—in vaguely radical ideas,

and after she has dutifully taken them all in, Lolenka creatively (mis)interprets what Veretitsyn has taught her, and she uses it to transform her life. In the end the male character becomes merely a vehicle for the heroine's development: Lolenka turns out to be the extraordinary one, as evidenced by her ability to pull herself out of the provincial slough.

The Boarding School Girl is structured around the conversations that lead to Lolenka's transformation. All these exchanges take place over a fence, a physical barrier that evokes both the battle lines drawn between the characters—they are "facing off"—and the borders dividing the horrid town of N from the rest of the world.[63] These conversations turn out to be a test of wills in a way that Veretitsyn did not anticipate, since he initiated the exchange only out of boredom and spite: in the book's opening passage he looks over the fence at the girl studying in her garden and declares, "I don't want her to be happy! . . . She'll learn to be miserable! . . . I'll teach her to be bored."[64]

Veretitsyn wants Lolenka to recognize the pointlessness of her entire life: he does his best to convince her that her studies, her music, her efforts to be a dutiful daughter—as well as Romantic ideals, "great men," and history generally—are without meaning or value. "You're memorizing nonsense—and that's the way it has to be!"[65] "You're a fine, obedient, affectionate daughter: you're only doing your duty. Always behave that way. Always live that way. Always live entirely for your father and mother. . . . *You're their property* . . . you have no right to ask to live any way you want."[66] Veretitsyn is simply echoing and mildly ironizing the patriarchal injunctions that are constantly being directed at Lolenka from other sources. Thus her mother scolds her, "how dare you not want what your father and I want!" and the matchmaker who has found Lolenka a loathsome suitor tells her bluntly, "just submit, you have to submit."[67]

Lolenka offers some resistance to her opponent's bitter irony—but I like studying, she objects weakly, and even embroidering is not so bad—but Veretitsyn wins the battle handily. Indeed at this point, Lolenka would seem to have lost everything: acceding to the truth of Veretitsyn's indictments, she deliberately fails out of school and provokes her parents' terrible ire. Veretitsyn then rubs salt in her wounds, mocking her for acting on his words, upbraiding her for what he now describes as a useless and selfish act of rebellion. Disclaiming all responsibility for Lolenka's actions, he again invokes patriarchal norms, this time virtually without irony: "a young girl should be modest, industrious, respectful toward her parents, satisfied with everything . . . and what are you?" "Willfulness causes disorder. Be satisfied with what you're given." "How are you going to get by in the world? . . . Sentimentality and willfulness have unhappy and even unseemly consequences. . . . People must coexist somehow. That's why laws, rules, proprieties were invented to hold them together."[68]

In her despair Lolenka adopts the familiar interrogative mode of the radical intelligentsia (what is to be done?), repeating over and over to herself the classic how-to-live questions: "What kind of life is this? What's housework? Swearing, nonsense, racket. . . . What kind of people are these? What are studies but useless memorization?"[69] "Living this way was impossible [*tak zhit' nel'zia*]; everything was totally wrong . . . other people lived differently . . . the peasants seemed to live better . . . why embroider a collar? . . . Was there nothing else?"[70] "It's impossible to live like this."[71] At times her vocabulary is explicitly political, a protest against "tyranny," as when she cries, "I am not a slave!"[72]

As the words "I am not a slave" suggest, there is always the possibility of physical violence in this text, though most of it happens offstage or is just hinted at. Lolenka goes home to "supper and abuse"[73]; the entire household fears her father's rage; her schoolmates will be beaten for failing exams; her little brothers are tied to table legs to force them to study. Occasionally Khvoshchinskaia comes close to representing the abuse: Lolenka's siblings are beaten, and after Lolenka fails her exams, we are told in passing that "her mother beat her, and not just once."[74] All of this violence, whether depicted or alluded to, is domestic; Veretitsyn, for example, suffers no physical violence as a result of his political crime. In fact domesticity in this book basically *is* institutionalized violence, with a little forced labor thrown in; child-raising and family life are at best pointless drudgery. In Khvoshchinskaia's critique of domesticity we see most clearly her book's relationship to the radical novel: as Herzen did in *Who Is to Blame?* (1847) and as Chernyshevsky would soon do in *What Is to be done?* (1863), Khvoshchinskaia focuses on domesticity and women's liberation as a way of raising questions about politics and about everyone's liberation.[75] At the end of the book we learn that Veretitsyn's love, the angelic Sofia, has devoted herself to a specifically domestic version of feminine self-abnegation, forsaking all personal satisfactions in order to serve her family in an offstage world that we never see—a solution Veretitsyn says makes Sofia a saint and a martyr, but not an option that the text would seem to be endorsing.

Given the meagerness of the resources (cultural, social, and economic) at Lolenka's disposal, and the formidable power of her adversaries, the reader expects her to give up and "submit." But instead Lolenka rebels, thereby effecting her own transformation: having formed the "stubborn, ardent, burning conviction" that her life is bad, she *acts on* this conviction.[76] And since Khvoshchinskaia does not illuminate the source of her heroine's strength, when we read the final words in what seems to be the main body of the book—"Mama, you can kill me on the spot, but I will not marry"—we are struck above all by the *inexplicability* of Lolenka's metamorphosis.[77] Immediately after these dramatic words, we encounter an ellipsis, then a chapter break, and finally a chapter that functions as a kind of epilogue.

At this point—"you can kill me" followed by an ellipsis—the reader is likely to assume that Lolenka has either died or has been consigned to a death-in-life provincial existence: so convincingly has Khvoshchinskaia described the hellish constraints of provincial life that any other ending seems impossible. However, the next words we read are "eight years had passed since that time": having just left Lolenka a virtual prisoner in a provincial hellhole, we now meet her—suddenly, miraculously—as a free subject in the midst of utter cultural plenitude: she is sitting in the Hermitage.[78] Lolenka is now an artist, serenely occupying the museum's Spanish Room and painting copies on commission (a fact to which I will return in a moment). We are left with the question: how did Lolenka get here? And why is her escape—so obviously a crucial juncture in the story—*not narrated*?

The text makes quick work of the implausible development, informing us that Lolenka wrote a desperate letter to her aunt/godmother in Petersburg, with the result that the aunt rescued her: apparently the only mechanism Khvoshchinskaia could find to ensure Lolenka's deliverance was an auntie-*ex-machina*. Once in Petersburg, the brief explanation concludes, Lolenka studied art and languages, living with her aunt; when she was able to support herself through translations and paintings, she stopped accepting any help from her relation. Indeed Lolenka insists tiresomely on her economic independence, often belaboring the point; she will not even accept a gift of opera tickets from her aunt, so as not to risk becoming "a burden" ("I don't cost her a thing," she says).[79]

Not only does Khvoshchinskaia deposit her heroine in Petersburg and make her an economically self-sufficient knowledge worker, she also situates her as a member of a genuine *public*. Before describing the new-and-improved Lolenka, the novel's final chapter opens with a careful description of the "unusually large number of visitors . . . gathered inside the halls of the Hermitage" that day, detailing the great variety of people who have come together in this open public space to look at art ("well-dressed ladies," "ladies less well-dressed but with a noticeable claim to the right to knowledge and understanding," "very respectable people . . . who looked at one object for a long time . . . and talked among themselves softly and animatedly," "provincial men and women with unfeigned emotion," even "common people [*prostye liudi*]").[80] In Russia in 1861, such an audience for art was, if not a fantasy, then at best a work in progress—certainly not an uncontested reality. All the more interesting, then, that Khvoshchinskaia signals Lolenka's unexpected triumph by locating her as a member of this (fantasy?) public.

Lolenka has not only escaped the provinces, she has made her way to the anti-*gorod N*: against N's deadly cultural attenuation, the capital—which is represented, none too realistically, as a giant museum open to all—is a distillation of everything that capital-C Culture can do for you. One thing the capital does for Lolenka is allow her to win the battle that Veretitsyn initiated in their far-off provincial town. There Lolenka would have lost, but in Petersburg the roles are reversed, and she wins: in the Hermitage it is she who first observes and identifies Veretitsyn, laughing at his confusion; she is serene while he is flustered. Above all Lolenka makes a strong case for the life she has chosen, justifying her "abandonment" of her parents against Veretitsyn's accusations of disloyalty and egoism. Veretitsyn charges that "as long as there were still people" (family members) to whom she had obligations, Lolenka had no right to escape, to which Lolenka retorts, "Injustice, persecution had reached an extreme . . . didn't I have the right to wish to tear myself away, to come to hate the memory of the past?"[81]

Even as Veretitsyn castigates Lolenka for the selfishness of her choice (selfishness, it seems, being the worst possible sin in a woman), Khvoshchinskaia has her heroine argue passionately for her right to forget her *personal* history. "I don't want to remember that time [in N]," Lolenka insists, "it brings back so many absurdities . . . it's past—and finished. I live in the present." "I remember nothing. . . . Haven't I said that already? . . . If you had [truly] known me [in N], you would not be surprised that I've cast off my yoke and that I choose not to remember anything about it. . . . There's nothing painful or difficult! I don't remember, so I don't burden my memory."[82] Lolenka has appropriated a cultural heritage—a vast one, all that is represented by the words "the Hermitage"—and has used it to replace her personal history. By earning money in a modern economy, she integrates herself into the circuits of print culture and sociality that make possible an explicitly modern way of life in the metropole. Her rooms, we are told, are full of newspapers; she "[knows] and continually [reads] a great deal," conversing easily with a group of educated peers on political topics of the day.[83] Khvoshchinskaia's heroine has joined *history*, history in the sense of "public time" ("time experienced by the individual as public being, conscious of a framework of public institutions in and through which events, processes and changes happened to the society of which he perceives himself to be part")—a history to which the provincial Town of N provided no access.[84]

Lolenka casts Veretitsyn and his peers as "people of the 40s" against her own ascendant "people of the 60s" generation: "*You* carried things to the point where *we* had to fight and suffer in order to escape from under that oppression, and devise for ourselves some possibility of living more easily!" she says, "why did you allow yourselves to be broken? Why didn't you renounce your prejudices, conquer your weaknesses, work more energetically? You're bored, full of melancholy and bitterness because you're always regretting something and remembering something."[85] To remember is to be "bored" and ineffectual; clearly, it is better to forget. It would seem that Lolenka has effectively turned the tables on her adversary.

However, as Veretitsyn urges Lolenka to recognize, now that she has "won," the result is that she is completely alone. Lolenka has no intimate ties, nor any mutual obligations that cannot be immediately dissolved by economic exchange, as we see when her obsession with autonomy leads her to pay her aunt back with money for a freely offered gift. And the ever-ticking clock in her room—a room organized around what the text describes as "strenuous, uninterrupted work calculated by the clock"—suggests the dry and perhaps sterile regimentation of a life that excludes all possibility of romantic love.[86]

Khvoshchinskaia herself denied that the ending of *The Boarding School Girl* was supposed to be happy, or that Lolenka was supposed to represent an "ideal contemporary working woman."[87] But more interesting than what Khvoshchinskaia said about her novel is how the text itself goes about trying to imagine a *way out* for a girl whose situation, in reality, would likely have afforded none at all. This way out involves—in fact necessitates—both a shift to the capital, and an emphatic rejection of romantic love. In fact perhaps one useful way to think of *The Boarding School Girl* is to conceive it as the polar opposite of a romantic comedy, a genre that has been described as "entertainment in the service of the biological imperative": romantic comedy exists to assure us that boy and girl will hook up and stay hooked, simply because, as Shakespeare's Benedick says in *Much Ado About Nothing*, "the world must be peopled."[88] In *The Boarding School Girl* Lolenka decides that there is no worse fate than peopling the world. Watching her mother beat her little brothers, she wonders numbly, "will I really have children one day? Will I really live like this?"[89]

The main reason she must escape *provintsiia* is that *provintsiia* represents the obligations of family, from which Khvoshchinskaia's heroine must unbind herself in order to live an authentic life (a message that could not be further from the one we will take from Tolstoy's two great novels, which generally represent family life as the only authentic life there is). Khvoshchinskaia allows for no possibility of forward movement through reproduction: when Lolenka is obliged to care for small children, it is not for her own offspring but for her younger siblings, which means she does not even have the option of convincing herself—as reproductive futurism would have us believe—that these children somehow represent her future.[90] In the end Lolenka's vision of the future, like the visions we find in many utopian fictions, would have difficulty accommodating the bearing and raising of children, a detail that does not bode well for its sustainability.

Only in the metropolis can Khvoshchinskaia's heroine recreate herself as a markedly modern subject; her only possibility of a future is located in the capital, where she can replace the vertical relationships that structured her past life with the up-to-date horizontal idea of the cohort ("our generation," as she says repeatedly). If in the end the alternatives Khvoshchinskaia imagines seem imperfect as well as improbable (as is suggested by the stridently doctrinaire nature of her heroine's diatribes: "Slavery, the family! . . . Precepts of submission to tyranny!

. . . She's guilty, your Sofia! She serves evil, teaches evil"[91]), it is not hard to understand why: the text's unconvincing ending—much like the flimsy ellipsis that stands in for any real explanation of exactly *how* a girl like Lolenka might escape the provinces in order to make her way to Petersburg and modernity—signals to us that *The Boarding School Girl* is probably trying to imagine an escape that is not yet quite imaginable.

For provincial women writers, geographic marginality underscored the marginality of femaleness. And while the *provintsialki* were not regionalists (they often settled outside their native *gubernii*, and their narratives tend to be set simply "in the provinces" rather than in a specific location), literary history has treated them much as it has treated the regionalists who are the subject of the next chapter: both groups have been seen as not quite "universal" enough to attain to the status of the highest art. It is therefore not surprising that the *provintsialki* felt obliged to make a case, whether explicit or implicit, for the significance and the aesthetic highness of their work. Elena Gan, by depicting "exceptional women" who were tragically isolated and misunderstood in provincial society, evoked the sad fate of the Romantic (male) genius who figured in so many canonical texts. Mariia Zhukova, by arguing for a close relationship between the provinces and ordinary, "real" life, implied that provincial settings were especially well-suited to literary realism, a mode of writing that in her time was deemed respectably up-to-date. Nadezhda Khvoshchinskaia adapted the provinces/capital opposition to her own purposes by using it to plot an escape route for her heroine, one that gestures toward a future in which women and provincials would be able to join progressive history.

In structural terms, the feminine and the provincial occupy similar positions. Both are typically imagined as secondary and dependent, limited to the particular, lacking the weighty and *universal* significance of things male and *stolichnye*. "Man is by his very nature more universal than woman," writes Belinsky in an essay on Zhukova, since man is able to "detach himself from his individual personality and transfer himself to many different situations . . . while woman is locked within herself."[92] Capitals make the same claim to universality: they "create the appearance of unity" for the entire nation by "taking upon [themselves] the role of *complete* spokesman for *all* national and state interests and opinions."[93]

In the next chapter we will have occasion to revisit the structural relationship between women's writing and provincial or regional writing by men. In the 1870s a male journalist whose focus is his native region feels compelled to issue a plaintive reminder: "the provinces *truly exist*," he insists.[94] Here we note a clear parallel with women's writing, the very existence of which is perennially called into question. Even when a feminist scholar like Irina Savkina asks "whether there in fact exists [in Russia] a specifically woman's literary tradition," she feels compelled to conclude that the answer is probably no: in Russia as elsewhere, what Germaine Greer once called "the transience of female literary fame" makes the development of such a tradition exceedingly difficult.[95] As a result, Elaine Showalter writes, "each generation of women writers has found itself, in a sense, without a history."[96] As we have seen in preceding chapters, to be without an accessible and coherent history is the same problem that haunts provincials: like the culture of Kukshina's provincial town in *Fathers and Sons*, the culture of women's writing burns down again and again, leaving no evidence that might certify its existence as a tradition, just a few disconnected artifacts.

Thus when the nineteenth-century critic Nikolai Shelgunov diagnoses the provinces' eternal "dependence" and "submissiveness," he might easily be talking about a sex—the second one—rather than a place: "There is something that makes the provinces the provinces . . . and that 'something' is their dependence on some power lying outside themselves—a dependence that is acutely felt, and that places on them a stamp of well-known submissiveness, a consciousness of non-autonomy, a second-rate position, depriving the provinces of any boldness, sureness of themselves, authority."[97] Like what is female, what is provincial is essential, but not primary. Both require defending and redeeming, and neither has an easy way of laying claim to the kind of uncontested universality thought to characterize the highest art. As the American poet Claudia Rankine has noted in another context, "Transcendence is unevenly distributed and experienced."[98]

CHAPTER EIGHT

Melnikov and Leskov, or What is Regionalism in Russia?

Le centre . . . transforme tout ce qu'il reçoit, il boit la vie brute, et elle
se transfigure. Les provinces se regardent en lui; en lui elles s'aiment et
s'admirent sous une forme supérieure . . . Cette belle centralisation, par
quoi la France est la France.

—Jules Michelet, 1833

Certain places are "regions" . . . while certain other places are not.

—Raymond Williams, 1983

The woods are full of regional writers, and it is the horror of every
serious Southern writer that he will become one.

—Flannery O'Connor, 1957

If *provintsiia* is not a wasteland of anonymity, repetition, and stasis, then what
is it? Regional writers, like women writers, were among those who approached
the question by trying to develop alternative ways of representing Russian
space. This chapter is *not* meant as an exhaustive catalogue of these alternatives,
and certainly not as a complete account of Russian regionalist writing; rather, it
is meant to give a sense of certain discourses that were capable of challenging the
powerful and familiar trope of provincial meaninglessness. The main authors of
fiction addressed here are Pavel Melnikov-Pechersky (hereafter Melnikov) and,
more briefly, Nikolai Leskov, both of whom imagine geographies that are not
organized around a simple provinces-capital divide. Melnikov focuses explicitly
and exclusively on a particular region (the Volga), and I read his fiction alongside

the tradition of local scholarship that fostered his intensely local point of view. Leskov, by contrast, often imagines Russian space as open and uncentered, populated by wanderers and off-the-grid characters whose movements take little account of the *provintsiia-stolitsa* opposition.

Both writers resist the polarized symbolic geography that is this book's focus, and although their resistance takes different forms, they share an interest in specific places that they invest with specific meanings. And yet as I will argue, when it comes to reception and canonization, a nuanced representation of Russian space seems not to have worked to either writer's advantage. In fact, the fates of Melnikov and Leskov suggest that a Russian prose writer who is actively *not* associated with a center risks being demoted to second-rate status, seen as a repository of raw material rather than as a generator of his or her own ideas. Melnikov and Leskov are prime examples of such a fate, from which their supporters are still trying to rescue them today.[1]

As I suggested in this book's introduction, and as I discuss in the present chapter, it may be that in Russian narrative art the very idea of high culture tends to be associated with a center. This would help explain why in Russian literary discourse, as we will see, attempts to replace clichés of *provintsiia* with more nuanced views of the local proved less successful than they did in nonfictional writing. Even as journalists and historians outside the capitals were paying close attention to their specific localities, fiction was perhaps less likely to be canonized as "high" if it remained focused on what was perceived as specifically and narrowly "local." And if it was not easy for writers to make a case for the strictly artistic significance of literature that was not written in, about, or from the viewpoint of the capitals, perhaps this is because the (symbolic) geographic center was often seen as sole locus of the *universality* and *unity* thought to characterize "real art." Capitals, as noted in the previous chapter, lay claim to both: a capital "creates the appearance of unity" by "taking upon itself the role of complete spokesman for *all* national and state interests and opinions."[2] Compare again Jules Michelet, writing from the absolute center of another absolutely centralized culture. For Michelet, the center—Paris—represents both the annihilation and the transformation of local *specificity* ("l'annihilation de tout esprit local, de toute provincialité"), which it transmutes into something of *general* significance ("Le centre . . . transforme tout ce qu'il reçoit, il boit la vie brute, et elle se transfigure").[3]

Finally, this chapter will note again the parallel we saw at the end of the preceding chapter—the structural similarities of regionalist literature, *provintsial'nost'*, and women's writing. Provincial places, even when they are figured as specific regions, are also figured as feminine. At times the parallel is drawn explicitly (e.g., the provinces or regions as a "big-breasted mother" charged with feeding her little son, Petersburg),[4] though more often the message is implied (as in Nikolai

Shelgunov's evocation of the provinces' eternal "dependence" and "submissiveness," their "second-rate position," etc., cited in chapter 7).[5] In all cases, what is
being called into question by the center—and defended by those who are outside
the center, whether geographically or symbolically—is the worth of the detail, the
local, and the particular—including what is embodied in modes of writing that
work to produce "an active resistance to what we now call world literature."[6]

An Aside on Ostrovsky

The playwright Alexander Ostrovsky has come to be associated with the same general region that preoccupied Melnikov (the Volga); Melnikov reviewed Ostrovsky's
work; in certain ways their projects might be seen as overlapping. Why, then, do
I include only an *aside* on Ostrovsky here? Because Ostrovsky's plays, no matter
how strongly they have come to be associated with a certain image of the provincial town, form part of another system altogether. If his work now calls to mind
provincial places (especially in the now-familiar toponym Kalinov, the imaginary
Volga locale where *The Storm* [*Groza*] and a few other plays are set), nonetheless
his primary topic is in no way the provinces or provincialism or even the provincial town. It is, rather, a backward caste and its particular backward culture,
surviving not only in isolated towns but also in Moscow merchants' houses (as
we see in *We'll Settle our Accounts, Mad Money* [*Svoi liudi—sochtemsia, Beshenye
den'gi*] and other important works set in the capital). By and large Ostrovsky's
plays target the old-fashioned *samodur*, a patriarch-tyrant who reigns despotically
over a realm the critic Dobroliubov famously named the Kingdom of Darkness.

This kingdom is not necessarily located in the provinces, and indeed the
word "provincial" does not necessarily carry a negative meaning for Ostrovsky.
Among the most positive characters in the play *Mad Money*, for instance, is Savva
Gennadich Vasilkov, whom Ostrovsky introduces as "a provincial [*provintsial*]
of about thirty-five years of age" who has been educated in England and has
absorbed the habits of honest work. When Ostrovsky notes the "provincialism
[*provintsial'nost'*] evident in his dress" and in his folksy speech ("sayings typical
of the Middle Volga"), we sense immediately that "provincial" in this instance is
meant to signal things traditional, countryside, small-town, regional, local, possibly even "authentic"; thus it resonates more with *glush'* and *derevnia* than with
gubernskii gorod (or even *uezdnyi gorod*).

Such examples should caution us, I think, against seeing Ostrovsky's oeuvre
as a *seminal* moment in the trope this book is describing, a trope that in any
case had taken clear shape well before his plays were written and staged (in the
period between 1849 and 1872). It seems, however, that some of his settings (like
Kalinov) have nonetheless assumed a place in the Russian cultural imaginary as

examples of "the entire deep [*glukhoi*] provinces in miniature form" (as we are informed by a website that provides easy overviews of historical and literary topics for students).[7] In this sense Ostrovsky's plays—even those set in Moscow—have to some degree been retroactively assimilated into the *provintsiia* trope, even if their origins are not traceable to it.

Regional Histories and the Case for the Particular

In many traditions literary regionalism has made available noncentralized ways of picturing the nation, even though its cultural work has by no means been constant in different times and places. In America, for instance, virtually all canonical nineteenth-century authors were strongly identified with a particular part of the country, and readers knew to expect different kinds of stories to be set in different regions.[8] In England, too, literature has taught us to expect something entirely different from a story set in the Home Counties than we do from a story set on the "Celtic Fringe." (In fact one wonders if the prominence of female novelists in the English tradition is related to the fact that England's symbolic geography is not structured by a strong provinces-capital binary: Jane Austen, the Brontes, and George Eliot need not worry that by adopting settings and points of view other than London, they risk being judged as second-rate.) In German-speaking lands, the novel enjoyed great popularity a time when no single city had a clear claim to the status of "capital"; as a result, most of nineteenth-century German prose fiction might be described as regional. Latin America, Canada, South Africa—in all these literatures regionalism has had an important role to play.

Regionalism is about what is *particular*. And as I noted in the previous chapter, what is perceived as particular will tend to collide with the (often unarticulated) assumption that art's highness depends, or might very well depend, on transcending particulars. An implicit "imperialism of the universal"[9] makes it difficult for women and regionalists to make a case for the high significance of their work, simply because this work treats subjects perceived to be nonuniversal. Just as what is male can pretend to encompass what is female, so the geographic center can claim to reflect or even contain everything else, thereby magically universalizing (per Michelet) what were previously mere particulars—including the merely regional. We have already seen how female writers have been denigrated for their use of details, charged with producing "'pointless' or 'plotless' narratives stuffed with strange minutiae."[10] Clearly, if art's highness is seen to depend on transcending details, this vision will place a special burden on writers of regionalist fiction, precisely as it has done to women.

However, the regionalist association with the particular—the local, the detailed, the trivial—seems not to have been quite as stigmatizing for Russian writers of *non*-fiction, who had more success challenging the capitals' pretensions to be all-encompassing. Outside of the strictly literary realm, attempts to correct the center's persistent neglect and misrepresentation of the provinces were made by local journalists (as well as by geographers, ethnographers, statesmen, and military strategists) whose work attests to the fact that in some contexts, Russians did recognize and value regional specificity. Certainly by the mid-nineteenth century, educated people with strong attachments to their native places were using amateur scholarly discourse as a way of building up forms of local knowledge that could counter received ideas about provincial homogeneity, monotony, and dependence. In doing so, they created categories of localness (*krai, mestnost', oblast'*, etc.) around which real-world regional identities could take shape. Recent historiography's attention to these discourses of regional specificity has complicated the "state-centered tradition of Russian history," a body of scholarship that has persistently represented what is local as "inert, passive, awaiting the dynamism of the outside" (to quote Susan Smith-Peter's description of this approach, which she critiques).[11] In Smith-Peter's words, "Russian history increasingly seems to be a history of regions."[12]

But Russian *literature* is generally *not* a literature of regionalisms. Even as new historical research cautions us not to assume that Imperial Russia can be adequately summed up as a centralized state with "little or no room for initiative from below," the fact is that when it comes to accounting for literary production, as I discuss in chapter 1 of this book, the old model usually works better.[13] Literature of the high canon tends to reproduce an image of Russia in which the local (that is, the non-capital, because capitals are never "local") is eternal and static, only occasionally roused from its torpor by the action of outside (usually state) agents. Such is the image familiar to us from the state-vs.-society paradigm of Russian history that Smith-Peter and others are working to complicate.[14] One of this chapter's goals is to explore the contrast between these two discourses—roughly, the historical versus the literary—in order to understand why regionalism's role in Russian literature is not more significant than it is.

In 1876, the Nizhnii Novgorod journalist Aleksandr Gatsitskii (1838–93) published a widely read pamphlet with the arresting title *The death of the provinces, or not?*[15] The essay amounts to an impassioned defense of provincial culture's role in the life of the nation—indeed a defense of the very existence of provincial culture and its "right to an independent life outside the center."[16] Again and again the pamphlet argues that *provintsiia* has a right to life: "we protest against the swallowing-up of the provinces by a single center, against the failure to recognize the provinces' human rights."[17] Clearly, the fact that intellectuals outside the capitals felt compelled to make a case like the one Gatsitskii articulates says much about the role assigned to the provinces in the Russian cultural imaginary. But who exactly would argue against Gatsitskii's claims, and why?

The death of the provinces, or not? responds to an overview of provincial journalism that had recently appeared in the Petersburg journal *Delo*—an article by
Daniil Mordovtsev titled "The Provincial Press," in which Gatsitskii is put forth as
a representative example of intellectual activity outside Moscow and Petersburg.[18]
Mordovtsev's assessment of provincial journalism (and of Gatsitskii) is only mod-
erately unflattering, but his comments on the larger cultural and social process of
"centralization" leave no doubt as to the profoundly unequal relationship between
province and metropole. This relationship, Mordovtsev argues, would inevitably
be shaped by what he called "the law of centralization": provincial places are forever engaged in "a battle with the centers, in the fullest sense of the term—a battle
for existence" against a centripetal force that "threatens to suck out of the provinces all of their best spiritual and economic powers, relegating them to a sterile
existence." Their fate is to be raw material (*pitatel'naia materiia*).[19] The battle's outcome is a foregone conclusion, thanks to nature's law: "it is natural that everything
in the provinces be drawn to the centers," just as the "natural laws of life and
development" dictate that giant beasts live in forests and whales in great oceans.[20]
"All the brightest examples of good and evil, of virtue and vice—all this will flow
toward the centers, while the rest of the earthly sphere will be obliged to play the
role of backward provincial [*otstalogo provintsiala*]."[21] The provinces will and must
be left behind, "widowed in all respects."[22]

While Mordovtsev argues that only the ever-greater concentration of forces
in a center can facilitate progress (a familiar argument in Russian historiography
from at least Karamzin on), Gatsitskii counters with a case for decentralization:
the strength of the nation resides in the combined strength of "numberless" regional centers, he says, and only the "widest possible *dissemination*" of enlightenment constitutes genuine progress.[23] But Mordovtsev likens Gatsitskii's research
on his home region to that of "a German pedant who has devoted his whole life to
studying his favorite minute aquatic creature." For long years, Mordovtsev charges,
Gatsitskii has focused on "his one little scrap of the Povolzhe," and seems intent to
go on doing so, year after year, "from Vetluga to the Kerzhenets and Tesha, from
Krasnaia Ramen to Vyksa and Pochinki."[24] (Again here we note a parallel between
the provincial and the feminine, both thought to be characterized by a preoccupation with inconsequential details that fail to cohere into a meaningful whole.)

Despite the disdainful tone, Mordovtsev is essentially correct in his assessment
of Gatsitskii, in the sense that the latter did indeed devote his entire career to his
region. As one scholar describes it, his was a life that "began and ended on the
local level."[25] In his own words Gatsitskii's project was to "publish *everything*"—
even "the smallest ethnographic characteristics"—concerning his home region. "We are interested *specifically* in the physiognomy of the Nizhegorodskoe
Povolzhe," he writes, and in order to understand it, "we must collect *all* the traits

that characterize the locality."[26] Again and again over the course of his career, Gatsitskii restates this ambition ("the investigation of *all possible aspects* of the popular life of the Nizhegorodskoe Povolzhe in its past and its present . . . from an eternal and all-embracing rather than a temporary perspective"),[27] going so far as to maintain that "if it were possible, history should take as its task *the detailed biography of each and every person on the earth without exception.*"[28]

Gatsitskii's priority is not the forest but the trees. While the "centralist-ethnographer" (*tsentralist-etnograf*) would be content to know that Russian tradition generally involves a ceremonial pre-wedding meeting of bride's and groom's parents, he says, the "writer-provincial" (*pisatel'-provintsial*) would want to know precisely what forms this tradition took in various micro-regions.[29] And therefore local intellectuals "need to [catalogue] the *tiniest traits* of the Nizhegorodskoe Povolzhe district; we need to know *how it differs* from every other locality—how does the inhabitant of the far bank of the Kudma [river] differ from the inhabitant of this side, and why on this side of the river is the term 'Zakudemskii' [meaning "from over the river"] considered an insult; we need to know why across the Volga the *posidelki* cannot do without young men, but in the hills . . . they maintain the custom of chasing off the young men from the *posidelki* . . . and so on, and so on."[30] Just as "only the superficial observer" believes the Russian peasant is everywhere the same, so only the superficial observer will believe that all Russian towns are the same: even though every town's streets have the same names and even though "in all these towns it is dull to live," nonetheless if one looks more closely at these "supposedly dull towns," one will see that "Nizhnii in no way resembles Tambov, and Penza does not look like Kaluga, even though each town is inconceivable without its Nobility Street."[31]

For Gatsitskii, only by collecting masses of data can we approach the truth, because only masses of data can reveal the differences (rather than the similarities or patterns) in which he believes truth resides. Clearly this idea of what would constitute adequate local knowledge demands an extraordinary, even fantastical, degree of specificity and copiousness. Yet Gatsitskii's goal is not just to amass information about a region, but to defend the value of the emphatically local knowledge that forms the basis of a certain epistemology. When Mordovtsev asserts that the job of the provincial intellectual is merely to collect raw data and "send it to the capitals" where it will be subjected to "more sophisticated treatment [*iskusstnoi otdelki*],"[32] Gatsitskii counters that the gathering and collating of local knowledge requires as much expertise as any other intellectual labor. (And as to intellectuals in the capitals who claim to be "processing" or "polishing" what has been collected elsewhere, Gatsitskii implies that they are simply appropriating others' labor, in keeping with the capitals' habit of treating the provinces as "a big-breasted mother whose sole obligation is to provide healthy milk to her child, Petersburg": clearly Gatsitskii understood the consequences of figuring *provintsiia* as feminine.)[33]

"Many provinces had their Gatsitskiis," as Catherine Evtuhov, Smith-Peter, and others have shown.[34] The same holds true today: the contemporary *kraevedy* (local historians) N. V. Frolov and E. V. Frolova, for example, organize their inquiries exclusively around a location (the Vladimir *oblast'* town of Kovrov and its environs); their topic is nothing less—and nothing more—than "the entire span of Kovrov's history, from prehistoric times to the present."[35] For this sort of scholar, "local history is the sum total of sources relating to a locale, organized into a narrative," and as a result, "any source dealing with Kovrov is relevant."[36] In other words, for the Frolovs, Kovrov is the only organizing "theory" their work requires: such historians have tended to eschew theoretical frameworks linking facts to ideas, preferring instead an "exclusive attention to the unique nature of [their] subject," at times even "consciously and explicitly [rejecting] theoretical formulations" and aiming instead to amass the "scientific raw material" necessary for "the total description of the local environment in all its possible dimensions."[37] If local historians like these remain little known to nonspecialists in our time, it is because their avowed aim has never been "to contribute to historical debates taking place in the center"; their goal, rather, has been "to give a fuller, richer, more detailed narrative of some aspect of local history."[38]

Debates like Mordovtsev's and Gatsitskii's (which attracted considerable attention) reveal that in journalism and historiography, regionalist thinking—an approach that recognizes and values local particularities—was able to establish a degree of legitimacy. But as we see from their exchange, an exclusive focus on the local can imply that regional scholars' best shot at respect involves deferentially abstaining from participation in capital-centered discourses of national history, which in turn implies acceptance of the capitals' intellectual dominance. Scholars of regional history are always at risk of being positioned as objects rather than subjects, providers of historical raw material that can reveal its value only after being intellectually processed—that is, *placed in relation to larger systems of knowledge*—by scholars in the center.[39] Thus while Mordovtsev acknowledges some value in the regional press's data-gathering activities, he also insists that without the capitals' "refining" interventions, everything provincial researchers collect will be "archeological, sepulchral, dry-as-dust."[40] Here I use "dry-as-dust" to render *grobokopatel'noe*, which literally means "grave-digging": the best provincials can do, this claim implies, is dig up dead artifacts, which later might, or might not, be reanimated by the life-giving powers of the capitals.[41]

Melnikov and the Status of the Local

In certain respects the life of writer, ethnographer, journalist, and bureaucrat Pavel Melnikov parallels that of Gatsitskii.[42] Born two decades apart, both men came to be strongly identified with their native province of Nizhnii Novgorod;

both worked tirelessly in provincial journalism (for the *Gubernskie vedomosti*); both made careers that capitalized on their prodigious local knowledge. Like Gatsitskii, Melnikov contributed enthusiastically to mid-century information-gathering efforts organized by the tsarist state—in the 1850s, he was employed by the Ministry of Internal Affairs in Petersburg to compile statistical surveys of various aspects of regional life—but his activities were more wide-ranging than Gatsitskii's, and more closely linked to the central government.[43]

In 1839, after a minor political indiscretion sent him briefly into internal exile in Perm, Melnikov published a series of travel notes that took an amateur ethnographer's "semi-scholarly" approach to the "exoticism, real and invented," of the Urals region, which he represented as an exotic foreign land.[44] A similar point of view—that of an outsider who is far more sophisticated than the locals he is observing—informs the fictional works that would later make Melnikov famous. Virtually all these narratives are set in his native region: first a series of stories, and later the (monstrously long) works of fiction *In the Forests* (1871–74) and *In the Hills* (1875–81). My focus here will be on one of his earlier tales ("The Krasilnikovs," 1852) and *In the Forests*, the more successful of his longer fictions. As these works reveal, Melnikov's regionalist writing is inseparable from his career as a loyal government servitor.

Melnikov's early story "The Krasilnikovs" is narrated by someone like Melnikov, a bureaucrat who has been dispatched to "district town S" (we get no further information about its location) to gather information on the tanning industry. The narrator is a sophisticated traveler who recounts for us what he finds in a decidedly unsophisticated place; thus provincial life is immediately figured as an object of perusal by more worldly outsiders. In fact the first thing Melnikov's narrator notices in "S" is that the ancient cathedral has been "disfigured" by additions "in the newest taste"[45]—entirely in line with what literature has taught us to expect from a story of this period that begins with an outsider's arrival in an unnamed provincial town.

The narrator seeks information from an elderly, prosperous, and very traditional leather merchant, Kornyla Egorych Krasilnikov, whose house, like the cathedral, bears marks of a specifically provincial version of cultural incoherence: displayed in Krasilnikov's front window are an expensive bronze clock set alongside a green parrot, a multi-colored cat, and "modest plaster busts" of Voltaire and Suvorov. Broken panes are covered with scraps of colored paper (some of which, inexplicably, have been cut into the shape of a horse and the letter "F"); everything smells of tar and leather.[46] Inside the house the incoherence intensifies: in Krasilnikov's "*zala*" (presumably from French *salle*, and in quotation marks), all the furnishings have been brought from Petersburg, and all are marked as incongruous imports.[47] Krasilnikov "had bought everything indiscriminately," and "everything was inappropriate": the walls are covered with marble, but from the ceiling hangs a cheap birdcage with a quail in it; patched canvases are thrown over the furniture; luxurious lamps have never been filled with oil because no one in the town of S knows how to light them.[48] The old man himself is acutely ill at ease in this room, but because he is unwilling to lose face before his neighbors, he cannot bring himself to abandon the house in which everything is to him "alien and estranged": "here even what is his own is not his own" (*zdes' emu i svoe ne svoe*).[49]

The old merchant's emphatic rejection of all "book learning" prompts the narrator to elicit his story.[50] It turns out that Krasilnikov's son Mitka was seduced—seduced, that is, in his father's interpretation—by his fancy education, and ended up falling in love with the German governess on a nearby estate. Upon learning that the couple had married without his consent, Krasilnikov killed the girl, leaving his gifted, beloved son to go mad from grief: the narrator sees Mitka wandering around the filthy leather factory, muttering to himself in French and singing songs about champagne.[51] The father blames this tragedy entirely on his son's schooling: "it all comes from book learning, from all those damned fashions [*mody prokliatye*]."[52]

Krasilnikov's account of Mitka's education is the story of a gradual estrangement from clan and class, expressed as an incremental geographic removal from one's place of origin—from "district school" to "provincial town capital" to "Moscow University" to places "over the sea" (*uezdnoe uchilishche, gubernskii gorod, Moskovskii universitet, iz-za moria*). The old man had allowed Mitka to study in the hopes that his learning would one day make the family rich, his decision having been swayed by a lavish dinner (complete with wine and pretty gentry girls) where the governor himself extolled the benefits of allowing the brilliant boy to attend university in Moscow. Thus the elder Krasilnikov, too, has been seduced by promises of a life beyond the local, and in this way his assessment of the tragedy is accurate: it is indeed the fault of "damned fashion." If we understand *moda* in the broadest sense, with its inescapable ties to modernity and to the distinctly modern belief that change is inevitable, then indeed Krasilnikov's family has been undone by fashion, "this engine that never stops, and makes the provinces feel old and ugly and jealous—and seduces them forever and a day."[53]

The characters who populate regionalist texts are generally immune to or simply outside of fashion in this sense, as I will discuss below; in fact they are defined by their removal from its flux, which stands for the flux of cosmopolitan modernity itself. In many times and places, not only does fashion constitute "one of the main routes of access to modernity,"[54] it can also serve as a constant reminder that one is, or might be, trailing behind; it is a reminder never to stop measuring oneself again the center's standard. The merchant Krasilnikov is not willing to abandon the garish house he hates, and to this extent he is a provincial. But he *is* willing to murder his daughter-in-law and drive his son mad in order to restore his values to what he sees as their rightful place, a place where they cannot be measured (and found wanting) against the external yardstick of enlightenment, modernity, and the capitals. To this extent, Melnikov's brutal old man effectively resists being "provincialized." But of course, Melnikov's text in no way endorses Krasilnikov's resistance; rather, it invites us to see his family tragedy as a consequence of provincials' ignorance and recalcitrance, their inability or unwillingness to assimilate to the enlightened culture offered to them by the center.

If we assess "The Krasilnikovs" against standard definitions of literary regionalism, there is little that is regionalist about it, nonstandard language and remote (but unspecified) setting notwithstanding. Regionalist literature typically reflects some variety of nostalgia for a lost or disappearing past, along with some antipathy to historical change: the past that Kornyla Egorych Krasilnikov represents is a curiosity, but not one that would seem to be worthy of preservation or even mourning. The narrators of regionalist texts often experience their encounters with "local" places and characters as a vaguely therapeutic "reconnection with one's roots," a return to "a locus of original identity,"[55] or as a salutary (brief) immersion in something "rustic-domestic":[56] not so here. Regionalist texts often tend to be concerned with "the character of the district or region rather than with the individual": again, not really the case in this story.[57] In the end "The Krasilnikovs" draws less on regionalist techniques than it does on the trope that is the topic of this book, the trope of Russia's backward *provintsiia*.

Approximately twenty years separate the composition of "The Krasilnikovs" from that of *In the Forests* and *In the Hills*. During the early years of this period, while working for the Ministry of Internal Affairs, Melnikov made his most important contribution to Petersburg's information-gathering efforts: he researched and wrote, in 1853–54, a secret report on Nizhnii Novgorod's Old Believer community, a document that has been described as "an extraordinary accomplishment of ethnographic research."[58] However, what is perhaps most extraordinary about this document is that its explicit purpose was to encourage and facilitate the state's destruction of the Old Believer culture it was describing: Melnikov's main recommendation to the central government was, in his own words, "*to destroy the sketes completely*" (emphasis in the original).[59]

In a striking fact that speaks to paradoxes of literary regionalism generally, the same Old Believer culture that Melnikov was helping to extirpate serves as setting and primary material, two decades later, for his most famous works of fiction, *In the Forests* and *In the Hills*.[60] While regionalism plays different roles in different traditions, in general it tends to commemorate, often somewhat complacently, what is believed to be "slipping away" (i.e., those subcultures that were succumbing to seemingly inexorable historical forces). Rarely, though, are writers such direct agents of this destruction as Melnikov was (and as he perhaps knew himself to be: in 1875 he urged his contemporaries to "gather these precious fragments [of Russian antiquity and folklore] while there is still time . . . the Russian way of life is changing").[61] If he was willing not just to memorialize Old Believer culture but also to help dismantle it, this is because in the end he saw himself as a representative of the Russian capital's modernizing and enlightening mission, the only force that he, like most of Russia's elites, believed capable of overcoming the provinces' inertia so as to bring them into progressive history, history in the sense of "public time."[62]

This is not the same story that all cultures tell themselves about center-periphery relations, whether in history or in literature. America, for instance, tends to cast its own history as a story of spreading-out and dissemination, the ever-greater devolution of power to small units and far-off places, whereas Russia tells itself a story of centralization, a "gathering" of "Russian" lands. American literary history, too, reveals little emphasis on a geographic center's role as the indispensable agent of progress. Instead, in the postbellum period, one task assigned to American literary regionalism was to help reunify the broken (imaginary) nation by promoting a vision of peaceful coexistence, locating sectional differences in a picturesque past—a delicate story-telling process that involved considerable repression of contemporary realities.[63] Melnikov's vision was in a sense more honest: it came closer to confronting the fact that the task of regionalism is to memorialize what it also plays a role in exterminating.[64]

The impulse behind *In the Forests* can be traced directly to the imperial center's desire for a certain kind of story about this periphery. In 1861, when Melnikov was invited to accompany Tsarevich Nikolai Alexandrovich on a Volga tour, the young heir was reportedly so enthralled by Melnikov's tales of the region that he asked him to "write all of this down—depict the legends and lore, everything about the daily life of the people [*narod*] on the left side of the Volga."[65] A decade or so later (and after the tsarevich's early death), Melnikov complied. By the time he began *In the Forests* in the 1870s, the region's Old Believer culture, previously the object of his (and the state's) intense interest, was a topic for memorialization rather than study: not only had the central government followed Melnikov's recommendation to work toward destroying the Old Belief in Nizhnii Novgorod province, but all of Russian society was changing rapidly under the influence of the Great Reforms. By setting *In the Forests* in the 1850s, Melnikov was choosing to focus on aspects of Volga Old Believer culture that were already more or less gone, a decision reflecting regionalism's familiar tendency to represent their subjects as "self-contained [forms] belonging to the past," rather than living forces "still adapting in the present."[66]

The setting of *In the Forests* would certainly have struck most Russian readers as remote and exotic, a culture that was, if not yet entirely gone, then certainly entirely *hidden* "within the depths of . . . remote Russian forests."[67] As Jane Costlow writes, this is "a novel written for urbanized literate Russians, which transported them *somewhere else*—an elsewhere they could situate on a map, but which they could only really travel to in this tale."[68] To read *In the Forests* is to be focused on and immersed in this setting, its rich nature and folklore (both Christian and pagan).[69] The novel begins with an invocation of place that is at once mythical (locating it in the same world as "the invisible city of Kitezh") and geographically concrete (carefully distinguishing the upper Trans-Volga [*Verkhovoe Zavolzhe*] from adjacent areas "beyond the Kama," etc.). This opening passage makes explicit that the Zavolzhe *stands for* Russia, or more specifically, for Rus: "Rus stands there from ancient times, in all its purity," Melnikov writes.[70] Thus we read the rest of the novel with the constant awareness that its setting stands in a synecdochic relationship to "Russia" as a whole (a typical strategy of regionalist literature, which often makes this kind of case for its own significance, if implicitly).

Yet Melnikov reveals the world of *In the Forests* to be not entirely unconnected to the one "outside." His practical Old Believers engage in trade—that is, they make their living in ways that typically require at least some movement and circulation and a working knowledge of what lies beyond one's own micro-region; thus larger cities, not necessarily the capitals but regional economic centers like Samara, play a role in their activities.[71] While they lead somewhat isolated lives, they are nonetheless aware of specific distances and of what is required to get from one place to another. The gold-seeking "pilgrim" (*palomnik*) Patap Maksimych, for instance, knows that the provincial capital is sixty versts from the village, other travelers know that the Krasnoiarskii *skete* is twenty versts further down the road, etc.[72]

In this sense the setting of *In the Forests*, though decidedly "far away" from the reader, differs from a place like Goncharov's imaginary village of Oblomovka, which is definitively *cut off* from everyplace else. For the inhabitants of Oblomovka, who engage in virtually no trade, almost all geographic space is untraversable and immeasurable; their imaginary geography involves "the world on the back of a fish."[73] They live in what Bakhtin calls (in his description of Greek romance) "an *abstract* expanse of space,"[74] a thoroughly premodern image structured by what Franco Moretti terms the "absolute distance" between "Home" and "the Wide World" outside.[75] By contrast, Melnikov's Old Believers, even when they cover relatively small distances, conceive of space not as the Oblomovka villagers do, but as does Stolz, Goncharov's ideal proto-capitalist. As I have argued elsewhere, Stolz perceives space in terms of modernity's (and literary realism's) "relative distance," "distance [that] has been brought down to earth: it can be measured, understood; it is no longer a function of Fate."[76] Melnikov's industrious Old Believers seem to be moving in this direction as well: and in fact, though *In the Forests* allies them with folk culture, religion, and nature, they have at times been read as harbingers of Russia's entry into economic modernity.[77]

Nonetheless, in the region's life and history, sheer geographic distance plays a significant role, even a determinative one, because while the dense forest is one factor that contributes to its isolation, another factor is simply that its inhabitants are far away from imperial and religious authorities in the capitals.[78] A priest who did not want to obey orders from the Moscow metropolitan could simply slip away, we are told, never to be found; the same went for others—whether debtors, run-away serfs, or gentry Old Believers—seeking to flee any representative of the central powers.[79] Melnikov tells the history of the region as a protracted effort to elude the center's ongoing attempts to control and subdue: "The Khlynov priests did not want to recognize Moscow with her metropolitan—and [the priests'] spiritual followers [*dukhovnye chada*] did not want to recognize the tsars' military authorities [*tsarskikh voevod*]; they evaded paying taxes, governed themselves by way of elections, organized their own rough justice [*sudili samosudom*], did not submit to Moscow's laws. The moment an emissary of the *voevod* or the patriarchal authority [*patriarshii desiatil'nik*] appeared at the edge the forest, they abandoned their houses and went off into the deep forests."[80]

Occasionally a character makes his way to Moscow and returns with novelties like new songs and trinkets (including decorative Easter eggs, deemed blasphemous by the pious),[81] but no one gazes longingly toward the far-off capitals or measures herself against their standards of style or enlightenment.[82] When, for instance, a prosperous father from Kazan (Patap) dreams of marrying his daughter to a rich Muscovite, he does not dream of going to Moscow, or of sending the girl to live there; rather, the fantasy is that she will return home in glory, bringing with her enough money for him to buy a steamship.[83] The prevailing sentiment seems to be that what happens in the capitals should stay in the capitals: when Patap catches himself daydreaming about getting rich and building a stone house in Petersburg, he immediately recoils from his own thoughts in shame and fear, recalling scandalous stories of ladies dancing half-naked at balls in the capitals ("all their clothes are made by Frenchmen!").[84]

In the end this vision of the licentious and fashion-driven life of the capitals strengthens Patap's resolve not to let his daughter marry a suitor who turns up from Moscow. When the prospective bridegroom is brought to meet his potential in-laws, the young man's attire reveals strenuous attempts at modern stylishness—frock coat, watch chain, and white gloves, all "according to fashion" ("*po-modnomu*"). Melnikov puts *po-modnomu* in quotation marks, thus underscoring the alienness of *moda* in this environment—and indeed fashion is what ends up discrediting the Muscovite suitor in the eyes of Patap and his wife. The young man's mother tries to apologize for her son's strange dress ("please don't

look at his clothes"), reassuring the potential in-laws that these are merely youthful affectations. But while the fiancée's mother replies charitably ("They're young,
immature. . . . It will pass. . . . They will come to love the staid dress that has been
sanctified by our blessed fathers"),[85] the marriage arrangements do not come off.
Far from making this young man a desirable representative of the capital's superior culture, the fashion sense he has developed in Moscow has rendered him
unmarriageable back home.

Moda is only intermittently and weakly present in the Volga region, at least as
Melnikov represents it. His Old Believers show themselves quite capable of resisting fashion's attraction, despite the fact that a few of their coreligionists in Moscow,
including the prospective bridegroom, have taken to it: "Mikhailo Danilych was
one of the 'educated Old Believers' who had appeared not long before in the capitals, and then twenty years or so after that began to show themselves in the provinces [*v guberniiakh*] as well. . . . They didn't believe that foreigners' clothes—or
clubs, theaters, or masquerades—were particularly sinful, and Mikhailo Danilych
had more than once . . . with a cigar between his lips and a glass of champagne,
laughed heartily along with others who had, like him, been exhorted and cursed
by the Rogozhskii [Old Believer] priest Ivan Matveich, who saw in the new ways
the final death of the Old Belief."[86] His modern ways, of which his clothes are just
a sign, make him unassimilable in the Povolzhe, thanks to the locals' powerful and
abiding sense of us-versus-them (*nashi* versus *chuzhie*). Theirs is a subculture capable of pushing back hard against the incursions of an imperialist modernity; "it
might be worse," they say, "but it's ours."[87] Given the power of these sentiments, it
is hard to imagine how the phenomenon of fashionability could ever be integrated
into the self-contained world imagined in Melnikov's regionalist work.

By leaving the words *po-modnomu* in quotation marks, Melnikov draws attention to fashion's profound alienness in a Nizhegorodskoe Povolzhe village,
suggesting that Old Belief and *moda* are mutually exclusive. In this setting what
is most discordant about Mikhailo Danilych's clothing is its evident commitment to what one art historian calls "the ineluctable *movement* of fashion," the
origins of which can be traced to its "essential presumptuousness," "its constant
pushiness, its middle-class mobility" (as sumptuary laws attest).[88] And in Russia,
thanks to Peter's peremptory sartorial reforms imposing Western dress on the
nobility, innovations in clothing were explicitly linked to modernization; as Luba
Golburt writes, Petrine vestimentary decrees initiated (some) Russians into "a
temporality that was externalized, wearable, foreign, unpredictable, and ultimately accelerated."[89]

But if "the commitment to change . . . is the essence of fashion,"[90] the essence
of the society described in *In the Forests* is the commitment to not changing. Page
after page of *In the Forests* is devoted to detailed accounts of this essentially static

subculture (static, I would again emphasize, according to Melnikov's depiction: reality might well have been a different matter), from folkways and legends to lexical peculiarities, foods, and crafts. In such passages the author's ethnographic knowledge is on ostentatious display, as when we are treated to regional vocabulary regarding, say, bogs, winter huts, and insects.[91] Passages like this underscore the stability of the subculture Melnikov represents, as well as the extremely local nature of what is being documented, as when he notes that a certain type of sled, hat, or food originates in one particular village and not in any other.

Such observations also signal to us that Melnikov, like Gatsitskii, is deeply committed to the *particular* (*this* village's handiwork, *this* type of sled, etc.). And one might argue that the particular is often opposed to the modern: in Goncharov's *An Ordinary Story*, as we saw, urban modernity is shaped by large-scale systems that generate many instances of the same thing, or rather, many instances of almost the same thing. This combination—scale and repetition leading to regularity with slight variation—teaches the capital's inhabitants to recognize and prioritize not singular details, but repeating patterns. In Goncharov's text only the naïve provincial Alexander thinks in terms of what is singular and never-again ("the heart loves but once!"). Becoming modern requires him to learn that in fact the heart loves over and over; as his uncle tells him, love stories have been more or less the same since Adam and Eve, "with slight variations."[92] Instead of being attentive to what is unique or extraordinary, modern people—people in the capital—must attend to ordinariness and repetition, because ordinariness and repetition create the patterns that make life in the metropolis intelligible.

Throughout most of *In the Forests*, place is more important than time, and dates are rarely mentioned. So while we know that the narrative must be set before the government's systematic persecution of the province's Old Believers in the mid-1850s, the past-ness of this past is not heavily emphasized; instead, history simply seems to be held at a remove ("a world in which time stood still," Costlow says).[93] Yet we know what happens next. We are aware that change is coming, aware that soon enough the sketes will be "*destroyed completely.*" As Vladimir Korolenko put it twenty years after the appearance of *In the Forests*, Melnikov "described [Old Believer] communities wonderfully—but he destroyed them even better."[94] Partly as a result of his efforts, isolated populations like those of *In the Forests* were being drawn into various transformative relationships, participating more and more in the modern economy, with its emphasis on boundary-crossing, exchange, and circulation. And a place that enters into money transactions will have a hard time choosing to remain isolated because money *penetrates*, dissolving things into abstractions. This is so not only because trade and traffic let the outside in, but also because (as we saw in *An Ordinary Story*) the money economy can abolish any object's "qualitative physical difference and specific history"—all that is local, material, fixed, and specific, like *this one village*'s traditional handi-work—by rendering it liquid and exchangeable. "The moment of exchange of a material commodity into money universalizes and abstracts qualitative physical difference and specific history":[95] in other words, the modern economy poses a threat to the kind of particularity that regionalists like Gatsitskii and (sometimes) Melnikov deem most valuable.[96]

Leskov's Un-Centered Space

Nikolai Leskov shares with Melnikov and Gatsitskii a rejection of, or simply a lack of interest in, theories that would claim to synthesize details into overarch-ing metanarratives. Yet Leskov is by no means a regionalist in the sense that they are: Melnikov's oeuvre is deeply rooted in a single and carefully delimited region, while Leskov's texts range all over Russia. Thus while Leskov's symbolic geography departs just as significantly from the *stolitsa-provintsiia* binary (almost none of his texts are organized around these two poles), its challenge to the binary takes different forms. Some of his characters originate in specific Russian towns with specific identities and histories, as is announced in titles like "The Tale of Cross-eyed Lefty from Tula and the Steel Flea" and "Lady Macbeth of Mtsensk," while other titles underscore the far-away nature of their settings ("On the Edge of the World"). *Cathedral Folk* takes place in an town with a vaguely archetypal name (*Stargorod*, "Old City"), a location that is—like the Volga region of Melnikov's *In the Forests*—simultaneously imaginary and situated in a specific part of the Russian empire (in this case the western borderlands), and where the characters and the culture strike us as simultaneously old-fashioned and representative of "real" Russia. Finally, and perhaps most significantly, many of Leskov's characters inhabit in-between or far-off spots, spending plenty of time in places where they rarely think about the distant metropole ("The Sealed Angel," "The Enchanted Wanderer"). When they pass through what we would think of as a center, it means little to them: "and so we made it to Moscow, but all I can say about that is, Woe unto thee, Moscow!" (Melnikov's characters say the same: "What's your Moscow to us? . . . Thrice-damned Babylon!").[97] Finally, they often travel not from center to periphery or vice versa, but from one "peripheral" place to another.

In the terms articulated by Vladimir Paperny in *Culture Two* (*Kul'tura "Dva"*), Leskov's symbolic geography recalls that of the early Soviet period, the 1920s, rather than the 1930s: like writers of the 1920s, Leskov assumes "a spatial para-digm asserting horizontality, a centrifugal dynamic, [and] mobility" (as opposed to the 1930s' emphasis on "the vertical, centripetal, static, symmetrical, and hi-erarchical").[98] Because Leskov's narratives tend to ignore not only the *stolitsa-provintsiia* opposition but also other familiar binaries (e.g., east vs. west, Russia vs. Europe), his characters' movements tend not to imply hierarchical relationships among places. What happens in Moscow is not necessarily going to be more meaningful than what happens anywhere else: there is no assumption of semiotic entropy as you move away from a center. By contrast, even the symbolic geography of Leskov's younger contemporary Chekhov, who was famously well traveled within Russia and famously adept at representing regions and social milieus left untouched by most writers, reveals a far more conventional view of Russian space; indeed, as I discuss in chapter 10, Chekhov's provincial characters are often wholly defined by a painful awareness of their distance from a center.

One of Leskov's lesser-known stories, "Voyage with a Nihilist" (1882), illuminates these issues with striking clarity in just a few pages.[99] The plot is slight. While traveling overnight on a decidedly minor train line ("a little branch of the railway . . . far removed from the great world"), a small group of passengers manage to convince themselves that one of their compartment mates is a "nihilist" and that the package on the seat across from him must be a bomb. In conformity with what readers had already learned to expect from stories set in train compartments, Leskov gives us a conventionally disparate group of passengers: an officer, a deacon, a merchant, a Jew, the unidentified narrator, and the supposed nihilist. The nihilist repeatedly declines to stow the package sitting across from him, offering no explanation beyond the words "I prefer not to"; his refusal leads his fellow travelers to elaborate various implausible theories about his identity. In the end it turns out that the package in question does not belong to the supposed nihilist but to the Jewish tailor; the nihilist is in reality a government official who is about to be respectfully received at the station by "his excellency."

Seen from one point of view, "Voyage with a Nihilist" might be read simply as an addition to the long list of canonical nineteenth-century narratives in which at least part of the action takes place in a train compartment (*Winter Notes on Summer Impressions, Anna Karenina, The Idiot, Kreutzer Sonata*, various Chekhov stories, and so on). Clearly, for writers the train is a godsend: imagining passengers thrown together in a confined but public space was a convenient way of imagining the heterogeneous populations of larger social collectives. And as a venue for the kind of chance encounters that generate narrative, the train compartment was as useful to nineteenth-century writers as the roadside inn was to story-tellers of previous centuries.[100] But Leskov, unlike his contemporaries, rarely incorporated train travel into his texts, and "Voyage with a Nihilist" does not conform to our expectations of how railroads function in narrative.

The symbolic geography that underlies Leskov's worldview and that of his characters helps explain why trains do not play an especially significant role in his work. Many of Leskov's stories are populated by wanderers (like the eponymous "Enchanted Wanderer")—and trains are not made for wandering. For a character whose entire life is built largely on the act of walking around—as for the narrator of "The Sealed Angel," who asks, "where didn't we walk together? Seems we walked all over Russia"—railroads make little sense.[101] Trains are made for goal-directed travel, for moving from one point to another in a way that allows one to skip over everything in between.[102] Leskov says as much quite explicitly in the prologue to "The Pearl Necklace": remarking on the supposed impoverishment of "invention [and] plot" in contemporary literature, Leskov's narrator attributes this decline to the spread of railways. Trains are "very useful when it comes to trade but harmful when it comes to artistic literature," he says, because when everything is "slipping by," travelers have no time to form "strong impressions."[103] It is the goal-directed nature of train travel that links it to the modern economy, making it the preferred mode of transport for capitalists like *Oblomov*'s Stolz, who is closely associated with railroads.

Railroads are also implicated in modern ideological conflicts. Like Stolz, the revolutionaries in Dostoevsky's *Demons* are moving to *get somewhere*, taking advantage of the railroad's grid in order to travel purposefully and quickly from one anonymous city to another. "Voyage with a Nihilist" was published at a time when ideologues of various stripes were preoccupied with technologies of transportation, a time when trains were strongly associated both with economic modernization and with political instability and terrorism.[104] Yet despite the fact that real-life revolutionaries were keen to blow up trains, Leskov, writing just a year after the tsar's assassination, gently mocks this link. In this sense "Voyage with a Nihilist" suggests a certain disinterest in big ideas like World Revolution, ideas that are often generated in the center (the capitals) and shipped out to the periphery by trains and other modern modes of dissemination. (Leskov did care enough about politics to write two somewhat garbled "anti-nihilist" novels, but it is perhaps telling that these texts are little read, and both are judged to be among his least successful works.)[105]

If Leskov's characters happen to register the fact that they are located on a periphery (and often they do not register it), this means almost nothing to them—because they are capable of envisioning relationships among peripheral places that have nothing to do with these places' relationships to Moscow or Petersburg. This brings us back to trains: if you worry about being on the periphery, you think about trains because they are what connect you to a *hub*. Leskov's characters spend virtually no time thinking about trains or hubs, just as they do not sit on their provincial porches and repeat "to Moscow! To Moscow!" the way that Chekhov's Prozorovs do in *Three Sisters*. Here once again Leskov's work recalls the early Soviet period: one thinks of literary celebrations of the Turksib railway, a major railroad line notable for "[linking] two peripheries independent of any historic centers."[106] In New York City subway terms, if Leskov's characters have to take a train, they would prefer one that carries you from Brooklyn to Queens without taking you through Manhattan.

Hence the unusual nature of rail travel as depicted in "Voyage with a Nihilist." In nineteenth-century fiction the railroad stands for technology, modernity, speed, rationality, westernization, spatial integration, economic progress—in short, what Dostoevsky saw as the Crystal Palace-ization of the world, harbinger of an often catastrophic modernity. Leskov, by contrast, pointedly de-emphasizes the train's modernity: train travel in "Voyage with a Nihilist" is *not* speedy, organized, comfortable, orderly, or predictable.[107] This "little side-branch" of the railway, the narrator tells us, is "not even finished yet"; the trains do not run on time; they stop and start; it is freezing cold in the compartment and there is no buffet. Leskov, in short, is not interested in railroads as an emblem of modernization, social change, or radical politics, and the characters in "Voyage with a Nihilist" might as well be in a post carriage. His lack of interest in modernization metanarratives (or in any metanarratives) goes along with his refusal to take the center more seriously than other places. And what we might describe as his *uncentered* geography relates to the "minor" genres in which he chose to work, as well as to the major genre he generally avoided: his reason for rejecting what he called "the unnatural form of the novel" was precisely that it he believed it to demand "*the concentration of everything around one main center*."[108]

Furthermore, I would argue that this refusal of a center helps explain Leskov's notoriously problematic place in the Russian canon. Leskov has never been consistently acknowledged as a writer of the "highest" order. Scholars who write about him outside of Russia can be made to feel that they should defend this choice, which they tend to do by asserting his enduring popularity among Russian readers. Given his reliance on wordplay and *skaz* (stories told in the chatty and often substandard language of a "simple" person), it is not hard to see why Leskov is not widely read in translation. But even in Russian scholarship, as one of Leskov's staunchest defenders concedes, he is not really placed "*among* the major nineteenth-century writers," but instead "*near*" to them.[109] Might Leskov's refusal to "[concentrate] everything around one main center" be part of what makes his work resistant to being certified as "high," even as it is lauded for being quintessentially Russian? From Leskov's own time until today, critics have insisted on his ur-Russian quality; in Gorky's words, Leskov is "Russian through and through."[110] This ur-Russianness has always been linked to the fact that his stories are set in *provintsiia*, which in Leskov's work is certainly not a Gogolian wasteland of anonymous gorod Ns but rather, as these same critics constantly tell us, "the very heart of Russia."[111]

In such characterizations, it seems that Leskov's work is being defended not quite for its own sake, but instead as a crucial raw material. Tsvetaeva calls his writing "a native source"; Dmitry Likhachev claims that without him "Russian literature would have been deprived of a significant share of its national coloring"; Alexander Gorelov locates Leskov's value in his "portrayal of an Old Russia [*Rus'*] that is disappearing"; Kuzmin calls him "a treasury of Russian speech."[112] Exactly the same kind of language recurs in assessments of Melnikov, who has often been treated as a repository, "an unparalleled imaginative compendium" crucial to various other (higher) artists' "quests for aesthetic resources."[113] And in our own time Melnikov is once again being described as an "encyclopedia," now with emphasis on his value for those who would embrace a "return" to "Christian" and "family values." Finally, even more than Leskov, who, as we have seen, has been placed "near" the most canonical authors instead of "among" them, Melnikov is generally assumed to have produced what D. S. Mirsky describes as "not really first-class literature."[114]

Leskov and Melnikov are to the high literary canon as *provintsiia* is to *stolitsa*: eternally secondary and absolutely essential; the symbolic repository of timeless, static meaning; a "nucleus of typicality."[115] Like *provintsiia*, they exist to be mined for resources (they are "a native source"). In cultural terms, what is mined in *provintsiia*/Leskov/Melnikov is not only the raw material of meaning, but also an authenticity that is no longer available elsewhere ("an Old Russia that is disappearing"). As we saw in the Gatsitskii-Mordovtsev debate, it is generally assumed that once such resources have been extracted, they must then be processed in the capitals—or, to take literature's equivalent of the capitals, by the "truly great" writers—if they are ever to be transmuted into the highest kind of knowledge or art. It is not difficult to see how such a schema could work against Leskov's and Melnikov's achievement of first-rung canonical status: this is a symbolic system that makes writers like them essential, but never primary. It is the price they pay for being genuinely interested in peripheral places for their own sake.

And here we can return to Nabokov's remarks dismissing regionalism as the quintessentially "boring" literature. "I always detested regional literature full of quaint old-timers and imitated pronunciation," he says, calling writers like Grigorovich, Korolenko, and Mamin-Sibiriak "stupefying bores," "comparable to American 'regional writers.'"[116] To call such writing "boring" is to say that it cannot be situated in a discourse that would allow someone like Nabokov to see it as Great Art. From the point of view of a Nabokov, regionalist art (like women's writing, which is frequently deemed "boring" too) lacks the right kind of history, the rich context that is a necessary (if not sufficient) condition of being seen as truly "high" (because somewhat paradoxically, being enmeshed in history and tradition is what allows a work of art to "transcend" time and place). Writers like Nabokov represent "the 'old' modernist intellectual—fundamentally a *déraciné*—[who] saw literature as 'a strategy of permanent exile,' as a fundamental dis-placement": again, the opposite of regionalism.[117]

The deracinated cosmopolitan intellectual—whose standards, it seems, still inform our own—wants art to be universal (which helps explain why Milan Kundera, another proud *déraciné*, goes so far as to claim that reading a work of great literature, a work that has attained to universality, *in translation* is every bit as good as reading it in the language in which it was written).[118] Nabokov and Kundera, Brodsky, and Conrad: such multilingual modernist prodigies who made their homes in art (sometimes having been forced to do so by historical events) tend to cast specificities as limitations, and to see these limitations as versions of provincialism. It is partly as a result of their enduring influence that Boris Eikhenbaum locates both Melnikov and Leskov in a "minor line" (*mladshaia liniia*) of nineteenth-century Russian writers, a tradition he describes as "crushed and forgotten"—or as Mordovtsev describes the provinces, "widowed in all respects"—"in the age of Dostoevsky and Tolstoy."[119]

· CHAPTER NINE ·

Centering and Decentering in Dostoevsky and Tolstoy

La province n'existe pas par elle-même.
—Honoré de Balzac, 1841

Even though we're provincials and we're most certainly worthy of
pity for that, nonetheless we know that so far in the world nothing
so new has happened that we would weep for having missed it.
—Fyodor Dostoevsky, 1872

"All these new ideas, reforms, and theories—it's all reached us out in the provinces, but to see everything and see it clearly, one must be in Petersburg": thus does a character in *Crime and Punishment* explain what he hopes to gain from coming to the capital.[1] And judging from Dostoevsky's own career, he concurred: as much as he professed his love for the common people or hinted at the spiritual riches to be found in the Russian countryside, he showed little inclination to remove himself from the center—that is, from Petersburg. Not only was the capital the seat of print culture and state power, it also seems to have struck him as the only *point of view* from which one might "see everything and see it clearly." Dostoevsky would have agreed with Jules Michelet's description of Paris as "the center [that] knows itself and knows all the rest," the only place where the provinces can "see themselves" and thus learn to "love and admire themselves in a superior form."[2]

Tolstoy's symbolic geography is radically different: for him the capital—any capital—is no place for seeing clearly. Tolstoy's family property and noble lineage afforded him his own center, the estate at Iasnaia Poliana, where he felt supremely at home and which provided him a stable vantage point from which he would always view the world. Dostoevsky's background connected him to a significantly lower and more precarious stratum of the gentry, which perhaps helps explain why gentry estates rarely appear as meaningful "centers" in his work. With no Iasnaia Poliana to retire to, he made his way to the capital—the undisputed center of Russian intellectual and especially journalistic life—where he proceeded to make a name for himself. Here the new (to Russia) mechanisms of print culture allowed him to publish works that could then be distributed far and wide: so even as Dostoevsky's texts sometimes critique the idea of a center that serves as an organizing Logos, making meanings for and dispensing them to passive "outliers," in his own life he was careful to locate himself in such a center so as to make use of its power to spread ideas.

This chapter begins with a brief look at Tolstoy's symbolic geography, an imaginary landscape that is by no means structured around a *provintsiia/stolitsa* binary and is thus an exception to the rule that is the subject of this book. The overview of Tolstoy serves as background to a closer analysis of Dostoevsky's geography, an analysis focused on *Demons*—a novel in which both the *provintsiia/stolitsa* binary and the trope of Russia's empty provinces take on great determinative power. If Dostoevsky at times recapitulates familiar images of the provinces, in *Demons* he also makes ideological use of them in ways that are strikingly original, dwelling on the essentialized difference between center and periphery in order to underscore how provincial isolation fosters a dangerous kind of intellectual vulnerability.

Tolstoy's Uncentered Heartland

The comparative insignificance of the *provintsiia/stolitsa* opposition in Tolstoy's world is perhaps best exemplified by *The Death of Ivan Ilych* (1886). Tolstoy's always-already-dying state servitor begins his life in Petersburg, advances his career by moving around to various provincial postings, and finally secures a position back in the imperial capital. While Ivan's return to Petersburg is associated with his ascent in the bureaucracy, his life there is fundamentally no different from his life in provincial places. Indeed one must read fairly closely to notice when he finally moves (back) to Petersburg, and neither in the story's opening lines nor elsewhere in the narrative is the location made definite. Literature has taught us to expect that an ambitious provincial bureaucrat (particularly one who, like Ivan Ilych, is originally from Petersburg and is married to a status-conscious wife) will have his eyes on that prize, the imperial capital, above all others—indeed, that he will be obsessed with the capital. Such expectations are not fulfilled in Tolstoy's text. Ivan Ilych has spent years in provincial posts, but he never seems to be intent on moving back to the capital: so uninterested is Tolstoy in the *provintsiia-stolitsa* binary that he is willing to make his bureaucrat protagonist almost implausibly indifferent to geography.

Which is not to say that Tolstoy's work neglects the capitals: Moscow and Petersburg feature prominently in *War and Peace* and *Anna Karenina*, novels that contributed significantly to the distinctive mythologies of both cities. Here Tolstoy helped to consolidate images that had taken shape in literature over the preceding decades in a series of texts, which often defined Moscow and Petersburg by comparing them to each other. *Eugene Onegin*, for instance, sets homey Moscow against worldly Petersburg, and essays by Gogol, Herzen, and Belinsky juxtapose the two capitals in order to bring the salient features of each into sharp relief. (As I have noted before, the incessantly recurring juxtaposition of Moscow and Petersburg seems to have reinforced the tendency to collapse everything outside of them into the category of "the provinces.") Tolstoy, too, sets the two capitals against each other, but he almost never implies comparisons between the (blank) provinces and the (meaningful) capitals.

War and Peace begins in the two capitals, but it soon moves outside of them. This "decentralizing design," as Ani Kokobobo writes, reflects the historical events of 1812, when "the regions of Smolensk, Yaroslavl, and other cities [came to] embody the image of Russia as a larger whole"—thereby making the point that neither Moscow nor Petersburg was capable of *representing* all of Russia. In fact Napoleon's grave error is to assume that Moscow—what he calls "the Asiatic capital of this great empire, the sacred city of Alexander's people"—stands in for the entire country, whereas Kutuzov, by contrast, "realizes that Russia is greater than one city."[3] Hence the "progressive decentralization" Kokobobo traces in Tolstoy's novel, as we follow "characters originating in Russia's centers [who] relocate themselves to other parts of the country in order to escape the French invasion."[4]

War and Peace makes explicit the symbolic content of the nation's real physical space, and this space is definitely not blank *provintsiia*. Our attention is directed to Russia's actual geography: specific rivers crossed, plains surveyed, redoubts fortified, cities taken and abandoned, etc. Clearly Tolstoy is taking part in the process by which the events of 1812 were used to "[fill Russian] geography with symbolic content," as one historian has put it[5]—a process that becomes visible if we plot on a map the many place names that Tolstoy mentions. In addition to a significant cluster of place indicators in Austria (representing the 1805 campaign), the most striking feature of such a map would be the great density of references in the large area around Moscow: here the map is so crowded with "pins" that we cannot even read the place names. What this tells us is what we already know—namely, that the main sites of the 1812 campaign are the book's symbolic focal point. Finally, we can clearly see an east-west *line* of references, the line that traces the French army's advance and retreat across the continent.

As this line on the map suggests, a narrative that focuses on an invading army and on efforts to repulse the invaders will probably be shaped by a certain type of symbolic geography. This geography is likely to reveal an acute awareness of borders and borderlands, and to pay close attention to actual distances: in *War and Peace* we will find nothing like *Dead Souls'* baffling assertion that the story's setting is "not far from both capitals."[6] Furthermore, any story about driving out invaders is unlikely to leave much of the nation's space blank and unworthy of attention (an elision that the provinces-capitals binary tends to encourage). A war story cannot afford to assume that any space is necessarily going to be insignificant, because in a war, almost *anyplace* (for instance, Borodino) might prove to be the most important place of all. Tolstoy makes a point of telling us that a day before the great battle, his characters do not know how to pronounce the name of this still-obscure town (which, as Saul Morson points out, is like an American saying "Gettysville" instead of "Gettysburg," or not knowing how to pronounce "Antietam").[7] *War and Peace* reminds us that Borodino was not *yet* an iconic place name, radiant with national meaning and heroic memory.

The anonymous provincial towns that serve as ground zero of provinciality in other authors' work do not feature in Tolstoy's most famous novels. When Tolstoy does depict provincial towns he gives us their names; their *provintsial'nost'* is not emphasized—that is, they do not serve to showcase a monotonous, derivative, or second-rate culture. For instance when *War and Peace* takes us briefly to Voronezh, what happens there (matchmaking for Nikolai and Maria) is every bit as significant as what happens anywhere else. If Voronezh is marked as "provincial" in the sense of backward, it is so only in Nikolai's own thinking: here he adopts an uncharacteristically free manner of dancing, Tolstoy tells us, because he "feels the need to surprise them with something unusual, something that they would have to accept as being the usual thing in the capitals despite being unknown to them in the provinces [*v provintsii*]."[8] And when *Anna Karenina*'s Levin goes to Kashin for *zemstvo* elections, the town itself is left virtually undescribed; all the focus is on Levin and the other noble landowners who have converged there to vote, and who can in no sense be construed as provincials.

In place of the empty provinces trope, Tolstoy's major works typically imagine a decentralized agricultural heartland organized around a number of gentry estates, with the estates serving as focal points toward which nearby surrounding areas direct their resources and attention. The word "surrounding" is important: we might imagine the geography implied by Tolstoy's texts as a continuous and relatively homogeneous stretch of space punctuated by dots of concentrated significance and activity. Surrounding these dots are tracts of rural land that are organically connected to the estates. The estate-dots are not exactly "nodes" since they are not usually represented as connecting points in a network; instead of emphasizing how these places are linked to each other by roads or other lines of communication, Tolstoy tends to depict each estate as a more or less self-sufficient world in a more or less symbiotic relationship with the directly adjacent countryside.[9]

Tolstoy's gentry estates seem "real" in the sense that they are carefully drawn places capable of fostering genuine (organic, nonimitative) culture, but we feel little need to locate them on a map. Except in *War and Peace* when the French army is approaching, in general we remain only vaguely conscious of precisely where in European Russia the various Rostovs, Bolkonskys, Levins, and Oblonskys have their homes. It is possible to figure out the estates' approximate locations—we can establish, for instance, that in *War and Peace* Bald Hills is further from Moscow than is Bogucharovo—but the information is not crucial. The same holds for *Anna Karenina*: here as in *War and Peace*, every estate is a distinct mini-civilization, but the distinctiveness has little to do with location (and once again it is instructive to recall the American literary tradition, in which it is impossible to imagine a generic "farm" that could be in either, say, Kansas or New Hampshire). Thus Tolstoy gives us a degree of geographic and topographic specificity, but instead of being pressed into the service of imagining regional particularity, specificity is used to emphasize national unity. In other words, this is not regionalism.

Tolstoyan estates are often not especially lavish, but they are almost always the locus of an authentic and coherent culture; they are often inward-looking, but not exactly isolated and usually not sealed off from "the world outside." His Rostovs and Bolkonskys and Levins move back and forth between estate and capital (something that Gogol's provincial gentry, for instance, never do); both worlds are thoroughly real and accessible to Tolstoy's characters, though they may prefer one or the other. Even his most modest and unsophisticated estates, the ones that are indeed isolated and insular, cannot be called provincial. The landed noblemen who inhabit them, whether rich or poor, feel themselves to be utterly *at home* in these places, and they are not comparing themselves to a distant standard (and as we have seen, anxious comparison is a prerequisite of provinciality). An extreme instance of this authenticity would be the tiny, self-contained world of "Uncle's" estate in *War and Peace* (books VII and VIII), a place where imitation is inconceivable because there can be nothing from "outside" available for imitation in a place whose culture is so thoroughly constant, homogeneous, and internally consistent. Even when Tolstoy represents an estate falling into inauthenticity—as does Anna's and Vronsky's English-inflected "play farm" toward the end of *Anna Karenina*—it does not become provincial in the sense of being behind or culturally incoherent. Instead it becomes just self-consciously modern, too deracinated and flimsy to serve as a setting for what Tolstoy deems real life.

Both *War and Peace* and *Anna Karenina* imply a close accord between the peasantry and the traditional gentry, strongly suggesting that whatever essence the two classes supposedly have in common is the basis of an "organic" Russian culture—and what is organic is the opposite of what is provincial. In other words, Tolstoy finesses the relationship between peasant/rural culture and estate culture (or to put it differently, between pastoral and provinciality) in order to draw on peasant authenticity, and peasant permanence, for his own ends. In order to be at risk of being provincial, you must be striving to be modern; unlike someone who is adhering to a supposedly timeless code (as do peasants and genuine noblemen, in Tolstoy's view), someone who tries to keep up with the times is bound to fail at least on occasion, at which point he or she has no "authenticity" to fall back on. As I have discussed in previous chapters, the very phenomenon of provinciality is closely tied to modernity and progress—and Tolstoy did not view modernity and progress as ideals. In his major fiction, a lack of interest in provincial towns goes along with a lack of interest in most of the distinctly modernizing types who were in reality transforming Russia in the post-Reform era, like *raznochintsy*, merchant capitalists, members of the professions, and other elements of the messy "middle strata" that shaped urban life.[10]

Tolstoy's various paeans to traditional class hierarchy (most notably in *Childhood* and *War and Peace*) seem to be motivated as much by revulsion at the adulterated nature of modern social categories as they are by simple nostalgia for the past. His more admirable characters tend to register displeasure when they notice what they take to be modernity's unpalatable incursions into peasants' lives, as for example in his early work "Morning of a Landowner," when a flashy, modern reproduction of a general's portrait in a peasant's hut bodes ill. Peasants are supposed to stay peasants; as long as they do so, they certainly cannot be provincials (though they are subject to other vices). In Tolstoy's view staying the same is a large part of what defines peasants, and ideally noblemen as well; there is nothing less appropriate to a supposedly timeless essence than following changing "fashions" or generally mixing it up in any way.

In the post-emancipation world of *Anna Karenina*, Levin is disgusted by the social indeterminateness of a smarmy upstart merchant, who is, in class terms, neither fish nor fowl. At the end of the novel when Oblonsky goes to work for the railway, we are meant to see his decision as a capitulation to a mongrelized and ethic-less modernity, a cloudy medium into which the essence of Russia's old nobility will be dissolved. Levin, by contrast, insists that he himself is something pure and apart. Consider for example his proud retort to the accusation that he is a "reactionary": "I've never really thought about who I am. I am Konstantin Levin, that's all."[11] In other words, Levin naturalizes his class position, presenting it as an immutable fact that he does not even have to think about (not true, of course:

Levin thinks about his class position all the time). For Tolstoy, it seems, peasants are fine, noblemen are fine, even priests are fine: but *mixtures* are not so fine. And mixtures are the stuff that both modernity and provinciality are made of.

Dostoevsky and the "Fantastic Center"

Tolstoy asks us to pay equal attention to a wide variety of Russian places: his texts generally discourage the semiotic privileging of the capitals, pushing back against the familiar tendency to allow centers to become oversaturated with meaning at the expense of other locations. Dostoevsky, by contrast, is much more likely to reproduce the symbolic geography we have seen over and over from the 1830s on—an imaginary landscape in which significance and authority are so intensely concentrated in the capitals that the rest of Russian space risks being reduced to blankness. As early as his feuilletons of 1847, Dostoevsky assumes what we might call the radical centrality of Russia's capital, a quasi-magical location that is also a force, a mysterious power capable of bringing together Russianness, modernity, and the future. In the Russian capital, he writes,

> with every step, you hear, feel and see the contemporary moment and the idea of the present moment. . . . [Petersburg] is still in the process of becoming, of creating itself; its future is in an idea; but the idea belongs to Peter I, and it is taking form . . . not just in the Petersburg swamp but throughout *all of Russia, all of which lives by Petersburg alone.* Everyone has already felt in themselves the force and the blessing of the Petrine direction [*napravleniia*]. . . . Therefore all are beginning to live. . . . Everything lives and is supported by Petersburg alone. (18:26)

"All of Russia, all of which lives by Petersburg alone": here we could not be further from the geography of *War and Peace*, with its emphatically decentralized geography and its attention to local realities.

Only in fleeting moments does Dostoevsky seem willing to critique such a worldview. For instance, toward the very end of his life, in an 1881 installment of *Diary of a Writer*, he appears to contradict his earlier remarks on the all-powerful and all-encompassing nature of the Russian center. Railing against those who would take Petersburg to represent all of Russia, even if the capital might believe itself capable of doing so, he writes:

> Petersburg has got to the point where it definitively considers itself to be all of Russia. . . . In this sense Petersburg is following the example set by Paris, despite the fact that it doesn't resemble Paris at all! Paris took shape historically in such a way that it swallowed up all of France, the whole significance of her political and social

life, her whole import. Take Paris away from France, and what's left?—nothing but a geographic definition. Some of us imagine that it's the same here as in Paris, that in Petersburg all of Russia has been brought together. But Petersburg is by no means Russia. . . . Take one look outside Petersburg and you'll see the ocean of the Russian land, an ocean vast and bottomless. (27:14)

Here he seems to edge toward an understanding of Russian geography that might allow what is local and specific to exist meaningfully on its own terms ("Petersburg is by no means Russia")—but a page or two later he quickly retreats from this possibility:

Our people [*narod nash*], in their various locales [*i po mestam sidia*], will say exactly the same thing they would say were they all together—for they are one. Whether they are scattered or brought together, they are one because their spirit is one. Each place [*mestnost'*] would contribute only its local particularity, while on the whole, in general, everything would be in agreement and unified. (27:21)

Yes, he sees value in talking to the people (*narod*) scattered across Russia's far-flung locales ("locally, in district towns," etc.): but if you investigate these places, he says, you will simply find *the same thing* again and again ("on the whole, in general, everything would be in agreement and unified"). "Local particularities" are acknowledged, but the provinces/capital binary is preserved, even reinforced. Having urged his readers to "look outside Petersburg" for the real Russia, Dostoevsky immediately assures us that the search should not take long, since every Russian place is sure to recapitulate the same idea.

Russian *unity* was a key value for Dostoevsky, who claimed elsewhere in the *Diary* (in 1876) that Europeans might well envy the "force of political unity" (*sila politicheskogo edinstva*) that characterized Russia (22:111). And such unity seems to have presupposed for him a high degree of centralization. Dostoevsky's faith in centralization finds expression in his response to the Gatsitskii-Mordovtsev exchange of 1875 (analyzed in the previous chapter), a debate concerning the proper role of provincial (or "regional," *oblastnaia*) culture in Russia's intellectual and cultural life. After the Petersburg journalist Mordovtsev made a case for "the law of centralization" ("it is natural that everything in the provinces be drawn to the centers"),[12] Gatsitskii and other provincial intellectuals responded with arguments for decentralization (the nation is only as strong as its "numberless" regional centers, and real progress assumes the "widest possible *dissemination*" of enlightenment).[13] When Dostoevsky weighs in with "A Regional New Word"—"*Oblastnoe novoe slovo*," an 1876 entry in *Diary of a Writer*—he comes down firmly on the side of centralization. Though he acknowledges the provinces' desire to "virtually emancipate themselves from the capitals" and "say their own word," he nonetheless downplays the importance of regional uniqueness in favor of Russian unity. The particularities of regions will be important only because they will confirm that "in each place throughout Russia, all of Russia exists" (23:6–7). The relationship of the provinces to Russia is at best synecdochic: the provinces are worthy of representation when a provincial part can stand in for the Russian whole.

This is not to say that Dostoevsky fails to see provincial places as integral parts of Russia. In *Diary of a Writer*, for instance, he often turns his gaze to the provinces. Many of the *Diary*'s entries are devoted to aggregating and (re)disseminating information from provincial publications and letters received from far-flung readers— but the aggregating, interpreting, and re-disseminating of provincial information is being done in and by a center. Here Dostoevsky is not so different from those educated Russians who had long been lamenting the center's dearth of knowledge about the provinces and calling for information-gathering efforts to render these places more useful to the centralized state, a phenomenon I have discussed in earlier chapters. His approach, like theirs, assumes both that the provinces have something essential to contribute to the life of the nation and that this contribution can only be made via the capital. As Luzhin says in *Crime and Punishment*, "to see everything and see it clearly, one must be in Petersburg" (6:115).

Dostoevsky's tendency to view centralization as key to Russia's strength does not prevent him from recognizing the distortions that inevitably attend such centralization. The risks posed by the center's hyperconcentration of authority and power are made especially clear in *Demons*, a novel that reflects on how an intensely centralized view of the nation's geographic space affects and in fact deforms Russian ways of thinking, especially political thinking. Here Dostoevsky both reproduces and critiques a conceptual geography that reduces provincial Russia to a meaningless blank or an appendage of the capitals. By taking an infamous real-life Moscow event, the so-called "Nechaev Affair," and moving it to a nameless provincial city, *Demons* responds to an imaginary geography that can locate meaning only in a center, whatever or wherever the center may be.

Every contemporary reader would be expected to know about the events Dostoevsky used as *Demons*' point of departure, and to know that these events took place in Moscow. In November of 1869 the revolutionary Sergei Nechaev, recently returned from Europe, incited a group of young radicals at Moscow's Petrovsky Agricultural Academy to kill a fellow member of their political circle.[14] The murder took place on the grounds of the academy. But *Demons* is set not in Moscow but rather in what the elusive and decidedly provincial narrator constantly refers to as *u nas*, meaning "in our province" or "in our (provincial) town." Where exactly is this town supposed to be, and what does it matter? A few very general features of the unidentified provincial city recall Tver, where Dostoevsky spent part of the year 1860: the town in *Demons* is divided by a river and there is a textile factory on the outskirts.[15] Such, however, would seem to be the extent of the topographical correspondence. Tver's specific topography, its monuments, history, and regional character all fail to play any important role in the narrative. When Dostoevsky's narrator remarks that "our town" has "a big marketplace" and "a decrepit church of the Nativity that is a most notable antiquity" (10:252), he is saying nothing that might not be said about many, many Russian towns. Thus the setting of *Demons* is not Tver in the way that, for example, the setting of Nikolai Leskov's "Levsha" is Tula: at most *Demons* might be said to refer to a kind of Tver-in-quotation-marks, another quintessentially average town evoking the average-ness of provincial places generally.[16]

In fact on the novel's first page, the narrator introduces "our town" as a place that "up till now was not remarkable for anything" (10:7)—thereby signaling to us that *Demons* makes explicit what will be implicit in, say, the town of Skotoprigonevsk in *Brothers Karamazov*. For while the setting of *Brothers Karamazov* is given a name, it is no more specifically characterized than is *Demons'* anonymous and imaginary *gubernskii gorod*. Like the setting of *Demons*, Skotoprigonevsk is de-fined largely by its averageness, its ability to stand in for any provincial place.[17] Dostoevsky seems to have based Skotoprigonevsk to some extent on the town of Staraia Russa, but in *Brothers Karamazov* we learn no more about Staraia Russa *per se* than we do about Tver in *Demons*, simply because neither novel is much concerned with the specificities of life in a *particular* Russian place. Besides this averageness, the other defining characteristic of both towns is isolation (the narra-tor of *Brothers Karamazov* tells us that Skotoprigonevsk is seventy or eighty versts from the nearest railroad station, which makes it even more isolated than the set-ting of *Demons*)[18]—and *Demons* will make explicit the fact that provincial isola-tion encourages ideological vulnerability.

Like others before him, Dostoevsky is relying on the trope of the provincial backwater to make an argument about Russia itself. The point is not that the be-nighted characters in *Demons* are provincials; the point is that all of Russia has placed itself in a provincial relationship to European culture, as is illustrated by the radicals' wholesale acceptance of imported ideas. Moving the action from Moscow to the provinces serves to underscore this fact. Because provincial cul-ture can so convincingly be represented as derivative and meager, it is not hard to understand why it puts up no resistance to ideas that come in from outside, thereby allowing these ideas to run amok. In this way the provincial town simply stands in for the nation as a whole; as one character asserts, "Russia is now . . . the place in the whole world where anything you like can happen with the least resistance" (10:287).[19] Were *Demons* set in Moscow, it would be more difficult for Dostoevsky to convey the power of the spurious *idée fixe* that animates nearly all of the characters, simply because in Moscow these characters would have had to contend with the metropolis's proliferation of competing ideologies and its myriad claims on their attention (witness what happens to Raskolnikov's thinking when he tries to pursue one grand idea to its conclusion in Petersburg). Certainly if *Demons* were set in the capital, Dostoevsky would have to work harder to make the grandly general points about morality, Russianness and Western influence that he is clearly interested in making.

The placelessness of *Demons'* provincial place relies on a symbolic geography in which only the center has the power to confer meaning on the chaotic phenomena of life. In this novel as in so many other texts, the provinces are a place where it is hard to make sense of things, a place where meanings are more likely to dissolve than to coalesce. Dostoevsky's static provincial town, animated only by the promiscuous circulation of rumor and gossip, clearly recalls Gogol's in various *gorod Ns*: all are characterized by what *Demons'* narrator calls "mental anarchy" (10:509).[20] Like the characters in *Dead Souls* and *The Inspector General*, Dostoevsky's provincials keep their eyes trained on a distant center (whether Petersburg, Moscow, or Paris) because there is nothing local that signifies. In Dostoevsky's text as in Gogol's, provincial society does of course have its local mores (*gubernskie poriadki*, the narrator calls them; 10:234), but the self-identified *gubernskii gorod* never forgets its own provinciality, its subordination to and dependence on some far-off central place.

One result of knowing oneself to be provincial is a constant readiness to take orders from someplace else. Virtually every character in *Demons* is convinced that real life is happening somewhere far away, somewhere "out there." Even more important, all are convinced that for those who are in the provinces, meaning can accrue only to actions that are sanctioned or directed from afar by some "central" intelligence or force. The provincial radicals, we are told, are always ready to change their minds "at the first hint from our progressive corners in the capital" (10:28). Thus Pyotr Verkhovensky gains power in large part by associating himself, in the minds of the provincials, with a place that he constantly refers to as "there." For example, in the key conversations in which he manages to manipulate first the dim-witted provincial governor and then his own followers, Verkhovensky repeats various forms of the word "there" over and over. To the governor he says, "no one *there* has yet issued any orders . . . I have not yet taken upon myself any such orders from *there*. . . . I could have chosen . . . to fly straight over *there*, that is there where I first gave my explanations," and so on.[21] In this brief passage forms denoting location or motion to or from "there" (*tam*, *tuda*, and *ottuda*) occur seven times, and five times they are actually in italics, as part of Verkhovensky's successful attempt to convince the governor that he (Verkhovensky) is allied with the powers-that-be in Petersburg.

Later Verkhovensky uses the same vocabulary to convince his provincial followers that he speaks for the radical masterminds who are supposedly directing the revolutionary show from somewhere abroad: he assures them that everything is "known *there*"; "*there* they don't lose track of a single hair or a single speck of dust" (10:420; italics in the original).[22] In such passages it is clear that this authoritative *tam* need not be specified geographically. The important thing is that it is not here (on the edge) but rather there (in the center); what provincials yearn for is always somewhere else, "not here, not at this place, but 'there,'" as Epstein writes.[23] Ideas reach the provinces only after having passed through "there" (usually, but not always, Petersburg), and the provincials are ready to credit virtually any idea that comes to them by way of this path. For while we might be inclined to assume that the substance of real life would naturally be "here" (where one actually *is*), to these characters "here" seems utterly insubstantial; only "there" can they locate a fullness of meaning that approaches the real.

The little cabal in *Demons* can exist only as long as it can see itself as one of an interconnected series of similar *piaterki* (revolutionary cells, groups of five) all tied together, in a way that they themselves cannot understand but must take on faith, by an all-seeing, all-ordering consciousness somewhere "out there." Thus the conspirators prove themselves more than ready to believe that Verkhovensky is "an emissary come from abroad with full plenary powers" (10:302). And Verkhovensky is successful in manipulating them precisely because he has painted what one of the conspirators calls "a picture of Russia covered by an endless network [*set'iu*] of knots" (10:418). It is the provincials' acceptance of this oft-repeated spatial image—"a whole network of *piaterki*," "an endless multitude [of *piaterki*] . . . the whole of Russia covered with a network"—that leads them to listen so eagerly to talk of the "central committee" (*tsentral'nyi komitet*) directing everything from afar (10:510, 424).

In fact the recurrence of the root *tsentr*—"this fantastic center," "our foreign centers," "a central but up till now unknown to us . . . committee" (10:416, 424, 418)—signals the provincials' faith that only a center has the power to render meaningful whatever they do, including something as senseless as an unmotivated murder. "I am acting on instructions from the central committee," Verkhovensky tells them, "and you must obey" (10:424). Elsewhere he drives home the connection between the central power that he represents and the necessity of submission: "You are only a single knot in an endless network of knots, and [thus] you owe blind obedience to the center," he declares (10:418). Having chosen to believe that "their unit is only one of hundreds and thousands of similar *piaterki*, just like theirs, scattered all over Russia, all depending on some sort of central, huge but secret place, in turn organically linked to the European universal revolution" (10:303), the provincials must also resign themselves to the belief that their actions can have no meaning without this network. If you are out in the provinces, and you accept that all power and significance are located in some far-off center (in this case, wherever the "European universal revolution" may be happening), then of course it pays to think that your peripheral place is indeed "organically linked" (albeit by an *invisible* web) to something that really counts, something central. And if you believe yourself to be merely "one among hundreds and thousands," each one indistinguishable from the next and each utterly insignificant on its own, you are uniquely vulnerable to ideas like Verkhovensky's.

Dostoevsky evokes the conspirators' intensely provincial worldview through repetition of the word *set'* (net, network, circuit, system) and the visual and spatial image this word conveys—a picture of Russia as an unvarying plain stretching out into the distance, randomly dotted with identical specks.[24] The picture is by no means unfamiliar: one thinks, for example, of the Russian landscape in *Dead Souls*, which Gogol famously describes as "exposed, desolate, and flat . . . like specks, like dots [*tochki, znachki*] are the low-lying towns scattered over the plains."[25] An even more extreme example is the setting of Dmitry Grigorovich's *Anton Goremyka*, where the only discernible "landmarks" are *holes*; here the empty, flat space is so unreadable that even a local can lose his way amidst "boundless fields stretched outward among [still] other fields and swamps," "endless flat fields" traversed by a "dead road."[26] *Demons* draws on such images of Russia as a vast homogeneous plain lacking legible markers, a space where nameless towns are seen merely as "specks" on the low horizon—although, as I have argued, Dostoevsky's provincials choose to believe that these insignificant specks can assume importance if they can become "knots" (*uzly*) by being placed in relationship to some higher organizing power. Once linked to such a center, Dostoevsky's characters believe, the dots have a chance of becoming nodes in a system of meaning.[27]

And it matters little whether or not the "network" really exists: what is important is the worldview that allows *Demons'* provincials to be duped into believing that it does. As Verkhovensky manipulates his followers into murdering their former comrade Shatov, it is this belief that makes the conspirators feel "like flies caught in the web of a huge spider"—a telling simile that links the novel's pervasive imagery of nets and networks (including the train lines entangling the countryside "like a spider web") with the characters' inability to extricate themselves from Verkhovensky's plot (10:421, 375). Shatov himself, who knows that Verkhovensky's network is a fiction, nonetheless dreams in the hours before his death that he is tangled up in ropes that leave him unable to move (10:432)—yet another evocation of the tightening web in which these characters find themselves trapped.

When Stavrogin carefully hangs himself on a "strong silk cord" (10:516), his chosen method of suicide resonates again with this imagery of webs, knots, and nets, plotted lines and (self-imposed?) traps. This suggests that even though Stavrogin has not participated actively in the townspeople's never-ending circuit of gossip and rumor (the fuel on which *Demons*' narrative engine runs) and has instead remained intriguingly silent, he is nonetheless as thoroughly enmeshed in their system as are his various satellites. And as the absent presence around whom the provincial revolutionaries hover—toward whom they look for the fullness of meaning that they trust will be revealed in and by ideology—Stavrogin is of course closely identified with the geographic and cultural fact of Petersburg.

Both Stavrogin and Petersburg embody what one of the provincial conspirators calls a "fantastic center" (*fantasticheskii tsentr*, 10:416), "fantastic" in the sense that it does not and perhaps cannot truly exist. The fact that Stavrogin has left Petersburg suggests as much: having found no *there* in the capital, he returns to the provincial periphery, where his ideological development ceases and where he comes to serve merely as a way for the provincials to delude themselves into thinking that what they are doing has coherence and purpose. Once again the parallel with Gogol's vision of the provinces/capital relationship becomes apparent. In *The Inspector General*, for example, far-off Petersburg serves as the patently unreal and quasi-magical ideal that motivates every character in the play. In Donald Fanger's words, Petersburg in Gogol's text (like Stavrogin in Dostoevsky's) is a "conferring power," a "seat of authority, ground of judgment"—but by the end of *The Inspector General* the capital proves to be an *empty* idea, functioning only as "a powerful absence" in the play.[28]

Near the end of *Demons* an outed conspirator, who by this point should understand that Verkhovensky's plot was almost certainly a sham, nonetheless continues to assert hysterically that there exists an "endless multitude" of *piaterki* linked by the mysterious network (10:510). By the time the cabal is disintegrating, the conspirators' panic is fueled above all by the fear that the network is a fiction, that "this fantastic center" might not exist at all; thus as things fall apart, the conspirators demand that Verkhovensky clarify his position "as a representative of the central but up till now unknown to us and practically fantastic committee" (10:416, 418). One would-be revolutionary challenges him in despair, "I think that our foreign centers have forgotten Russian reality and have broken every tie and are simply raving . . . I even think that instead of many hundreds of *piaterki* in Russia we are the only one and there's no network at all" (10:424).

The plural noun ("our foreign centers") suggests that for the provincial revolutionaries who are eager to follow Verkhovensky, this idea of the *tsentr* need not refer to a single, specific geographic incarnation in order to do its conceptual work. Here Epstein's remarks on the role of centralized political power in Russian culture are suggestive: at certain historical moments, Epstein argues, the center itself could "lose its geographic incarnation [*plot*']" because the autocracy's geographic transfers of power were capable of "[provincializing] the entire world that had been abandoned, torn away from the capital-throne" ("in Russian history even the capital not infrequently was transformed into a province, inasmuch as the sovereign would transfer his seat to a specially created or minimally populated 'center'"). Thus even Moscow and Petersburg might be figured as provinces "in relationship to an imperial power that was always [both] elusive and transcendental."[29] The imperial state and its *portable* apparatus of "central" power seem to have conditioned the way Russian culture conceives of an organizing center—which perhaps helps explain why, in *Demons*, the vague possibility of the movement or proliferation of centers (whatever that might mean) does not lead to the collapse of the basic binary (all-meaningful "there" *vs.* insignificant "here") that governs characters' conceptions of space.

In *Demons* the "elusive and transcendental" entity (or entities) in relationship to which characters experience their own provinciality in fact seems to have become so thoroughly elusive and transcendental as to defy embodiment in any concrete institution. The result is a symbolic geography that reduces much of Russia's physical space to blankness, thereby giving rise to the tormenting sense of insignificance that encourages provincials to seek meaning by envisioning their place as one "knot" in a mysterious network. At the moment when Verkhovensky is about to embark on the train that will allow him to make his escape, leaving behind his doomed associates, he claims to have "plenty of such knots in the general network [*etikh uzlov obshchei seti u menia dovol'no*]," although he concedes that "an extra knot can't hurt" (10:478).

The noun *uzel* occurs over and over in *Demons*.[30] In addition to designating a knot, a node, or a nerve center, it can also signify a juncture in a road—thereby drawing our attention to the ways in which *Demons'* image of a vast net of conspiracy stretching out over the Russian landscape resonates with the text's depiction of the railroads. Railroads and trains are mentioned frequently in the novel. A character prophesies, for example, that "what with the railroads" he cannot believe in "the Russian God" (and in any case everything in Russia will soon "dissolve into mud"); one of the conspirators has worked for the railroad; student radicals travel by railroad to distribute incendiary leaflets (whereas the itinerant peddler of religious texts seems to travel by foot—*khodit i Evangelie prodaet*; 10:287, 303, 304, 488). Seen as a whole, railroad tracks are shown to form a network of interconnected *uzly* spreading web-like across Russia's open spaces.

As such references remind us, *Demons* was being written and serialized within just a few years of *Anna Karenina*. But in *Anna Karenina*, unlike in *Demons*, our attention is drawn to the narrative function of the train itself: Tolstoy's locomotive is an image of modernity, technology, industrialization, and speed; the locus of an unprecedented kind of class mixing; and a driving force behind the era's new social mobility and the dissolution of traditional social bonds and local attachments. In this sense the Dostoevsky text that most clearly recalls Tolstoy's paradigmatic rail-road novel is not *Demons* but rather *The Idiot*, in which onrushing trains serve as emblems of sexual passion, violence, and a pernicious version of modernity. In *The Idiot* as in *Anna Karenina*, the locomotive evokes teleological movement (no matter what that *telos* is or whether or not one deems it to be a worthy goal).[31] But *Demons*, by contrast, is not dominated by the image of the train, but rather is structured around images of the *tracks*, a *set'* that is associated less with forward movement than with circulation and distribution.

This contrast points to two ways of considering the relationship between rail-roads and narrative, whether in Dostoevsky's work or anywhere else: you can focus either on the train itself or on the system created by the rail lines. The first approach (that is, concentrating on the train) tends to privilege questions of time: by drawing our attention to speed, duration, trajectory, and the effort to arrive at a goal, the image of the locomotive tends to foreground a narrative's end-directed quality. It is this image that Jean Cocteau, for example, was drawing on when he wrote that "everything one does in life . . . occurs in an express train racing to-wards death."[32] But if we take the second approach (that is, if we concentrate on the system of interlocking tracks, as *Demons* seems to require), we will instead privilege questions of space: the railroad as a network calls attention to such issues as the legibility or illegibility of the landscape; the relationship between narrative developments and topographic features; the ways in which narrative can repre-sent such oppositions as distance vs. nearness, connectedness vs. isolation, and differentiated vs. homogeneous spaces.

While Dostoevsky's thematics in *Demons* have little in common with Tolstoy's in *Anna Karenina*, both writers tell stories that would not have been possible with-out the transportation technology that was transforming how Russians experi-enced distance and geographic space. Characters in *Demons* are constantly coming and going—"turning up abroad" or "suddenly appearing" in town. Stavrogin and Verkhovensky arrive unexpectedly on the train (10:157). We last see Verkhovensky at the train station, and Stavrogin spends his final days "six stations away [from town], at the stationmaster's house," before coming home "on the early train" to hang himself (10:515). The conspirators' itinerancy is linked to their efforts to disseminate political tracts across Russia. One just-arrived *studentka-nigilistka*, for example, attends the conspirators' meeting "practically still in her traveling clothes," "intending to stay only a day or two and then go on further and further" distributing propaganda along the way (10:302, 304).

So itinerant are these characters that it is almost impossible to track their move-ments. Paris, Geneva, Petersburg, Moscow, America, Switzerland, Gottingen, Frankfurt, Dresden, Iceland, Greece, Jerusalem, Egypt: an attempt to map the various voyages mentioned in the book reveals only that the effort of precise mapping yields little in the way of useful information or telling patterns, simply because this is not a narrative in which a character is likely to follow a trajectory through space that corresponds in any way to a "development" (whereas a text like *War and Peace* establishes "a strong link between *Bildung* and geographical mobility").[33] Movement in *Demons* is less about development or progress than it is about circulation, whether of people, printed texts, gossip, or ideas. Furthermore, all of this frantic, swirling movement occurs outside the bounds of what is narrated. We never witness any of these voyages, and as we sit in the provincial city with the narrator, who seems never to have left town in his life, we experience this pervasive transience merely as report and rumor. The result is a feeling of torpid stasis *surrounded by* constant movement, movement made possible, somewhere out there, by an ever-ramifying network of connect-the-dot train tracks.[34]

In fact *Demons'* whole plot (in both senses of the word) hinges on the workings of this network, simply because it hinges on the possibility of moving relatively quickly through space, and doing so in a particular way: moving from one point to another, from one "knot" to another in the net, and *skipping over everything in between*. As many nineteenth-century European observers noted, even as railroads linked places together, they did so by destroying the lived reality of space between points, which is to say almost everyplace.[35] In 1840 a French writer asserted, "[the railroads] serve only the points of departure, the way-stations, and the terminals, which are mostly at great distances from each other. . . . They are of no use whatsoever for the intervening spaces, which they traverse with disdain and provide only with a useless spectacle."[36] In the words of one historian, the railroads' "industrialization of time and space" meant that "the region that could be reached by train from Paris . . . [came to appear] as the product or appendage of the railroad."[37]

"The product or appendage of the railroad": this statement suggests the degree to which the railroad's advent might serve to reinforce or even create a sense of provinciality or peripheralness, a sense of inescapable dependency on a far-off "hub." Thus *Demons'* insistence on the train tracks' ever-extending web resonates not only with the characters' paranoia and conspiracy theorizing, but also with their inability to see their own physical place, their "here," as meaningful in its own right. The railroad encourages them to experience their own geographic reality as nothing more than a "province," an appendage—because as will see in the following chapter, a location experiences itself as provincial only once it is made aware of another more important location (a "center"), and the distance dividing it from this center. This is exactly what was accomplished by technologies like the railroad over the course of the nineteenth century. The arrival of the railroad means that a place is no longer its own place, but rather a place that is close (or close enough) to another, more central place—as we will see in Chekhov's *Cherry Orchard*, for instance.

Dostoevsky uses an isolated (but not wholly isolated) *gubernskii gorod* to reflect on how a particular symbolic geography can form and deform Russian ways of thinking, especially political thinking. By and large *Demons* reproduces a familiar, intensely centralized conceptual geography—but at certain points it begins to critique this geography as well, registering its problematic ability to reduce provincial Russia to a meaningless blank or an appendage of the capitals. For instance, one of the provincial conspirators challenges Verkhovensky, "Excuse me, sir . . . even though we're provincials [*provintsialy*] and we're most certainly worthy of pity for that, nonetheless we know that so far in the world nothing so new has happened that we would weep for having missed it" (10:313–14). His assertion implies a healthy skepticism about any hierarchy of meaning that would definitively subordinate "provincial" places to a far-off center.

In fact *Demons* concludes by challenging any symbolic geography that would represent the Russian provinces as an undifferentiated, illegible expanse covered with insignificant little dots waiting to be connected by a higher power. In the novel's second-to-last chapter, Stepan Trofimovich, the maundering old "man of the 40s" whom Dostoevsky uses to indict the intelligentsia for its failings, wanders off into the countryside, first on foot and then in a peasant's cart. Stepan Trofimovich wants to flee the provincial town, but he wants to flee without going *to* any specific place. In fact, the narrator tells us, "at this moment his chief suffering stemmed from his absolute inability to name or specify a place [*nazvat' i naznachit' mesto on ni za chto ne mog*]," precisely because he sensed that "the instant he were to decide on [going to] *any particular city*, the ridiculousness and impossibility of his undertaking would become clear in his own eyes: . . . for what was he supposed to do precisely in this town, and why not go to some other?" (10:480–81; emphasis mine). Since Stepan Trofimovich, as an *intelligent* (member of the intelligentsia) who knows nothing of the common people or Russian reality, assumes that all provincial places mean the same thing (which is to say, they mean nothing), it must be better, he decides, simply to "take to the high road [*luchshe prosto bol'shaia doroga*]" (10:480).

And here the text takes careful note of the quintessentially Russian topography that Stepan Trofimovich encounters as he finds himself (perhaps for the first time in his life) alone and on foot in the middle of his country's vast, flat landscape. Significantly, though the high road "passes just half a verst" from the estate where he has lived for decades, he manages to embark on this road only as if by accident ("strangely, he did not even notice at first how he had come upon it," the narrator tells us; 10:481). Only after walking almost unconsciously for quite a distance does he look around to try to see where he actually is. And where he *is*, is in Russia, in an almost exaggeratedly monotonous version of the illegible landscape that by Dostoevsky's day had frustrated the aestheticizing efforts of educated observers for nearly a century:

> The old, black and deeply rutted road stretched out before him in an endless thread, planted with its willow trees; to the right—a bare place [*goloe mesto*], fields harvested long ago; to the left—bushes, and further beyond them, woods. And far, far off, the barely noticeable line of the railroad tracks running obliquely, with the smoke of some train hanging over them. (10:481)

Having insisted on the landscape's tedium and featurelessness, thereby acknowledging the difficulty of extracting meaning from such a "bare place," the description ends by drawing our attention to the railroad line that is barely visible in the furthest distance. In this passage the train can only be "far off"—insubstantial as smoke and in effect irrelevant—now that Stepan Trofimovich has stepped off the grid, as it were, and into the Russian landscape.

The people who inhabit this landscape are *muzhiki*, the peasants whom the lost intellectual encounters in the passage immediately following the landscape description. And while Stepan Trofimovich had hoped to take grandly and abstractly "to the high road," the peasants keep asking him exactly where he is going. They want to know the name of the actual village that is his destination—and as they repeatedly ask the bewildered old man whether he is headed to Khatovo, Spasov, or Usteevo, we realize that these peasants live in real geographic space (10:483ff). While they know that "visiting foreigners come by rail sometimes [*inostrantsy zaezhie po chugunke inoi priezhaiut*, 10:482]," they themselves move through space not on a network of train tracks, but on foot and in the carts, steamer-boats, and coaches to which they repeatedly refer. Thus in the book's final pages we are introduced to a way of seeing Russian places not as a series of nameless and interchangeable dots against a blank background of "provinciality," but rather as a collection of real individual locations with their own associations and meanings. The image of Russian space that has informed much of the narrative is replaced by a markedly different image, one that works to undermine the assumption that the whole expanse of provincial Russia constitutes a blank on the map of the nation.

And in a narrative that has been structured by the image of a network that simultaneously facilitates and constrains travel (you go where the train takes you, or where the masterminds in Geneva tell you to go), we conclude instead with an image of unstructured, unpurposeful movement, the kind of movement that is in fact suggested by the chapter title "Stepan Trofimovich's Last Pilgrimage" (*Poslednee stranstvovanie Stepana Trofimovicha* [10:479], in which one might also translate pilgrimage as wandering, journeying, or peregrination). A pilgrim (*strannik*—Leskov's *ocharovannyi strannik*, "enchanted pilgrim," for example) does not move from point to point on a network, experiencing all the spaces in between points as blanks; a *strannik* is more likely to attend equally to all of the space that he covers, as do the peasants who live in and pay attention to the off-the-grid places that have no significance for "visiting foreigners [who] come by rail."

Why, though, is this called Stepan Trofimovich's *last* pilgrimage—have there been others? In this sense the title of *Demons'* penultimate chapter brings us back to a claim I made above—that is, the idea that Dostoevsky is using the provinces quite intentionally as a way of developing ideas about Russia as a whole. Stepan Trofimovich, deracinated *intelligent* that he is, has never *not* been "wandering" in the way that Pyotr Chaadaev, in his oft-quoted "First Philosophical Letter," describes his "nomadic" countrymen doing. "Does it not seem that we [Russians] are all in transit? We all resemble travelers," Chaadaev writes. "We do not even have homes [point même de foyer domestique]. . . . In our houses, we are like wayfarers [dans nos maisons, nous avons l'air de camper]; in our families, we are like strangers; in our cities, we are like nomads, more nomadic than those who wander our steppes, for they are more attached to their deserts than we are to our towns."[38] Stepan Trofimovich is a wanderer not only in the Russian countryside, where he speaks French to the peasants; he is so thoroughly a product of imported ideas that he is a wanderer anywhere in Russia.

Or perhaps it is more accurate to say that the version of Russian culture Stepan Trofimovich represents is one that threatens to render all Russians permanently "alien to themselves"—to adapt Epstein's description of the "alienation from itself" that is a structural characteristic of the provinces—by placing them in a provincial relationship to European culture. To be provincial in this sense is not only to feel oneself eternally exiled, with one's "own center . . . taken out of [oneself] and transferred to some other space or time," transferred, that is, to the elusive *tam* toward which Dostoevsky's characters direct a gaze full of longing and submission.[39] More importantly, as *Demons* makes clear, to be provincial is to be dangerously susceptible to conspiracy theorizing, manipulation, demagoguery—a point *Demons* reinforces by enlisting a resonant spatial trope to do its ideological work.

And by linking the trope of blank *provintsiia* to his era's most dramatic new technology, the railroad, Dostoevsky incorporates this technology into a vision of Russian geographic space that is at once familiar, evocative, and ideologically significant. Russia's various apostles of progress generally depicted railways as a connective technology promising prosperity and unity. As *Notes of the Fatherland* put it in an editorial of 1839, railroads would soon take "people who have been separated" and render them "tightly joined together by the bonds of fellow-feeling and mutual interest."[40] Decades later the student radical Nikolai Kibalchich depicted the railroad as just this sort of system: "covering Russia by sections with an interconnected network of railroads," he declared, his countrymen would soon "overtake the rich and advanced nations of Western Europe."[41] Kibalchich's vision suggests a landscape divided into a series of legible sectors, all placed into rational relationship with one other by the rail lines' connecting and organizing grid. But in *Demons*, the railway system instead mirrors and reinforces an insidious net-like conspiracy spreading out across Russia's open spaces.[42] Railroads may promise connection, Dostoevsky suggests, but as one character in *The Idiot* tells us, they cannot serve as "an idea tying contemporary humanity together" (*sviazuiushchaia nastoiashchee chelovechestvo mysl'*)—for while past ages were unified by a religious ideal, there is no such unifying principle "in our age of vice and railways!" (8:315).

In *Demons* it is particularly clear that Dostoevsky places little hope in Kibalchich's project of "covering Russia by sections with an interconnected network" of train tracks. Such networks generally have a hub, an organizing center, but not an end-point; in fact, the *set'* of the tracks can suggest a system linking everything, but going nowhere. Rather than the precipitous movement of the train itself, the tracks are likely to evoke stasis, even entrapment, as is suggested by *Demons'* picture of the railroads as a spider web. A narrative dominated by the image of such a network implies a certain structure—a structure quite unlike that of *The Idiot*, which is dominated instead by the image of a locomotive, and which seems always to be pointing toward its own climax.[43] *Demons*, in keeping with its focus on the *set'* of the tracks, ends not with any decisive climax, but with a kind of dispersal. Like the cabal of would-be revolutionaries in Turgenev's *Virgin Soil*, this group, too, disintegrates having accomplished virtually nothing. Stavrogin's death is anticlimactic, even trivial, and Verkhovensky slips away on the train to continue his fundamentally pointless "revolutionary" activities. There is no closure here, almost no "ending"—as is suggested by the fact that Verkhovensky himself seems not to believe in any *end*, but rather in an ongoing end*game*. In the novel's closing chapters, it is this image of the railroad as system—a network linking everything but going nowhere, a grid you cannot escape—that lingers in our minds, the reflection of an endgame that never resolves itself in an ending.

The symbolic geography that structures *Demons* is, I would argue, a version of the one that underlies almost all of Dostoevsky's works. This vision attends very little to the particularity and variety of Russian places. In the working notebooks for *Demons*, Dostoevsky has his narrator make the point explicitly: "I am not describing the city, its layout, daily life, people, and official positions, nor its social relations, nor the curious shifts in these relations peculiar to the provincial life of our city, as consequences of the ancient, customary mores according to which the city has taken shape or as consequences of new disturbances in these mores owing to recent reforms. *I don't have time to occupy myself with a picture of our little corner of the world.*" The narrator concedes that "since the affair took place not in the sky but, after all, among us, then it's really impossible for me never to touch, purely picturesquely, on the everyday side of our provincial life," but he warns, "I will do this only as much as is required by absolute necessity. I will not deliberately undertake any description of our contemporary daily life" (11:240–41; emphasis mine).

In the end *Demons* highlights, confirms, and complicates the pattern we see developed over the course of its author's career: what matters most to Dostoevsky are not particular places, but instead a "central" place with the power to confer meaning on all the other ones. As he puts it in the feuilleton entry cited above, "all of Russia . . . lives by Petersburg alone" (18:26). This central place is often elusive—or as *Demons* suggests, it might even be nonexistent—but nonetheless it functions as an essential force, one that not only holds together and animates but seems almost to *create* Russia. Once again we could not be further from Tolstoy's geography in *War and Peace*, with its insistently decentralized view of the country's space and its frequent recurrence to the specific lived realities of many places, diverse and dispersed. Indeed at times Dostoevsky might almost be writing directly against Tolstoy's Kutuzov, who intuitively understands that Russia cannot be embodied in or reduced to a single center. If *War and Peace* reminds us that any place might someday turn out to be the most important place, Dostoevsky's works are more likely to remind us that without the central place—the capital, elusive as it may be—Russia itself would hardly exist.

· CHAPTER TEN ·

"Everything Here Is Accidental": Chekhov's Geography of Meaninglessness

En province, la pluie devient une distraction.

—Frères Goncourt, 1866

What isn't done in the provinces out of boredom, how many useless and foolish things!

—Anton Chekhov, 1898

Over and over in *Three Sisters*, the Prozorov women invoke "Moscow," repeating the name of the Russian capital lovingly, obsessively, urgently, dreamily, until it ends up sounding like a talisman intended to stave off some dark truth about provincial lives. Very often the city's name is in the accusative case, suggesting movement toward something, movement that in this play is never initiated. Olga cries, "Yes! Quickly to Moscow!" and Irina concurs, "Go away to Moscow. Sell the house, finish with everything here and—to Moscow . . ."[1] The last lines of Act II (spoken by Irina) are "To Moscow! To Moscow! To Moscow!" The last lines of Act III (also spoken by Irina) are, "Only to go to Moscow! I beg you, let us go! There's nothing on earth better than Moscow! Let us go, Olia! Let us go!" (14:156, 171).

We know that Moscow in *Three Sisters* is "symbolic," that it stands in some way for a rich life that is beyond the characters' reach. But beyond that, its definition is left unspecified, and we have little way of knowing to what degree the name stands for a real place. The same holds true for the play's setting: stage directions describe it only as "a provincial town" (*v gubernskom gorode*), and it would seem to be a version of the anonymous, could-be-anywhere provincial city made available by a long series of literary predecessors. Chekhov elaborates on the setting very slightly in one of his letters by describing it as "a provincial town, like Perm."[2] But as their endless invocations of the capital suggest, the sisters' dwelling place might best be described simply as *not*-Moscow. Beyond that, it is hard to say—and it is perhaps not very important to say, either, since in the world of this play there is little to suggest that the differences between one provincial town and another are particularly significant. As Chekhov writes elsewhere, "In Russia, all towns are the same. Ekaterinburg is exactly like Perm or Tula, or like Sumy and Gadyach" (*Pis'ma* 4:72).

Chekhov makes this dubious assertion in an 1890 letter to his sister, and he repeats it virtually word for word in another letter. Clearly the statement is not meant to be taken literally, but it is nonetheless puzzling when we consider that Chekhov was among the writers most engaged with the realities of life in Russia's provinces. He was not only born in the provinces but maintained close ties there, traveling throughout the empire and involving himself in various provincial institutions; certainly no one could say of him, as was said of Gogol, that he "knew nothing of real Russian life."[3] Furthermore, Chekhov wrote famously sensitive descriptions of Russian, Ukrainian, and Siberian landscapes, and in the course of an overland voyage to Sakhalin he noted differences among the towns along the way. In short, there is much in Chekhov's writing to belie the claim that specificities of place meant nothing to him in real life, or that he subscribed to a view that collapsed regional differences into the category of "the provinces." And yet, the statement I have quoted ("in Russia, all towns are the same") suggests that, thanks to the powerful and distorting geographic images that have been the subject of previous chapters, Chekhov is on occasion willing to assimilate specific provincial places to the idea of "the Russian town," indistinguishable from all other "Russian towns."

I would argue that for Chekhov certain particularities of place matter in a way they often do not for other writers. The questions this chapter asks are where, how, and how much? In "Ward No. Six," for instance, is the hideous provincial life the story describes—a life of confinement, cruelty, cultural deformation—specific to a certain place? Are things so bad here actually *because* they are in the provinces—in yet another "dirty, wretched little town" located "two hundred versts from a railway station" (8:78)—or is this geographic peculiarity finally incidental to the misery Chekhov depicts? In other words, do Chekhov's provinces stand for the provinces, or do they stand for something else? I have argued that for Gogol the provinces never really stand for the provinces, since his symbolic geography never allows us to imagine that a better life might be found in some other real place, whether Petersburg, Moscow, Paris, or anywhere else. But Chekhov's provinces, notwithstanding their clearly and even insistently symbolic import, are often locations that we could imagine pinpointing on a map of Russia: the specificities of place do matter in Chekhov's world, if in subtle ways. And perhaps most importantly, a place's meanings can change over time.

"Ward No. Six" and *My Life*: Are the Provinces Everywhere?

The town that provides the setting of "Ward No. Six" (1892) is perhaps the most darkly and irremediably provincial place in Chekhov's oeuvre. The story's indictment of the provinces is articulated in familiar terms (its "stifling" character, its society "without any higher interests" leading a "dull, senseless life"; 8:76), but these criticisms take on unusual power from the narrative's opening paragraphs, which require the reader to follow the narrator ("if you are not afraid of being stung by the nettles, walk down the narrow footpath . . .") past heaps of moldering trash and a fence topped with upturned nails into the prison-like hospital yard, and finally into a stinking room dominated by more images of decay, "disfigurement," and captivity (8:72–73). Only once we have been led into this closed space and entombed there with the rest of the characters does the action of the narrative begin. Having opened with profoundly disturbing images of enclosure and confinement, the story manages to condense all the horror of provincial stasis, isolation, powerlessness, and injustice into one tiny space.

The setting in "Ward No. Six" is explicitly "provincial," but beyond that its location is unspecified. For many of the story's interpreters, this lack of geographic specificity helps to allow the town and the hospital to be seen as stand-ins for all of Russia, for the suffering and injustice that were thought to grip the whole country in the late imperial period. As Leskov said, "'Ward No. Six' is everywhere. . . . This is Russia."[4] The characters' tendency to philosophize and thereby generalize the significance of their own sufferings has probably encouraged the tendency to see the story's details as symbolic of something "bigger" than a description of the provinces—"all of Russia," perhaps, or even "the human condition."

However, if we read "Ward No. Six" in this way—that is, if we assume that its critique is aimed at a far more general phenomenon than the provincial town—we are aligning ourselves with the story's most morally corrupt character, the doctor Andrei Efimych Ragin, who justifies his passivity in face of the suffering all around him by recourse to "bigger" thoughts. Ragin tells himself that nothing matters, that there is ultimately "no difference between the best Viennese clinic and my hospital," simply because in the end death will win out all the same. The doctor knows that there has recently transpired a genuine revolution in medicine

(Pasteur, Koch), that there are ways of saving people and alleviating suffering; he even acknowledges to himself that "such an abomination as Ward No. Six is possible only two hundred versts from a railroad station" in a town run by "half-literate petty merchants." "Anywhere else," he thinks, "the public and the newspapers would long ago have torn to pieces this little Bastille" (8:91–92). But he convinces himself that none of this matters, just as he tries to convince one of his incarcerated patients that there is no real difference between his (the patient's) life and that of a philosopher in ancient Greece (the patient begs to differ; 8:100).

If we do not want to follow the doctor's lead, we must consider the possibility that the grotesque existence depicted in "Ward No. Six"—a "senseless life enlivened only by violence, coarse dissipation, and hypocrisy"—is partly the result of real-world geography. Perhaps the abuses the story chronicles are not a manifestation of the "human condition," but are instead "possible only two hundred versts from a railroad station" in a "dirty, wretched little town." As Ragin himself says, "in our town it's agonizingly boring . . . there are no new people . . . but judging by everything [that we hear], in our capitals there's no intellectual stagnation, there's movement—which means there must be real people there" (8:97–98). The ills described in "Ward No. Six" might be specific to this provincial place—or rather, they might be specific to the provincialism of this place, this city that could be any provincial city. The individuating details of life in this one town may not matter, but the fact that this town is not the capital matters very much.

Similarly, in the 1896 novella *My Life* (*A Provincial's Story*), the subtitle explicitly invites us to connect the failure and incoherence of the narrator's life with the place where he lives—yet another nameless provincial town, described in the same terms of sameness, repetition, stupidity, and incoherence we have learned to expect. As is often the case in Chekhov, railroads serve to define this location's relationship to the wider world: thanks to the townspeople's ill-considered refusal to pay the appropriate bribe, the closest railroad station is several miles away, a fact that underscores the town's seemingly irremediable isolation. Needlessly grim material conditions like bad food and dirty water point to the inhabitants' moral failings: endemic corruption, "coldness and narrowness of opinions"—"how these people lived, it was shameful to say!" (9:205–6). The story concludes with a passionate indictment: "Our town has existed for hundreds of years, and in all that time it has produced not one . . . useful person." Were this "useless" place to disappear suddenly from the face of the earth, the narrator declares, not one soul would lament its passing (9:278).

The only answer is to get out of town, which is what the narrator's intelligent and sensitive wife does when she finally abandons him. Her husband does not blame her for her decision, and the text as a whole does not seem to invite us to blame her, either. When it comes to extracting oneself from the provincial mire, perhaps *sauve-qui-peut* is a defensible course of action, because to stay in the provincial town—a dead end, a virtual cul-de-sac in space and time—is to embrace stagnation and pointlessness. However, we have no idea what happens to the narrator's wife once she reaches the capital. And Chekhov's work gives us no reason to assume that living in the capital *guarantees* a meaningful life; witness, for instance, the main character in "Lady with a Little Dog," who constructs for himself a perfectly empty existence in Moscow. The best we can assume is that this character has seized for herself the *possibility* of a different life. The details remain to be worked out, and for Chekhov, details are everything.

Complicating the Binary: "The Fiancée" and *Three Years*

In a sense the 1903 story "The Fiancée" can be read as a coda to *My Life*, filling in the story of a lively young woman who abandons her provincial life and runs off to the capital. By fleeing a wretched Town of N (and a wretched husband-to-be) and going off to educate herself in Petersburg, the heroine of "The Fiancée" saves her own life and at the same time ruins the life of the family she leaves behind in *provintsiia*. Here Chekhov reprises not only *My Life* but also the basic plot of Khvoshchinskaia's *Boarding School Girl* (see chapter 7): an intelligent young woman, faced with spending a lifetime immured in a dirty, stagnant, oppressive provincial town, surprises us by making a break for it and succeeding, if at the cost of nearly all her social and familial ties. In each case, the impetus to act comes from an intellectual man who, in the end, proves to be a less worthy and consequential character than the woman he goads into action. Both Chekhov's and Khvoshchinskaia's anonymous towns are characterized by obstruction and confinement (fences, walls), filth and disorder (dead flies, dust), and slow but pervasive violence (class oppression, child abuse). Both narratives begin with the heroine embedded in the steeply vertical hierarchy of the provincial social order; both end with her having joined her cohort in the capital's new world of horizontally organized "generations."

But while "The Fiancée" initially appears to lay out the same sort of unambiguous capital-vs.-provinces binary that structures *The Boarding School Girl*, Chekhov's narrative soon complicates that binary considerably. In Khvoshchinskaia's novella the contrast between capital and Town of N could not be drawn in starker terms: here Petersburg represents life and progress; the provinces—death and stagnation. Once in the capital, Lolenka declares that she has abandoned her provincial past, entirely and irrevocably ("I've cast off my yoke and I choose not to remember anything about it"; "it's past—and finished. I live in the present").[5] There is no going back and no combining the two worlds, which seem practically to exist on different ontological planes; the heroine must choose one and leave the other behind forever. By contrast, as I will show, in Chekhov's world the situation is considerably more ambiguous—even if the heroine of "The Fiancée" does not recognize this ambiguity. While Nadya herself may echo the rhetoric of Khvoshchinskaia's heroine, Chekhov's narrator consistently undercuts her suggestion of any impassable divide or absolute opposition between *provintsiia* and *stolitsa*.

"The Fiancée" dwells on the vulgarity of provincial culture, calling attention to it so heavy-handedly that we cannot fail to recognize the moral dimension of its coarseness. Nadya's widowed mother, pitiful and half-educated, lives as a dependent in her mother-in-law's house. "Tightly corseted" and wearing a pince-nez, she makes herself weep with vague talk of hypnotism and "philosophy"; she is "deeply moved" by her own incoherent ideas even as she sits down to dine on spiced cherries and "an enormous, juicy turkey" (10:204–5). The turkey reminds us once again of what literature has been telling us from the 1830s on: existence in the provinces is above all corporeal, mired in what is *merely* physical, from mud to borscht. In Chekhov's story, food and filth signal the same unredeemed materiality we saw in Sollogub's "barbarous and horrid" provincial places. But while in the 1840s Sollogub required lists of prosaic nouns to make his point ("nails, flour, lard"; "an enormous puddle that never dries out"),[6] by Chekhov's time the trope is so familiar that he need only gesture toward it (spiced cherries, flies) and we know immediately where we are.

The setting of "The Fiancée" is evoked with a few familiar details, the same physical markers we have seen authors use to evoke Towns of N for decades. The streets are wide and the fences drab; dust covers everything, "rising in clouds" from the empty streets; Nadya's house, like all the other old houses, is repeatedly described as low and dark, "very small and squat" (10:217). But here comfort and modern amenities can be as vulgar, as morally suspect, as flies and stench. A case in point is when Nadya's fiancé complacently shows off the cistern that is to provide their new bathroom with running water. The newly built house where Nadya and her husband are to live highlights deformations of taste that are of course intensified rather than masked by the expense that has been incurred to obtain them. The house's defining feature is "a large oil painting in a gilt frame, a picture of a naked lady beside a purple vase with a broken handle"—an object that serves to taint everything around it with an air of unwholesome sexuality. The unsavory nude recalls the picture hanging on the wall of Gogol's provincial inn in *Dead Souls* ("a nymph with breasts so large the reader has probably never seen the like"),[7] though unlike Gogol, Chekhov seems to find no humor in the aesthetic failure. All Nadya can see in the house and its furnishings, he writes, is "vulgarity [*poshlost'*], stupid, naïve, unbearable vulgarity" (10:210).

Nadya's escape from this life is straightforwardly narrated (unlike in *The Boarding School Girl*, where the narrative obscures the mechanics of the heroine's escape simply because such a happy outcome was, in 1861, so deeply implausible). Chekhov's heroine sends her family a telegram, buys a train ticket, goes to Petersburg, and begins to "study." Telegraphs and railways, nonexistent in the provincial Russia of *The Boarding School Girl*, are critical to Chekhov's story; clearly, in practical terms, the provincial town is no longer as isolated as it once was. But in symbolic terms, in this story at least, it remains radically cut off from all that is happening in the rest of the world. Russia in 1903 was in upheaval: the preceding decade had seen famine, pogroms, rural dislocation, rapid urbanization, severe political unrest, and strikes; Lenin, abroad, was keeping his eye on the growing anarchy, and at home the Socialist Revolutionaries were laying their plans. But none of these events seems to have touched the life of the provincial town as Chekhov depicts it: as Nadya's friend tells her, "everything's the same here as it was twenty years ago, no change at all" (10:203). Nadya's transformation begins when she recognizes this fact ("and for some reason it seemed things would be like this her whole life, without changing, forever and ever!" 10:202) and begins to feel "a passionate longing to live, to be in Petersburg" (10:219). The only way to *live* is to be in the capital—"life" is simply not present in the provincial town.

As in *The Boarding School Girl*, where provincial *skuka* reaches a virtually apocalyptic pitch, perhaps even presaging "the end of the world,"[8] in "The Fiancée" too, the empty tedium of *provintsiia* cannot be named ("something was missing," Nadya thinks, 10:218), but it points unmistakably toward things far worse than boredom and idleness. Khvoshchinskaia's Lolenka insists, in politically strident terms, that the way of life in her provincial town is utterly evil (anyone who submits to this life's precepts is "serving evil, teaching evil," she declares).[9] Chekhov's Nadya likewise conceives of the problem in terms that are at once extreme and vague, as when she concludes that absolutely everything about her past must and will be consigned to oblivion (10:217). "The past had been torn away from her and had disappeared, as if burned in a fire, its ashes scattered to the wind," she thinks (10:219–20). Having decided to run away, Nadya quite melodramatically declares herself "ready for anything, for death itself" (10:214).

Sasha, the old friend who convinces her to flee to Petersburg, provides the language in which Nadya's escape is imagined—the language of radical rupture, even political revolution. Sasha is a poor artist who is dying of consumption, but he insists that a glorious future lies ahead. The old world, the world exemplified by the provincial town, is about to die, and a new one is about to be born, he assures Nadya: "Once you've turned your whole life upside down [*perevernete vashu zhizn'*], then everything will change. The important thing is to turn your life upside down [*perevernut'*], nothing else matters" (10: 214). In Sasha's recurrence to vocabulary drawn from the same root as *perevorot* (revolution, upheaval, radical change) we read a utopian political message: the rupture is going to usher in "the kingdom of heaven on earth":

> In this town of yours not one stone will be left on another [cf. Jesus's words in Luke 21:6: "there shall not be left one stone upon another"]—everything will be turned topsy-turvy [*poletit vverkh dnom*], everything will change, as if by magic. And then there will be enormous, splendid buildings, wonderful gardens, amazing fountains, extraordinary people . . . But that's not the important thing. The important thing is that the crowd, in our sense of the word, will no longer exist; that evil will no longer exist, because every person will have faith and every person will know what he is living for, and no one will seek support from the crowd. My dear, my darling, go away! Show everyone that you've had enough of this stagnant, gray, sinful life! (10:208)

And Nadya herself, once she is seated in a railway car watching telegraph poles fly by, imagines her future in terms of radical "freedom" (*volia*), "running away to join the Cossacks" (10:215). Of the two Russian nouns for the English "freedom," *volia* and *svoboda*, *volia* emphasizes will and even willfulness, including the desire to break away from constraints, whether illegitimate or legitimate; *volia* was what serfs dreamt of when they fled their masters. Nadya's choice of vocabulary, like her urge to "run away to join the Cossacks," does not suggest a particularly judicious decision-making process.

Later when Nadya thinks about her provincial town, her verdict is again expressed in Sasha's language:

> It seemed to her that everything in her town had long been getting old, that it had outlived its time and was only waiting, either for the end or for the beginning of something young and fresh. Oh, if only this new, bright life would come soon, when one would be able to look one's fate in the eye, directly and boldly, knowing oneself to be right, happy, and free! . . . Soon the time would come when not a trace of her grandmother's house would be left. (10:219)

Contemporary reviewers seem to have taken such rhetoric at face value, reading it as evidence of a new emphasis on positive action rather than what they saw as Chekhov's usual melancholy.[10] But there is little that is plausible in Sasha's Chernyshevskian vision or Nadya's flights of fancy, and virtually nothing that coincides with Chekhov's own inclinations (which were famously nonideological in an era of high ideological commitment). Given that such eschatological vocabulary is quite alien to Chekhov, whose work almost always ironizes or subtly undercuts this sort of rhetoric, it is not surprising to discern the narrator's hints that Nadya may be deceiving herself. The entire passage quoted above is of course prefaced by "it seemed to her," and the story's closing line is ironized by another Chekhovian hedge: "the next morning she said good-bye to her family, and in a lively and gay mood she left the town—*as she supposed*, forever" (10:220; emphasis mine).

Nadya wants to believe that provincial stagnation can be left behind in the provinces; her way of life in the anonymous town has "outlived its day," she thinks, and is "forever and irrevocably lost" to her (10:217). But we are not necessarily invited to embrace this belief along with her. For one thing, Sasha lives *in Moscow* amid garbage and disorder (dead flies and stench, just as in Nadya's grandmother's house); his life in the capital city strikes Nadya as "drab and provincial" (in fact the only time the word "provincial" is used in the story is to describe his Moscow existence). When Sasha dies of consumption, he dies in Saratov, where he has gone to take a cure; the fact that he has lived in a capital rather than in the provinces does little to redeem his life. And most importantly, the very fact that Nadya returns to her town to visit, and that the narrative ends in this deeply provincial place, suggests that the discontinuity between provinces and capital, and the rupture between past and present, cannot be as decisive or permanent as the characters in "The Fiancée" imagine it to be.

Nadya's decision to go to Petersburg opens the way to a life that is neither perfect nor a complete break with her past (unlike what Khvoshchinskaia imagines in *The Boarding School Girl*)—but what she gains in the capital is undeniably better than what she leaves behind in the provinces. Chekhov is a chronicler of nuances, of small differences (clean linen, a nearby railway station) that matter in concrete and often cumulative ways. In his world there is a difference between capitals and province, but he does not allow this binary to obscure *other* differences that matter.

The novella *Three Years* (1895) is built less on a strict opposition between capital and province than on a kind of counterpoint between the two. The narrative moves between Moscow and an unnamed provincial town, following the characters as they travel back and forth by train, repeatedly and easily. We sense no real barrier between the two locations—and certainly no intimation that they exist on different ontological levels, as we have found in some earlier texts. Instead they are separated by a kind of porous membrane, traversable with an ease that would have been almost inconceivable in the literature of earlier decades. The only character who insists on an absolute opposition between capital and province (mocking "cultured people in the capitals" for failing to recognize that "in the provinces . . . there's nothing lyrical at all, there's just barbarism, meanness, and nastiness") is the least reliable and most morally compromised figure in the text (9:13–14). The rest of the narrative suggests instead that the attributes of *stolichnost'* and *provintsial'nost'* are more fluid and mutable than such a binary would imply, as when the main character, Laptev, writes of his fiancée, "she is a provincial but she studied in Moscow, and she loves our Moscow, and for that I love her" (9:16). As Laptev's description implies, characters in *Three Years* are perhaps not definitively Muscovite or definitively provincial; they are from here and there, they move and drift.

The story opens with Laptev visiting his sister in the provinces and dreaming of Moscow. But unlike, say, in *Three Sisters*, in *Three Years* Moscow is quite accessible, and while it possesses significant advantages over other places, it is no utopia. One might even adapt Bazarov's dismissive formula—"a [provincial] town like any other"—and say that Moscow in *Three Years* is "a capital like any other." Laptev's childhood and youth in the capital were narrow and oppressive; to grow up in a Moscow merchant family, Chekhov suggests, is to grow up not so much in the metropole as in the middle ages (a point that is also made by Ostrovsky's plays, as noted in chapter 8). Even outside the merchant milieu, the city as Chekhov describes it is lively, but not particularly sophisticated; it is stimulating, but not radiant with significance. If in *Three Years* life in a provincial town is marked by cultural meagerness and bad taste (e.g., the provincial doctor's house with its "poor, common decorations, its wretched pictures," "like an uninhabited place, a huge barn, [where] no one could feel at home"; 9:25), such cultural deficits and incongruences are found in the capital as well (e.g., Laptev's Moscow home, decorated with "paintings of large dimensions but inferior quality"; 9:65). When a Moscow clerk strains against the limits of his vocabulary and intellect in an effort to sound clever (e.g., "the congruity of life with the conceit of the personality"; 9:85), we hear the same kind of trying-too-hard incoherence that literature has used for decades to characterize "provincial" cultural failings. When the same clerk asks a waiter for "a plateful of the source of all slander and evil-speaking, with mashed potatoes" (9:88), we might as well be back in the provincial inn of Sollogub's *Tarantas* (see chapter 3), trying to decipher menu items like "soup the soup" and "chicken with lynx."[11]

Moscow in this text—unlike in certain others—is simply a real place. But upon sober assessment, it is a better place than most. Certainly compared to the story's provincial town—with its inevitable "grey fences, pitiful little houses, and thickets of nettles" and its "provincial way of life that was monotonous and poor in events and yet not serene"—Moscow is "entertaining" (9:15–23). And entertaining is important: thanks to the capital's diversions, Laptev's wife Iulia is able to reconcile herself to her unhappy marriage.

> Iulia Sergeyevna considered her marriage a mistake, a misfortune, and if she had had to live with her husband in any other town but Moscow, it seemed to her that she could not have endured the horror of it. Moscow entertained her—she loves its streets, houses, and churches; and had it been possible to drive around Moscow in those splendid sledges with expensive horses, to drive the whole day from morning

till night, and with the swift motion to breathe in cold autumn air, then maybe she would not have felt herself so unhappy. (9:37)

In fact when Iulia decides to marry, she does so on the basis of an entirely realistic accounting of the differences between Moscow and her hometown:

> There were no eligible men in the [provincial] town. She pictured all the men she knew—clerks, teachers, officers—and some of them were already married, their family lives striking for their emptiness and triviality, while others were uninteresting, colorless, dull, immoral. *Laptev was in any case a Muscovite,* he had graduated from the university, he spoke French; he lived in the capital, where there were many clever, rich, remarkable people, where there was activity, fine theaters, musical parties, outstanding dressmakers and confectioners. (9:23, italics mine)

Plenty of good confectioners: we are a long way here from the Prozorov sisters' luminous ideal.

Yet Chekhov is not condemning his character's eminently reasonable decision to marry in order to get to Moscow, any more than he is condemning Nadya, in "The Fiancée," for doing what she needs to do in order to flee her Town of N. In both these texts—"The Fiancée" and *Three Years*—capital and province exist on the same real-world geographic continuum; their attributes can be weighed one against the other; characters can travel back and forth between them, and can themselves become more and less "provincial" depending on time and circumstance.

Moscow as Unattainable Ideal: *Three Sisters, Uncle Vanya, The Seagull,* and "On Official Business"

This is by no means the case in Chekhov's plays, in which the difference between capital and province is not just stark but definitive, unbridgeable. In *Three Sisters,* when Irina cries "To Moscow! To Moscow! To Moscow!" and Olga echoes her "Only to go to Moscow! I beg you, let us go! There's nothing on earth better than Moscow!" (13:156, 171), we understand that in the world of this play, such a journey is entirely impossible: hence the irony behind Mandelshtam's impatient quip that the sisters should just buy a train ticket, already. Furthermore, even if we were to imagine the sisters in Moscow, we could not believe that their lives would thereby become rich and significant. For the Prozorov sisters—or rather, from the position that the sisters occupy—"Moscow" does not exist. If we try to conceive of them setting out for the capital, we picture something like what we recall from Dal's 1839 tale *The Unlucky One* (see chapter 3). Here a hapless "little man" tries to travel from his provincial town to the capital—either capital—but he can do nothing but repeatedly cover and re-cover the same ground, passing and re-passing through a series of provincial towns and "never setting eyes on" Moscow or Petersburg. In *The Unlucky One*, not unlike in *Three Sisters*, for a provincial the capital is always unreachable; it represents a strictly unrealizable ideal. In such texts, capitals and provinces would seem to stand in a relationship of mutual non-existence: you just can't get there from here.

In Chekhov's plays the fact that the characters will never go to Moscow does nothing to change what the capitals—or the provinces, for that matter—*mean* to them. Consider *Uncle Vanya*, in which once again the reality of the capital offers no solution. We listen to Serebriakov's litany of complaints about the "sepulcher" of provincial life ("trivial conversations . . . like being in exile . . . as though I've fallen off the earth and landed on some alien planet" [13:77, 98]), in full awareness of the fact that he made nothing of his years "in the city." And yet for those who were laboring and sacrificing for him back on the provincial estate, the belief that Serebriakov was doing something consequential in a far-off luminous "there" (comparable to the "there" in Dostoevsky's *Demons*) had once given meaning to their lives: "I worshiped that professor . . . I worked like a dog for him! . . . I was proud of him, proud of his learning, it was like the breath of life to me," says the disillusioned Voinitsky (13:80). In *Three Sisters* and *Uncle Vanya* as in *Dead Souls* and *Demons*, even if the distant capital cannot possibly be what provincials believe it to be, it is nonetheless the ever-elusive signifying ideal, promising an irresistible hope even while confirming the insignificance of provincial lives.

For earlier generations, life on a country estate, as opposed to life in a provincial town, could at times be experienced as something other than provincial—but in Chekhov's plays, we are never given good reason to believe in a salient difference between provincial estate and provincial town. In *Uncle Vanya*, Astrov calls on the putative difference between the two in trying to dissuade Elena Andreevna from going to live "in town": "You're better off here, in the lap of nature, than in some Kharkov or Kursk," he says, "Here at least it's poetic . . . here there are the woods, and the dilapidated manor house in the style of Turgenev . . ." (13:110). Lap of nature, poetic, in the style of Turgenev: the irony here signals an awareness that the heyday of the sophisticated manor house is past, and that the outdated image of a shabby-chic gentry nest can do nothing to obviate the overwhelming sense of provincial stasis that holds all of *Uncle Vanya*'s characters in its grip. Life "in some Kharkov or Kursk" might be even worse, even more provincial, but the difference is quantitative rather than qualitative (again, Chekhov attends to nuances of difference).[12]

The same holds true for *The Seagull*, in which we sense again that the country estate exists not apart from *provintsiia*, but on the same continuum as the various provincial cities that characters happen to mention. The country estate as a cordoned-off space of creativity, freedom, and possibility is clearly no longer viable. Even when the opposition between provinces and capital is complicated or blurred—as it is in *The Seagull*, which is not organized around a straightforward province/capital binary—still the fantastic ideal of a center endures, with Moscow always figuring prominently in characters' dreams. Nina, the aspiring actress, goes to the capital to "begin a new life," and her failure is denoted by her slow descent into ever smaller and more miserably provincial towns—"I must go to Yelets, third class . . . there the educated merchants will pester me with their attentions. It's a coarse life!" (13:44, 57). Even when there is ample evidence that the center is an illusion, still it continues to stand for the significance that will always be lacking in desultory provincial lives.

In *Three Sisters* Andrei evokes the purposelessness of life in his town with a long series of negative constructions: "Our town has been in existence for two hundred years, there are 100,000 inhabitants in it, and there is not a single one who does not resemble all the others, not one hero [*podvizhnik*] either in the past or in the present, not one scholar, not one artist, not one person in the least bit remarkable." There is nothing to indicate that this town is distinguishable from any other, and nothing to indicate that this will ever change: all the town's inhabitants inevitably become, as Andrei puts it, "the same pathetic, identical corpses as their fathers and mothers" (13:181–82). Using thoroughly Gogolian techniques (negation, repetition, people likened to "identical corpses," etc.), Andrei evokes a thoroughly Gogolian Town of N, thus connecting the play's setting to the long tradition of nameless provincial places that are not just backward but vaguely sinister. And as in *My Life (A Provincial's Story)*, the town is defined not just by its predictable vices and deficits but also by its *unintelligibility*: as the narrator of *My Life* says repeatedly, "I couldn't understand how these 60,000 inhabitants were living" (9:269). Again and again he insists on the town's incomprehensibility, declaring himself unable to figure out what this place is and why it is that way: "I couldn't understand why and how these 65,000 people were living . . . What our town was and what is was doing, I did not know" (9:205).

The unanswerable questions to which the narrator keeps returning in *My Life* ("why is [life here] so boring, so undistinguished, why in not one of these houses . . . are there people from whom I might learn how to live in such a way as not to be culpable?" 9:278) are precisely the kinds of questions and non-answers that proliferate in *Three Sisters*. When Vershinin declares, for example, that "the railway station is twenty versts away [from the town], and *no one knows why*," Solionyi offers an inane "reason" for this geographical peculiarity: "because if the station were near, then it wouldn't be far, and if it's far, then that means it's not near" (13:128; emphasis mine). The only thing explained by the brazenly absurd non-explanation is the following: not only is the provincial town of *Three Sisters* not Moscow, and not only is it not connected to Moscow or to anyplace else, but also there is *no reason* for any of this.

Similar moments of unintelligibility recur in the play. One character's incoherent French phrases, another's non sequitur literary citations, half-hearted efforts at fortune-telling in an effort to predict whether they will ever get to go to the capital—all leave us with a sense that it is going to be very hard to extract any meaning from life in this place. This impression is reinforced by the frequently random quality of exchanges between characters: as Andrei daydreams aloud of sitting in a Moscow restaurant, the addled old servant Ferapont replies, "And a workman was telling how in Moscow some sort of merchants were eating bliny, and the one that ate forty bliny, looks like he died. Forty or fifty, I can't remember." A moment later Ferapont continues, just as inexplicably, "and you know, that same workman, he was saying how they got a rope stretched all the way across Moscow . . ." (13:141).

When Irina complains that her work in the telegraph office is "without poetry, without meaning," she is pointing not only to high culture's failure to signify properly in *provintsiia* (a complaint that we have heard in many texts about provincial life, as for example in Turgenev's "Hamlet of Shchigrov"). Rather, Irina's lament is an indictment of their lives overall: *everything* here is "without meaning" (13:144). She cries in despair, "My God! I've forgotten everything, everything . . . everything is all muddled up in my head. I can't remember how to say window or ceiling in Italian . . . I'm forgetting everything, every day I'm forgetting . . . *and we will never go to Moscow*" (13:166; emphasis mine). In *Three Sisters* as in *The Inspector General*, what the capital can confer is coherence, meaningfulness. Being in Moscow, going to Moscow, or at the very least believing that one might one day go to Moscow are the only things that can stave off the pointlessness of the sisters' lives, which are threatening to slip into pure randomness. The sisters' elaborate education gains them nothing: Masha declares that in a place so "backward and vulgar," "knowing three languages is a useless luxury. Not even a luxury, but some sort of useless appendage, like a sixth finger" (13:131). The grotesque image of a useless physical appendage suggests the purposelessness of life in a place that is itself superfluous, since it is merely one in a series of indistinguishable Ns.

Belief in the capital's transfiguring power is articulated most directly and powerfully in "On Official Business" (1899), the story I cited to open this book (see chapter 1). The main character is a young government official named Lyzhin, originally from Moscow but now assigned to serve in an unspecified Russian province. From this posting he has been sent out to investigate the mysterious suicide of another official, which has occurred in an even more remote province. In a wretched village called Syrnia (which is named but not located), Chekhov's bureaucrat must spend the night alone in a hut alongside the suicide's corpse— that is, he finds himself in circumstances that strike the reader as quite frighten- ing. But Lyzhin declares that it is not possible to be afraid in this place, simply because nothing here can be *meaningful* enough to be frightening: "If this person had killed himself in Moscow or someplace near Moscow . . . then it would have been interesting, important, even frightening," he thinks, "but here, a thousand versts from Moscow, all this was somehow seen in a different light, all this was not life, not people. . . . It would leave not the least trace in the memory and would be forgotten as soon as he departed." In this "remote" place, it is not possible for phenomena to be anything but "alien," "trivial," and "uninteresting" (10:92–93).

Chekhov's bureaucrat makes explicit what has been implicit in so many ac- counts of provincial life: what is wrong with the provinces is that things here do not and in fact cannot *mean* anything. "Everything here is accidental [*sluchaino*]," Lyzhin thinks, "there can be no conclusion drawn from it." All evidence seems to him to suggest that "here there is no life, but rather bits of life, fragments; ev- erything here is accidental." Hence his longing for what he calls the *kul'turnaia sreda*, the cultural center: "where nothing is accidental, where everything is in accordance with reason and law, where . . . every suicide is comprehensible and one can explain why it is and what significance it has in the general scheme of things" (10:92, 96).

To reiterate: in "On Official Business," a government official is confined over- night in a cold, dirty hut with a dead body, a blizzard raging outside. But what pains him are not the myriad horrors that attend this event (poverty, ignorance, injustice, filth, violence), but rather the fact that this backwater has no power to confer significance on any of them. For him the worst thing about the situation is simply how far it is from the center, because this distance renders phenomena unbearably trivial. (And in this context both Moscow and Petersburg can func- tion as centers, as we see from Lyzhin's easy conflation of the two capitals: "Our homeland, the real Russia, is Moscow and Petersburg," he thinks, "but here is just the provinces, the colonies [*provintsiia, koloniia*]," 10:93.) According to the geo- graphic imaginary that shapes this character's thinking, the meaninglessness of what happens in this place is an inevitable consequence of where it has happened.

Chekhov is certainly not endorsing Lyzhin's claim that "to live, you have to be in Moscow," not any more than he is endorsing such a claim in "The Fiancée" when Nadya says the same thing about Russia's other capital (to live, she thinks, one has to be in Petersburg). "On Official Business" even has Lyzhin realize, in a half-dream combining disorientation and lucidity, how wrong he was to think that real life does not exist outside the capitals, how wrong he was to tell himself, "all this isn't life, it isn't people . . . to live, you have to be in Moscow" (10:92–93). Half-asleep, he gropes toward the realization that "some tie, unseen but meaningful and essential, exists . . . between all people"; "even in the most desolate desert, nothing is accidental, everything is full of one common idea" (10:99). Briefly, then, Chekhov allows his character to free himself from the belief that all significance and coherence are located in the center, which monopolizes everything capable of making life good. Nonetheless, it is precisely this symbolic geography—the one that Lyzhin seems briefly to renounce—that haunts not just "On Official Business" but also much of Chekhov's oeuvre. Again and again it returns as a kind of shadow structure underlying even those narratives that seem to want to free themselves of its distortions and constraints: such is the power of *provintsiia* as trope.

Becoming Provincial: "At Home" and *The Cherry Orchard*

If a place is provincial, has it always been so, and will it always remain so? In Gogol's world, for instance, it is difficult to imagine the Towns of N in *The Inspector General* and *Dead Souls* as having once been or as one day becoming anything *in particular*, anything other than general embodiments of provinciality. Immutability and stasis, like sameness, are part of what defines provinciality. In the literary imagination, *provintsiia* rarely changes because it is imagined as being fundamentally ahistorical; thus Bakhtin describes the provinces as event-less, mired in a "viscous and sticky time that drags itself slowly through space."[13] Provincials struggle to catch up—to follow fashions and news from the far-off centers—but they are doomed to run in place. This rule would seem to apply to certain Chekhov texts as well—the setting of *Three Sisters*, for example, strikes us as irremediably and ahistorically provincial. But elsewhere in Chekhov, we witness places in the (historical) process of *being provincialized*: if a place is provincial because "its own center has been taken out of itself and transferred to some other space or time" (to quote once again Mikhail Epstein's definition), in some texts we seem to be watching such a transfer take place.[14]

Take, for example, the story "At Home" (1897). When we begin reading, it is not immediately clear either to us or to the main character that we are in the provinces, because we are (also) on the steppes. Vera, another of Chekhov's spirited, intelligent and doomed young women, has just finished her studies in Moscow and is traveling on the Donets railway line to her family's steppe estate, which she believes to be located in a far-off and exotic land. "At Home" tells the story of Vera's realization that while the steppes might once have been a frontier, they are now just the provinces—thanks largely to the train on which she has arrived.

As she disembarks at the "cheerless railway station" and sees "steppe, steppe, nothing but steppe," "without a shadow, without a single human being," Vera wants to believe she has arrived in a wilderness—"so spacious, so free" (9:313). But it soon becomes clear that by the later decades of the nineteenth century, the steppes no longer qualify as wild. The train tracks with which the story opens have succeeded in physically linking the steppe region to the far-off centers, but the result has not been the magically animating energy of true connection that was long anticipated by Russia's various apostles of railroads (see chapter 9), who had long held that once Russia was "[covered] by sections with an interconnected network of railroads," it was sure to "prosper and blossom forth with unheard-of progress," and "civilization would go rapidly forward."[15]

In Chekhov's representation, the new accessibility brought about by physical lines of connection does not lead to genuine connectedness or "civilization." Rather, as we will see in *The Cherry Orchard* too, railroads create a new sense of proximity that can in fact drain places of their former meanings, turning previously exotic or independent places into mere provinces. In "At Home," the railroads that bind the steppe to distant economic centers support the development of factories and mines, thus making what used to be a wild region much less wild—but not more civilized or culturally meaningful. The town near Vera's estate combines the usual narrowness of provincial sociality (fastidious manners, gossip) with intimations of a new urban chaos and unrest, as suggested by the late-night sounds of drunken workers carousing and passersby being robbed near the mining pits (9:318). In such passages Chekhov registers the rapid industrialization of the steppe region, which by 1880 or so was crisscrossed by train tracks. By this time even Russian peasants migrating to the steppe lands could do so by train, paying specially reduced "migrant rates" and obtaining official admittance documents from existing settlements (thus mirroring the processes by which Montana and Nebraska, having been "emptied" of their native inhabitants, were being "filled up" with the help of railroad corporations at around the same time).[16]

The Russian state, having long seen the land's emptiness as a problem, was making considerable progress toward filling it up. In taking account of such changes, "At Home" acknowledges what Chekhov seems deliberately to repress in his earlier story *The Steppe* (1888), which represents the same landscape, the same region, as if it were virtually untouched by modernity—despite the fact that by 1876 a wistful tourist could already declare that "[these] once-virgin lands are all plowed out."[17] In "At Home" the steppe is still big and empty, but its people and culture are straightforwardly provincial. On the estate Vera meets an aging aunt, mincing and tightly corseted, and a grandfather who misses the days when he could flog serfs; cowed servants run around trying to meet their demands. The estate swallows everything: nothing here is made or grown ("there was no farming being done"), and everything is eaten (upon seeing a sheep Vera thinks, "Grandfather will eat that," 9:317). Life in the nearby industrial town is no better. "Culture" here is limited to card-playing and polkas, and people spend their time "arguing about things they [do] not understand." Even the educated townspeople are ignorant and coarse; cut off from the ideas and connections that animate life elsewhere, they appear to Vera to have "no homeland, no religion, no public interests" (9:319).

In desperation Vera agrees to marry an eligible but stupid doctor who works at the iron works. Everything about this man—from his inarticulateness to his "cloying" expression and tasteless clothing—confirms that Vera is trapped in deepest *provintsiia*. Like Khvoshchinskaia's Lolenka, Vera asks the classic intelligentsia questions ("What to do? Where to go?" 9:319), but she finds no answers. And like the Prozorovs in *Three Sisters*, Vera is in possession of a fine education. She speaks three foreign languages and has traveled abroad and read widely: but for Vera as for her counterparts in the play, *provintsiia* is the end of the line. The difference is that while it is impossible for us to imagine the setting of *Three Sisters* as anything but eternally provincial, in "At Home," Chekhov reflects on the process by which a *particular* place (e.g., a place that was once a steppe frontier like the setting of Aksakov's *Family Chronicle*) can be turned into just another instantiation of *provintsiia*.

In *The Cherry Orchard*, too, we bear witness to such a transformation. The characters in Chekhov's last play can remember a time when they did not live in the anonymous provinces, but instead in a very particular place—on a singular estate with a singularly important orchard. Over and over they recur to a day when this orchard was *its own center*. Gaev reminds everyone that the orchard is mentioned in the *Encyclopedia*, Firs recalls how they used to send cartloads of dried cherries off to Kharkov and Moscow, and Liubov' Andreevna declares, "if there's one thing in this whole province that's interesting, even remarkable, it's our cherry orchard"—"without the orchard I cannot understand my own life," she cries. All are referring to a time before their own place had been provincialized by its new proximity to something else, something more important. As the merchant Lopakhin understands, the orchard is no longer its own place, but rather a place that is close (enough) to another, more central place—it is now simply land that is "only twenty versts from town," with "the railroad close by" (13:233, 205–6). Once it has been provincialized in this way, the country estate and the orchard can be definitively transformed into real estate, easily divisible into plots for summer cottages.

When Liubov Andreevna cries that "without the orchard [she] cannot understand [her] own life," the cherry orchard is made to occupy the same position that "Moscow" occupies in *Three Sisters*—touchstone, organizing principle, and bearer of meaning. But what becomes clear in *The Cherry Orchard* is that provincialism depends as much on proximity as it does on distance. Hence the importance of Chekhov's notes on the set: in addition to the dilapidated garden, the orchard, and the road leading to the manor house, there is "a row of telegraph poles" and in the distance the outline of "a large town" (13:215). As in *Three Sisters*, here again railroad lines and telegraph poles figure prominently, as they do in so many of Chekhov's works with provincial settings (*My Life*, "The Fiancée," and "At Home," as well as "In the Ravine," "Murder," *The Duel*, "Lights," and "Champagne," among others); indeed, these technologies of travel and communication are frequently incorporated into the plot (e.g., Irina's job as a telegraph operator in *Three Sisters*).

In virtually every such instance, Chekhov makes it clear that lines of tracks and wires stretching off into a vague distance do not guarantee a meaningful link between a provincial place and anyplace else. The long tale *Peasants*, for instance, ends with a mournful reminder that technologies of modernity are likely to skip over vast swaths of land, connecting only a few isolated nodes and thereby reducing everyplace else to what we would today call fly-over space. In the story's closing lines, a peasant woman reduced to living as an itinerant beggar walks with her small daughter along a country road, traversing a landscape that seems entirely rural (there are farms, skylarks, crakes)—until Chekhov notes the line of telegraph poles extending out to the horizon, and over the characters' heads, wires "humming mysteriously" (9:312). The telegraph has nothing to do with the reality of the characters' lives or that of the space they inhabit: Chekhov's radically deracinated peasants occupy the space that wires and tracks have passed over, both literally and figuratively. Much as we see at the end of Dostoevsky's *Demons*, when Stepan Trofimovich wanders out into the countryside and encounters peasants who live "off the grid" (see chapter 9), here again we meet characters who have no choice but to be *in* modernity, but are certainly not *of* it.[18] In both texts, connective technologies serve only "the points of departure, the way-stations, and the terminals, which are mostly at great distances from each other," as a French writer put it in 1840; they are "of no use whatsoever" for the spaces in between, "which they traverse with disdain and provide only with a useless spectacle."[19]

Of course, technologies like the railroad effected many conceptual-geographic transformations in the nineteenth century, and in Russia during Chekhov's lifetime, they did so in a dramatically compressed period of time. Chekhov's texts, by returning again and again to tracks and trains and stations and telegraph lines, register the *changing* meanings of Russia's geography: what used to be far becomes less far, what used to be inaccessible becomes a tourist destination, what used to be on the way is out of the way once the rail line has bypassed it, what used to be a place to stop overnight becomes a place through which one travels without slowing down. Thus while Chekhov's provinces may reprise the "filth, vulgarity and asiaticism" (as Trofimov says in *The Cherry Orchard*) that literature has taught us to expect of such places, they are rarely characterized by the utter stasis that tends to prevail in other writers' Towns of N, simply because Chekhov's vision is capable of acknowledging, whether implicitly or explicitly, the possibility of change and movement. Given this mutability, it is not surprising that Chekhov's works are rarely structured around a rigid binary that collapses all noncapital space into a homogeneous *provintsiia*; rather, they tend to acknowledge gradations of provinciality, just as they acknowledge gradations of everything.

And yet—in some sense the quality of *provintsial'nost'* remains nearly as elusive and even mysterious in Chekhov's world as it does in Gogol's. For one thing, this quality is not confined to the Russian interior or to the unambiguously native "heartland." The quintessentially provincial setting of *Three Sisters* might even be in the Urals, Chekhov hints ("in a provincial town like Perm," as he writes in a letter),[20] which is a region considerably more remote than what comes to mind when we imagine Russian *provintsiia*. In "At Home," as we have seen, what used to be a steppe frontier has become the provinces thanks to the railway, and in "The Fiancée," it is possible to live a markedly provincial life in Moscow. And one might easily list more examples from Chekhov texts I have not considered here. In "Lights," for instance, a coastal hamlet on the train line to the Caucasus proves to be as grim and "provincial" as any steppe town ("life in a seaside Town of N . . . for someone from the capital, can be as dull and comfortless as in any Chukhloma or Kashira"; 7:112–13). In *The Duel*, even the Caucasus region itself—in literature perhaps the only locus of undisputed sublimity within the Russian empire, virtually never represented as provincial but instead as reliably exotic—is likened to "languishing at the bottom of a very deep well" ("if I were offered the choice of a chimney-sweep in Petersburg or a prince in the Caucasus, I should choose the job of chimney-sweep," says one character; 7:359).

Chekhov's last play is a meditation on the fact that a place can come to experience itself as "provincial" only after it is made acutely aware of some other, "central" place, as well as its own distance from that central place and thus from everything that counts as significant. *The Cherry Orchard* shows us a formerly remote location in the process of being brought just close enough to a "center" so as to be made constantly aware of its fundamental distance from and dependence on that center, wherever it might be. And Chekhov explicitly invites us to make the comparison between this newly provincialized place (the orchard) and Russia itself: "all of Russia is our orchard," Trofimov declares.

The main opposition at work in *The Cherry Orchard* is not between province and capital, but between Russia and Europe. Characters arrive not from the Russian capitals but from abroad (from Paris, the distilled essence of "Europe"), they talk of traveling back and forth not to Moscow and Petersburg but to Yaroslavl and Kharkov, "Moscow" is mentioned only in passing, in the same breath as Kiev as a "holy place"—and all are symbolically opposed to Europe. As characters speak of coming from and going to Paris, with even the least sophisticated among them having learned to bemoan Russia's "barbarism" and "ignorance" (13:236, 247), Russia is made to resemble a little town on the steppe that becomes definitively provincial once the railroad and the telegraph arrive. In other words, the more closely Russia is brought into contact with Europe, the more acutely it experiences its own provinciality.

CHAPTER ELEVEN

In the End: Shchedrin, Sologub, and Terminal Provinciality

"It's no Paris here."
"Oh, indeed, it's no Paris."

—Fyodor Sologub, 1913

Provincial life is a great school, but a filthy one.
—Saltykov-Shchedrin, 1852

In the nineteenth-century discourse of *provintsiia*, Mikhail Saltykov-Shchedrin (hereafter Shchedrin) and Fyodor Sologub feel like end points: they evoke what one might call a *terminal* provinciality. At the same time, their texts point forward to how the provinces trope will make itself felt in the twentieth century. Thus they offer us an appropriate place to end this book's examination of what the provinces have meant in the literature of nineteenth-century Russia, as well as a way to begin looking ahead to what they will mean in the following period. Shchedrin's *The Golovlyov Family* and Sologub's *Petty Demon* are separated in time by approximately two decades (*The Golovlyov Family* was serialized between 1875 and 1880; *Petty Demon* came out between 1892 and 1902); Shchedrin's text is set on an estate, Sologub's in an unnamed provincial town. But both these settings strike us as *the end of the line*, places where narrative itself is so congealed in a mire of sticky *provintsial'nost'* that forward movement has become virtually impossible.

Shchedrin's Golovlyovo: The Provinces as Coffin

The Golovlyov Family was not Shchedrin's first work to treat the "swamp" of provincial life. After being exiled to Vyatka from 1848 to 1856 (for having published a novella that caught the authorities' attention in the aftermath of the 1848 revolutions), he published a series of *Provincial Sketches* (*Gubernskie ocherki*) upon his return to Petersburg. If in his later satirical work *History of a Town,* the provincial capital quite clearly stands for all of Russia and the town's history for Russia's history (so clearly, in fact, that I do not treat it here: because *History of a Town* is too allegorical to be *about* the provinces), in *Provincial Sketches* the provinces stand for the provinces—the place that Shchedrin was desperate to escape throughout his seven-year banishment. His provincial exile was by no means brutal; he simply served as a bureaucrat, much as Herzen and Melnikov had done during their exiles in the 1830s and 1840s (exiles which also produced memoirs). Nonetheless these years left Shchedrin with exceedingly bitter memories: the thought of having to live out his life in the provinces, as he wrote to his brother, was "so repellent it made [his] hair stand on end."[1]

The *Provincial Sketches* are set in an imaginary town "at the end of the world"; the moment you enter, Shchedrin writes, "you know you can never again ask anything of life."[2] Recapitulating virtually every *provintsiia* trope (filth, repetition, stasis, bureaucratic corruption, vile predictability), recurring over and over to the familiar provincial images of slime and swamp (*tina* and *boloto*), Shchedrin, like Herzen, dwells on the provinces' power to rot and defile: in a sketch aptly titled "Boredom" ("Skuka") he writes, "Oh provinces, you corrupt people!" (*o provintsiia, ty rasstlevaesh' liudei*).[3] Anyone is liable to "drown in the swamp of provincial life": "pity the young man who is cast out into the provinces! Imperceptibly, little by little, he sinks into a mire of trivialities" (the Russian here is *tina melochei,* words that we have seen in descriptions of *provintsiia* from the 1830s on).[4] "Provincial stench and filth will creep up on you until one fine day you find yourself sitting up to your ears in all the trivial vileness . . . that abounds in the life of a small town," living a life that destroys the desire for anything beyond the physical.[5]

Life in the *Provincial Sketches*' imaginary town strikes us as foul, but not as an irreversible catastrophe on a metaphysical level: in other words, it is quite possible to imagine the wrongs Shchedrin describes in the *Sketches* being righted. One might build a railway line to the town, say, or fire the most corrupt bureaucrats, or open a lending library. The text does not assign the town's negative qualities the status of terminal, irreparable spiritual deficiencies; this provincial place is not a void that will forever resist being filled up. Like Herzen in *Who Is to Blame?* Shchedrin is interested in milieu and its effects—an interest that leaves open the possibility of change. And since the provinces/capital binary shapes this text's symbolic geography, people in the provincial town can dream of going to the capital, and at times they do go. Even if the town in *Provincial Sketches* is the last stop on the road, it is not the last stop for narrative itself: something might still *happen.*

The same cannot be said about *The Golovlyov Family*, a book that has been called "one long obituary."[6] Shchedrin tells the story of sixteen deaths in three generations, all in the same gentry family—the matriarch Arina Petrovna and her three sons Stepan, Pavel, and Porfiry (the last of whom is known as "Little Judas"), Arina's husband, Vladimir, her daughter Anna, her five children who die at birth, three more of her grandchildren (two by suicide and one in prison), and a fourth illegitimate grandchild sent off to die in a foundling hospital. Her final grandchild is on the verge of death as the novel ends.[7] For the reader, these deaths—almost all of which result from the same pathological stinginess and neglect—become nearly indistinguishable from one another. The narrative is not structured by any plot (it opens with denouement, as one critic says) but rather by repetition and rhythm in a series of largely static portraits or scenes.[8] Even the province/capital binary that conditions the meaning of *provintsiia* in so many nineteenth-century texts has faded away in *The Golovlyov Family*: here the capital seems hardly to exist, even as a dream. Characters who try to escape Golovlyovo can do so only temporarily (to the army, to a bureaucratic post in Petersburg, to work as an actress in a provincial theater); soon enough they are drawn back "home" to this least homey of places. Golovlyovo can never be a home, as one granddaughter realizes when she returns, desperate and starving, to find nothing but "desolation, comfortlessness, alienation."[9]

All we know about the estate's location is that it is far away from everything else; indeed, it is so cut off from the rest of the world that other places seem thoroughly illusory. When the matriarch Arina Petrovna considers banishing one son to the Suzdal monastery, she cannot even be sure that this famous place is real:[10] once you are interred at Golovlyovo, the rest of the world recedes and all avenues out are occluded. The horizon here is low and the land flat; you could be anywhere on the open steppe. The seasons are unremittingly hostile: July is stifling, the October skies pour rain, winter is a "desolate, dreary desert," and throughout the year the clouds hang heavy and motionless.[11] Even the wind stands still at Golovlyovo.

So illegible is the surrounding landscape that it threatens to obliterate meaning by rendering all things indistinguishable from one another. We see the space around Golovlyovo as eternally obscured, whether covered with a "uniform shroud of blackness," "a blinding haze," "an endless winding sheet of snow," or a blizzard in which "everything [disappears] in a whirling mist."[12] From the manor house, people in the distance appear as "black dots in gray autumn fog," "black specks" and "dots."[13] "Bare, endless fields" dissolve all distinctions that might have rendered the space decipherable, and characters can stare out the window for hours without making any sense of what they see.[14] We are repeatedly told that everything within view melts together or disappears: topography here actively defies attempts to render it significant or even comprehensible.

This is what Berdiaev would soon describe as the "gloom of deep *provintsiia*," the empty open space in which Russian culture always "feared it would drown."[15] In the vast, flat, all-the-same steppe where everything blurs together, no signs are readable, and the system of *contrasts* upon which Saussurean meaning-making depends seems to be disabled. Here we recall again the landscape that engulfs us in *Dead Souls*—"exposed, desolate, and flat," with "low-lying towns scattered over the plains like specks, like dots"[16]—and in texts like Dostoevsky's *Demons*, Chekhov's *Steppe*, Grigorovich's *Anton Goremyka*, and so many others: empty, relentlessly horizontal, and unreadable. *The Golovlyov Family* takes this emptiness and meaninglessness to the last extreme. The space surrounding Golovlyovo is not just silent and monotonous, but would seem instead to represent an irremediable lack, a void that is simply not amenable to any kind of improvement or "filling up."

No news reaches the estate ("no books, no newspapers, no letters," no "connection with the outside world").[17] Under such circumstances there can be no engagement with historical forces or historical meanings, and thus life here cannot be anything other than "blind, unexpected, haphazard," as Shchedrin describes the Golovlyovs' existence (*slepo, ne gadano, ne dumano*).[18] Only dimly aware of the great historic upheavals of their age (the emancipation of the serfs, the decline of the patriarchal order, radical changes in the economy), Shchedrin's protagonists simply "grow like nettles along a fence," with "no work, no connection with public life, no political importance."[19] Hence what he describes as the purposeless freedom of the provincial landowner, "a freedom so limitless that there [is] nothing but a gaping void."[20]

The provinces disable narrative and expunge memory, collapsing time into what this novel calls the "grim and bare present."[21] As each character approaches death, there is "neither past nor future, but only the present moment to be lived through," as not only historical memory but personal recollections become increasingly fragmented and intermittent.[22] For Stepan, "a thick wall" arises "between that which had been and was now" ("the past did not respond with a single recollection," only "senseless and disconnected" images); Arina, too, can recall her past only intermittently and in "disconnected fragments."[23]

The deaths follow a nearly identical pattern, beginning with repetition and paralysis. The first to go is Stepan, who paces in a tiny room, sensing only "a succession of dull, hideous days, swallowed up one after the other in the gray, yawning abyss of time": "the grim and bare present claimed him."[24]

> All there was before him was the present, in the shape of a tightly locked prison in which the idea of space and time disappeared without a trace. The room, the stove, three windows, a creaky wooden bed with a thin hard mattress on it, the table with the bottle of vodka—this was the horizon beyond which his mind could not penetrate.[25]

When the darkness recedes, Stepan confronts a light that is worse: "space filled by phosphorescent brilliance," "a dead, endless void, sinister and luminous, without a single sound of life . . . no doors, no windows—nothing but the boundless, garish void."[26] For Porfiry and Anninka too, as death approaches, their surroundings are "obliterated by a luminous void."[27] Emptiness, monotony, silence—these words recur over and over.

The Golovlyovs occupy "a dead, endless void"—and yet this void is full of physical objects: room, stove, windows, bed, mattress, table, bottle.[28] When Stepan awakens full of "anguish, disgust, and hatred," he directs his attention toward these objects: "His inflamed eyes dwelt first on one object and then another. . . . The stove was in front of him, and his mind was so occupied with taking it in that it was impervious to any other impression. Then the window replaced the stove; window, window, window . . . ."[29] Nothing about these things is worthy of attention, but for characters who are aware of nothing beyond the body and its demands, the world of the senses expands to fill the whole consciousness. Even language acquires a physical presence—a degraded one—at Golovlyovo. Porfiry's constant, poisonous babble is called a "sticky stream" of corrupt and corrupting words, a material force that, as a peasant remarks, can "rot a man" with its "putrid" effect, "like an open, festering sore."[30]

All reality at Golovlyovo is reduced to the physical, to mere things. Because physical objects are "empty of emotional content and devoid of spiritual value," as Ehre writes, "the Golovlyovs stand before an incoherence of things, a reality turned into nightmare."[31] And to be embedded in this material world is to be mired in filth. As Stepan lies on his deathbed, the narrative dwells on the squalor of his surroundings:

> The room was so grimy, dusty, and filthy. . . . The ceiling was black, the wallpaper had cracked and hung in tatters in many places, the window-sills were dark under a thick layer of ashes, the pillows lay on the slimy floor, a crumpled sheet, gray with dirt, was thrown on the bed . . . the air smelt of a hideous mixture of cheap vodka, coarse tobacco, and wet sheepskins.[32]

Stepan's brother Pavel inhabits a nearly identical environment:

> The rooms . . . were in semi-darkness; the windows were covered with green curtains . . . ; the stagnant air was filled with an unpleasant mixture of different smells, including the smell of fruit, plasters, lamp oil, and the odors that unmistakably suggest disease and death.[33]

Clouds of flies swarm about the room, alighting sometimes on the sick man; on his deathbed, Pavel rants about beetles, moles, and rotten hay.[34]

The grossly material quality of the Golovlyovs' world is underscored by the book's preoccupation with food and eating. By Shchedrin's time literature had long associated *provintsiia* with grotesque excesses of consumption: think of Sollogub's lists of dainties, Gogol's lovingly described meals, and Herzen's references to "food that would kill anyone accustomed to a European diet"—all serving as indices for what Herzen calls the purely "animal desires" (*zhivotnye zhelaniia*) that shape provincial life.[35] But Shchedrin's focus on food is accompanied by constant references to hunger and want—an old auntie starved to death, a disgraced uncle forced to eat from a dog's bowl.[36] Arina withholds food from her dying son Stepan, who thinks of nothing but what is being eaten at the manor house (snipe or mutton? liver, mushrooms in sour cream, custard cakes?); she herself is later starved by her son Porfiry and spends her hungry old age dreaming of carp, mushrooms, and poultry. When Arina is obliged to feed her children and grandchildren, she gives them putrid meat and sour milk.[37]

Yet the Golovlyovo property is rich and vast; provisions pile up in great quantities as the peasants pay their taxes in kind. Recurring lists of foodstuffs ("dried mushrooms, berries, eggs, vegetables, and so on")[38] remind us that wealth on the provincial estate exists almost solely in physical and usually organic form. But all this organic material is more likely to rot than to be consumed; people go hungry in the midst of abundance because everything is hidden away to decompose in "the yawning abyss of the cellars."[39] The narrative returns constantly to images of corruption and decay: as hoarded foodstuffs go bad, giving off a putrid smell, they are fed to the servants and children even as fresh supplies are being stored away to spoil, sacrificed to what Shchedrin calls elsewhere "the greed of the future."[40] By the end of the novel, Porfiry Petrovich, having locked himself away in one room of his huge house, is piling up money as though it were food. Unable to conceive of any form of "investment"—that is, unable to believe that one must feed people today so as to keep them alive tomorrow, or spend money now in order to realize a return next year—the Golovlyovs are out of circulation in every sense.[41] They represent the final devolution of the traditional rural gentry that was already beginning to decay in Gogol's "Old World Landowners" and Goncharov's *Oblomov*, characters whose torpid mushroom-fueled idylls were always at the point of sliding into mere rot. And if in *The Cherry Orchard* we watch Russia's ruling class wither into dry dust and blow away (in the characters' desultory dispersal at the play's end), gentry rot as staged in *The Golovlyov Family* is decidedly moist, a family decomposing in the stagnant pond it has dredged for itself: terminal stasis.

Thus do the Golovlyovs live out the last stage of what Odoevsky called the "bestial dream" (*zhivotnyi son*) of provincial life, where reality is densely and *merely* physical.[42] Again we find ourselves in the polar opposite of the Acmeists' world, which Mandelshtam imagines as a place where the things surrounding human beings are not "indifferent objects" but "utensils" filled with purpose and meaning. In the Acmeist dream, objects can serve to "unite the external world to humanity," resulting in "the humanization of the surrounding world, the environment heated with the most delicate teleological warmth."[43] But in Shchedrin's novel, every object is aggressively indifferent; nothing is capable of "[uniting] the external world to humanity." Like *Dead Souls*, *The Golovlyov Family* imagines a space that is at once empty (characterized by "eventlessness and nonbeing [*nebytie*]," as one critic sums up *Dead Souls*)[44] *and* crammed full of things; in both texts we encounter an excessive, oppressive physicality that coexists with what Gogol calls "the highest degree of Emptiness"[45]—or what Shchedrin terms the "dead, endless void."

The setting of *The Golovlyov Family* is repeatedly called a tomb, a grave, a coffin, a vault, a sepulcher. If death is virtually the only thing that happens in this book, perhaps this is because death is the only thing that *can* happen on the remote provincial estate in this, its final iteration. Your story is over the moment you arrive at Golovlyovo: upon Stepan's return we read that "the doors of the sepulchral vault opened, let him in—and slammed shut."[46] Stepan sees his mother's house and thinks, "Grave! Grave! Grave!"[47] In fact every return amounts to an entombment: "This is my grave, my grave, my grave!"[48] "Golovlyovo is death itself," Anninka thinks.[49] And if in *Dead Souls* and *Demons* an outsider arrives in an inert provincial place and thereby generates narrative, in Shchedrin's text anyone who arrives at Golovlyovo is instead consumed—"eaten up," as the characters say over and over—by the black hole of provincial life. Not only is there "no future, no escape" (as one character thinks), but in fact *"nothing can happen"*:[50] the provincial estate has swallowed up the very possibility of narrative.

Sologub's Town of N: This Is Not Paris

Like Shchedrin, Fyodor Sologub (1863–1927) was forced to spend years in Russia's provinces and was deeply marked by the experience.[51] Sologub was a descendant of serfs and the son of an illiterate mother; when he became a schoolteacher, his profession required him to serve much of his career in isolated towns. His biographers, basing their judgments on Sologub's own accounts, represent his various provincial postings as a living hell: "years of vulgar existence" during which he had to endure "the petty vulgarity of life in a small provincial town" with its "meddlesome incompetence and tyranny" and "coarse philistinism."[52] But throughout his years in *provintsiia*, Sologub assiduously followed the newest developments in literary life—especially symbolism—in the capitals and Europe. He even made a special trip to Petersburg in 1889 to meet the avant-garde writers Dmitry Merezhkovsky and Nikolai Minsky, after which he returned to the provinces for several more years. Given the intensity of this contrast, it is difficult to imagine a situation more conducive to sharpening one's sense of the chasm between center and periphery—and indeed the "nightmare of soul-destroying provincial life" (in one critic's words) informs more than one of his works.[53] *Bad Dreams* (1895), *Petty Demon* (1907), and *Sweeter Than Poison* (1912) are all set in more or less this same milieu, and all were written after he escaped the provinces for Petersburg in 1892.

A foreword to the seventh edition of *Petty Demon* (1913) announces, "'This isn't Paris!' 'Oh no, it's certainly not Paris!'"[54] The novel is set in an anonymous provincial town, and although the word *provintsiia* occurs only once (when a character asks, "Now you see what's meant by a provincial milieu?"),[55] there is no need for it to recur: the fact that we are not in Paris is abundantly clear. To the extent that the narrative has a plot, it is as follows: an unpleasant, suspicious schoolteacher named Peredonov loses his grip on reality as his paranoia intensifies. The characters surrounding Peredonov are by and large as limited, animalistic, repellent and even subhuman as he is. (The exception is a rather mysterious subplot involving the young lovers Liudmila and Sasha, whose erotic games hold out the vague possibility of an embodied experience that is something other than degraded.)

Although we do not begin to exhaust the meaning of *Petty Demon* by saying it is about *provintsiia* (it is about many things, including perhaps the nature of evil or even "life in its entirety"),[56] it certainly could not have been set anywhere else. And more importantly, it could not have been written without the preceding century's development of the *provintsiia* trope: *Petty Demon* is virtually unimaginable without its various intertexts—*Dead Souls*, *Demons*, "The Man in a Case," and others—which are recalled in nearly every chapter. Gogol is ever present, especially in the way Sologub's seemingly dead characters attempt to "prop up their hollowness by insignia of rank," for instance, and in the constant parallels between these characters and animals.[57] *Petty Demon* takes all we have come to associate with a nameless Town of N and pushes it not just to the point of surrealism (since literature's provincial towns had been a prime locus of the surreal from at least Gogol's time on), but to the point of a terrifying, nauseating burlesque. The obsession with hierarchy, bureaucracy, and denunciations; food and eating as indices of degradation; a repetitive, ahistorical temporality; a nearly apocalyptic boredom—there is nothing new about Sologub's provincial town.

Things happen in *Petty Demon*, but there is no plot, no narrative trajectory driven by characters' desires. In fact only rarely can we identify reasons or "psychology" behind what people do in this text, so bizarrely abrupt and unmotivated are their behaviors. Rubbing a cat's fur the wrong way, tearing off strips of wallpaper: many actions in the novel are in some sense inexplicable (Peredonov's are often described as "sudden"), but the acts of petty destruction are perhaps the most strikingly so. Much as in *The Golovlyov Family*, where we are never expected to understand precisely *why* Arina would choose to starve her grandchildren while food rots in her cellars or *why* Porfiry would send his own son off to die, in *Petty Demon* we are not invited to ask why Peredonov and the other characters do what they do. Here again we see an intensification of a familiar *provintsiia* trope, in this case, the idea that what is done in provincial places is more likely to be motivated by an extremity of boredom—or by something we cannot name—than by plan or desire. Earlier depictions of provincial life have accustomed us to the vaguely senseless quality of characters' actions in such places (as in Chekhov's "A Man in a Case": "But what ridiculous things don't we do in the provinces, simply out of boredom!").[58] But in *Petty Demon,* provincial boredom and absurdity seem to have supplanted or blotted out interiority and psychology altogether. They have expanded, as it were, to the point that nothing in the text *can* make sense in terms of the kind of motivation we expect of literary realism; it simply becomes impossible to imagine such characters having reasons for doing what they do. The very world of *Petty Demon* has no reason to exist: "Depressing silence reigned in the streets, and it seemed *as if all these pitiful houses had sprung up to no purpose,* as if their hopelessly decrepit shapes hinted at the poor, tedious, and boring life within their walls."[59]

Marked by a near-total absence of interiority, Sologub's characters are less people than they are puppets, puppets in the sense Bakhtin describes such figures in his characterization of the "Romantic grotesque"—"the puppet as the victim of alien inhuman force, which rules over men by turning them into marionettes," devoid of what we would call psychology.[60] This shell-like quality links *Petty Demon* once again to *The Golovlyov Family* (e.g., "the protective layer of empty and thoroughly rotten aphorisms with which [Porfiry has] cloaked himself from head to toe"),[61] as well as to the longer history of the *provintsiia* trope. The one-note townspeople of *Dead Souls* and *The Inspector General,* the "beasts" and "savages" Herzen met during his provincial exile, the mask-like Stavrogin in *Demons,* Chekhov's various provincial automata eating their way through life, Dal's pitiful "unlucky one": all these figures point to an enduring link between *provintsiia* and the refusal of deep psychology. This refusal often marks the grotesque as well; indeed Ani Kokobobo's apt characterization of *The Golovlyov Family* as an example of "grotesque realism" can be extended to *Petty Demon.* In both texts, an exaggeratedly provincial milieu serves as incubator and intensifier of the grotesque—which makes perfect sense, given what we have seen to be literature's long history of using *provintsiia* as a laboratory for exploring hybridity, incoherence, dehumanization, and gross corporeality. Thus it is unsurprising that in the last decades of the Imperial period—when Russian prose fiction, as Kokobobo argues, responded to social upheaval and extreme instability by infusing realism with elements of the grotesque[62]—the provinces serve as a locus for such narrative experimentation.

Life in *Petty Demon* amounts to a monotonous and never-ending competition for scarce resources; to build a plot around Sologub's characters would be like trying to tell the "story" of amoebas fighting for survival in a pond.[63] If Shchedrin's Golovlyovs are living the bestial dream of provincial life, Sologub's characters seem to have even descended even further down the scale of being; as Zamiatin puts it, Peredonov is a species of "mold" that "grows everywhere all by itself,"[64] without being planted or cultivated (by comparison Shchedrin's landowners are "growing like nettles along a fence"). And if in Shchedrin's morbid attention to the Golovlyovs' degeneracy and their obsession with feeding themselves we sense the influence of popularized Darwinian theory, in *Petty Demon* such theory is invoked openly: "It's a struggle for survival! They can't all be inspectors!" Peredonov declares.[65] Like amoebas in a pond, Sologub's protagonists have "no goals, only habits"—and habits do not generate narratives with clear forward trajectories, clear *stories*.[66] Thus *Petty Demon* reads like a series of "incidents" strung together, with little in the way of the cause-effect relationships we expect from a plot—just "a tremendous and confusing number of encounters . . . which neither advance the story nor give us insight into the characters."[67] (*The Golovlyov Family*, similarly lacking in plot and forward trajectory, reads like a series of tableaux, more *morts* than *vivants*.)

In a narrative like Sologub's, the passage of time—whether historical, familial, or seasonal—is so hard to trace that it comes to seem irrelevant. Indeed as *Petty Demon* progresses, it is increasingly dominated by imperfective verbs, suggesting not progress or development but rather a hell of repetition and accretion.[68] Here we note the intensification of another familiar trope: the nauseating repetition long associated with *provintsiia* reaches an apotheosis, an extreme which would be difficult to exceed. Peredonov—who, like all of Sologub's characters, both speaks and is described in a severely limited lexicon—repeats the same phrases over and over, invoking and re-invoking senseless "spells" and "counter-spells" intended to protect him from his enemies; other characters, too, compulsively repeat themselves, "unable to stop, retelling the very same thing in a variety of ways."[69] Such verbal tics recall Porfiry's mechanical prayers and clichés in *The Golovlyov Family*. In both texts linguistic compulsions are motivated by fear, and in both, language takes on a kind of morbid, even putrid materiality. Peredonov's words seem to be the source of the elusive *nedotykomka*, a malign little creature that takes shape to torment him; likewise Shchedrin's Porfiry, as we have seen, produces a "sticky stream" of corrupt and corrupting speech.[70]

Sologub's characters, like Shchedrin's, are mired in an exaggerated form of the sticky, degraded materiality that has long marked literature's depictions of provincial places. Often likened to various animals, the town's inhabitants are constantly shown to be guzzling food and drink (Peredonov gorges himself on dirty raisins)[71] and seeking to indulge carnal appetites: they are at one with the filth of their environment. The young widow Grushina, for instance—who lives in a "slovenly" little house with three children who are "shabby, dirty, stupid, and mean"[72]—is described almost entirely in terms of the various kinds of dirt covering her body:

> She was slender, her dry skin covered with fine little wrinkles that seemed to be full of dust. He face wasn't unpleasant, but her teeth were dirty and black. Her hands were slender, her fingers long and grasping, with dirty fingernails. At first glance she didn't seem very dirty, but she gave the impression that she never washed but instead just beat the dust out of herself along with her clothes. One felt that if one were to hit her a few times with a carpet beater, a column of dust would rise all the way up to the sky. Her clothing hung in wrinkled folds, as though it had just been unpacked from a tightly wrapped bundle where it had lain crumpled up for a long time.[73]

Filth in *Petty Demon* is ubiquitous (forms of the word *griaz'*—dirt—recur constantly); the very earth under the town is "unclean" (*nechistoi*).[74] At times the streets are covered with dust; at other times they are thick with viscous, impassable mud.[75]

Indeed by the time of *Petty Demon* and *The Golovlyov Family*, literature seems to have concluded that the defining attributes of Russian *provintsiia* are simply filth and mud. Since the 1830s we have known to expect the word *griaz'* (dirt) in any description of a provincial place, often alongside swamp, slime, dust, and mud; the words puddle, unpaved, and impassable come up frequently as well.[76] The pattern becomes ever more obvious over the course of the century. A mid-nineteenth-century travel sketch characterizes the town of Vesegonsk, for instance, with reference to the "three swamps (*bolota*) right in the middle of town," which "never dry up." We even encounter towns that effectively *are* swamps (*gorod-boloto*), as in Nemirovich-Danchenko's description of Elets: "the whole town seemed like a large puddle in which countless pigs were lolling about."[77] Finally, by the time of Bely's *Silver Dove* (1910), all inhabitants of the godforsaken town of Likhov (the only notable features of which are mud and dust) can be divided into two parties, the mud party and the dust party.[78] Such pervasive filth suggests not just degradation but also the intellectual and spiritual *disorder* that has come to be associated with the provinces: dirt is "matter out of place," and the provinces are where nothing can ever be where it should be.[79]

Even though Sologub's characters, like Shchedrin's, have their eyes trained on pleasures that are strictly corporeal (since they know nothing different or higher), their physical environments offer them no succor or harmony, and the filth in which they live marks their fallenness. The built environment in *Petty Demon* recapitulates almost exactly the ugly and illegible version of pseudo-public space that has characterized literature's Towns of N since *Dead Souls*: lopsided "hovels" separated by barren spaces, an asymmetrical public "square" unpaved and over-grown with grass, a muddy courtyard.[80] This is the Town of N as we have seen it for decades—"one dirty street lined with submissively stooped little houses . . . resembling beggars in their rags" (Vladimir Sollogub), "more a disordered pile of huts than a town" (Shchedrin), etc.[81] Peredonov and the others devote themselves to defiling this "unclean" environment even further, spitting on the wallpaper, soaking it with beer, throwing balls of chewed-up bread onto the ceiling.[82] The only difference is that Sologub is more explicit than his predecessors in assign-ing meaning to the disorder and filth, telling us that in a place like this one, "in the grip of alienation from the sky," everything—from the "hopelessly decrepit" houses to the "murky light"—stands for "barbarity and ineradicable sorrow."[83]

The domestic objects that surround Sologub's characters are as hostile as those that surround Shchedrin's Golovlyovs. In *Petty Demon*, wine is served in glasses meant for coffee, vodka in glasses with their bases broken off so they cannot be set down. Furniture in the mayor's reception rooms is "strained and rigid," uncom-fortable as stones, "as if it were toy furniture that had been many times enlarged."[84] This is an aggressively alien and alienating material environment, again the polar opposite of Mandelshtam's harmonious, luminously significant Acmeist world. And while Shchedrin is a committed materialist, never gesturing toward mean-ings underneath or beyond the physical, rarely are we able to forget that Sologub is a Symbolist: and as a result, the grotesque nature of *Petty Demon*'s physical world strikes us as even more repellent. If, as one critic writes, "the artistic method through which *poshlost'* is integrated with the demonic is the grotesque," then the *poshlost'* and grotesquerie of Peredonov and his surroundings point toward some-thing worse—the evil, whether petty or not, signaled by the demon of the title.[85]

"Divorced from Time"

Poshlost', of course, is a Russian untranslatable, encompassing, in Svetlana Boym's description, at once "triviality, vulgarity, sexual promiscuity, and a lack of spiritu-ality."[86] Nabokov's famous riff defines it as "vulgar clichés . . . imitations of imita-tions, bogus profundities, crude, moronic and dishonest," "not only the obviously trashy but mainly the falsely important, the falsely beautiful."[87] As Nabokov's re-marks suggest, *poshlost'* assumes a certain striving and meretriciousness that are unlikely to characterize the very lowest classes. Rather than being linked to peas-ants or workers, *poshlost'* in literature is likely to be associated with the middling sort, including members of the *meshchanstvo* (very roughly, the philistine petite bourgeoisie) and the lower gentry. The semantic fields of *poshlost'* and *mesh-chanstvo* also overlap with that of *byt* ("daily life" in the grimmest sense). In the literary tradition, *provintsiia* is the main site where these three phenomena—*byt, meshchanstvo, poshlost'*—tend to find expression.

The provincial worlds of *The Golovlyov Family* and *Petty Demon* might be described as congealed *poshlost'*. All real action has been suspended: these worlds stand outside of historical time, and the only thing their characters can know is what Shchedrin's novel calls "the grim and bare present."[88] In these settings as in Pushkin's Goriukhino, the unstructured time and space of deep *provintsiia* cannot be assimilated to history, to "time experienced by the individual as a public being" who is conscious of historical changes.[89] Shchedrin's Golovlyovo and Sologub's Town of N are *cut off*, and their geographic insularity creates a temporal disjunction (as one critic describes the Golovlyovs, they are "unhinged from the dimension of time").[90] This disjunction in turn deprives events of meaning by divesting them of connections to larger systems. Neither psychology nor plot—both of which imply movement, development, and change—can exist in the environments imagined by Shchedrin and Sologub.

One can compare here Chaadaev, who locates *all of Russia* in space and time that is insufficiently structured—unmoored, unregulated, unbordered ("in our own houses we seem to be camping . . . in our cities we look like nomads")—and thus resistant to meaning. Spatial isolation results in temporal stasis or confusion: "we live only in the narrowest of presents, without past and without future, in the midst of a flat calm," he writes.[91] Chaadaev's insistence on Russia's isolation from "that wonderful interconnection of human ideas throughout the ages" anticipates Mikhail Bakhtin's description of *provintsiia* as chronotope: because the provincial town's isolation allows for "no advancing historical movement," Bakhtin says, in literature it cannot accommodate "events," but "only 'doings' that constantly repeat themselves."[92] When Bakhtin describes how provincial insularity creates a temporal disjunction that deprives events of larger meaning, leading to repetition and stagnation, he reprises Chaadaev's view of how time works for Russia as a whole: like Chaadaev's Russians, Bakhtin's provincials are "outside of time."[93]

Much the same can be said about time as it is represented by Shchedrin and Sologub. In fact *The Golovlyov Family* and *Petty Demon* remind us again that representations of provincial temporality have often served as commentaries on Russian history, which was long thought to defy European and supposedly universal rules of orderly progress and development: instead of a steady march forward, Russia's history (so the story went) was marked by contingency, with alternating periods of chaos and stagnation. As Lotman put it, the "inconsequentiality" of Russia's past was always threatening to render the nation's history "'inorganic,' illusory, or nonexistent" ('*neorganichnymi,' prizrachnymi, nesushchestvuiushchimi*).[94]

Lotman's adjectives—inorganic, illusory, nonexistent—might well be enlisted to describe the worlds imagined in the two novels this chapter has examined, worlds at once grossly material and in some sense phantasmagoric. As it is in *Dead Souls*—which also combines grotesque materiality with a pervasive sense of desolation and vacuity—so it is in *The Golovlyov Family* and *Petty Demon*: provincial stasis and isolation render change and movement nearly impossible, leaving characters outside of historical development, capable only of repeating their own words and actions. But as the last chapter of this book will argue, even as some Russians mourned their nation's failure to follow standard trajectories of historical development, literature's recurrence to the *provintsiia* trope could also serve to call into question the universality of European models, suggesting other ways of imagining historical time and raising the possibility that the chronological and spatial disorder of *provintsiia*/Russia might not prove to be as barren as any "flat calm" diagnosis would have it.

· CHAPTER TWELVE ·

Conclusion: The Provinces in the Twentieth Century

> Once again I am overcome with melancholy, once again I am in 'Tambov,'
> which in the future will become for me some kind of symbol.
> —Andrei Platonov, 1926

rovintsiia can be read as the prehistory of *byt*, that untranslatable Russian noun denoting what is pointedly untranscendent about "daily life," forever mired in the trivial and the material. The provinces trope prepares the ground for the modernists' strenuous rejection of all things daily and banal; indeed, before *byt* assumed its sharply negative connotations in the modernist and early Soviet period, the idea of provinciality did much of the same cultural work. Materiality, repetition, routine, food, stasis, the anti-aesthetic and the anti-poetic: "the provinces" tend to function much as "the daily grind" will do for Mayakovsky and others. When we read that for Mayakovsky *byt* signified "the general enslavement of man to physical, biological, and social necessity," we could well be reading about *provintsiia* and Herzen (or Gogol or Chekhov or any number of nineteenth-century writers).[1] It is no surprise that even modernists who tend to treat *byt* as a metaphysical category often locate it geographically in provincial places.

This book has been devoted to the process by which nineteenth-century Russian writers imagined the provinces into being, thereby figuring alienation in geographic terms that have proven powerfully enduring. In the coda below, I glance ahead at the trope's afterlives in the twentieth century, considering briefly how Silver Age and Soviet writers made use of the geographic imaginary that they inherited. Finally, I conclude by reflecting on the relationship between Russian provinciality and the problematic (Western) idea of "World Literature"—a category

from which Russian texts, no matter how "worldly" or how widely circulated, have
been almost wholly excluded.

The Provinces Trope in the Twentieth Century

Not so long after Sologub published the final version of *Petty Demon*, he wrote a
poem about a Russian provincial town that seems nothing at all like the novel's
grim, nameless setting. Not only is the poem's subject identified as a real place
(Kostroma), it is infused with precisely the kind of luminous significance whose
very absence defines the nameless setting of *Petty Demon*:

> Сквозь туман едва заметный
> Тихо блещет Кострома,
> Словно Китеж, град заветный,-
> Храмы, башни, терема.
> Кострома—воспоминанья,
> Исторические сны,
> Легендарные сказанья,
> Голос русской старины,
> Уголок седого быта,
> Новых фабрик и купцов,
> Где так много было скрыто
> Чистых сил и вещих снов.

> Through the fog, barely seen,
> Softly flickers Kostroma.
> Like Kitezh, the sacred city,
> Temples, towers, palaces.
> Kostroma is memories,
> Historic dreams,
> Legendary tales,
> The voice of Russia's olden times.
> A little corner of grey *byt*,
> Of new factories and tradesmen,
> Where lie hidden such
> Pure forces and prophetic dreams.[2]

In another context, the toponym "Kostroma" might evoke much the same feeling that, say, "Kharkov" evokes in Chekhov ("Kharkov in Chekhov is a symbol of nowhere," as Lawrence Senelick writes), a place where characters can

be dispatched to a provincial death-in-life.[3] But in Sologub's suggestive lyric, Kostroma instead becomes a source of cultural and even spiritual treasures: one must see through whatever is grey or bleak or *bytovoi* about it (*bytovoi*, derived from *byt*, evoking the low commonness of daily life) in order to perceive the mystical riches lying underneath.

I would emphasize that this particular Silver Age way of imagining of the provinces has little to do with the *provintsiia* trope this book has traced. Rather, it draws on ideas about the cultural authenticity of *glush'* (remote rural places, as I have discussed in connection with Leskov and Melnikov) and a certain version of *derevnia* (the village or gentry estate, *Onegin*-style). We note the distinction immediately in the popular turn-of-the-century journal *Capital and Estate* (*Stolitsa i usad'ba*), the first issue of which announces its focus on "remote provincial corners" (*glukhie provintsial'nye ugolki*) as "repositories of [the nation's] enormous wealth."[4] Here as in Sologub's poem and in other lyric poetry of the time, the provinces play the role not of repellent Other but of storehouse charged with preserving *ourselves, our own* Russian authenticity—a reservoir of what Sologub's poem calls "pure forces and prophetic dreams," or what Akhmatova evokes in the lines "Mysterious, dark hamlets—/ *Repositories* of prayers and labor."[5] Towns as well as estates can be called upon to fulfill this function, as in Sologub's paean to Kostroma and in Gumilev's strikingly similar "Little Town" ("Gorodok," 1916), both of which represent the Russian hamlet as a model of cultural harmony.[6] Yet even in such idealized visions of *provintsiia*, we are never far from the decay that threatens any Russian provincial idyll: Akhmatova's lovely picture of the manor house opens with "Of flowers and *lifeless* things," and goes on to mention the slime [*tina*] we are so used to seeing in provincial places (even if for Akhmatova this pond scum now "resembles brocade").[7]

In general these lyrics are of a piece with the era's intensified interest in *kraevedenie* (regional studies) and ethnography. Hence the popularity of texts like N. N. Vrangel's series of articles detailing his travels through Russia's "quiet provincial towns and estates" (*po tikhim provintsial'nym gorodam i pomest'iam*), published in the journal *Olden Times* (*Starye gody*) under the title "Landlord's Russia" ("Pomeshchich'ia Rossiia," 1910).[8] A decade or two earlier, it is unlikely that any of these keywords—olden times, landlord's, estates, quiet provincial towns—would have been expected to call up such positive connotations (and a decade or two later, many of these associations will have been forcibly altered or negated).

Silver Age texts often imply a chronotope according to which, as Liudmila Zaionts writes, meaning and value are located "not *today and here*—that is, in the present moment and in the capital, [which remained] the point of reference—but *yesterday and there*, that is, in the past and outside-the-capital, or in other words, in the long-ago life of provincial Russia."[9] In effect we see here another expression of the Russian cultural condition that Lotman described: "what is yet to come into existence . . . and is 'someone else's' is highly valued."[10] In other words, Russia has usually felt itself to be in some sense provincial, and thus has longed for an elusive and far-off something or someplace. For a decade or two in the early twentieth century, the only difference is that the values assigned to the two poles (capital and province) are reversed as the culture's ideal is briefly relocated to an elusive and far-off version of the *provintsiia*.

But even in the Silver Age's spatial imagination, *provintsiia* is always more object than subject. Furthermore, it remains static, homogeneous, predictable: hence its function as reservoir. The qualities Sologub attributes to Kostroma are precisely those that other poets as well as popular journals are attributing to "the Russian provinces" generally; in fact during this period the same images and clichés are recurring constantly in texts poetic, journalistic, and scholarly. Gumilev's poem "Old Estates" ("Starye usad'by," 1913), for instance, recapitulates virtually point by point the "gallery of images" (pond, drying house, bells, etc.) appearing in texts like Vrangel's: the idea is never to describe a specific place, but to evoke *all* of the "Old estates scattered / Across mysterious Rus," as Gumilev writes.[11] The pattern even holds in local guidebooks of the period, which tend to celebrate the presence of exactly the same—"picturesque"—features in each town. Thus a genre that one expects to focus on local specificities reveals instead a "striving for typicality" so intense that even locally produced texts end up recapitulating the center's point of view.[12] Indeed these texts seem "unable to see in [a small town] anything besides what is typical," unable to describe it "outside of its 'typicality.'"[13] And in the provincial estate they seek not the provinces *as* the provinces, but the provinces as an image of the nation itself (*natsional'nyi lik*), "a poetic hypostasis of Russia."[14]

Here we recall Dostoevsky's assumption, decades earlier, that the best a specific provincial locality can hope for is to fulfill its synecdochic function as representative part of the national whole, thereby providing confirmation that "in each place throughout Russia, all of Russia exists."[15] The provinces remain trapped in the iterative mode, even when they are represented in positive terms. Attempts to imagine *provintsiia* as what one critic calls a *zapovednik*—a preserve or monument of some sort[16]—end up freezing this culture, rendering it at best benignly predictable, and at worst, inert and sterile.

In the Soviet period the geographic and conceptual category of *provintsiia* was immediately complicated by new ideological demands. For a brief time in the 1920s, Soviet cultural production tended to reject the provinces-capital binary altogether, assuming instead (in Vladimir Paperny's description) "a spatial paradigm asserting horizontality, a centrifugal dynamic, [and] mobility."[17] One thinks here of works like Dziga Vertov's film *A Sixth Part of the World* and Boris Pilniak's novel *The Volga Falls into the Caspian Sea*. But as early as the late 1920s we see a renewed focus on what is "vertical, centripetal, static, symmetrical, and hierarchical."[18] And here one recalls instead Mayakovsky's lines of 1927—*nachinaetsia zemlia, kak izvestno, ot Kremlia* (the world begins, as is well known, from the Kremlin).[19] In Andrei Platonov's story "Doubting Makar" (1929), the peasant protagonist sets off for Moscow "in order to stand *at the very center*," "the middle of the central city and the center of the entire state." Having determined that this point is near the Bolshoi Theater, Makar goes there and holds perfectly still, "[experiencing] a feeling of respect for himself and for his state."[20]

Texts of the 1930s generally reflect this belief in Moscow as the center of all centers. However, in Platonov's day as in earlier times, on occasion what was supposed to be a solid and immutable center could be re-imagined as something much less stable, becoming instead unfixed and elusive. Indeed despite this era's insistence on Moscow's centrality, we discern hints that it was still possible to lose hold of the center, and even to experience all of Russia as a periphery characterized by chaos and entropy. In 1932, the Soviet official Alexander Arosev, describing his journey through Germany and Poland on the way to Moscow, imagines himself to be approaching not a center but a ragged edge: "After the Polish border, the train became dirtier and the staff, less disciplined and more confused. *It was as if everything gradually began to lose meaning.* Such is the terrible difference between a European and the resident of the Russo-Polish Plain. The latter does not seem quite sure why he was born or what his place in the world should be, while the European, by the age of seventeen, knows all this, as well as when he will die and how much capital he will leave behind."[21] Arosev's vision here calls to mind Vladimir Kagansky's schematic account of the Russian spatial imaginary (see chapter 1), which starts in a center—where meaning and sense are concentrated—and moves outward from there, with amorphousness and disorder increasing gradually along the way.

Arosev's words show that even for a Communist official, while approaching Moscow *might* mean approaching the center of the world, if one is leaving Europe it also might mean falling off the edge of it, descending into anarchic space where "everything gradually [begins] to lose meaning." Striking as it is to hear such claims from a good Bolshevik like Arosev, it is even more striking to hear him echo (inadvertently, no doubt) Chaadaev's famous description of Russia from the First Philosophical Letter of 1829: "Look around you. Doesn't everyone seem to have one foot in the air? One would think that everyone is in transit. No one has a fixed sphere of existence; there are no proper habits, no rules governing anything. We do not even have homes [point même de foyer domestique]; there is nothing to attach us, nothing that arouses your sympathies and affections, nothing that endures, nothing that lasts. Everything passes, everything flows away, leaving no trace either outside us or within us. In our homes, we are like guests; in our families, we are like strangers; and in our cities we seem like nomads, even more so than those who wander our steppes, for they are more attached to their deserts than we are to our cities."[22]

Of course socialism was supposed to solve all such problems, dispelling chaos and uncertainty in part by providing an interpretative framework capable of establishing the clear and necessary meanings of all places and all times. And *provintsiia* itself—like everything retrograde and corrupt—was supposed to die along with the old regime. However, not only did the provinces survive the revolution, they continued to serve as the foul "natural habitat" of the revolution's enemy, the philistine everyman (*obyvatel'*).[23] The metaphor of *provintsiia* as swamp was quickly repurposed after 1917 as an image for the contamination that was always threatening revolutionary purity, "[seeping] into homes, souls, and Bolshevik reading circles."[24] For Bolshevik thinkers, as Yuri Slezkine explains, the small town represented a morass of "protocapitalist acquisitiveness [combined] with the 'primeval and utter swinishness' of provincial backwardness," "a swamp where time stands still and dreams come to die."[25] The words "primeval and utter swinishness" belong to the Bolshevik critic and editor Alexander Voronsky, who in 1927 described his hometown of Tambov as a "swamp [that] bubbled, rumbled, rotted, and gurgled, exhaling foul odors."[26]

The swamp-towns of Herzen, Shchedrin, Sollogub and others seem to haunt early Soviet literature, as do the debased pastorals we recall from Gogol and Goncharov, whose idylls always risked taking a turn "into the realm of the squalid and the mundane, or even into the realm of nightmare" (one minute you are drinking tea with jam, the next you are rotting to death in your own filth).[27] In Pilniak's *The Naked Year* (1922), the town of Ordynin reeks of rotten pork; in Yuri Libedinsky's *A Week* (1922), the kitchen table is covered with lace doilies and cockroaches, and flies buzz around the icons in the corner.[28] (But of course according to the revolutionaries, with the disappearance of private property, the heretofore degraded and degrading material world—doilies, cockroaches—would be redeemed: thus Voronsky sounds almost like an Acmeist when he writes that "in a fully developed Communist society . . . *Things* will once again become the source of joy that they are in Homer's *Odyssey*.")[29]

In the 1930s we hear occasional assertions that Soviet reality does not accommodate the category of the provincial at all: *Pravda* announced in 1937, "the gloomy word '*provintsiia*' has lost its right to residence in our country," since, as *Literaturnaia gazeta* had declared in 1937, "there no longer exists any '*provintsiia*,' backward and dark."[30] And yet we know that the idea of *provintsiia* lived on, since the Soviets kept trying to kill it. Gorky repeatedly attacked authors who used "provincialisms" (as well as "regionalisms" and "local patois"), excoriating those who wrote "not in Russian but in the language of Vyatka or Balakhna."[31] And in his dark warnings against the *meshchanstvo* (roughly, petty bourgeois philistinism) lurking in "small towns" (*uezdnye goroda*), it is clear that the backwardness and pollution Gorky believes to be threatening the new regime are specifically *provincial* phenomena: "In the Union of Soviets, philistinism [*meshchanstvo*] has been displaced, driven out of its lair, out of hundreds of district [*uezdnykh*] towns, has scattered everywhere and, as we know, has penetrated even into Lenin's Party, whence it is forcibly ejected during every Party purge. Nevertheless, it remains and acts like a microbe, causing shameful maladies."[32] The phenomenon of *provintsial'nost'* has gone underground—much as the word *provintsiia* has at times been subsumed by vocabulary like *meshchanstvo, poshlost'*, and *byt*—but it retains a latent power to adulterate and shame, and it might return at any moment to defile the unified, coherent culture that the center seeks to impose throughout the country.

Thanks to the Soviet period's hypercentralization of power, at times it could seem that most of the vast country's space bore the marks of peripheralness, with "everything outside the Kremlin walls [appearing] almost equally a part of the periphery."[33] Thus in a radio play of 1959, one character asks another where she is from and receives the reply, "The provinces . . . though now they say the periphery and they think it's better."[34] For a quintessentially Soviet text like Venedikt Erofeev's *Moscow-Petushki*, so powerfully central is the Kremlin that everything and everywhere else are effectively provincialized (in fact this is the phenomenon Erofeev parodies by preventing his hero from ever reaching the Kremlin). And in our own post-Soviet times, the provinces continue to accrue meanings both positive and negative, in books, films, and television series that veer back and forth between versions of the Silver Age myth (*provintsiia* as repository of purity and cultural authenticity) and much darker views that once again depict *provintsiia* as locus of degradation and moral decay.[35]

Provincialism, "World Literature," and Russian Time

As we have seen over and over, because Russian literature's provincials believe themselves to be in the wrong place, they are often convinced that they are in the wrong time too; or perhaps better, because they feel themselves to be in the wrong time, they conclude that this must be a result of being in the wrong place. Somewhat strangely, contemporary Western accounts of what has come to be called "World Literature" often reproduce precisely this view of the relationship between geographic space and progressive time. For instance, Pascale Casanova's *The World Republic of Letters*, perhaps the most influential among these analyses, makes Paris both the undisputed "center" of the literary world and the vanguard of a literary "progress" that is essentially linear. Paris is the "Greenwich meridian" of culture, a point both spatial ("the center of all centers") and temporal ("a basis for measuring the time that is peculiar to literature").[36] And for Casanova as for most other World Literature theorists, spatial "peripheries" are dependent and sterile because they are temporally "behind."[37] Thus Western models of World Literature tend to leave writers and national literary traditions with two options: you can be cosmopolitan, or you can be provincial.

In order to arrive at such a binary, this symbolic geography of the literary world has to leave out Russia altogether. Thus with the exception of a few passing references (to Nabokov, predictably), Russia is nowhere to be found in *The World Republic of Letters*, or in most other accounts of World Literature. Occasionally an individual author rates a mention (Fredric Jameson's influential essay "Third-World Literature in the Era of Multinational Capitalism," for instance, adduces "Dostoevsky" as a decontextualized, denationalized example of "great literature").[38] But the Russian literary *tradition* has no place in these systems: the 2012 *Routledge Companion to World Literature*, for instance, makes virtually no mention of either Russia or the Soviet Union.[39] This despite the fact that few writers, it seems, could be described as more "World Lit" than the Great Russian Writers of the nineteenth and twentieth centuries. (Indeed the baggy-monster Russian realists can be seen as precursors of Salman Rushdie and the other big, messy, hybrid—and mostly male—geniuses who perch at the top of the World Lit canon.)[40]

The *provintsiia* trope that this book has examined helps explain why Russian literature cannot be assimilated to systems like Casanova's, and indeed how Russian texts end up mounting a kind of resistance (sometimes passive, sometimes less passive) to a Paris-centered map of the literary world. Indeed, by focusing so intently on *provintsiia* as a problem—sometimes even as a mystery—nineteenth-century Russian texts might be said to foretell their own neglect by later Western models of literary development. Above all it is provincial temporality that poses a challenge to totalizing systems: because as we have seen, the provinces as we encounter them in literature tend not to be simply "behind." Rather, they often exist in a strange and ambiguous space that is not in *any* (single) time. According to Casanova, Paris (or rather "Paris") is the "Greenwich meridian of literature" because it has successfully coerced more or less everyone into measuring their own modernity against the French capital. But *provintsiia* and *provintsial'nost'* foreground the fact that Russia—which is neither "modern" nor straightforwardly "backward"—does not fit comfortably into the "Eurochronology" that habitually represents itself as a universal standard.[41]

Russians are not, of course, the only people who have had to contend with what Casanova describes as the "decentering" and "disadvantaged remoteness" experienced by those on a cultural periphery who feel stranded "in a place outside real time and history."[42] When Casanova quotes Octavio Paz's account of his own coming of age in Mexico, it reads like a citation from Chaadaev:

> I felt dislodged from the present. . . . The real present was somewhere else. . . . For us Spanish Americans this present was not in our own countries: it was the time lived by others—by the English, the French, the Germans. It was the time of New York, Paris, London.[43]

This belief, Paz explains, gave rise to his urgent need to find "the gateway to the present": "I wanted to belong to my time and to my century. . . . My search for modernity had begun."[44] Paz's alienation is the result of a geographic localization of cultural authority so intense that it forces those on the periphery to judge their own reality by Casanova's "Greenwich meridian of literature" (i.e., Paris and the standards it supposedly embodies).[45] As Casanova shows, once spatial decentering (being on the physical periphery) is experienced as temporal decentering (being outside of "modern," "real" time), the quest for modernity in literature can take on a desperate urgency.

A Mexican like Paz could quite easily cast this quest in geographic terms, confidently locating the present he seeks in real geographic space ("New York, Paris, London"): but as we have seen, this has generally not been the case for Russians, who have often felt themselves to be in the wrong time no matter where they were in space. For Russians it was not simply a matter of going to Paris. Nor was it a matter of going to Moscow or Petersburg, because thanks to Russia's particular relationship to the standard embodied by European culture, its own capital(s) played a far more ambiguous role in Russian high culture than Paris played in the French-administered empire of world literature. Russians—like provincials— were liable to confront "alienation from themselves" no matter where they were, because "a province is located, as it were, not in itself; it is alien not in regards to someone or something else, but to itself, inasmuch as its own center has been taken out of itself and transferred to some other space or time."[46]

As a result, Russians found it more difficult to embrace wholeheartedly the belief that Petersburg or Moscow or Paris—or anyplace else—might "save [them] from provincialism," as the Peruvian writer Vargas Llosa says he once expected Sartre (i.e., Paris) to do for him and his peers.[47] The townspeople in *Dead Souls*, the provincial revolutionaries in *Demons*, and the Prozorovs in *Three Sisters* all long for a distant center, wherever they may imagine that center to be—but the narratives in which these characters are embedded make it clear to us that their hopes of locating any geographic ground zero of meaningfulness and modernity are illusory. Rarely can Russians fully embrace the belief that if only they were able to *monter à Peterbourg*, Balzac-style, all of their semiotic problems would be solved.

Quite unlike Paris, that indisputable center of all centers, Russia's elusive capital has almost always been, to adapt Luce Irigaray's feminist formulation, "un centre qui n'en est pas un."[48] Even as the Russian capital has exerted authority over the provinces, it could not quite be pinned down, either geographically or semiotically; in Lotman's terms, it "[did] not have its own point of view on itself."[49] Never fully believing in their center's centrality, Russians have continued to search the distance for what Rimbaud called "la vraie vie [qui] est absente."[50] Reading Rimbaud's words we recall once again both Lotman's and Epstein's analyses of Russia's spatial semiotics: in such a system, "what is yet to come into existence . . . and is 'someone else's' is highly valued" (Lotman); one longs for what is "not here, not at this place, but 'there'" (Epstein).[51]

The ambiguities of Russia's situation—maybe peripheral but definitely not small, European but also Asian, behind but possibly ahead, Christian but perhaps not exactly Christendom in the sense of "the West"—help explain why the *provintsiia* trope came to play such a complicated and *useful* role in its literature. Many Russians aimed to connect their country to the only timeline that mattered to them, the normative chronology of European history. Chaadaev himself wrote a mollifying follow-up to his scandalous letter, arguing that Russia's backwardness was a boon that would allow the country to skip stages of historical development through which other nations had been obliged to pass (advantage: Russia).[52] As Chaadaev's emendation demonstrates, long before Trotsky elaborated his well-known ideas on "unevenness," "the privilege of historic backwardness," and "the law of combined development" (all of which, he claimed, would allow Russia to make "leaps," "drawing together . . . different stages of the [historical] journey"),[53] some Russians tried to seize on the advantages that might be inherent in a late arrival to civilization, thereby opening up the possibility of "line-jumping" in or into History.

But the *provintsiia* trope is different: it is *not* a way of arguing that Russia can go back to get ahead. Nor does the trope locate value in an idealized version of some coherent past (any such ideal would have to be located in *derevnia*, not *provintsiia*, as we see in the Silver Age texts referenced above). In fact rarely does *provintsiia's* temporal mode imply the possibility of any "straight line" of historical progress. Representations of provincial culture suggest no clear trajectory of development, no chronological telos; rather, the jumble of provincial life—a mishmash of objects and styles and words, debris washed up on the provincial shore—gives the impression of utterly disordered temporality, a confused relationship to normative periodizations of history and progress.

What the idea of provinciality can do is to suggest other ways of imagining time, raising the possibility that Russia is not necessarily destined to move through history *along the same trajectory* as other nations. As Michael Holquist argues, some Russians aimed to "universalize [the] dilemma" of being off of any heaven-ordained timeline, outside of any "transcendent system for ensuring order."[54] Holquist shows how Lermontov's *Hero of Our Time*, for example, anticipates Lukacs's famous diagnosis of the "transcendental homelessness" that defines the modern subject. Instead of simply getting ahead of everyone else ("everyone else" being the West) while moving along the same axis, Russians might actually redefine what it meant for *everyone* to be modern.[55]

If the *provintsiia* trope represents a way of thinking not about backwardness per se but about the relationship between cultural syncretism and Russian time, one question the trope implies is what consequences will ensue if Russia remains permanently outside of the normative chronology supplied by European history. In Monika Greenleaf's analysis (cited in chapter 6), Russian literature has long borrowed ideas that were "sometimes up-to-the-minute but more often chronologically out of sync with European fashion," and having borrowed them, has gone on to "conflate and play off of [them] *simultaneously*."[56] Literary representations of *provintsiia* as hodgepodge—say, Melnikov's provincial merchant's house where a stuffed parrot stands next to a bust of Voltaire[57]—draw on precisely this sense of simultaneity and non-synchronicity. Anything might appear at any moment, because as *Dead Souls* tells us, "there [is] no way of knowing how or why" such artifacts turn up in deepest *provintsiia*.[58]

And perhaps anything might *happen*, too: because in Gogol's words once again, "more events take place in Russia in ten years than occur in other states in half a century."[59] For Gogol as for Dostoevsky, simultaneity seems to be linked— somehow, vaguely—to modernity. Both authors imply that there is something about the strange, jumbled-up quality of Russian space and time that might prove fruitful and modern rather than sterile and behind. In other words, we might read Russian writers' focus on provinciality as a response to thinkers who see all peripheries as sterile and dependent, always in need of catching up. This, I think, is where we should look for the utility of the *provintsiia* trope, with its insistence on all that is ad hoc and syncretic in Russian culture. By asking whether the chronological and spatial disorder of *provintsiia*/Russia might not prove to be as barren as Chaadaev's "flat calm" diagnosis would have it, images of *provintsiia* can raise the possibility of a connection between chaotic simultaneity and creative potential. The *provintsiia* trope, then, signals not just the conflation and out-of-syncness that Greenleaf says are characteristic of Russian literature, but also Russians' productive *awareness* of these phenomena.

If this is so, then perhaps Russian literature's persistent focus on provincial chaos points toward a fundamentally modern insight: *all* culture is syncretic, not just that of the provinces, or that of Russia. In Edward Said's words, "all cultures are involved in one another; none is simple and pure, all are hybrid, heterogeneous,

extraordinarily differentiated and unmonolithic."[60] When Gogol's contemporary
Nikolai Nadezhdin describes his era's prose as "a confusion of all the European
idioms having overgrown in successive layers the wild mass of the undeveloped
Russian word," he is identifying precisely those phenomena from which Gogol's
art would draw its greatest power.[61] In fact we might even read a text like *Dead
Souls* alongside Salman Rushdie's commentary on his own novel *The Satanic
Verses*, another scandalous rebuke to the idea of cultural purity:

> *The Satanic Verses* celebrates hybridity, impurity, intermingling, the transformation
> that comes of new and unexpected combinations of human beings, cultures, ideas,
> politics, movies, songs. It rejoices in mongrelization and fears the absolutism of the
> Pure. Mélange, hotch-potch, a bit of this and a bit of that is how newness enters the
> world. . . . *The Satanic Verses* is for change-by-fusion, change-by-conjoining. It is a
> love song to our mongrel selves.[62]

Viewed in this light, the Russian fascination with provincial detritus might be
seen not only as a sustained reflection on having to make art from adulterated
materials, but also as a semi-horrified love song to our mongrel, modern selves.

A contemporary Russian scholar writes that *provintsial'nost'*, "like ethnicity,
is a fact of self-consciousness": provincial origins leave such an indelible mark
(*kleimo*) on a person that this mark becomes an "ontological trait."[63] Clearly the
idea of *provintsiia* has never disappeared, even if it has at times gone underground
or been hidden behind terms like *byt* and *poshlost'*. It endures in part because it
has proven so useful, serving as a laboratory for exploring the cultural condition Chaadaev diagnosed (or perhaps better, the condition that he, by diagnosing, helped to create) when he described Russia as "a culture based entirely on
borrowing and imitation," in which "new ideas sweep away the old ones because
they do not grow out of the latter, but arise among us from who knows where."[64]
Chaadaev's diagnosis, as this book has shown, finds fictional embodiment in
nineteenth-century literature's addled, hilarious, mournful, and fascinating provincials, always casting about for the next new idea. The resulting mess—a culture
"outside of time," he says, out of step with "that wonderful interconnection of
human ideas throughout the ages"[65]—cannot be separated from the enormously
productive cultural syncretism that made possible Russia's modern literary tradition. In other words, provincialism, though a form of marginalism or peripheral-
ism, is central to Russian culture.

The confused and confusing version of provincial culture—the shameful mélange represented by literature's various Kukshinas, Manilovs, and even
Golovlyovs—in the end held far more aesthetic interest and promise than the
harmonious frozen world of the Silver Age's *provintsiia*. In the Soviet period,

texts that treated *provintsiia* as a crude hodgepodge helped nourish the weird peripheral modernisms of writers like Platonov, Zoshchenko, and Dobychin.[66] Platonov writes, "Once again I am overcome with melancholy, once again I am in 'Tambov,' which in the future will become for me some kind of symbol."[67] He admits that life in a "Gogolian province"—this Tambov-in-quotation-marks—was a "nightmare" that at times tried his faith in art: "Wandering these backwaters, I've seen such dreary things that it was hard for me to believe there somewhere exists magnificent Moscow, art, *et cetera*."[68] Moscow and art—it would be difficult to find a more direct expression of the Russian tendency to link the geographically central with the culturally high.

But at this point Platonov adds a crucial, cryptic sentence that I have quoted before: "And yet it seems to me that genuine art and thought can in fact only appear in such a backwater."[69] His emendation recalls Andrei Sinyavsky's claim that all art "has the provinces in its blood." "Art is provincial in principle," Sinyavsky writes, "preserving for itself a naïve, external, astonished and envious look."[70] Both statements help illuminate the fruitful and *sophisticated* nature of Russia's provinciality. As this book has argued, thanks to the peculiarities of their country's historical situation—its inside/outside relationship to Western high culture—Russians have developed a more nuanced understanding of center/periphery relations than those who occupy undisputed centers.[71] We would not be incorrect to describe Russia as "utterly and deeply provincial in its very essence,"[72] as long as we keep our eyes trained on what is, in the end, the aesthetically miraculous nature of this provincialism.

LIST OF ABBREVIATIONS

MTR   *Russkaia provintsiia: mif—tekst—real'nost'*, eds. A. F. Belousov, T. V.
       Tsivian, and V. N. Sazhin (Moscow: Nauchnyi sovet po istorii mirovoi
       kul'tury Rossiiskoi Akademii Nauk, 2000)
PKR   *Provintsiia kak real'nost' i ob"ekt osmysleniia*, eds. A. F. Belousov, M. V.
       Stroganov, A. Iu. Sorochan (Tver': Tverskoi gosudarstvennyi universitet,
       2001)
TP   *Tsentr-provintsiia. Istorichesko-psikhologicheskie problemy. Materialy vse-
       rossiiskoi nauchnoi konferentsii, 6–7 dekabria 2001 g*, ed. S. N. Poltoraka
       (Petersburg: Nestor, 2001)
ZP   *Zhizn' provintsii kak fenomen dukhovnosti*, ed. N. M. Fortunatov (Nizhnii
       Novgorod: izd. Vektor T i S, 2004)

NOTES

Chapter One

1. A. P. Chekhov, *Polnoe sobranie sochinenii i pisem v 30-i tomakh* (Moscow: Nauka, 1978), 10:96.

2. Chekhov, *PSS*, 10:96.

3. Chekhov, *PSS*, 10:93.

4. Chekhov, *PSS*, 10:92–93.

5. Chekhov, *PSS*, 10:99.

6. Maria Todorova, *Imagining the Balkans* (Oxford: Oxford University Press, 1997), 7.

7. V.V. Maiakovskii, "Prochti i katai v Parizh i v Kitai," *Polnoe sobranie sochinenii Maia-kovskogo v 13 tomakh* (Moscow: Goslitizdat, 1955), 10: 257.

8. *Tsentr, serdtse, iadro, zerno, nutro, korennnoi, vnutrennyi, sredinnyi*. Cited in Leonid Gorizontov, "The 'Great Circle' of Interior Russia: Representations of the Imperial Center in the Nineteenth and Early Twentieth Centuries," in *Russian Empire: Space, People, Power, 1700–1930*, ed. Jane Burbank, Mark von Hagen, and Anatolyi Remnev (Bloomington: Indiana University Press, 2007), 67–93. Pushkin, for example, referred to Moscow as *sredinnyi grad*. A.S. Pushkin, *Polnoe sobranie sochinenii v 10-i tomakh* (Leningrad: Nauka, 1978), 7:187–90, 439–40.

9. The ethnographer is S. V. Maksimov. F. N. Glinka, *Pis'ma k drugu* (Moscow: Sovre-mennik, 1990), 439–40. (F. N. Glinka, 1786–1880, was the vaguely Slavophilic cousin of the composer, and the author of a widely read memoir of the Napoleonic Wars.) Both quoted in Gorizontov, "The 'Great Circle' of Interior Russia," 70, 69.

10. *Karmannyi pochtovyi atlas vsei Rossiiskoi Imperii, razdelennoi na gubernii s pokaza-niem glavnykh pochtovykh dorog* (St. Petersburg: Sobstvennyi Ego Imperatorskogo Velich-estva Departament Kart, 1808), 16. I am grateful to John Randolph for sharing this image as well as his knowledge of the post relay system.

11. Reproduced in Philip Fisher, *Still the New World: American Literature in a Culture of Creative Destruction* (Cambridge, MA: Harvard University Press, 1999), 43.

12. Fisher, *Still the New World*, 43–44.

13. Fisher, *Still the New World*, 44.

14. As will be made clear in the chapters that follow, the kind of representativeness made possible by the American grid is very different from the interchangeableness of Russian provincial places. When Russian writers claim that having seen one provincial town

you have seen them all, they are not saying that each of these towns is capable of standing for all of Russia. Rather, they are implying that in Russia only the metropoles can lay claim, simultaneously and paradoxically, both to particularity (they merit detailed descriptions) and to representativeness (they stand for "all of Russia").

15. Fisher, *Still the New World*, 44.

16. V. L. Kaganskii, "Tsentr-provintsiia-periferiia-granitsa. Osnovnye zony kul'turnogo landshafta," *Kul'turnyi landshaft: voprosy teorii i metologii issledovaniia*, edited by V. V. Valebnyi et al. (Moscow: Izd. SGU, 1998), 76–77.

17. M. O. Koialovich quoted in Gorizontov, "The 'Great Circle' of Interior Russia," 72–3.

18. Michelet is cited in Stephane Gerson, "Parisian Litterateurs, Provincial Journeys and the Construction of National Unity in Post-Revolutionary France," *Past and Present* 151, no. 1 (May 1996): 168–69. Gerson writes that the French capital is "a crucible which melts down all provincial characteristics and produces an educated, sophisticated, critical Parisian 'type,'" representing "a central authority . . . for which Paris is a metaphor."

19. Gerson, "Parisian Litterateurs," 168.

20. Gerson, "Parisian Litterateurs," 160.

21. This idea can be transposed into the literary sphere: a "big" national literature can be thought (spuriously, no doubt) to "contain" all others. To illustrate and support such claims Milan Kundera cites Polish essayist Kazimierz Brandys, who writes in his *Paris Notebooks* that "the French student has greater gaps in his knowledge of world culture than the Polish student, but he can get away with it, for his own culture contains more or less all the aspects, all the possibilities and phases, of the world's evolution." Milan Kundera, "Die Weltliteratur: European novelists and modernism," *New Yorker* (January 8, 2007): 30.

22. Fonvizin and Glinka are quoted in Sara Dickinson, *Breaking Ground: Travel and National Culture in Russia from Peter I to the Era of Pushkin* (Amsterdam: Rodopi, 2006), 150–52. Cf. John Sexton, speaking as President of New York University: "New York is literally the miniaturization of the world." *New York Magazine*, November 14, 2010, accessed July 26, 2018. http://nymag.com/news/features/69482/index4.html.

23. "Encyclopedic and universal city" is from Edmond Texier in *Tableau de Paris*, 1852, but one can marshal seemingly endless quotes expressing the same idea. Texier is quoted in Pascale Casanova, *The World Republic of Letters* (Cambridge, MA: Harvard University Press, 2004), 27. The Musée de l'Homme inscription reminds us that if a capital contains everything, this is so because it has taken it all from someplace/someone else.

24. The role of Moscow in Soviet times provides another example of "hypercentralization," as a result of which the whole country was in effect marginalized. Kaganskii, "Tsentr-provintsiia-periferiia-granitsa," 96.

25. P. I. Didenko, "Istoricheskie formy oppozitsii 'tsentr-provintsiia,'" in *Tsentr-provintsiia. Istorichesko-psikhologicheskie problemy. Materialy vserossiiskoi nauchnoi konferentsii, 6–7 dekabria 2001 g.*, ed. S. N. Poltoraka (St. Petersburg: Nestor, 2001), 4, hereafter *TP*. See also N. G. Baranets, "Faktor provintsializma v universitetskoi filosofii v Rossii kontsa XX-ogo veka," *TP*, 177–80. Baranets describes provincial academics' belief that their own scholarship is not capable of developing large, synthesizing ideas, but only of addressing "particular problems"— leaving the synthesizing, the actual making of significance, to the center. *TP*, 177.

26. V. A. Koshelev, "O 'literaturnoi' provintsii i literaturnoi 'provintsial'nosti' novogo vremeni: Zametki," in *Russkaia provintsiia: mif—tekst—real'nost'*, ed. A. F. Belousov, T. V. Tsivian, and V. N. Sazhin, (Moscow: Nauchnyi sovet po istorii mirovoi kul'tury Rossiiskoi Akademii Nauk, 2000), 41, hereafter *MTR*.

27. The underlying spatial semiotics of pre-Petrine texts—including both maps and documents like the *Life* of the Archpriest Avvakum—differ radically from those of the later period. For example, as Susan Smith-Peter writes, the works of seventeenth-century cartographer and architect Semyon Remezov "[place his] Siberian town of Tobol'sk at the center, not only of Russia, but also of the universe." Smith-Peter, "Making Empty Provinces: Eighteenth-Century Enlightenment Regionalism in Russian Provincial Journals," *REGION: Regional Studies of Russia, Eastern Europe, and Central Asia* 4, no. 1 (2015): 7–29. See also Valerie Ann Kivelson, *Cartographies of Tsardom: The Land and Its Meanings in Seventeenth-Century Russia* (Ithaca, NY: Cornell University Press, 2006). Kivelson notes that Remezov's map, which leaves out Moscow altogether, "effectively [creates] a center in a place more commonly understood as a periphery" (Kivelson, 138).

28. Yuri M. Lotman, *Universe of the Mind: A Semiotic Theory of Culture*, trans. Ann Shukman, intro. Umberto Eco (London; New York: I. B. Tauris, 2001), 191.

29. Lotman, *Universe of the Mind*, 192.

30. N. V. Gogol', *Polnoe sobranie sochinenii* (Moscow: Akademiia Nauk SSSR, 1937–52), 7:177, emphasis mine.

31. Andrei Bely, *Petersburg*, trans. and ed. Robert A. Maguire and John E. Malmstad (Bloomington: Indiana University Press, 1978), 2.

32. Il'ia Il'f, Evgenii Petrov, *Dvenadtsat' stul'ev* (Moscow: Vagrius, 1998), 374–75.

33. Toni Morrison, *Playing in the Dark: Whiteness and the Literary Imagination* (New York: Vintage, 1993).

34. Lotman, *Universe of the Mind*, 195, 198.

35. Lotman, *Universe of the Mind*, 198–99.

36. Lotman, *Universe of the Mind*, 192. The spectator "'as it were exists'" for the actors, and the actor "'as it were exists'" for the spectator: "from the point of view of stage space the only things that is real is stage existence, while from the point of view of behind-the-scenes space, stage existence is just play and convention." They live in "a mutual relationship of non-existence." Lotman, *Universe of the Mind*, 197, 199.

37. Mikhail Epstein, *Bog detalei: Narodnaia dusha i chastnaia zhizn' v Rossii na iskhode imperii* (New York: Slovo, 1997), 33–34.

38. Epstein, *Bog detalei*, 30, 32.

39. I am using the words "provincialism" and "provinciality" more or less interchangeably, because it seems to me that in normal usage there is no clear or consistently observed difference between the two terms, despite occasional—prescriptive—attempts to draw such a distinction: see, for example, M. V. Stroganov, "Provintsializm/provintsial'nost': opyt definitsii," *MTR*, 30–37, for an unconvincing attempt to distinguish between these two Russian nouns.

40. Willard Sunderland, *Taming the Wild Field: Colonization and Empire on the Russia Steppe* (Ithaca, NY: Cornell University Press, 2004), 208.

41. Sunderland, *Taming the Wild Field*, 171.

42. See in particular the debates surrounding Alexander Etkind's (problematic) *Internal Colonization: Russia's Imperial Experience* (Cambridge, UK: Polity Press, 2011), including my review of it in *Russian Review* 72, no. 1 (January 2013): 156–60. See also Vitaly Chernetsky, Nancy Condee, Harsha Ram, and Gayatri Chakravorty Spivak, "Are We Post-Colonial? Post-Soviet Space," *PMLA* 121, no. 3 (May 2006): 828–36, as well as Jonathan Platt, ed., *Ulbandus: The Slavic Review of Columbia University* 7 (2003)—an issue that carries the formidable and tellingly complex subtitle *Empire, Union, Center, Satellite: The Place of Post-Colonial Theory In Slavic/Central and East European/(Post-) Soviet Studies*. On Russian as an imperial power see for instance Olga Maiorova, *From the Shadow of Empire: Defining the Russian Nation through Cultural Mythology, 1855–1870* (Madison: University of Wisconsin Press, 2010) and Edyta Bojanowska, A *World of Empires: The Russian Voyage of the Frigate Pallada* (Cambridge, MA: Harvard University Press, 2018).

43. Sunderland, *Taming the Wild Field*, 89.

44. Chekhov, *PSS*, 13:233, 205–6.

45. Gorizontov, "The 'Great Circle' of Interior Russia," 85.

46. Gogol', *PSS*, 4:12, emphasis mine.

47. Gorizontov, "The 'Great Circle' of Interior Russia," 85.

48. Sunderland, *Taming the Wild Field*, 112–13.

49. Kaganskii, "Tsentr-provintsiia-periferiia-granitsa," 76; "eternal and indestructible" is from Vasilii Shchukin, "Krizis stolits ili kompleks provintsii?" *Novoe literaturnoe obozrenie* 34 (1998), 350–54.

50. V. A. Ushakov, "Tsentr-provintsiia v SShA: put' preodoleniia razlichii," *TP*, 26; L. O. Zaionts, "Provintsiia kak termin," *MTR*, 12. Most classicists, however, seem to dispute this etymology.

51. For detailed accounts of the history of the terminology, see Evgeniia Kirichenko and Elena Shcheboleva, *Russkaia provintsiia* (Moscow: Nash dom, 1997), 11, 46–48; L. O. Zaionts, "Istoriia slova i poniatiia 'provintsiia' v russkoi kul'ture," *Russian Literature* 53, no. 3 (2003): 307–30; Ia. E. Akhapkipa, "Provintsiia, periferiia—problema nominatsii," in *Provintsiia kak real'nost' i ob"ekt osmysleniia*, ed. A. F. Belousov, M. V. Stroganov, A. Iu. Sorochan (Tver': Tverskoi gosudarstvennyi universitet, 2001), 6–8 and 22, hereafter *PKR*; Introduction to *MTR*, 9–14; E. N. Stroganova, "'Miniatiurnyi mir': provintsiia v russkoi proze 1830-kh–pervoi poloviny 1840-kh gg. Ekskiz," in *MTR*, 196–204; and Zaionts, "Provintsiia kak termin," in *MTR, 12–20.*

52. Zaionts, "Istoriia slova i poniatiia 'provintsiia,'" 315.

53. Zaionts, "Istoriia slova i poniatiia 'provintsiia,'" 314. The vocabulary remained unstable for decades. For example, Ianovskii's *Novyi slovotolkovatel'* dictionary (1803–06) offered as synonyms for *provintsiia* the terms *uezd, okruga, okol'nye sela, volosti i derevni*, and *podsudnye provintsial'nomu gorodu*—all of which suggest that *provintsiia* could still be used to designate both countryside and towns, and that its definition was not strictly negative ("not the capitals"). Between 1806 and 1822, the *Slovar' Akademii Rossiiskoi* did not include the word *provintsiia* at all, and when it reappeared in 1847, it was labeled a colloquialism (defined as "*oblast', okrug*"); in his 1863–66 dictionary, Dal' has as synonyms *guberniia, oblast', okrug; uezd*. See Stroganova, "'Miniatiurnyi mir,'" 197.

54. Akhapkipa, "Provintsiia, periferiia—problema nominatsii," 6. Along the same lines, Akhapkipa notes, Chudinov's dictionary of 1900 defines *provintsiia* as "a separate part of the country . . . in opposition to the capital." Akhapkipa, 6.

55. Introduction to *MTR*, 9.

56. Franco Moretti, *Atlas of the European Novel, 1800–1900* (London: Verso, 1998), 65.

57. I. A. Razumova and E. V. Kuleshov, "K fenomenologii provintsii," in *PKR*, 22.

58. Alexander Herzen, *My Past and Thoughts*, trans. Constance Garnett, intro. Isaiah Berlin (Berkeley: University of California Press, 1973), 173, and A. I. Gertsen, *Sobranie sochinenii v 30-i tomakh* (Moscow: Izd. Akademii Nauk SSSR, 1954), 8:237. On the link between *provintsiia* and words like *tina, boloto,* and *luzha* (slime, swamp, and puddle), see M. L. Lur'e, "'Ves'egonsk gorodishko prebedneishii' (vzgliad na uezdnyi gorod v putevykh zametkakh XIX veka)," in *PKR*, 124–40, and Akhapkipa, "Provintsiia, periferiia—problem nominatsii," 9.

59. Coastal places seem to be immune to the worst forms of provinciality. Even in a text like *Oblomov*, where a version of *provintsiia* (Oblomovka) plays a key role, the seaside location where Olga and Stolz finally settle down is remote but not provincial: it is a place which is its own place, and which is also quite explicitly connected to the rest of the world ("from one side . . . the sea could be seen," and "from the other, the road to town"). *Oblomov* in I. A. Goncharov, *Sobranie sochinenii v 8-i tomakh.* (Moscow: Gosudarstvennoe izdatel'stvo khudozhestvennoi literatury, 1953), 4:459–60. Even in Brodsky's famous line about *glukhaia provintsiia* ("if it's your fate to be born in an Empire / it's better to live in the deepest provinces, by the sea [*v glukhoi provintsii u moria*]"), this province's proximity to the ocean means that it is not in fact provincial. In general *provintsiia* is an inside space, a closed space, one that is not a center but strives toward a center, whereas the place Brodsky describes is *open*—thanks to the sea, which in effect leads to everywhere. Iosif Brodskii, "Pis'ma rimskomu drugu," in Iosif Brodskii, *Bog sokhraniaet vse* (Moscow: Mif, 1992), 66.

60. F. M. Dostoevskii, *Polnoe sobranie sochinenii v 30-i tomakh* (Leningrad: Nauka, 1974), 10:483ff.

61. M. N. Zagoskin, "Tri zhenikha (provintsial'nye ocherki)," in *Russkie povesti XIX v., 20-kh–30-kh godov*, ed. B. S. Meilakh (Moscow: Izdatel'stvo khudozhestvennoi literatury, 1950), 2:451.

62. Hence the bitterness expressed by a Nizhnii Novgorod journalist-intellectual in the 1870s, complaining that elites in the capitals obsess endlessly over "the common people" (*narod*) while remaining content to "know virtually nothing about *provintsiia*." A. S. Gatsitskii, *Smert' provintsii ili net?* (Nizhnii Novgorod: Tip. Nizh. gub. pravleniia, 1876), 19–20.

63. Various scholars have made this observation. See Kirichenko and Shchebol-eva, *Russkaia provintsiia*, 81; L. O. Zaionts, "Russkii provintsial'nyi 'mif' (k probleme kul'turnoi tipologii)," in *Geopanorama russkoi kul'tury. Provintsiia i ee lokal'nye teksty*, ed. L. O. Zaionts, V. V. Abashev, A. F. Belousov, and T. V. Tsivian (Moscow: Iazyki slavianskoi kul'tury, 2004), 427–56; Marica Fazolini, "Vzgliad na usad'bu, ili predstavlenie provintsi-alov o russkoi stolichnoi zhizni," in *MTR*, 176–85.

64. V. A. Koshelev, "O 'literaturnoi' provintsii i literaturnoi 'provintsial'nosti' novogo vremeni," in *MTR*, 38.

65. I. M. Dolgorukov, *Povest' o rozhdenii moem*, ed. N. V. Kuznetsova and M. O. Mel'tsin (St. Petersburg: Nauka, 2004), 1:164. Torzhok is the subject of a chapter in Alexander Radishchev's 1790 *Journey from St. Petersburg to Moscow*.

66. John Randolph, *The House in the Garden: The Bakunin Family and the Romance of Russian Idealism* (Ithaca, NY: Cornell University Press, 2007), 36, 24.

67. Randolph, *The House in the Garden*, 38.

68. Tom Nairn, "The British Political Elite," *New Left Review* 23 (January–February 1964): 22. Some Russian estates succeeded in these terms: see Patricia Roosevelt, *Life on the Russian Country Estate* (New Haven, CT: Yale University Press, 1995), esp. ch. 11, "Ideal Worlds: The Idyll of the Russian Intelligentsia."

69. In another passage that resonates powerfully with nineteenth-century Russian culture, Nairn writes that the necessary counterpart of the British estate's intense meaningfulness is the "meaninglessness" of the "modern British town": "Culturally, as an artifact of real civilization, [the British town] has never existed, because civilization went on elsewhere, in the residences of the territorial aristocracy and gentry." Nairn, "The British Political Elite," 22. As Marica Fazolini writes of the Russian estate, it is "the representative of the city in the provinces . . . a sign gesturing toward another culture." Fazolini, "Vzgliad na usad'bu," 176.

70. Koshelev, "O 'literaturnoi' provintsii," 50. *Stolitsa i usad'ba* was a sort of "lifestyle" magazine along the lines of *Better Homes and Gardens* in mid-century America.

71. M. A. Glushkova, "Mir russkoi usad'by v lirike Afanasiia Feta," *Zhizn' provintsii kak fenomen dukhovnosti*, ed. N. M. Fortunatov (Nizhnii Novgorod: izd. Vektor T i S, 2004), 237, hereafter *ZP*.

72. The idea of estate self-sufficiency could take various forms, ranging from early nineteenth-century paeans to life in *glush'* and Polevoi's romanticized descriptions of *sel'skaia zhizn'* (rural or village life) as a model of social harmony (both of which can be linked to the eighteenth century's sentimental cult of village or estate life) to the high-culture pleasure palaces of the upper aristocracy. On Polevoi, see I. Z. Kokovina, "Provintsial'nyi byt v strukture khudozhestvennogo proizvedeniia XIX veka," in *PKR*, 101–7; on the high aristocracy's estates, see Roosevelt, *Life on the Russian Country Estate*, and William F. Broomfield, "Dvorianskaia idiliia. Neoklassicheskaia arkhitektura v epokhu Ekateriny Velikoi," in *ZP*, 188–92.

73. The Russian is "vkus byl na maner stolichnyi." A. A. Fet, "Dve lipki," *Sochineniia v dvukh tomakh* (Moscow: Khudozhestvennaia literatura, 1982), 1:487.

74. Susan Smith-Peter, "How to Write a Region: Local and Regional Historiography," *Kritika* 5, no. 3 (Summer 2004): 535. For more scholarship challenging the old paradigm, see Catherine Evtuhov, *Portrait of a Russian Province: Economy, Society, and Civilization in Nineteenth-Century Nizhnii Novgorod* (Pittsburgh, PA: University of Pittsburgh Press, 2011), as well as the following works by Smith-Peter: *Imagining Russian Regions: Subnational Identity and Civil Society in Nineteenth-Century Russia* (Leiden: Brill, 2017); "The Russian Provincial Newspaper and Its Public, 1788–1864" *The Carl Beck Papers in Russian & East European Studies* 1908 (2008); "Making Empty Provinces: Eighteenth-Century Enlightenment Regionalism in Russian Provincial Journals," *REGION: Regional Studies of Russia, Eastern Europe, and Central Asia* 4, no. 1 (2015): 7–29. Other important works in this vein include Daniel R. Brower, *The Russian City between Tradition and Modernity,*

1850–1900 (Berkeley: University of California Press, 1990); V. V. Abashev, *Perm' kak tekst. Perm' v russkoi kul'ture i literature XX veka* (Moscow-Berlin: Direct Media, 2014); Kate Pickering-Antonova, *An Ordinary Marriage: The World of a Gentry Family in Provincial Russia* (Oxford: Oxford University Press, 2013). See also the essays collected in the four seminal post-Soviet volumes for which I have listed abbreviations above.

75. See Pierre Bourdieu, *The Rules of Art: Genesis and Structure of the Literary Field* (Stanford: Stanford University Press, 1996).

76. See interview with Nabokov conducted on September 25, 27, 28, and 29, 1966, at Montreux, Switzerland, published in *Wisconsin Studies in Contemporary Literature* 8, no. 2 (Spring 1967), and available at http://lib.ru/NABOKOW/Inter06.txt_with-big-pictures .html, accessed March 10, 2017. See also Vladimir Nabokov, *Speak, Memory: An Autobiography Revisited* (New York: Vintage International, 1989), 160.

77. And the system certainly does not work the same way when it comes to music and painting, as attested by even a cursory look at the backgrounds, self-mythologizations, and ongoing provincial involvements of the Mighty Handful (composers) and the *peredvizhniki* (painters) of nineteenth-century Russia.

78. The world of Fet's lyric poetry, for instance, is a gentry estate that serves as a wholly legitimate center. Fet's *usad'ba* is not only the home of nature (which *provintsiia* is not), it is also the focus of an ordered, hierarchical, and traditional culture out of which poetry can appear to grow naturally. This kind of art does not require a *stolichnyi* point of view in order to avoid the taint of provinciality.

79. Dostoevskii, *PSS*, 6:115. These words are spoken by Luzhin, one of the least insightful and more pernicious characters in the novel, but Dostoevsky made a habit of using "bad" characters to articulate "good" ideas.

80. Katie Trumpener writes, "London functions [in literature] not so much as the source and center of Englishness but as the nerve center—and blind spot—of a patched-together empire. As the place from which the empire is ruled, it gathers a cross-section of intellectuals, aristocrats and merchants from every domain. A place from which all of the isles seem visible, it can really give only the most misleading sense of the empire's cultural coherence, its actual political or economic conditions." Katie Trumpener, *Bardic Nationalism: The Romantic Novel and the British Empire* (Princeton, NJ: Princeton University Press, 1997), 15–16. The parallels with Imperial Russia are striking.

81. Philip Roth made this point himself in an interview: Al Alvarez, "The Long Road Home," *The Guardian*, September 11, 2004, accessed July 21, 2017, http://donswaim.com /guardian.uk.rothprofile.html.

82. V. F. Odoevsky, "Sil'fida" (1837), accessed November 1, 2016, http://rulibrary.ru /odoevskiy/silfida/3.

83. F. K. Sologub, *Melkii bes* (St. Petersburg: Nauka, 2004), 74.

84. Sologub, *Melkii bes*, 516.

85. Gogol', *PSS*, 6:692.

86. Mikhail Bakhtin, "Forms of Time and Chronotope in the Novel," in *The Dialogic Imagination: Four Essays by M. M. Bakhtin*, ed. Michael Holquist, trans. Caryl Emerson and Michael Holquist (Austin: University of Texas Press, 1981), 247–48.

87. Fisher, *Still the New World*, 52.

88. For recent scholarship on provincial (middling) elites with strong local affiliations, see Antonova, *An Ordinary Marriage*, and Evtuhov, *Portrait of a Russian Province*.

89. Peter Kolchin, *Unfree Labor: American Slavery and Russian Serfdom* (Cambridge, MA: Harvard University Press, 1987), 169, emphasis mine.

90. Moretti, *Atlas of the European Novel*, 70.

91. Moretti, *Atlas of the European Novel*, 16, 19–21.

92. Gorizontov, "The 'Great Circle' of Interior Russia," 68. See also Dickinson, *Breaking Ground*, 200–201, on the post-1812 period's increasing tendency to locate the nation's strength in "the rural provinces and the *narod*." But again, this kind of focus on rural Russia was not about regional particularity.

93. Dostoevskii, *PSS*, 23:6–7.

94. V. A. Sollogub, *Tarantas*, in *Povesti i rasskazy*, intro. E. Kiiko (Moscow: Gosudarstvennoe izdatel'stvo khudozhestvennoi literatury, 1962), 199, 186.

95. Chekhov, *PSS*, 13:110.

96. "The action in *The Brothers Karamazov* could have developed in any other town of a similar size and location . . . Skotoprigon'evsk stands for the province, it is the small town typically opposed to the metropolis, to the urban area traditionally well-known to Dostoevsky's readers." The town "has little significance of its own," just as it has "no boundaries, no historic centre, no particularly relevant or evocative monuments for the action to revolve around. There is only a monastery, but at about a verst or more away, immediately suggesting, in fact, that it belongs to another world." Gian Piero Piretto, "Staraia Russa and Petersburg; Provincial Realities and Metropolitan Reminiscences in *The Brothers Karamazov*," *Dostoevsky Studies* 7 (1986): 82–83.

97. Edward Said, *Culture and Imperialism* (New York: Vintage Books, 1994), 74, 72.

98. Kirichenko and Shcheboleva, *Russkaia provintsiia*, 62–63, 123. Dolgorukov also comments on provincials' awareness of this hierarchy as we will see in chapter 3: Petersburg is thought to be "above" Moscow, just as both capitals are "above" provincial cities. I. M. Dolgorukov, "Slavny bubny za gorami, ili puteshestvie moe koe-kuda 1810 goda," in *Chteniia v Imperatorskom Obshchestve Istorii i Drevnostei Rossiiskikh* 2: Materialy otechestvennye (April–June 1869), 8.

99. Razumova and Kuleshov, "K fenomenologii provintsii," *PKR*, 25. Only in a few Russian cities were the old arrangements preserved, with houses facing different directions.

100. Evtuhov, *Portrait of a Russian Province*, 46.

101. Brower, *The Russian City*, 15, 10. See also Kirichenko and Shcheboleva, *Russkaia provintsiia*, 50–62; L. O. Zaionts, "Istoriia slova i poniatiia 'provintsiia' v russkoi kul'ture"; and Razumova and Kuleshov, "K fenomenologii provintsii," *PKR*, 24.

102. Smith-Peter, *Imagining Russian Regions*, ch. 1.

103. Smith-Peter in *Imagining Russian Regions* also explains that certain categories of Russian towns and settlements (most notably the *uezd*, or district town) were less subject to the state's systematizing efforts than others.

104. Dolgorukov, "Slavny bubny za gorami," 67.

105. "Precisely at this moment [later eighteenth/early nineteenth century] . . . the idea of 'provincial backwardness' takes shape, linked . . . to idea of progress, a unified historical

process." T. V. Klubkova and P. A. Klubkov, "Russkii provintsial'nyi gorod i stereotipy provintsial'nosti," in *MTR*, 22. On how the countryside came to be seen as backward, see Yanni Kotsonis, *Making Peasants Backward: Agricultural Cooperatives and the Agrarian Question in Russia, 1861–1914* (New York: Palgrave Macmillan, 1999).

106. Both *pomeshchik* and *dvorianin* were used to denote a member of the gentry, but with different emphases: *dvorianin* designates legal membership in the nobility (it derives from the word for court), whereas *pomeshchik* (derived from the word for an estate given to a nobleman by the tsar) calls to mind the nobleman's relationship to his land. For an analysis of the crucial role played by this figure in eighteenth- and early nineteenth-century literature, see Bella Grigoryan, *Noble Subjects: The Russian Novel and the Gentry, 1762–1861* (DeKalb, IL: Northern Illinois University Press, 2018). As Grigoryan's work demonstrates, the landowner in this era's literature was a far more complex (and at times a more positive and promising) figure than the caricature I have sketched out here, particularly as writers began to imagine him as a potential citizen.

107. These negative representations were tempered, at the end of the eighteenth century and in the early decades of the nineteenth, by Romanticism's sentimental reappraisal of things rural (in texts like Karamzin's *Poor Liza*, for example), as I discuss in ch. 2.

108. One inheritor of this eighteenth-century satirical tradition is perhaps Alexander Ostrovsky, whose plays vilify the figure of the domestic tyrant (*samodur*) associated with Russia's hidebound merchant caste. Ostrovsky's famous *samodury* (who were only sometimes provincials: Moscow, too, was a congenial milieu for them) serve as targets much in the same way that benighted rural noblemen do in earlier texts.

109. N. I. Novikov, "Pis'mo uezdnogo dvorianina k ego synu," accessed April 15, 2018, http://rvb.ru/18vek/novikov/01text/01prose/05.htm. As I discuss in ch. 2, by the turn of the century (e.g., in Karamzin's 1811 *Memoir on Old and New Russia*), we note more favorable depictions of the rural gentry, often highlighting the patriarchal virtues that were to appear even more virtuous in the aftermath of 1812. These texts are likely one source for the wholesome *glush'*-dwellers we begin to see a bit later, like Pushkin's Larin family.

110. N. I. Novikov, cited in David MacLaren McDonald, "Razmyshleniia o poniatii 'glush'": provintsiia, gosudarstvo i dvoriantsvo v Rossii," *Russkii sbornik. Issledovaniia po istorii Rossii*, vol. 5, ed. O. R. Airapetov et al. (Moscow: Modest Kolerov, 2008), 67–92, accessed April 4, 2018, http://nlr.ru/domplekhanova/dep/artupload/dp/article/70/NA1914.pdf

111. I. S. Turgenev, *Polnoe sobranie sochinenii i pisem v 30-i tomakh* (Moscow: Nauka, 1978), 7:62.

112. Turgenev, *PSS*, 7:63–64; Pavel Mel'nikov-Pecherskii, "Krasil'nikovy," in *Sobranie sochinenii v 6-i tomakh* (Moscow: Knizhnyi Klub Knigovek, 2010), 1:17.

113. Turgenev, *PSS*, 7:258–9, 265, 262.

114. Quoted in Rosalind H. Williams, *Dream Worlds: Mass Consumption in Late Nineteenth-Century France* (Berkeley: University of California Press, 1982), 355.

115. O. M. Somov, *Roman v dvukh pis'makh*, in Somov, *Selected Prose in Russian*, ed. John Mersereau and George Harjan (Ann Arbor: University of Michigan Press, 1974), 54–55.

116. Casanova, *World Republic of Letters*, 88–89.

117. Casanova, *World Republic of Letters*, 75.

118. Pierre Bourdieu, *Distinction: A Social Critique of the Judgement of Taste*, trans. Richard Nice (Cambridge, MA: Harvard University Press, 1984), 68.

119. Bourdieu, *Distinction*, 95.

120. M. E. Saltykov-Shchedrin, *Sobranie sochinenii v 20-i tomakh* (Moscow: Khudo-zhestvennaia literatura, 1965–77), 8:407.

121. Saltykov-Shchedrin, *SS*, 2:79.

122. Saltykov-Shchedrin, *SS*, 2:225.

123. Gertsen, *SS*, 4:37.

124. Turgenev, *PSS*, 7:63–4; Gogol', *PSS* 6:95, 115.

125. Dolgorukov, "Slavny bubny za gorami," 67.

126. I. M. Dolgorukov, *Povest' o rozhdenii moem*, vol. 1, 166. In nineteenth-century fiction provincial social circles are almost always characterized by motleyness ("fenomen 'pestrogo'") and contradiction. Koshelev, "O 'literaturnoi' provintsii," 47.

127. Gertsen, *SS*, 4:33.

128. Gogol', *PSS*, 6:26, 163.

129. Honoré de Balzac, *Lost Illusions*, intro. Richard Howard, trans. Kathleen Raine, notes by James Madden (New York: Modern Library, 1997), 195, emphasis mine.

130. T. S. Eliot, "What is a Classic?," in *Selected Prose of T. S. Eliot*, ed. Frank Kermode (New York: Farrar, Straus and Giroux), 129, emphasis mine.

131. Eliot, "What is a Classic?," 129, emphasis mine. Pascale Casanova concurs: "the classic" functions above all as a standard, a "unit of measurement for everything that is or will be recognized as literary." Casanova, *World Republic of Letters*, 15.

132. Eliot, "What is a Classic?," 122, 129.

133. Eliot, "What is a Classic?," 130, 124, emphasis mine.

134. V. G. Belinskii, *Polnoe sobranie sochinenii* (Moscow: Akademiia Nauk, 1953), 7:46.

135. Eliot, "What is a Classic?," 122–23.

136. Koshelev, "O 'literaturnoi' provintsii," 52.

137. This is the Paris that Casanova takes as her subject in *The World Republic of Letters*, first published in French as *La république mondiale des lettres* (Paris: Editions du Seuil, 1999). Casanova's work is to a significant degree a transposition into the literary sphere of certain historians' ideas about space, power, and force (particularly the thought of Immanuel Wallerstein and Fernand Braudel).

Chapter Two

1. The toponym "Goriukhino" appears again in *The Tales of Belkin*, a work that is also attributed to the same imaginary "compiler," Belkin (see note 37 below). *Povesti pokoinogo Ivana Petrovicha Belkina*, in A. P. Pushkin, *Polnoe sobranie sochinenii v 17-i tomakh* (Moscow: Akademiia nauk SSSR, 1937–59), 8 (1): 57–124. Hereafter all Pushkin citations are from this edition and appear parenthetically in the main text. The setting of *The Tales of Belkin*—a remote provincial area—is consistently designated as *derevnia*, never *provintsiia*.

It has much in common with the Larins' home; indeed, one might imagine these imaginary spots occupying adjacent space on a map of Russia.

2. However, even after the steppe came to be seen as part of "European Russia," it was *not* taken to be part of "interior," "central," or "essential" Russia. See Leonid Gorizontov, "The 'Great Circle' of Interior Russia: Representations of the Imperial Center in the Nineteenth and Early Twentieth Centuries," in *Russian Empire: Space, People, Power, 1700–1930*, ed. Jane Burbank, Mark von Hagen, and Anatolyi Remnev (Bloomington: Indiana University Press, 2007), 67–93.

3. As a result the southern border was where Russia "defined her identity vis-à-vis both Europe and the Asian territories she incorporated into her empire. In a sense, it was here that Russia determined where that all-important border between east and west lay, and whether Russia belonged to Asia or, as a *practitioner* of Orientalist discourse, to Europe." Monika Greenleaf, *Pushkin and Romantic Fashion* (Stanford: Stanford University Press, 1994), 109.

4. Already in Pushkin's day, and certainly by the 1830s, Russia's southern regions were exotic in a thoroughly literary and even stylized way. The conquest of the Caucasus had been going on for a century, and Russians who wrote about the region drew on European Orientalist tropes made available to them by poets like Byron and Moore. Often these models had to be adjusted, particularly since the contiguous empire could make it difficult to tell precisely where Russia ended and not-Russia began (hence in *Journey to Erezrum*, Pushkin's narrator momentarily believes—hopes—that he has crossed the border and left Russia behind, but it turns out that he never actually has). In the post-Romantic period, with the rise of a self-consciously realist aesthetic, writers' interest shifted away from the exotic (Orient) and toward the typical (Russian).

5. The focus of idyll or pastoral (terms that are often used interchangeably, and are certainly interchangeable for my purposes) is "the peace and simplicity of the life of shepherds and other rural folk in an idealized natural setting," with the simple life being not necessarily that of shepherds, but also, say, that of children or the lower classes. M. H. Abrams, *A Glossary of Literary Terms* (New York: Harcourt Brace, 1999), 202–3. *Glush'*—derived from the same root as the word for "deep" and meaning more or less "rural backwater"—can be used to evoke such places and images as well. See ch. 1, note 110. Precisely this image of *derevnia* informs Pushkin's 1819 lyric by the same name ("Derevnia," 1819), which gives voice to the poet's love of his rural estate/village—a "haven of tranquility, labor, and inspiration" where he feels himself to be utterly at home, though this peace is marred by his awareness of serfdom's injustice. Pushkin, *PSS*, 2 (1): 89–91.

6. See ch. 1. On Polevoi, see I. Z. Kokovina, "Provintsial'nyi byt v strukture khudozhestvennogo proizvedeniia XIX veka," in *PKR*, 101–7.

7. This is the argument developed in David MacLaren McDonald, "Razmyshleniia o poniatii 'glush'": provintsiia, gosudarstvo i dvoriantsvo v Rossii," in *Russkii sbornik. Issledovaniia po istorii Rossii*, vol. 5, ed. O. R. Airapetov et al. (Moscow: Modest Kolerov, 2008), 67–92, accessed April 4, 2018. http://nlr.ru/domplekhanova/dep/artupload/dp/article/70/NA1914.pdf. Indeed, one might speculate that in the Sentimental/Romantic period, some

of the negative traits (like venality and pernicious backwardness) that earlier eighteenth-century literature had ascribed to nearly all *nestolichnye* (non-capital) places were being symbolically confined to *gubernskie goroda*—that is, the "provincial capitals" that served as the face of state power outside Petersburg and Moscow. This shift then freed up the estate/village/small town/countryside (categories that could be conveniently conflated as necessary) for symbolic use by members of the gentry looking to accumulate social and cultural capital, or by writers looking for a place to locate a version of Russian authenticity.

8. Vladimir Nabokov, trans. and commentary, *Eugene Onegin: A Novel in Verse*, vol. 2: Commentary and Index (Princeton, NJ: Princeton University Press, 1990), 31, 179. Nabokov locates the setting "on the basis of certain viatic data"—i.e., the time it takes Eugene to cover the distance between Petersburg and his estate near the Larins', which should therefore be "between parallels 56 and 57 . . . at the junction of the former provinces of Tver and Smolensk . . . and some 250 miles S of St. Petersburg" (31).

9. Abrams, *A Glossary of Literary Terms*, 202–3.

10. Unlike Petersburg, the Moscow of *Eugene Onegin* has much in common with *derevnia*: the old capital seems to stand for continuity and Russianness as opposed to the new capital's restlessly innovating modernity. Tatiana's Moscow relations, for instance, are unchanging ("No v nikh ne vidno peremeny; / Vse v nikh na staryi obrazets"). Pushkin evokes Moscow's ancient monuments and churches, its place "in the Russian heart" and Russian history (e.g., its proud refusal to give Napoleon the keys to "the ancient Kremlin"), and the folksy quality of daily life (monasteries and towers, streets bustling with merchants, Cossacks, etc.). Pushkin, *PSS*, 6:158, 155.

11. See I. A. Razumova and E. V. Kuleshov, "K fenomenologii provintsii," in *PKR*, 18–20, and Sara Dickinson, *Breaking Ground: Travel and National Culture in Russia from Peter I to the Era of Pushkin* (Amsterdam: Rodopi, 2006), 133.

12. Mikhail Bakhtin, "Forms of Time and Chronotope in the Novel," in *The Dialogic Imagination: Four Essays by M. M. Bakhtin*, ed. Michael Holquist, trans. Caryl Emerson and Michael Holquist (Austin: University of Texas Press, 1981), 225.

13. Razumova and Kuleshov, "K fenomenologii provintsii," *PKR*, 120.

14. Priscilla R. Roosevelt, "Tatiana's Garden: Noble Sensibilities and Estate Park Design in the Romantic Era," *Slavic Review* 49, no. 3 (Autumn 1990): 335.

15. The irony of nomenclature was not lost on Russians; the memoirist Andrei Bolotov even rejected the term "English" to describe this mode of landscaping, for which he advocated tirelessly. "Some Russian afficionadoes were defensive about the fact that the English garden in which they delighted, though made to appear natural, was clearly not native. . . . Bolotov did not even like the term 'English,' for all his passion for the style." Roosevelt, "Tatiana's Garden," 348.

16. Roosevelt, "Tatiana's Garden," 335. The garden's goal was supposedly to provide "an immediate and natural relationship with [one's] surroundings"; in England, designers often aimed to obscure the division between (pleasure) park and (working) countryside. Roosevelt, "Tatiana's Garden," 336, 339.

17. Roosevelt, "Tatiana's Garden," 339. "Russian owners of large estates . . . did not sentimentalize or simulate real rural life in their gardens. In fact, they cut themselves off from

it, whether by disguising their house serfs in European dress or by imposing physical bar-riers . . . physical [reminders] of the divide between the Europeanized owner in his equally European setting, and his Russian serfs in their villages." Roosevelt, "Tatiana's Garden," 347.

18. Tatiana's garden "[seems] meant to evoke, however briefly, the immediate relation-ship with nature that Romanticism demanded and, through this immediacy, to suggest the genuine harmony with rural Russia to which generations of Russian *intelligenty* would aspire. It is hardly surprising that Pushkin and his contemporaries were on the whole more at home in the isolated, often theatrical, and ultimately foreign English garden of the *vel'mozha* (grandee) than in a Russian village." Roosevelt, "Tatiana's Garden," 347, 349.

19. Roosevelt, "Tatiana's Garden," 336. And by contrast, the "huge, neglected" garden at Eugene's grander estate (6:31) rates no description at all.

20. Roosevelt, "Tatiana's Garden," 347; Thomas Newlin, "Rural Ruses: Illusion and Anx-iety on the Russian Estate, 1775–815," *Slavic Review* 57, no. 2 (Summer 1998): 307.

21. Newlin, "Rural Ruses," 307. Grand "natural" gardens were also exceedingly expen-sive to build and maintain, if one counts "free" serf labor as an expense (in Pushkin's story "Baryshnia-krestianka," gardening mania helps bankrupt one anglophile *pomeshchik*).

22. When Bolotov left government service and returned to his estate in 1762, the home he had remembered so fondly appeared "small, squalid, and a veritable prison. . . . Seeing everything through completely different eyes, I could not get over my surprise at how it all at first seemed somehow too small, too poor, and too meager, and not at all the way I had been accustomed to imagining everything ever since I was a child. In childhood all things seem to us somehow much bigger and grander than they really are. My old ponds now seemed like mere mud puddles to me; my gardens seemed utterly insignificant and were overgrown with all sorts of wild vegetation; the outbuildings all seemed totally rickety, run-down, and paltry, and looked more as if they belonged to peasants than to a nobleman; the layout of everything was as stupid and illogical as one could imagine." Thomas Newlin, "The Return of the Russian Odysseus: Pastoral Dreams and Rude Awakenings," *Russian Review* 55, no. 3 (July 1996): 454–55.

23. Newlin, "The Return of the Russian Odysseus," 449. Newlin continues, "Pushkin draws on [the eighteenth-century pastoral] tradition only to tip it slyly into the mud pud-dle of realism: it is a pastoral vision gone slightly awry. While the result may not qualify as nightmarish—quite yet, at least—the shift is in that direction; the sessile, cabbagey existence evoked here threatens to teeter even further afield, from a grubby realism, not yet entirely de-void of a certain residual and bedraggled picturesqueness, into a Gogolian *sur*realism" (450).

24. Tom Nairn, "The British Political Elite," *New Left Review* 23 (January–February 1964): 22.

25. "Derevnia zhe nash kabinet" is a line from Pushkin's unfinished "Novel in Letters" of 1829. Certainly the time Pushkin spent quarantined at his estate during the famous "Boldino autumn" of 1830, when he quickly penned a series of masterful works, suggests this association between rural (estate) seclusion and creative productivity. Newlin notes that the idea of the village estate as the Russian nobleman's study "had roots deep in the eighteenth century." Newlin, "The Return of the Russian Odysseus," 456. For examples of Russian estates that succeeded in these terms, see Patricia Roosevelt, *Life on the Russian*

Country Estate (New Haven, CT: Yale University Press, 1995), esp. ch. 11, "Ideal Worlds: The Idyll of the Russian Intelligentsia." See also William F. Broomfield, "Dvorianskaia idiliia. Neoklassicheskaia arkhitektura v epokhu Ekateriny Velikoi," in *ZP*, 188–92.

26. M. A. Glushkova, "Mir russkoi usad'by v lirike Afanasiia Feta," in *ZP*, 237.

27. Alexander Pushkin, *Eugene Onegin*, trans. James E. Falen (Oxford: Oxford University Press, 1990), 35. All English citations of *Onegin* are taken from this edition.

28. "Vkus byl, na maner stolichnyi, / Vo vsem fasade sokhranen otlichnyi." A. A. Fet, "Dve lipki," in *Sochineniia v dvukh tomakh* (Moscow: Khudozhestvennaia literatura, 1982), 1:487.

29. Nabokov, *Eugene Onegin*, 2:168, emphasis mine.

30. A. I. Gertsen, *Sobranie sochinenii v 30-i tomakh* (Moscow: Izd. Akademii Nauk SSSR, 1954), 1:298–99.

31. Falen, trans., *Eugene Onegin*, 191.

32. Falen, trans., *Eugene Onegin*, 192.

33. M. Iu. Lermontov, *Polnoe sobranie sochinenii v 6-i tomakh* (Moscow: Akademiia Nauk SSSR, 1954–57), 6:295–96, 276.

34. In fact these "inauthentic" characters are perhaps the only thing that allows us to perceive Pechorin as being in any sense "authentic" because, as I have noted elsewhere, "authentic" and "inauthentic" are in the end definable chiefly against each other, à la Saussure. We know a thing is authentic because it is not inauthentic.

35. Pierre Bourdieu, *Distinction: A Social Critique of the Judgement of Taste*, trans. Richard Nice (Cambridge, MA: Harvard University Press, 1984), 68, 95.

36. Pushkin's note reads, "Уездн.<ый> гор<од> не имеет истории." Pushkin, *PSS* 8 (2): 719. For English citations of "A History of the Village of Goriukhino" I have used Paul Debreczeny, trans., *Alexander Pushkin: Complete Prose Fiction* (Stanford, CA: Stanford University Press, 1983), amending as necessary.

37. At the same time Pushkin wrote "Goriukhino" he was working on *The Tales of Belkin* (see note 1 above). Unlike the deliberately naïve "Goriukhino" text, the Belkin tales are polished and self-consciously literary miniatures, masterfully arranged in a complex, puzzle-like structure that showcases Pushkin's sophisticated irony and his control of the genre system. Where "Goriukhino" underlines its own incoherence, the Belkin tales, with their marked insistence on genre formulas like mirroring, repetition, mistaken identity, implausible coincidences, and clichéd vocabulary, call attention to exaggerated forms of order and symmetry.

38. David M. Bethea and Sergei Davydov, "The History of the Village Gorjuxino: In Praise of Puškin's Folly," *Slavic and East European Journal* 28, no. 3 (Autumn 1984): 300.

39. Bethea and Davydov, "The History of the Village Gorjuxino," 300.

40. J. G. A. Pocock, "Modes of Political and Historical Time in Early Eighteenth-Century England," in *Virtue, Commerce, and History: Essays on Political Thought and History, Chiefly in the Eighteenth Century* (Cambridge, UK: Cambridge University Press, 1985), 91.

41. Bakhtin, "Forms of Time and Chronotope in the Novel," 247. In Bakhtin's system the difference between the negatively inflected chronotope of the provincial *town* and the more positively inflected chronotope of the (essentially rural) idyll seems to lie mainly in the

idyll's close relationship to nature, procreation, and cyclical time (none of which is central to the provincial town chronotope). Thus what Bakhtin calls "provincial novels" are set in rural spaces (not provincial towns) and draw on the temporality of the classical idyll. See Bakhtin, "Forms of Time and Chronotope in the Novel," 228–29. Yet as I note elsewhere, in the Russian tradition even what is idyllic or pastoral is often at risk of degradation.

42. Thus "the significance of all . . . stories depends in part on seeing their narrative relationship to expanding circles of plots within plots." Louis Mink, "Narrative Form as a Cognitive Instrument," in *The Writing of History*, ed. Robert H. Canary and Henry Kozicki (Madison: University of Wisconsin Press, 1978), 137.

43. White continues, "'the true' is identified with 'the real' only insofar as it can be shown to possess the character of narrativity." Hayden White, "The Value of Narrativity in the Representation of Reality," in *On Narrative*, ed. W. J. T. Mitchell (Chicago: University of Chicago Press, 1981), 5–6.

44. Bethea and Davydov, "The [Hi]story of the Village Gorjuxino," 295.

45. Mink, "Narrative Form as a Cognitive Instrument," 132. Mink's second pole corresponds to White's description of the philosophy of history, which consists of "nothing but plot" since "its story elements exist only as manifestations . . . of the plot structure." White, "The Value of Narrativity," 20.

46. M. [François] Guizot, *General History of Civilization in Europe: From the Fall of the Roman Empire to the French Revolution*, 9th American Edition (New York: D. Appleton, 1869), 253, cited in Alexander Dolinin, "Historicism or Providentialism? Pushkin's *History of Pugachev* in the Context of French Romantic Historiography," *Slavic Review* 58, no. 2, Special Issue: Aleksandr Pushkin 1799–1999 (Summer 1999), 294n13. Dolinin writes, "There is no doubt that Pushkin followed the newest trends in French history with keen interest," and writers such as Barante, Thierry, Thiers, Guizot, etc., were all "widely discussed" in Russian periodicals. Dolinin, "Historicism or Providentialism," 291–92, 292n3.

47. Svetlana Evdokimova, *Pushkin's Historical Imagination* (New Haven, CT: Yale University Press, 1999), 53, 54, 50.

48. Iurii Lotman, "'Pikovaia dama' i tema kart i kartochnye igry v russkoi literature nachala XIX veka," in *Izbrannye stat'i*, 3 vols. (Tallinn: Aleksandra, 1992), 2:397. See also ch. 2 ("Chance and Historical Necessity") in Evdokimova, *Pushkin's Historical Imagination*, and Dolinin, "Historicism or Providentialism," 291–308.

49. Pushkin also wrote a nonfiction account of the uprising, titled *A History of Pugachev*. The relationship between *A History of Pugachev* and *The Captain's Daughter* is similar to that between "A History of the Village of Goriukhino" and *The Captain's Daughter*: while Pushkin's fictional treatment of the rebellion (*The Captain's Daughter*) draws attention to its own orderly structure, his nonfiction account (*A History of Pugachev*) refuses to impose much order on the anarchy that is its subject matter; rather than explaining the confusion and violence, it offers a welter of details and facts. The result is something approaching mere chaos, an image of "social upheaval as a cluster of contingencies, an intrusion of chaos and unpredictability upon the established order." Dolinin, "Historicism or Providentialism," 297–98, 305.

50. For English citations of *The Captain's Daughter*, I have consulted Debreczeny, trans., *Alexander Pushkin: Complete Prose Fiction*, amending as necessary.

51. Michael Biggs, "Putting the State on the Map: Cartography, Territory, and European State Formation," *Comparative Studies in Society and History* 41, no. 2 (April 1999): 377.

52. Jane Austen, *Mansfield Park* (New York: W. W. Norton, 1998), 15. *Mansfield Park* was published in 1814; it is set mostly between 1810 and 1813, though some of the action extends back to 1785.

53. Bakhtin, "Forms of Time and Chronotope in the Novel," 226–29.

54. Bakhtin, "Forms of Time and Chronotope in the Novel," 225–26.

55. Bakhtin, "Forms of Time and Chronotope in the Novel," 226, italics mine.

56. Willard Sunderland, *Taming the Wild Field: Colonization and Empire on the Russia Steppe* (Ithaca, NY: Cornell University Press, 2004), 79–80.

57. Sunderland, *Taming the Wild Field*, 65, italics mine.

58. Sunderland, *Taming the Wild Field*, 52–53. In reality, of course, Russians had to work to imagine the steppe as empty—especially by settling, eradicating, and strategically forgetting about the land's nomadic inhabitants. This was a version of the same process that unfolded in the United States and Canada, Argentina and Australia: first colonizers imagine the land as unpeopled, and then they go about peopling it.

59. Sunderland, *Taming the Wild Field*, 70. "The adoption of the name of New Russia was in fact the most powerful statement imaginable of Russia's coming of age. There was now, it seemed, a recognizable and containable entity called Russia that could be replicated in a new place." Cf. New England, New Spain, New France, New Amsterdam, etc.

60. Grigory Kaganov, *Images of Space: St. Petersburg in the Visual and Verbal Arts*, trans. Sidney Monas (Stanford: Stanford University Press, 1997), 16.

61. Sunderland, *Taming the Wild Field*, 70.

62. At this time "the question 'where is Russia?' . . . had no commonly accepted answer." Mark Bassin, *Imperial Visions: Nationalist Imagination and Geographical Expansion in the Russian Far East, 1840–1865* (Cambridge, UK: Cambridge University Press, 1999), 14.

63. Sunderland, *Taming the Wild Field*, 65.

64. Jürgen Osterhammel, *The Transformation of the World: A Global History of the Nineteenth Century* (Princeton, NJ: Princeton University Press, 2014), 110–112, emphasis mine.

65. Michael Biggs, "Putting the State on the Map," 374.

66. K. I. Arsen'ev quoted in Gorizontov, "The 'Great Circle' of Interior Russia," 72.

67. I say *modern* state because, as Benedict Anderson notes, "in the older imagining, . . . states were defined by *centres*," not borders. Borders at this time were not clear but rather "porous and indistinct, and sovereignties faded imperceptibly into one another." Benedict Anderson, *Imagined Communities: Reflections on the Origin and Spread of Nationalism* (London: Verso, 1991 [1983]), 19, emphasis mine.

68. Belogorsk corresponds roughly to the location of Fort Tatishchev.

69. Cited in Christopher David Ely, *This Meager Nature: Landscape and National Identity in Imperial Russia* (DeKalb, IL: Northern Illinois University Press, 2002), 18.

70. In *A History of Pugachev* the list of named ethnic groups is longer: here Pushkin notes—in addition to Bashkirs, Kalmyks, and Cossacks—the Mordvin, Chivash, Cheremis,

Meshcheriaks, Kirgiz Kaisakhs, "and other peoples." Pushkin, *Istoriia Pugacheva, PSS* 8 (1): 3–367.

71. Pushkin was aware that the Russian state's perspective on the Cossacks was not the only way to understand them. This much is clear in his *History of Pugachev*, in which, as William Todd makes clear, the Cossacks are shown to possess their own culture and government, which were being suppressed by the Russian empire. See William Mills Todd III, "Pushkin's *History of Pugachev* and the Experience of Rebellion," unpublished paper cited by permission of author.

72. The Cossacks here recall the "Ukrainians" in Lermontov's "Taman," a section of *A Hero of Our Time* set in a seaside Ukrainian town—a town that turns out to be much more dangerous, and much more destabilizing to ethnic categories, than the straightforwardly foreign Caucasus mountains. In Valeria Sobol's analysis, what is threatening about this place is the fact that while the hero still seems to think he is "at home" here (that is, he thinks he is in Russia proper), the locals turn out to have hybrid and indeterminate identities and loyalties: "the world they inhabit [is] at the same time . . . familiar and banal ('a little coastal town,' one of many), and . . . unfamiliar and threatening—just as ethnographically the locals are simultaneously Russians and Ukrainians, 'self' and 'other.'" And these people's "indeterminate status" results "from the peculiar character of the Russian Empire itself, where the distinction between self and other, colonizer and colonized, is often rather difficult to draw." The hybrid nature of Lermontov's Ukrainians "problematizes the notion of the Russian Empire as a coherent whole with clearly drawn boundaries." Valeria Sobol, "The Uncanny Frontier of Russian Identity: Travel, Ethnography, and Empire in Lermontov's 'Taman,'" *The Russian Review* 70, no. 1 (January 2011): 71–73, 66.

73. Such characters, Moretti writes, "are all enemies of the new centralized power of the state, and the novel, obediently, sentences them to death; but on the other hand it presents them as generous, young, brave, passionate—and 'noble.'" Moretti, *Atlas of the European Novel, 1800–1900* (London: Verso, 1998), 37n18.

74. Sunderland, *Taming the Wild Field*, 18.

75. Gogol', *PSS*, 6:95.

76. Gertsen, *PSS*, 7:304 (*v strane molchaniia i nemoty*).

Chapter Three

1. A. I. Gertsen, *Sobranie sochinenii v 30-i tomakh* (Moscow: Izd. Akademii Nauk SSSR, 1954), 1:298–99. Here Herzen uses the word *provintsial'nyi*, whereas in designating the setting of *Who Is to Blame?* he uses the adjective *gubernskii* ("v gubernskom gorode NN"): as I explain in the introductory chapter, there is no significant difference between these two adjectives by the mid-1830s. Thus in *Who Is To Blame?*, for example, the two are used almost interchangeably, with the exception that *gubernskii* is required for official state designations (e.g., *gubernskii prokuror*). The same holds true in other texts of the period.

2. Gertsen, *SS*, 4:69, 169.

3. P. A. Klubkov, "'Zamkami slaven Tver', a Novgorod syrtiami,'" in *PKR*, 47.

4. V. A. Sollogub, *Tarantas*, in *Povesti i rasskazy*, intro. E. Kiiko (Moscow: Gosudarst-vennoe izdatel'stvo khudozhestvennoi literatury, 1962), 199.

5. Chekhov's words to his sister in a letter of 1890. A. P. Chekhov, *Polnoe sobranie so-chinenii i pisem v 30-i tomakh* (Moscow: Nauka, 1978), 4:72.

6. Susan Smith-Peter, *Imagining Russian Regions: Subnational Identity and Civil Society in Nineteenth-Century Russia* (Leiden: Brill, 2017), 27.

7. Smith-Peter, *Imagining Russian Regions*, 35. Smith-Peter cites GAVO, f. 410, op. 1, d. 88, l. 16. (N6, p. 34a).

8. Sollogub, *Tarantas*, 156.

9. Gertsen, *SS*, 7:303.

10. Gertsen, *SS*, 7:304.

11. Gertsen, *SS*, 4:69, 169. The tiny *gubernskii gorod* where Krutsifersky is from is designated NN; the seemingly larger provincial town where Beltov later meets him is designated ***.

12. Saikat Majumdar, *Prose of the World: Modernism and the Banality of Empire* (New York: Columbia University Press, 2013), 32.

13. Majumdar, *Prose of the World*, 32. Of course, under other circumstances a char-acter's stasis might signal a form of social power, whereas mobility might be associated with weakness or oppression. Thus the power of Balzac's moneylender in *Gobseck* (1830) is expressed in his stasis, and in Thomas Hardy's novels, impoverished (English) "natives" roam the countryside in desperate attempts to earn a living (e.g., in *Jude the Obscure*, 1895).

14. Sollogub, "Aptekarsha," in *Povesti i rasskazy*, 84. Greater distance from the capitals is equated with deeper misery—and as Herzen will explain in his memoirs, for political exiles, distance is thus associated with more severe punishment.

15. Dolgorukov had few models on which to base his writings about domestic voyages undertaken for pleasure, since existing modes of Russian travel writing paid little attention to the towns, estates, and historical sites that interested the prince. Sara Dickinson explains that eighteenth-century Russian writing about travel within the empire was generally state-sponsored, aimed at compiling useful data about natural resources, topographic features, etc. Later in the century, moralizing texts like Radishchev's *Journey from St. Petersburg to Moscow* (1790) and Fonvizin's "Notes on My First Journey Before 1762" (published in 1783) used travel writing as a way of calling attention to rural miseries, official corruption, and the peasants' plight. Neither genre provided models for someone like Dolgorukov, who simply wanted to see the sights and record his impressions. See ch. 2, "Radishchev and Domestic Description," in Sara Dickinson, *Breaking Ground: Travel and National Culture in Russia from Peter I to the Era of Pushkin* (Amsterdam; New York: Rodopi, 2006).

16. I. M. Dolgorukov, "Slavny bubny za gorami, ili puteshestvie moe koe-kuda 1810 goda," in *Chteniia v Imperatorskom Obshchestve Istorii i Drevnostei Rossiiskikh* 2 (April–June 1869), 1.

17. Sollogub, *Tarantas*, 199.

18. The vocabulary here indicates a blurring of the terms *provintsiia* and *guberniia* that is fairly characteristic of the period, as I discuss elsewhere: immediately after calling

Vladimir a *gubernskii gorod* Dolgorukov describes it as *nastoiashchaia provintsiia*. I. M. Dolgorukov, *Povest' o rozhdenii moem*, ed. N. V. Kuznetsova and M. O. Mel'tsin (St. Petersburg: Nauka, 2004), 1:266.

19. E.g., Gorbatov is "insignificant," Myt' "merits no remarks," Mokshan "is and will always be" small and poor, etc. I. M. Dolgorukov, "Zhurnal puteshestviia iz Moskvy v Nizhnii 1813 goda," in *Chteniia v Obshchestve Istorii i Drevnostei Rossiiskikh* 1 (1870): 106, 11, 66.

20. Dolgorukov, cited in Ugo Persi, "Russkaia stolitsa i russkaia provintsiia v memuarnykh tekstakh Ivana M. Dolgorukova," in *MTR*, 61.

21. Dolgorukov, "Slavny bubny za gorami," 54.

22. Not wanting to appear a "novice in my own home region [*gubernii*]" when arriving in Vladimir, Dolgorukov even asks the locals for advice on manners; one old man tells him he bows too much. Dolgorukov, *Povest' o rozhdenii moem*, 1:267.

23. Dolgorukov, "Zhurnal puteshestviia," 99.

24. Dolgorukov, "Slavny bubny za gorami," 15.

25. Dolgorukov, "Slavny bubny za gorami," 36.

26. Michael Holquist, *Dostoevsky and the Novel* (Evanston, IL: Northwestern University Press, 1977), 5–6.

27. Dolgorukov, "Slavny bubny za gorami," 18; Dolgorukov, I. M., *Povest' o rozhdenii moem*, vol. 1, 164.

28. Dolgorukov, *Povest' o rozhdenii moem*, 1:166. On the "*pestrota*" (motleyness) of provincial society, see V. A. Koshelev, "O 'literaturnoi' provintsii i literaturnoi 'provintsial'nosti' novogo vremeni," in *MTR*, 47–48.

29. Dolgorukov, "Slavny bubny za gorami," 8.

30. Dolgorukov, "Slavny bubny za gorami," 67.

31. On façade laws, see Daniel R. Brower, *The Russian City between Tradition and Modernity, 1850–1900* (Berkeley: University of California Press, 1990), 9–15. Today, of course, we know Poltava to be located in the sovereign nation of Ukraine, but such was not the case for Dolgorukov. While on the road, he is aware of moving from Russia to (the) Ukraine, but he experiences this change as a somewhat gradual transition, a kind of internal shift, rather than the abrupt crossing of a clear border. He is attentive to changes in language and landscape (for example, the steppe for him tends to be associated with Ukrainianness); when approaching Kharkov, he thinks about Mazeppa, Khmelnitskii, and watermelons, and he waxes uncharacteristically dreamy and metaphorical while spending the night under the moon on the southern steppe (*Nikolaevskaia step'*). But Dolgorukov also assumes that those in state service (*liudi chinovnye*) are "cosmopolitans with a shared language," who therefore "belong to all countries": "the rabble [*chern'*]" may "mark natural boundaries [*urochishcha*] between kingdoms [*Tsarstvami*]," but members of the upper classes serve "the same empire [*derzhava*]." Dolgorukov, "Slavny bubny za gorami," 64, 109. Such complexities do little to challenge Dolgorukov's concept of "Russia" (since his concept is based largely on the idea of Russia as an empire), but they do anticipate how, in later decades, works of literature will tend to represent Ukrainian space less as the Russian provinces than as an imperial periphery (e.g., Gogol's *Dikanka* tales and Antony Pogorelsky's novel *Monastyrka*, 1830–33).

32. Dolgorukov, "Slavny bubny za gorami," 68–69, 30.

33. See, for instance, Dolgorukov, "Slavny bubny za gorami," 105, 122, and "Zhurnal puteshestviia," 66.

34. Dolgorukov, "Slavny bubny za gorami," 99, 105–6, 122.

35. Dolgorukov, "Slavny bubny za gorami," 110–11.

36. "Exhausting uniformity" is K. I. Arsenev, quoted in Leonid Gorizontov, "The 'Great Circle' of Interior Russia: Representations of the Imperial Center in the Nineteenth and Early Twentieth Centuries," in *Russian Empire: Space, People, Power, 1700–1930*, ed. Jane Burbank, Mark von Hagen, and Anatolyi Remnev (Bloomington: Indiana University Press, 2007), 72; "desolate wastes" is from the late-eighteenth-century travel diary of A. G. Bobrinsky, but variations on this formula (*pustynia*) recur in many accounts; see Dickinson, *Breaking Ground*, 101.

37. P. Ia. Chaadaev, "Lettres philosophiques adressées à une dame. Lettre première," *Polnoe sobranie sochinenii i izbrannye pis'ma* (Moscow: Nauka, 1991), 1:90. Chaadaev wrote the letters in French. For the English, see *Philosophical Works of Peter Chaadaev*, ed. T. J. Blakeley, Guido Küng, and Nikolaus Lobkowicz (Netherlands: Springer Netherlands, 1991). See also Karamzin, cited in Dickinson, *Breaking Ground*, 99–100.

38. Nikolai Kostomarov, cited in Maxim Gorky, "On the Russian Peasantry," *Journal of Peasant Studies* 4, no.1 (October 1976 [1922]): 12.

39. E. N. Stroganova, "'Miniatiurnyi mir': Provintsiia v russkoi proze 1830-kh–pervoi poloviny 1840-kh gg. Ekskiz," in *MTR*, 198.

40. Stroganova, "Miniatiurnyi mir," 198.

41. M. N. Zagoskin, "Bogotonov ili provintsial v stolitse," *Sobranie sochinenii M. N. Zagoskina: Dramaticheskiia proizvedeniia* (St. Petersburg: Izdanie Tovarishchevstva M. O. Vol'f, 1901), 11:131–32. Bogotonov bemoans the fact that he speaks no French, only Russian: "every peasant speaks Russian! These days it would be better for us not to know [Russian] at all!"

42. Zagoskin wrote a sequel titled *Bogotonov in the Country* (*Bogotonov v derevne*, 1821): a straightforward story of Bogotonov's doomed attempt to impose "progressive" Western ways on his peasants back home (e.g., a peasant "parliament").

43. K. F. Ryleev, "Provintsial v Peterburge," in *Polnoe sobranie sochinenii* (Moscow: Academia, 1934), 304.

44. Ryleev, "Provintsial v Peterburge," 304.

45. Ryleev, *PSS*, 303–4.

46. Ryleev, *PSS*, 398.

47. Belinsky's dismissive "review" of *Three Suitors* reads: "Zagoskin was right to call his tale 'Provincial Sketches' [*Provintsial'nye ocherki*]: with this title he wrote the best possible critique of the work *a priori*." V. G. Belinskii, "Nichto o nichem, ili otchet g. izdateliu *Teleskopa* za poslednee polugodie (1835) russkoi literatury," Belinskii, *Polnoe sobranie sochinenii* (Moscow: Akademiia Nauk SSSR, 1953–59), 2:22.

48. M. N. Zagoskin, "Tri zhenikha (provintsial'nye ocherki)," in B. S. Meilakh, ed., *Russkie povesti XIX v., 20-kh–30-kh godov* (Moscow: Izdatel'stvo khudozhestvennoi literatury, 1950), 2:451.

49. For instance Gogol and Herzen use both *gubernskii* and *provintsial'nyi*, but *gubernskii* appears more often in their work because they focus on provincial towns and officials.

In other (nonofficial) uses, the English "provincial" (e.g., a "provincial ball"), could be and is rendered with either *gubernskii* or *provintsial'nyi* almost interchangeably. See ch. 1 for a brief survey of the history of *provintsiia* as a term, its relationship to other terms, and scholarship concerning evolving usage.

50. Sollogub, *Tarantas*, 186.

51. Sollogub, "Aptekarsha," 83. Somov's *A Novel in Two Letters* opens with a Petersburg dandy's letter to friends in the capital complaining about the boredom of provincial life; Sollogub's *Tarantas* opens on Tverskoi Boulevard before shifting to the provinces, etc.; Kul'chitskii's *An Unusual Duel* (*Neobyknovennyi poedinok*, 1845) opens with "In an imaginary provincial town," etc. Kul'chitskii, *An Unusual Duel*, accessed July 31, 2017, http://homlib.com/read/kulchickiy-aya/neobyknovennyy-poedinok.

52. Dostoevskii, *PSS*, 6:115.

53. A. N. Pleshcheev, *Zhiteiskie tseny*, in *Russkie povesti XIX veka 40–50-kh godov*, vol. 2, ed. B. S. Meilakh (Moscow: Gosudarstvennoe izdatel'stvo khudozhestvennoi literatury, 1952). Accessed July 31, 2017, http://az.lib.ru/p/plesheew_a_n/text_0130.shtml.

54. Gertsen, *SS*, 4:115.

55. Sollogub, *Tarantas*, 186.

56. Pleshcheev, *Zhiteiskie tseny*.

57. Sollogub, "Serezha," in *Povesti i rasskazy*, 17–18.

58. Sollogub, *Tarantas*, 207.

59. Sollogub, *Tarantas*, 199.

60. Thomas L. Dumm, *A Politics of the Ordinary* (New York: New York University Press, 1999), 14, cited in Majumdar, *Prose of the World*, 21.

61. Sollogub, "Aptekarsha," 131.

62. Sollogub, *Tarantas*, 186; Gertsen, *SS*, 4:41.

63. Gertsen, *SS*, 4:28. The merchant described in this passage is from Moscow, but as I discuss below, Moscow in *Who Is to Blame?* is provincial, and life there is explicitly described as being no different from life on the provincial estate.

64. Sollogub, *Tarantas*, 170; Zagoskin, "Tri zhenikha," 485.

65. Gertsen, *SS*, 8:237.

66. Gertsen, *SS*, 4:32.

67. Gertsen, *SS*, 7:247 and 8:294; Sollogub, *Tarantas*, 170.

68. Gertsen, *SS*, 1:294.

69. Gertsen, *SS*, 4:29. All this points to a paradox we will encounter in Gogol, in characteristically intensified form: provincial places are both the essence of Russianness and forbidding foreign territory, at once banal and utterly opaque to outsiders. In passages describing province-dwellers as savages, we are not far from *Dead Souls* (in which people are repeatedly likened to animals and inanimate objects) or *Selected Passages from Correspondence with Friends* (in which the provincial town is compared to a sick ward full of disgusting invalids). In *The Apothecary's Wife*, Sollogub's Petersburg lady points to the Gogol parallel herself: claiming never to have met any provincials, she imagines them as "monsters" like the ones she saw on stage in *The Inspector General*.

70. Gertsen, *SS*, 1:287.

71. Sollogub, "Aptekarsha," 87, 85.

72. O. M. Somov, *Roman v dvukh pis'makh*, in *Selected Prose in Russian*, ed. John Mersereau and George Harjan (Ann Arbor: University of Michigan Press, 1974), 58.

73. Sollogub, "Aptekarsha," 124. The provincial reacts in the same way again when he learns that the baron's vest is not from the Russian capital but from Paris itself.

74. Sollogub, "Aptekarsha," 85.

75. Sollogub, "Aptekarsha," 85.

76. Gertsen, *SS*, 9:53.

77. Somov, *Roman v dvukh pis'makh*, 59.

78. Quoted in Rosalind H. Williams, *Dream Worlds: Mass Consumption in Late Nineteenth-Century France* (Berkeley: University of California Press, 1982), 355, italics mine.

79. Pascale Casanova, *The World Republic of Letters* (Cambridge, MA: Harvard University Press, 2004), 88–89.

80. Gertsen, *SS*, 4:72

81. Somov, *Roman v dvukh pis'makh*, 54–55, 56.

82. Somov, *Roman v dvukh pis'makh*, 56. Again, fashion is not natural anywhere, but it can be made to look natural by those who possess the requisite social power.

83. Gertsen, *SS*, 8:294.

84. Somov, *Roman v dvukh pis'makh*, 55.

85. Gertsen, *SS*, 4:117–18.

86. Somov, *Roman v dvukh pis'makh*, 54–55.

87. Sollogub, "Serezha," 23, 24.

88. Sollogub, *Tarantas*, 182.

89. Sollogub, *Tarantas*, 180.

90. Gertsen, *SS*, 4:118.

91. Gertsen, *SS*, 4:115, 116.

92. Somov, *Roman v dvukh pis'makh*, 54.

93. Sollogub, "Aptekarsha," 90.

94. Sollogub, "Aptekarsha," 103, 116.

95. Sollogub, *Tarantas*, 294.

96. Gertsen, *SS*, 4:34 and 1:193.

97. William James, *The Varieties of Religious Experience: A Study in Human Nature* (New York, 1929); Mary Douglas, *Purity and Danger: An Analysis of Concepts of Pollution and Taboo* (London: Routledge and Kegan Paul, 1966).

98. Sollogub, "Aptekarsha," 83.

99. N. V. Gogol, "The Carriage," in *The Collected Tales of Nikolai Gogol*, trans. Richard Pevear and Larissa Volokhonsky (New York: Vintage Classics, 1998), 328. Gogol', *PSS*, 3: 178.

100. Sollogub, *Tarantas*, 224.

101. Sollogub, "Serezha," 17.

102. The effect is similar to what we encounter in nineteenth-century writings about steppe topography, where unrelieved horizontality and emptiness were thought to

undermine attempts to make the space intelligible (as I discuss in later in connection with Chekhov).

103. Osip Mandelshtam, "On the Nature of the Word," in *Osip Mandelshtam: Selected Essays*, trans. Sidney Monas (Austin: University of Texas Press, 1977), 75.

104. Sollogub, *Tarantas*, 165.

105. The Romantic object, by contrast, can create the desired effect through an accumulation of details or fragments, "[transmuting] . . . quantity into quality." Naomi Schor, *Reading in Detail: Aesthetics and the Feminine* (London: Routledge, 1987), 17–18.

106. It is difficult to name the opposite of the sublime with more precision than the "not-sublime." The sublime is traditionally masculine, hard, powerful, and high. It is sometimes conceived as an "anti-particularist aesthetic" (Schor, *Reading in Detail*, 5); but it can also be thought of as ungraspable, irrational, even resisting unity. In any case it is always opposed to detail: see, for example, Sir Joshua Reynolds's contention that details are incompatible both with the Ideal ("because of their material contingency") and with the Sublime ("because of their tendency to proliferation"). Schor, *Reading in Detail*, 15.

107. "Both as a social being and as an individual, woman is seen as more embedded in the concrete and the particular than man," more tightly linked to what the anthropologist Sherry Ortner calls "lower-level, socially fragmenting, particularistic . . . concerns," as opposed to "higher-level, integrative, universalistic" ones. Cited in Schor, *Reading in Detail*, 16–17.

108. Joanna Russ, *To Write Like a Woman: Essays in Feminism and Science Fiction* (Bloomington: Indiana University Press, 1995), 89. These are, in turn, the same terms in which Russian narrative art was often denigrated when it first came to Western critics' attention in the nineteenth century, as Russ points out: "Here we have other outsiders who are trying, in less than a century, to assimilate European myths, producing strange Russian hybrids (*A King Lear of the Steppes, Lady Macbeth of Mtsensk*), trying to work with literary patterns that do not suit their experiences and were not developed with them in mind. What do we get? Oddly digressive Pushkin. 'Formless' Dostoevsky. . . . Sprawling, glacial, all-inclusive Tolstoy. And of course 'lyrical' Chekhov, whose magnificent plays are called 'plotless' to this very day." Russ, *To Write Like a Woman*, 89.

109. Odoevsky, "Sil'fida," http://rulibrary.ru/odoevskiy/silfida/3, accessed November 1, 2016. Cf. Shchedrin's *Provincial Sketches* on the "petty lusts" (*melkie vozhdeleniia*) and "slime of pettiness" (*tina melochei*) that mar provincial life (Shchedrin, *Gubernskie ocherki*, http://rvb.ru/saltykov-shchedrin/01text/vol_02/01text/0034.htm, accessed July 31, 2017), Herzen on provincials' "narrow, petty" life and "petty gossip" (Gertsen, *SS*, 4:117–18), Elena Gan and other women writers on the "petty envy" (*melochnaia zavist'*) of the provincial town (Elena Gan, "Ideal," http://az.lib.ru/g/gan_e_a/text_0010.shtml, accessed May 30, 2017), etc.

110. V. F. Odoevsky, "Sil'fida" (1837), accessed November 1, 2016, http://rulibrary.ru/odoevskiy/silfida/3.

111. Gertsen, *SS*, 1:293, IV: 40.

112. Gertsen, *SS*, 4:157–58.

113. Gertsen, *SS*, 4:37. Compare Balzac, *La Femme de province* (1841): "Quelque grande, quelque belle, quelque forte que soit à son début une jeune fille née dans un département quelconque, si . . . elle se marie en province et si elle y reste, elle devient bientôt femme de province. . . . Les lieux communs, la médiocrité des idées, l'insouciance de la toilette, l'horticulture des vulgarités envahissent l'être sublime caché dans cette âme neuve, et tout est dit, la belle plante dépérit." Accessed August 27, 2018, http://www.bmlisieux.com /curiosa/balzac01.htm.

114. Gertsen, *SS*, 1:295.

115. Gertsen, *SS*, 1:294.

116. Gertsen, *SS*, 4:69.

117. Gertsen, *SS*, 4:122.

118. Gertsen, *SS*, 4:16.

119. Gertsen, *SS*, 8:124. The same might hold true even for Petersburg, Herzen suggests elsewhere in *My Past and Thoughts*: when Petersburg officials mock their counterparts in Vyatka, he writes, they ignore the fact that Petersburg is to Vyatka as a clean leather boot is to a dirty one of the same leather and design. *Byloe i dumy*, part 4: *Moskva, Peterburg i Novgorod (1840–1847)* (Moscow: Gosudarstvennoe izdatel'stvo khudozhestvennoi literatury, 1958). Accessed July 31, 2017, http://az.lib.ru/g/gercen_a_i/text_0130.shtml.

120. Mikhail Epstein, *Bog detalei: Narodnaia dusha i chastnaia zhizn' v Rossii na iskhode imperii* (New York: Slovo, 1997), 32.

121. Gertsen, *SS*, 1:287.

122. Gertsen, *SS*, 1:283.

123. Gertsen *SS*, 21:44. Cited in V. V. Abashev, *Perm' kak tekst. Perm' v russkoi kul'ture i literature XX veka* (Moscow-Berlin: Direct Media, 2014), 110.

124. Quotations are from Abashev, *Perm' kak tekst*, in order cited: Mel'nikov-Pecherskii, 92; Vigel, 59n42; Nebol'sin, 87; Mamin-Sibiriak, 88; Shmurlo, 92n76. Abashev writes that for Mamin-Sibiriak, "Perm as a city exists outside of space as it is saturated with historical memory, it inhabits the periphery of this space, in an empty landscape devoid of historical memory." Abashev, *Perm' kak tekst*, 88. Note that even Russian writers who might themselves be described as regionalists—Mel'nikov-Pecherskii and Mamin-Sibiriak—describe Perm as nothing but another provincial void, despite its "far away" location and rather exotic history. Abashev collects an enormous number of quotes to this effect in *Perm' kak tekst*.

125. V. Sh. Krivonos, "Gogol': Mif provintsial'nogo goroda," in *PKR*, 112.

126. Gertsen, *SS*, 1:287.

127. Dal''s story appeared in 1839, and Herzen's "Notes of a Young Man" in 1840–41. The toponym "Malinov" will be echoed later in Ostrovsky's Kalinov and other texts. On the use of this and other invented toponyms to designate provincial towns in literature, see A. F. Belousov, "Simvolika zakholust'ia (oboznachenie rossiiskogo provintsial'nogo goroda)," in *Geopanorama russkoi kul'tury: Provintsiia i ee lokal'nye teksty*, ed. L. O. Zaionts, V. V. Abashev, A. F. Belousov, and T. V. Tsivian (Moscow: Iazyki slavianskoi kul'tury, 2004), 457–81.

128. Dal', "Bedovik," in *Russkie povesti XIX v., 20-kh–30-kh godov*, ed. B. S. Meilakh (Moscow: Izdatel'stvo khudozhestvennoi literatury, 1950), 2:537.

129. Dal', "Bedovik," 528.

130. Dal', "Bedovik," 533.

131. Dal', "Bedovik," 546.

132. Dal', "Bedovik," 543.

133. Dal', "Bedovik," 554.

134. Dal', "Bedovik," 561, 573.

135. Sollogub, *Tarantas*, 294; Gertsen, *SS*, 4:122.

136. Gertsen, *SS*, 4:16, 38. In 1896 Chekhov's novella *My Life (A Provincial's Story)* will pose the question in almost identical terms: "I couldn't understand why and how these 65,000 people were living," the narrator says, "What our town was and what it was doing, I did not know." Were this "useless" place to disappear suddenly from the face of the earth, he declares, not one soul would lament its passing. Chekhov, *PSS*, IX: 278, 205.

137. N. V. Gogol', *Polnoe sobranie sochinenii* (Moscow: Akademiia Nauk SSSR, 1937–52), 6:692.

138. Gary Saul Morson, *Encyclopædia Britannica*, s.v. "Russian literature," accessed February 9, 2017, https://www.britannica.com/art/Russian-literature; Mixail Vajskopf, "Imperial Mythology and Negative Landscape in *Dead Souls*," in *Gogol: Exploring Absence: Negativity in Nineteenth-Century Russian Literature*, ed. Sven Spieker (Bloomington, IN: Slavica, 1999), 103–4.

Chapter Four

1. Thomas Seifrid, *Andrei Platonov: Uncertainties of Spirit* (Cambridge, UK: Cambridge University Press, 1992), 9; Andrei Platonov, *"Ia prozhil zhizn'." Pis'ma 1920–1950* (St. Petersburg: Astrel', 2013), 218–19.

2. N. V. Gogol', *Polnoe sobranie sochinenii* (Moscow: Akademiia Nauk SSSR, 1937–52), 6:692. Hereafter all Gogol citations are from this edition and appear parenthetically in main text.

3. See Edyta M. Bojanowska, *Nikolai Gogol: Between Ukrainian and Russian Nationalism* (Cambridge, MA: Harvard University Press, 2007). Bojanowska claims, for instance, that Ukraine as depicted in *Evenings on a Farm Near Dikanka* can be read as "an organic national community that struggles against dissolution in the imperial Russian state." Bojanowska, 37.

4. I. M. Dolgorukov, "Slavny bubny za gorami, ili puteshestvie moe koe-kuda 1810 goda," *Chteniia v Imperatorskom Obshchestve Istorii i Drevnostei Rossiiskikh* 2 (April–June 1869), 64, 109.

5. Paul Debreczeny, "Nikolay Gogol and his Contemporary Critics," *Transactions of the American Philosophical Society* 56, no. 3 (1966): 5.

6. Katie Trumpener, *Bardic Nationalism: The Romantic Novel and the British Empire* (Princeton, NJ: Princeton University Press, 1997). As Trumpener points out, through the eighteenth century Britain (like Russia) was primarily an "internal" empire, and I would note that British literary dynamics resulting from internal political inequalities resonate with those in Russia. Trumpener depicts Britain (itself a highly problematic designation) as an empire without a fully developed sense of nation: "British centralization implies not only the spread and enforced imposition but also the systematic underdevelopment of

Englishness. To the degree that England becomes the center of the empire, its own internal sense of culture accordingly fails to develop." Trumpener, 15–16. Her argument recalls the characterization of Russia by Geoffrey A. Hosking in *Russia: People and Empire, 1552–1917* (London: Harper Collins, 1997).

7. In any case, such a renunciation probably would not have been possible: unlike his contemporary Pushkin, who could choose to play up his own African descent as an exotic component of his authorial identity, Gogol was pretty much stuck with Ukrainianness. It was nonnegotiable.

8. Uilleam Blacker, "Blurred lines: Russian literature and cultural diversity in Ukraine," *The Calvert Journal*, March 14, 2014, accessed February 12, 2017, http://calvertjournal.com /comment/show/2176/russian-culture-in-ukraine-literature?hc_location=ufi.

9. M. N. Zagoskin, "Tri zhenikha (provintsial'nye ocherki)," in *Russkie povesti XIX v., 20-kh–30-kh godov*, ed. B. S. Meilakh (Moscow: Izdatel'stvo khudozhestvennoi literatury, 1950), 2:451.

10. Here the noun *provintsiia* appears in the locative plural, though today in this case and meaning it is used almost exclusively in the singular (*v provintsii*).

11. For other instances of *provintsiia* and its derivatives in *The Inspector General*, see 4:74, 76. Forms of *guberniia* occur less frequently in the play because it (unlike *Dead Souls*) is not set in a *gubernskii gorod* (a district capital) but rather in a small town (*uezdnyi gorod*).

12. Evgeniia Kirichenko and Elena Shcheboleva, *Russkaia provintsiia* (Moscow: Nash dom, 1997), 62–63, 123.

13. See Irina Reyfman, *How Russia Learned to Write: Literature and the Imperial Table of Ranks* (Madison: University of Wisconsin Press, 2016).

14. Daniel R. Brower, *The Russian City between Tradition and Modernity, 1850–1900* (Berkeley: University of California Press, 1990), 15. See also Kirichenko and Shcheboleva, *Russkaia provintsiia*, 50–62.

15. See ch. 2 in connection with Pushkin's *The Captain's Daughter* and *A History of Pugachev*. As Susan Smith-Peter explains, the first phase of provincial information-gathering was conducted in a cameralist spirit (aimed at "[extending] the reach of the sovereign by increasing his knowledge of his own lands"), whereas later, in Gogol's day, greater attention was paid to the population's productivity and quality of life. Susan Smith-Peter, "Defining the Russian People: Konstantin Arsen'ev and Russian Statistics before 1861," *History of Science* 45, no. 1 (2007): 47–48.

16. Smith-Peter, "Defining the Russian People," 7. On these efforts generally, see W. Bruce Lincoln, *In the Vanguard of Reform: Russia's Enlightened Bureaucrats 1825–1861* (DeKalb, IL: Northern Illinois University Press, 1982), 109–25. As Lincoln notes, the receptions these bureaucrats met in the provinces were often quite as bizarre as Khlestakov's in *The Inspector General*.

17. Quoted in Lincoln, *In the Vanguard of Reform*, 117.

18. Smith-Peter, "Defining the Russian People," 7.

19. Herzen quoted in Smith-Peter, "Defining the Russian People," 6.

20. Herzen quoted in Smith-Peter, "Defining the Russian People," 9.

21. S. A. Vengerov, "Gogol' sovershenno ne znal real'noi russkoi zhizni" (1911), *Sobranie sochinenii*, vol. 2, *Pisatel'-grazhdanin. Gogol'* (St. Petersburg: Prometei, 1913), 123–39. While Vengerov's literalism is perhaps naïve (since the amount of time Gogol spent in the Russian countryside matters very little to the artistic truth of *Dead Souls*), his criticism does speak to the unreal quality of the Russian provinces as Gogol represents them.

22. Smith-Peter, "Defining the Russian People," 7.

23. Peter Kolchin, *Unfree Labor: American Slavery and Russian Serfdom* (Cambridge, MA: Harvard University Press, 1987), 59. Recent scholarship has argued that middling landowners who spent virtually all their time on their estates—as opposed to the vastly wealthy and more itinerant few on whom Kolchin tends to focus—had stronger ties to their localities. See, for instance, Katherine Pickering Antonova, *An Ordinary Marriage: The World of a Gentry Family in Provincial Russia* (Oxford: Oxford University Press, 2012) and Catherine Evtuhov, *Portrait of a Russian Province: Economy, Society, and Civilization in Nineteenth-Century Nizhnii Novgorod* (Pittsburgh, PA: University of Pittsburgh Press, 2011).

24. Kirichenko and Shcheboleva, *Russkaia provintsiia*, 81; A. I. Gertsen, *Sobranie sochinenii v 30-i tomakh* (Moscow: Izd. Akademii Nauk SSSR, 1954), 8:237.

25. Monika Greenleaf, *Pushkin and Romantic Fashion* (Stanford: Stanford University Press, 1994), 15–16. Greenleaf's focus is the Romantic period, but her insights shed light on the tradition as a whole.

26. Donald Fanger, *The Creation of Nikolai Gogol* (Cambridge, MA: Harvard University Press, 1979), 135, 133.

27. In his more didactic texts Gogol makes the parallel between province and capital more explicit. In "Leaving the Theater after the Performance of a New Comedy" (written in response to the reception of *The Inspector General*), Gogol has one character declare that the vices just exposed on stage are not representative of life only "in a provincial town, but rather here, all around us"—that is, in the capital. Gogol', *PSS*, 5:155.

28. The exception to this may be Gogol's fragment "Rome," which imagines Italy as the home of a truly unified and organic culture.

29. Fanger, *The Creation of Nikolai Gogol*, 135, 133.

30. Mikhail Epstein, *Bog detalei: Narodnai dusha i chastnaia zhizn' v Rossii na iskhode imperii* (New York: Slovo, 1997), 30, 35.

31. Mikhail Epstein, "Good-bye to Objects, or, the Nabokovian in Nabokov," in *A Small Alpine Form: Studies in Nabokov's Short Fiction*, ed. by Gene Barabtarlo and Charles Nicol (New York: Garland, 1993), 217–24.

32. I draw here on Pevear and Volokhonsky's translation: "Little festoons! little festoons, little festoons all over: a pelerine of little festoons, sleeves with little festoons, epaulettes of little festoons, little festoons below, little festoons everywhere." Richard Pevear and Larissa Volokhonsky, trans., *Dead Souls* (New York: Vintage Books, 1997), 182–83. For more on the gendered nature of the detail, see chapters 3, 7, and 8: women writers, the provinces, and sometimes even Russian novels in general have been associated with an unseemly

excess of detail. Joanna Russ, *To Write Like a Woman: Essays in Feminism and Science Fiction* (Bloomington: Indiana University Press, 1995), 89.

33. For instance in "On Present-Day Architecture," when he imagines the colossal tower "rising to an incalculable height," the goal is to stun the viewer "into a kind of numbness": "people should huddle up against it and thereby magnify its grandeur by their smallness." Gogol', *PSS*, 8:62–63, 66. On Gogol and the sublime, see Sven Spieker, "Esthesis and Anesthesia: The Sublime in *Arabesques*," in *Gogol: Exploring Absence*, ed. Sven Spieker (Bloomington, IN: Slavica, 1999), 161–70. According to classical rhetoric, the sublime "literally blinds its addressee," seeking "less to persuade . . . than to *overpower*." Spieker, 162.

34. Here I draw again on Pevear and Volokhonsky's translation. Gogol, "The Carriage," in *The Collected Tales of Nikolai Gogol*, trans. Richard Pevear and Larissa Volokhonsky (New York: Vintage Classics, 1998), 328.

35. V. A. Sollogub, *Tarantas*, in *Povesti i rasskazy*, intro. E. Kiiko (Moscow: Gosudarstvennoe izdatel'stvo khudozhestvennoi literatury, 1962), 180; Gertsen, *Kto vinovat?*, in *SS*, 4:33.

36. Jarringly high language applied to paltry or squalid phenomena evokes a similar feeling of disproportion, as when Bely, in *Silver Dove*, uses high Slavonicisms to talk about provincial poverty and filth. M. L. Spivak, "'Zavetnye griazishchi' i 'slavnyi gorod Likhov' (provintsiia v tvorchestve Andreia Belogo)," in *MTR*, 245.

37. V. G. Belinskii, "Ob"iasnenie na ob"iasnenie po povodu poemy Gogolia 'Mertvye dushi,'" in *Polnoe sobranie sochinenii* (Moscow: Akademiia Nauk SSSR, 1955), 6:430–31.

38. V. A. Koshelev, "O 'literaturnoi' provintsii i literaturnoi 'provintsial'nosti' novogo vremeni. Zametki," in *MTR*, 52.

39. Abram Terts [pseud. Andrei Siniavskii], *V teni Gogolia* (London: Collins, 1975), 324, 322.

40. Terts, *V teni Gogolia*, 434. Platonov, cited in Seifrid, *Andrei Platonov*, 9; Platonov, "*Ia prozhil zhizn'*," 215.

41. T. S. Eliot, "What is a Classic?," in *Selected Prose of T. S. Eliot* (New York: Farrar, Straus, and Giroux, 1975), 129.

42. As I note in ch. 1, although Gogol played up his own outsider status in the capitals' literary circles (as a Ukrainian bumpkin, a *Khokhol*), he never allowed himself to be figured as an *object* by this society. Compare here Bourdieu's analysis of the "primitive" painter Henri Rousseau, an outsider who had to be constituted as a "real" artist by powerful supporters like Duchamp. Though Gogol was perhaps initially treated as a curiosity who has been discovered and made available for display in elite literary circles, he seized control of the situation for himself. He was never (as was Rousseau, according to Bourdieu), the artist "as object, who does something other than what he thinks he is doing, does not know what he does, because he knows nothing of the field he stumbles into, of which he is the plaything." Pierre Bourdieu, *The Field of Cultural Production: Essays on Art and Literature* (New York: Columbia University Press, 1993), 61. Here is another way in which Gogol's Ukrainianness may have proven useful, helping him to master the "artistic field" of his time and place: had he been merely a class outsider—a lower-class Russian—perhaps even his

extraordinary and bizarre talent would not have been enough to cause his contemporaries to grant him the status of the "outsider genius" who gets to make his own rules.

43. Terts, *V teni Gogolia*, 434.

44. Fanger, *The Creation of Nikolai Gogol*, 174. Again, it is useful to compare Henri Rousseau. As Bourdieu's analysis of this "naïve" painter makes clear, his primitive artwork affords us the pleasure of superiority (among other pleasures); our delectation depends partly on the happy knowledge that our eye makes his paintings into something the artist himself was supposedly incapable of intending or even understanding. We enjoy our clearly defined relationship to these paintings and to their provincial maker, a relationship from which we draw assurance of our own expertise and subtlety of understanding. Gogol's readers, by contrast, can easily be left with the impression that his texts are mocking or tricking them. On this, see my article "'Russia! What Do You Want of Me?': The Russian Reading Public in *Dead Souls*," *Slavic Review* 60, no. 2 (Summer 2001): 367–89.

Chapter Five

1. V. G. Belinskii, V. G. Belinskii to V. P. Botkin, March 15–17, 1847, in *Polnoe sobranie sochinenii* (Moscow, Akademiia Nauk, 1953), 12:352. Hereafter Belinsky texts will be referenced parenthetically by volume and page number of this edition.

2. The full title of the article is "Nichto o nichem, ili otchet g. izdateliu 'Teleskopa' za poslednee polugodie (1835) russkoi literatury."

3. It is worth pointing out that to assume such an ability is acquirable is to make a whole list of other assumptions as well: "the ideology of charisma regards taste in legitimate culture as a gift of nature, [but] scientific observation shows that cultural needs are the product of upbringing and education." Pierre Bourdieu, *Distinction: A Social Critique of the Judgement of Taste*, trans. Richard Nice (Cambridge, MA: Harvard University Press, 1984), 1.

4. Milton Ehre, *Oblomov and his Creator: Life and Art of Ivan Goncharov* (Princeton, NJ: Princeton University Press, 1974), 133–34.

5. Honoré de Balzac, *Lost Illusions*, trans. Kathleen Raine (New York: Modern Library, 1997), 162–63, emphasis mine.

6. Balzac, *Lost Illusions*, 164, 195, emphasis mine.

7. Balzac, *Lost Illusions*, 165.

8. Balzac, *Lost Illusions*, 164–69.

9. I. A. Goncharov, *Polnoe sobranie sochinenii i pisem v 20-i tomakh.* (St. Petersburg: Nauka, 1997), 1:387. Hereafter *Obyknovennaia istoriia* (*An Ordinary Story*) is cited parenthetically from this edition.

10. Lyn Lofland names and analyzes the "city of strangers" phenomenon in *A World of Strangers: Order and Action in Urban Public Space* (New York: Basic Books, 1973), ch. 1.

11. Elsewhere I have analyzed the implications of this lack of economic engagement in Goncharov's *Oblomov*. See Anne Lounsbery, "The World on the Back of a Fish: Mobility, Immobility, and Economics in *Oblomov*," *The Russian Review* 70, no. 1 (January 2011): 43–64.

12. Janet Sorensen, "'I talk to everybody in their own way': Defoe's Economics of Identity," in *The New Economic Criticism: Studies at the Intersection of Literature and Economics*, ed. Martha Woodmansee and Mark Osteen (London: Routledge, 1999), 82.

13. N. V. Gogol', *Polnoe sobranie sochinenii* (Moscow: Akademiia Nauk SSSR, 1937–52), 8:104, emphasis mine.

14. Gogol', *PSS*, 6:9.

15. William Mills Todd, III, *Fiction and Society in the Age of Pushkin: Ideology, Institutions, and Narrative* (Cambridge, MA: Harvard University Press, 1986), 3, 113.

16. In other words, what Goncharov represents as the provinces' supply of singularities—a particular linden tree beneath which Aduev first kissed a particular girl on a particular day—appears to Gogol as mere chaos. For instance, a bizarre painting hanging in Sobakevich's house in *Dead Souls* is certainly singular, but this radical singularity renders it incomprehensible. Gogol', *PSS*, 6:95.

17. For this crucial caveat I am indebted to two articles by Ilya Kliger: "Genre and Actuality in Belinskii, Herzen, and Goncharov: Toward a Genealogy of the Tragic Pattern in Russian Realism," *Slavic Review* 70, no. 1 (Spring 2011): 45–66; and "Hegel's Political Philosophy and the Social Imaginary of Early Russian Realism," *Studies in East European Thought* 65, no. 2–3 (2013): 189–99.

18. Balzac, *Lost Illusions*, 165.

19. Belinsky says the same in a review of Gogol. Belinskii, *PSS*, 1:283.

20. Here I think we catch of glimpse of what would later develop into the intelligentsia's truly fantastic faith in the supposedly universal appeal of high culture, their conviction that the common people, once exposed to literary works of high quality, would leave behind their various trashy entertainments.

21. Sometimes Belinsky uses the term *provintsial'nost'*, and sometimes he uses *provintsializm*. He makes no particular distinction between the two (nor do I).

22. *Teleskop* 21 (1834): 330. This writer is adapting a quotable line from Griboedov's *Woe from Wit*, in which Famusov threatens his maid Liza with exile to the *glush'*: *Ne byt' tebe v Moskve, ne zhit' tebe s liud'mi;/Podalee ot etikh khvatov,/V derevniu, k tetke, v glush', v Saratov,/Tam budesh' gore gorevat'/Za pial'tsami sidet', za sviattsami zevat'* (Act 4, Scene 14). A. S. Griboedov, *Sochineniia v stikhakh* (Leningrad: Izd. Sovetskii pisatel', 1967), 170.

23. N. Nadezhdin, "Zdravyi smysl i Baron Brambeus," *Teleskop* 21 (1834): 329–30.

24. Gogol', *PSS*, 8:164.

25. George Gutsche, "Puškin and Belinskij: The Role of the 'Offended Provincial,'" in *New Perspectives on Russian Nineteenth Century Prose*, ed. George J. Gutsche and Lauren G. Leighton (Columbus, OH: Slavica, 1982), 41–59. On the reader-from-Tver trope, see Melissa Frazier, who quotes such a "letter to the editor" by Senkovsky: "when we say—Tver' province," Senkovsky writes, "we mean by that all intelligent provinces, all of Russia." Frazier cites O. I. Senkovskii, "Pervoe pis'mo trekh tverskikh pomeshchikov k baronu Brambeusu," *Biblioteka dlia chteniia* 22, section 1 (1837): 72. Melissa Frazier, *Romantic Encounters: Writers, Readers, and the "Library for Reading"* (Stanford: Stanford University Press, 2007), 181.

26. A. S. Pushkin, *Polnoe sobranie sochinenii* (Moscow: Akademiia Nauk, 1937), 12:98. Quoted in Todd, *Fiction and Society in the Age of Pushkin*, 104.

27. P. A. Vyazemsky, review of *Revizor, Sovremennik* 2 (1836): 296; Pushkin, *PSS*, 12:96; quoted in Todd, *Fiction and Society in the Age of Pushkin*, 22.

28. Senkovsky, quoted in Donald Fanger, *The Creation of Nikolai Gogol* (Cambridge, MA: Harvard University Press, 1979): 43, emphasis mine. Frazier points out the relationship between Senkovsky's unsavory version of "personal criticism" and the much more reputable Romantic idea of criticism as a primary form of literary creativity. But she also notes how Senkovsky claims to "base his critical authority on his own personality while at the same time undermining the notion of his own personality through the use of pseudonyms." Frazier, *Romantic Encounters*, 71, 52.

29. See also, for instance, "O kritike i literaturnykh mneniiakh Moskovskogo Nabliudatelia" (1836), where he writes, "Theory is the systematic and harmonious uniting of the laws of the beautiful [*iziashchniago*]," Belinskii, *PSS*, 2:123.

30. F. M. Dostoevskii, *Polnoe sobranie sochinenii v 30-i tomakh* (Leningrad: Nauka, 1974), 10:28.

31. Fanger, *The Creation of Nikolai Gogol*, 73.

32. Gogol', *PSS*, 8: 166, 160, emphasis in original.

33. Gogol', *PSS*, 8: 162.

34. Melissa Frazier's book on *Library for Reading* draws a parallel between the journal's *raznoobraznaia smes'* and German Romantic theorists' conscious embrace of heterogeneity and fragmentariness. But for Belinsky, such indiscriminate combinations were clear signs of aesthetic failure resulting from lack of judgment: as Frazier acknowledges, for him, "this eclecticism pointed straight to the provinces." Frazier, *Romantic Encounters*, 132.

35. Gogol', *PSS*, 8:165. When it came to professional integrity, *Library for Reading* was exemplary: contributors were paid for their work, and the issues came out on time (which was not always the case with Russia's high-brow journals).

36. Todd, *Fiction and Society in the Age of Pushkin*, 96.

37. T. S. Eliot, "What is a Classic?," in *Selected Prose of T. S. Eliot*, ed. Frank Kermode (New York: Farrar, Straus and Giroux, 1975), 129.

38. Eliot, "What is a Classic?," 129. Pascale Casanova expresses a similar idea in The World Republic of Letters (Cambridge, MA: Harvard University Press, 2004), 15.

39. Note, too, the subtly gendered nature (*domashnii*, domestic) of the banal and the provincial.

40. T. S. Eliot, "Turgenev," *The Egoist* 4 (1917): 167.

41. Eliot calls this understanding a "maturity of mind" that "needs history, and the consciousness of history"; only "with maturity of mind [comes the] absence of provinciality." Eliot, "What is a Classic?," 122–23. The trait that Eliot labels "maturity of mind" is a version of what Casanova invokes when she claims that only an *old* tradition can be "rich" enough to make the rules for everyone: "The age of a national literature testifies to its 'wealth'—in the sense of number of texts—but also, and above all, to its 'nobility,'" and therefore to its right to serve as arbiter in all comparisons and as embodied standard of literariness. Casanova, *The World Republic of Letters*, 14.

42. Dmitrii Sergeevich Merezhkovskii, "Turgenev," *Rech'* 51 (February 22, 1909), accessed July 31, 2017, http://dugward.ru/library/merejkovskiy/merejkovskiy_turgenev .html.

43. Merezhkovskii, "Turgenev."

Chapter Six

1. Dmitrii Sergeevich Merezhkovskii, "Turgenev," *Rech'* 51 (February 22, 1909), accessed July 31, 2017, http://dugward.ru/library/merejkovskiy/merejkovskiy_turgenev.html.

2. V. Piatnitskii and N. Dobrokhotova-Maikova, "Parodii na Kharmsa o Turgeneve" (1971–72), accessed July 31, 2018, http://nasledie.turgenev.ru/stat/smeh/Peredelka/Harms /har.html.

3. Arjun Appadurai, *Modernity at Large: Cultural Dimensions of Globalization* (Minneapolis: University of Minnesota Press, 2000), 30. See also Appadurai, "Disjuncture and Difference in the Global Cultural Economy," in *Colonial Discourse and Post-Colonial Theory: A Reader*, ed. Patrick Williams and Laura Chrisman (New York: Columbia University Press, 1994), 324–39.

4. Roberto Maria Dainotto, "'All the Regions Do Smilingly Revolt': The Literature of Place and Region," *Critical Inquiry* 22, no. 3 (Spring 1996): 486.

5. I. S. Turgenev, *Polnoe sobranie sochinenii i pisem v 30-i tomakh* (Moscow: Nauka, 1978), 3:7. Hereafter Turgenev texts will be referenced parenthetically by volume and page number of this edition. For English versions I have consulted and amended as necessary the following translations by Richard Freeborn: *Nest of the Gentry* (New York: Penguin, 1987); *Rudin* (New York: Penguin, 1975); *Sketches from a Hunter's Album* (New York: Penguin, 1967). I have also consulted *Fathers and Sons*, trans. Michael Katz (New York: W.W. Norton, 1995); *Smoke*, trans. Michael Pursglove (Surrey, UK: Alma Classics, 2013); *Virgin Soil*, trans. Constance Garnett (New York: NYRB Classics, 2000).

6. In the sketch "Lgov," for instance: "Lgov is a large steppe village with a very ancient single-towered stone church and two mills on the marshy stream Rosota. Around five versts from Lgov this stream turns into a wide pond, overgrown at the edges and in parts of the middle by thick reeds known in Orel dialect as 'mayer,'" 3:75. And yet this is not quite regionalism because we sense that Turgenev's aim is to look at Orel Province in order to understand something about Russia generally rather than about this region specifically. For more on the metonymic assumptions that often inform Russian "regionalist" writing, see ch. 8. For a sensitive analysis of how Turgenev represents the specificities of the natural world and particular places, see Jane Tussey Costlow, *Heart-Pine Russia: Walking and Writing the Nineteenth-Century Forest* (Ithaca, NY: Cornell University Press, 2013), 18–40.

7. Michel Jeanneret, *A Feast of Words: Banquets and Table Talk in the Renaissance* (Chicago: University of Chicago Press, 1991), 260–61, emphasis mine.

8. Many texts of the period remark on provincials' unnerving curiosity concerning visitors from the capital. See T. V. Klubkova and P. A. Klubkov, "Russkii provintsial'nyi gorod i stereotipy provintsial'nosti," in *MTR*, 27.

9. Iurii Lotman, "The Poetics of Everyday Behavior in Eighteenth-Century Russian Culture," *The Semiotics of Russian Cultural History*, ed. Alexander D. and Alice Stone Nakhimovsky (Ithaca, NY: Cornell University Press, 1985), 69–70.

10. Mikhail Epstein, *Bog detalei: Narodnaia dusha i chastnaia zhizn' v Rossii na iskhode imperii* (New York: Slovo, 1997), 30, 35.

11. With some effort the reader can more or less figure out the locations of *Fathers and Sons'* four main settings (three estates plus the Town of N) in relationship to one another. The Kirsanovs' Marino is not far from an unnamed highway ("***") in what seems to be a fairly remote (also unnamed, possibly southern) Russian province; Bazarov's parents' home is thirty versts from the town of ***; Odintsova's estate is forty versts from the same town; Bazarov's and Odintsova's estates are about twenty-five versts from each other. The town of *** would thus seem to be somewhere more or less in the middle of these establishments. Turgenev, *PSS*, 7:7, 57, 73, 104. But it matters little, since these places impinge on each other only minimally: they seem to be separated by implied boundaries that isolate them from each other and from the rest of the world, almost as if Turgenev had devised each as its own distinct milieu or site of experimentation. Elizabeth Cheresh Allen has noted that space in Turgenev seems at times to be oddly discontinuous. See Allen, *Beyond Realism: Turgenev's Poetics of Secular Salvation* (Stanford: Stanford University Press, 1992), 76–79. This helps explain why, as Dale Peterson puts it, "problems of transport" often take on significance: "in Turgenev's Russia it is difficult to get anywhere." Dale Peterson, *The Clement Vision: Poetic Realism in Turgenev and James* (Port Washington, NY: Kennikat Press, 1975), 78.

12. *Rudin*, too, features an estate that in effect knows its own taste to be unimpeachably *stolichnyi* even though it is in the provinces: Daria Mikhailovna's manor house, constructed "according to Rastrelli's drawings in the taste of the last century," set on the summit of a hill and surrounded by fertile fields and a great river. Turgenev, *PSS*, 5:208.

13. Jane Tussey Costlow, *Worlds Within Worlds: The Novels of Ivan Turgenev* (Princeton, NJ: Princeton University Press, 1990), 123.

14. J. G. A. Pocock, "Modes of Political and Historical Time in Early Eighteenth-Century England," in *Virtue, Commerce, and History: Essays on Political Thought and History, Chiefly in the Eighteenth Century* (Cambridge, UK: Cambridge University Press, 1985), 91.

15. Pierre Bourdieu, *Distinction: A Social Critique of the Judgement of Taste*, trans. Richard Nice (Cambridge, MA: Harvard University Press, 1984), 68, 95.

16. The rule being that "art, to be recognized as such, requires grounding in . . . common culture"—in which the outsider artist is not grounded. Peter Schjeldahl, "Mystery Train. Martin Ramirez, Outsider," *New Yorker* (January 9, 2007), accessed July 28, 2018, https://www.newyorker.com/magazine/2007/01/29/mystery-train.

17. Costlow points out that Turgenev believes in and values ineffability (often comparing it favorably to such phenomena as Rudin's speechiness); among Turgenev's goals, she writes, is "the overcoming of romantic eloquence." Costlow, *Worlds*, 25.

18. See too the description of Lavretsky's estate at Vasilevskoe, at once ancient and timeless. Turgenev, *PSS*, 6:61–64.

19. Benedict Anderson, *Imagined Communities: Reflections on the Origin and Spread of Nationalism* (London: Verso, 1991 [1983]), 205.

20. Monika Greenleaf, *Pushkin and Romantic Fashion* (Stanford: Stanford University Press, 1994), 15–16. Greenleaf is referring to the Romantic period, but her insights shed light on the tradition as a whole.

Chapter Seven

1. Kelly's pioneering work focuses mostly on provincial tales featuring "exceptional" female protagonists with an acute need to "escape" the provinces, texts dating from around the 1850s and later. Catriona Kelly, *A History of Russian Women's Writing 1820–1992* (Oxford: Clarendon Press, 1994), 59–63. But as Irina Savkina has noted, the women writers of an earlier generation, including Elena Gan and Mariia Zhukova, tend instead to represent ordinary provincial women who do not necessarily aim for "escape." Irina Savkina, *Provintsialki russkoi literatury (zhenskaia proza 30–40-kh godov XIX veka)* (Wilhelmshorst, Germany: Verlag F. K. Göpfert, 1998), 68.

2. Kelly, *A History of Russian Women's Writing*, 62; Savkina, *Provintsialki*, 68.

3. In addition to Savkina, see two articles by Hilde Hoogenboom: "The Importance of Being Provincial: Nineteenth-Century Russian Women Writers and the Countryside," in *Gender and Landscape: Renegotiating Morality and Space*, ed. Josephine Carubia, Lorraine Dowler, and Bonj Szczygiel (London: Routledge, 2009), 242; and "The Society Tale as Pastiche: Mariia Zhukova's Heroines Move to the Country," in *The Society Tale in Russian Literature from Odoevskii to Tolstoi*, ed. Neil Cornwall (Amsterdam: Rodopi, 1998), 85–97.

4. For example, Zrazhevskaia's letters to her sister (cited by Savkina) from Staraia Russa in the 1840s bemoan the *skuka* and *melochi interesov* (boredom and triviality of interests) of her surroundings, describing a provincial life much like those we read about in Sollogub or Herzen.

5. Savkina, *Provintsialki*, 56ff. Hoogenboom makes the case that provincial women took advantage of their marginal position to develop a distinctive literary voice; this may be so, but such writers' continued marginality in the canon today suggests that they paid a high price. See Hoogenboom, "The Society Tale as Pastiche."

6. Margaret Cohen's *The Sentimental Education of the Novel* (Princeton, NJ: Princeton University Press, 1999), which treats nineteenth-century French novels written by women, conveys just how difficult it is to "reclaim" an aesthetic practice (in this case, Sentimentalism) that has been so long excluded from our view that it has become alien to us. Critics like Savkina and Diana Greene, among others, are undertaking this work for the Russian tradition. See Diana Greene, *Reinventing Romantic Poetry: Russian Women Poets of the Mid-Nineteenth Century* (Madison: University of Wisconsin Press, 2014), as well as Greene's forthcoming book on Russian women novelists.

7. For instance, Greene demonstrates that Russian women poets continued to write tales in verse (*povesti v stikhakh*) for decades after the genre was deemed "exhausted" in male writing. Greene, *Reinventing Romantic Poetry*, 244n23. For further discussion of how "periodization has been challenged as an organizational concept by feminist theory," see the essays collected in Bonnie Kime Scott, ed., *The Gender of Modernism* (Bloomington: Indiana University Press, 1990), 5ff.

8. Pascale Casanova, *The World Republic of Letters* (Cambridge, MA: Harvard University Press, 2004), 75.

9. Hoogenboom, "The Importance of Being Provincial," 243. Hoogenboom is referring here to Belinsky's 1840 review of Mariia Zhukova's work (Belinskii, *PSS*, 4:110–118). While it is true that Belinsky at times relegated women writers to a marginal position ("man is by his very nature more universal than woman," *PSS*, 4:115), at other times he expressed a nuanced view of their capabilities and of the extent to which these capabilities were socially conditioned, as we see in his 1843 review of Elena Gan's writing (*PSS*, 7:648–76).

10. See Kelly, *A History of Russian Women's Writing*, 22, 35–36.

11. Thus Balzacian realists elided a whole tradition of female Sentimentalist novelists in France, much the same way that Hawthorne and other ("serious," male) authors displaced the women who had written wildly popular (also Sentimentalist) fictions in antebellum America. A generation of feminist critics have worked to recuperate writers like Madame de Montpezat and Susan Warner, and similar work is underway in the Russian tradition (see note 6 above). My quotation marks around "realism" indicate the difficulty if not the impossibility of defining the term, whether at this period or any other. Indeed, rather than saying that Russian women were often excluded from the ranks of realist writers (since no one knew or knows exactly what a realist is), it is perhaps more useful to note that women were increasingly excluded from the ranks of real writers, i.e., socially committed professionals.

12. Belinskii, *PSS*, 7:650. See Kelly, *A History of Russian Women's Writing*, 24.

13. Kelly, *A History of Russian Women's Writing*, 62.

14. Savkina, *Provintsialki*, 57; Kelly, *A History of Russian Women's Writing*, 110.

15. Belinskii, "Sochineniia Zeneidy R-voi," *PSS*, 7:675.

16. E. A. Gan, "Sud Sveta," in *Dacha na Petergofskoi doroge: Proza russkikh pisatel'nits pervoi poloviny XIX veka*, ed. V. V. Uchenova (Moscow, Sovremmenik, 1986), 152.

17. E. A. Gan, "Ideal," in *Russkaia Romanticheskaia povest'*, comp. Vsevolod Sakharov (Moscow: Izd. Sovetskaia Rossiia, 1980). Accessed May 30, 2017, http://az.lib.ru/g/gan_e_a/text_0010.shtml. Here and throughout, for Gan's "Ideal" I have consulted Joe Andrew's translation in his *Russian Women's Shorter Fiction: An Anthology, 1835–1860* (Oxford: Oxford University Press, 1996).

18. Gan, "Ideal."

19. Kelly, *A History of Russian Women's Writing*, 112.

20. A. I. Gertsen, *Sobranie sochinenii v 30-i tomakh* (Moscow: Izd. Akademii Nauk SSSR, 1954), I: 298–99.

21. Gan, "Ideal."

22. Gan, "Ideal."

23. Gan, "Ideal."

24. Gan, "Ideal."

25. Gan, "Ideal."

26. Gan, "Sud Sveta," 150.

27. Gan, "Ideal."

28. Gan, "Sud Sveta," 200.

29. Gan, "Ideal."

30. See Savkina, *Provintsialki*, ch. 6 for Zhukova's biography.

31. M. S. Zhukova, "Provintsialka," in *Vechera na karpovke* (Moscow: Izdatel'stvo Sovetskaia Rossiia, 1986), 92.

32. Zhukova, "Provintsialka," 187–88

33. Zhukova, "Provintsialka," 188

34. Zhukova, "Provintsialka," 187–88, 190, 196.

35. Zhukova, "Provintsialka," 189

36. Zhukova, "Provintsialka," 212–13.

37. Zhukova, "Provintsialka," 211.

38. Zhukova, "Provintsialka," 206.

39. Zhukova, "Provintsialka," 207.

40. Zhukova, "Provintsialka," 208.

41. Zhukova, "Provintsialka," 206.

42. Zhukova, "Provintsialka," 207.

43. Zhukova, "Naden'ka," in *Serdtsa chutkogo prozren'em: Povesti i rasskazy russkikh pisatel'nits XIX v.* (Moscow: Sovetskaia Rossiia, 1991), 174, 234.

44. Zhukova, "Provintsialka," 221.

45. Zhukova, "Provintsialka," 222.

46. Zhukova, "Provintsialka," 222.

47. Zhukova, "Provintsialka," 243. Likewise, Zhukova says, novels and fairy tales emphasize the wholeness of a person's life, by focusing on one event or feeling, not following any further past the plot's denouement, at which time "another feeling, another life would violate the unity."

48. Zhukova, "Provintsialka," 221; Hoogenboom, "The Society Tale as Pastiche," 91. Hoogenboom notes that this technique "unsettled" Belinsky and other (male) critics, who criticized Zhukova's work for plotlessness.

49. Zhukova, "Provintsialka," 249.

50. Zhukova, "Naden'ka," 219.

51. Zhukova, "Naden'ka," 207, 177.

52. Zhukova, "Naden'ka," 181, 222.

53. Zhukova, "Naden'ka," 184–85.

54. Zhukova, "Naden'ka," 186, 196.

55. Zhukova, "Naden'ka," 176.

56. Zhukova, "Naden'ka," 172.

57. Zhukova, "Naden'ka," 195, 197.

58. Zhukova, "Naden'ka," 215–16, 207.

59. Christine D. Tomei, ed. *Dictionary of Russian Women Writers*, vol. 1 (New York: Garland, 1999), 261.

60. N. D. Khvoshchinskaia [V. Krestovskii, pseud.], "Pansionerka," in *Povesti i rasskazy* (Moscow: Khudozhestvennaia literatura, 1963), 134. I have also made use of the following translation: Nadezhda Khvoshchinskaya, *The Boarding School Girl*, trans. Karen Rosneck (Evanston, IL: Northwestern University Press, 2000).

61. Thomas L. Dumm, *A Politics of the Ordinary* (New York: New York University Press, 1999), 14, cited in Saikat Majumdar, *Prose of the World: Modernism and the Banality of Empire* (New York: Columbia University Press, 2013), 21.

62. Khvoshchinskaia, "Pansionerka," 92, 128.

63. Khvoshchinskaia, "Pansionerka," 136, 163, 170.

64. Khvoshchinskaia, "Pansionerka," 100–101.

65. Khvoshchinskaia, "Pansionerka," 119.

66. Khvoshchinskaia, "Pansionerka," 114.

67. Khvoshchinskaia, "Pansionerka," 127, 172.

68. Khvoshchinskaia, "Pansionerka," 149–50.

69. Khvoshchinskaia, "Pansionerka," 163–64.

70. Khvoshchinskaia, "Pansionerka," 154–55.

71. Khvoshchinskaia, "Pansionerka," 170.

72. Khvoshchinskaia, "Pansionerka," 141.

73. Khvoshchinskaia, "Pansionerka," 137.

74. Khvoshchinskaia, "Pansionerka," 145.

75. See Irina Paperno, *Chernyshevsky and the Age of Realism: A Study in the Semiotics of Behavior* (Stanford: Stanford University Press, 1988).

76. Khvoshchinskaia, "Pansionerka," 144.

77. Khvoshchinskaia, "Pansionerka," 175.

78. Khvoshchinskaia, "Pansionerka," 175.

79. Khvoshchinskaia, "Pansionerka," 180–81.

80. Khvoshchinskaia, "Pansionerka," 175. I have relied on Rosneck's translation in this passage.

81. Khvoshchinskaia, "Pansionerka," 186.

82. Khvoshchinskaia, "Pansionerka," 180, 182.

83. Khvoshchinskaia, "Pansionerka," 182. Cf. Benedict Anderson's famous remarks on the kind of community created by print culture—a collective (possibly a nation) "conceived as a deep, *horizontal* comradeship." This modern "horizontal" vision of the collective (horizontal in the sense that it is imagined as a vast fraternal web rather than as a hierarchy) relates to what Anderson calls the "horizontal" and secular *time* of modernity. Benedict Anderson, *Imagined Communities: Reflections on the Origin and Spread of Nationalism* (London: Verso, 1991 [1983]), 7, 24, emphasis mine.

84. J. G. A. Pocock, "Modes of Political and Historical Time in Early Eighteenth-Century England," in *Virtue, Commerce, and History: Essays on Political Thought and History, Chiefly in the Eighteenth Century* (Cambridge, UK: Cambridge University Press, 1985), 91.

85. Khvoshchinskaia, "Pansionerka," 180.

86. Khvoshchinskaia, "Pansionerka," 182. The ever-present clock also suggests the contrast between modern, measured time—time that is divided up and filled up—and the time of N, empty, endless and undifferentiated (hence the apocalyptic levels of *skuka* in *provintsiia*). Cf. once again Anderson's remarks on the relationship between modernity and "the steady onward clocking of homogeneous, empty time." Anderson, *Imagined Communities*, 33.

87. Khvoshchinskaia's demurral quoted in Rosneck, "Translator's Introduction," Khvosh-chinskaya, *The Boarding School Girl*, xiii.

88. David Denby, "A Fine Romance: The New Comedy of the Sexes," *New Yorker* (July 23, 2007), accessed July 28, 2018. https://www.newyorker.com/magazine/2007/07/23/a-fine-romance.

89. Khvoshchinskaia, "Pansionerka," 155.

90. Lee Edelman, *No Future: Queer Theory and the Death Drive* (Durham, NC: Duke University Press), 2004.

91. Khvoshchinskaia, "Pansionerka," 185.

92. Belinskii, "Povesti M. Zhukovoi," in *PSS*, 4:115.

93. V. A. Koshelev, "O 'literaturnoi' provintsii i literaturnoi 'provintsial'nosti' novogo vremeni: Zametki," in *MTR*, 41, emphasis mine.

94. A. S. Gatsitskii, *Smert' provintsii ili net?* (Nizhnii Novgorod: Tip. Nizh. gub. pravleniia, 1876), 19, emphasis mine.

95. Irina Savkina, "Kto i kak pishet istoriiu russkoi zhenskoi literatury," *Novoe literaturnoe obozrenie* 24 (1997), 359–72. Greer is quoted in Elaine Showalter, *A Literature of Their Own: British Women Novelists from Bronte to Lessing* (Princeton, NJ: Princeton University Press, 1999 [1977]), 11.

96. Showalter, *A Literature of Their Own*, 11–12.

97. Nikolai Shelgunov, *Ocherki russkoi zhizni* (St. Petersburg: O. N. Popova, 1895), cited in Ia. E. Akhapkipa, "Provintsiia, periferiia—problema nominatsii" in *PKR*, ed. A. F. Belousov, M. V. Stroganov, A. Iu. Sorochan (Tver': Tverskoi gosudarstvennyi universitet, 2001), 10.

98. Claudia Rankine and Beth Loffreda, "On Whiteness and the Racial Imaginary," *Literary Hub*, April 9, 2015, accessed March 9, 2017, http://lithub.com/on-whiteness-and-the-racial-imaginary/.

Chapter Eight

1. For an attempt to rescue Melnikov from the fate of being seen as merely a regionalist, see I. V. Kudriashchov, "Khronotop 'lesov' i 'gor' v filosofskom kontekste dialogii P. I. Mel'nikogo-Pecherskogo," in *ZP*, 252–55.

2. V. A. Koshelev, "O 'literaturnoi' provintsii i literaturnoi 'provintsial'nosti' novogo vremeni: Zametki," in *MTR*, 41, emphasis mine.

3. Jules Michelet, *Tableau de la France. Géographie physique, politique et morale* (Paris: A. Lacroix et Cie, 1875), 77–78.

4. A. S. Gatsitskii, *Smert' provintsii ili net?* (Nizhnii Novgorod: Tip. Nizh. gub. pravleniia, 1876), 20.

5. Nikolai Shelgunov, *Ocherki russkoi zhizni* (St. Petersburg: O. N. Popova, 1895), cited in Ia. E. Akhapkipa, "Provintsiia, periferiia—problema nominatsii" in *PKR*, ed. A. F. Belousov, M. V. Stroganov, A. Iu. Sorochan (Tver': Tverskoi gosudarstvennyi universitet, 2001), 10.

6. Toral Gujarawala, "Nagarjun's World Literature and the Problem of Fiction as Theory" (paper delivered at conference "World Literature and Its Discontent," NYU Abu Dhabi, March 31, 2016), cited by permission of the author.

7. A. N. Ostrovskii, *Beshenye den'gi* (1870), accessed April 16, 2018, http://rushist.com /index.php/rus-literature/5184-ostrovskij-beshenye-dengi-chitat-onlajn-polnostyu.

8. Richard Brodhead elaborates on these ideas in *Cultures of Letters: Scenes of Reading and Writing in Nineteenth-Century America* (Chicago: University of Chicago Press, 1993), 116. However, see ch. 7 for a discussion of the fact that even in the United States, women writers were more likely to be labeled and marginalized as regionalists than were men whose work treated similar material.

9. Pierre Bourdieu, "Deux impérialismes de l'universel," in *L'Amérique des Français*, ed. Christine Fauré and Tom Bishop (Paris: François Bourin, 1992), 149–55.

10. Joanna Russ, *To Write Like a Woman: Essays in Feminism and Science Fiction* (Bloomington: Indiana University Press, 1995), 89.

11. Susan Smith-Peter, "How to Write a Region: Local and Regional Historiography," *Kritika* 5, no 3 (Summer 2004): 527, 535.

12. Smith-Peter, "How to Write a Region," 527.

13. Catherine Evtuhov, *Portrait of a Russian Province: Economy, Society, and Civilization in Nineteenth-Century Nizhnii Novgorod* (Pittsburgh, PA: University of Pittsburgh Press, 2011), 249.

14. Smith-Peter, "How to Write a Region," 535. For examples of recent historiography that attends seriously to regional particularity and autonomy, see this and other works by Smith-Peter, including "The Russian Provincial Newspaper and Its Public, 1788–1864" and "Making Empty Provinces: Eighteenth-Century Enlightenment Regionalism in Russian Provincial Journals." Other important works in this vein include Evtuhov, *Portrait of a Russian Province*, cited above; Brower, *The Russian City*; Abashev, *Perm' kak tekst*; and Pickering-Antonova, *An Ordinary Marriage*. See also the essays collected in these four seminal post-Soviet volumes: *MTR, PKR, TP,* and *ZP* (see abbreviations list).

15. Gatsitskii, *Smert' provintsii*.

16. Gatsitskii, *Smert' provintsii*, 6. Here one might compare the words of twentieth-century Serbian writer Danilo Kis: "in order to exist it is necessary to pass through Paris." Quoted in Pascale Casanova, *The World Republic of Letters* (Cambridge, MA: Harvard University Press, 2004), 129.

17. Gatsitskii, *Smert' provintsii*, 8.

18. D. Mordovtsev, "Pechat' v provintsii," *Delo* 9 (September 1875): 44–74; see also "Pechat' v provintsii," *Delo* 10 (October 1875): 1–32. Gatsitskii was not the only provincial journalist who responded to Mordovtsev; even Dostoevsky weighed in. For an overview of the polemics, see Dostoevskii, *PSS*, 23:6–7.

19. Mordovtsev, "Pechat' v provintsii," *Delo* 9, 55, 59.

20. Mordovtsev, "Pechat' v provintsii," *Delo* 9, 44, 51, 48.

21. Mordovtsev, "Pechat' v provintsii," *Delo* 9, 51.

22. Mordovtsev, "Pechat' v provintsii," *Delo* 9, 51.

23. Gatsitskii, *Smert' provintsii*, 7, emphasis mine.

24. Mordovtsev, "Pechat' v provintsii," *Delo* 9, 54–55. "Povolzhe" means simply along the Volga River (and thus denotes Saratovskoe povolzh'e, Nizhegorodskoe povolzh'e, etc.,

or all such places taken together); "Zavolzh'e" means *beyond* the Volga and denotes the forested expanses north of the Volga.

25. Evtuhov, *Portrait of a Russian Province*, 247. Evtuhov makes a similar point about Melnikov, whose "early life was . . . purely local—something that had only just become possible for an educated person." Similarly, the vision Melnikov proposed at *Gubernskie vedomosti* "was above all *local.*" Evtuhov, *Portrait of a Russian Province*, 141–42.

26. Mordovtsev, "Pechat' v provintsii," *Delo* 9, 60, citing Gatsitskii. Emphasis mine.

27. Gatsitskii's words as cited and translated by Catherine Evtuhov, "The Provincial Intelligentsia and Social Values in Nižnij Novgorod, 1838–91," *Slavica Lundensia* 22 (2005): 86, emphasis mine.

28. Catherine Evtuhov, "The Provincial Intelligentsia and Social Values in Nižnij Novgorod," 89, emphasis mine. Evtuhov cites A. S. Gatsitskii, *Liudi Nizhegorodskogo Povolzh'ia* (Nizhnii Novgorod: Tip. Nizh. gub. pravleniia, 1887).

29. Mordovtsev, "Pechat' v provintsii," *Delo* 9, 63–65.

30. Mordovtsev, "Pechat' v provintsii," *Delo* 9, 60, emphasis mine. *Posidelki* were village gatherings held especially on winter nights for the purpose of socializing.

31. Mordovtsev, "Pechat' v provintsii," *Delo* 9, 64, citing Gatsitskii's words.

32. Gatsitskii, *Smert' provintsii*, 17, quoting Mordovtsev.

33. Gatsitskii, *Smert' provintsii*, 17, 20.

34. Evtuhov, *Portrait of a Russian Province*, 234. See also works by Susan Smith-Peter, "How to Write a Region," and "Making Empty Provinces." Other important works in this vein include Brower, *The Russian City*, and Abashev, *Perm' kak tekst*.

35. Smith-Peter, "How to Write a Region," 538.

36. Smith-Peter, "How to Write a Region," 538.

37. Evtuhov, *Portrait of a Russian Province*, 231. Even in our time the idea persists that scholarship by provincial academics is not capable of developing large, synthesizing ideas, but only of addressing "particular problems"—leaving the synthesizing, the actual making of significance, to scholars in the capitals. N. G. Baranets, "Faktor provintsializma v universitetskoi filosofii v Rossii kontsa XX- ogo veka," *TP*, 179.

38. Smith-Peter, "How to Write a Region," 540.

39. Scholars have pointed out a similar division of intellectual labor (locals provide raw facts, scholars in the center provide authoritative interpretative narratives) in other traditions as well. Evtuhov has a sensitive discussion of the delicate position occupied by Russian provincial intellectuals, whose "psychology . . . combined an acute sense of the extreme modesty of one's life task (occasionally slipping into a full-blown inferiority complex), together with an equally intense dedication." Evtuhov, *Portrait of a Russian Province*, 299.

40. Mordovtsev, "Pechat' v provintsii," *Delo* 10, 27.

41. Over the course of the nineteenth century the word *grobokopatel'nyi* came to be used quite often in association with archaeology. This passage, then, suggests that the provinces are virtually a graveyard with little value beyond the archaeological, a site of artifacts that are always already dead and buried. (My thanks to Michael Kunichika for this insight.)

42. From 1850 on, Melnikov wrote under the pseudonym Pechersky, derived from the name of the street where he lived.

43. See Evtuhov, *Portrait of a Russian Province*, 141–45, for an overview of Melnikov's career (which does not treat his fiction writing).

44. Thomas H. Hoisington, "Melnikov-Pechersky: Romancer of Provincial and Old Believer Life," *Slavic Review* 33, no. 4 (December 1974): 680, 681.

45. Pavel Mel'nikov-Pecherskii, "Krasil'nikovy," in *Sobranie sochinenii v 6-i tomakh* (Moscow: Knizhnyi Klub Knigovek, 2010), 1:17.

46. Mel'nikov, "Krasil'nikovy," 17.

47. Mel'nikov, "Krasil'nikovy," 19.

48. Mel'nikov, "Krasil'nikovy," 19.

49. Mel'nikov, "Krasil'nikovy," 20.

50. Mel'nikov, "Krasil'nikovy," 24–25.

51. Mel'nikov, "Krasil'nikovy," 27.

52. Mel'nikov, "Krasil'nikovy," 28.

53. Moretti, *Atlas of the European Novel, 1800–1900* (London: Verso, 1998), 65.

54. Casanova, *The World Republic of Letters*, 88–89.

55. Roberto Maria Dainotto, "'All the Regions Do Smilingly Revolt': The Literature of Place and Region," *Critical Inquiry* 22, no. 3 (Spring 1996): 499.

56. Richard Brodhead, *Cultures of Letters*, 132.

57. Donna M. Campbell, "Regionalism and Local Color Fiction, 1865–1895," *Literary Movements*, Dept. of English, Washington State University, last modified October 10, 2017, accessed July 29, 2018, http://public.wsu.edu/~campbelld/amlit/lcolor.html.

58. Evtuhov, *Portrait of a Russian Province*, 143.

59. Evtuhov, *Portrait of a Russian Province*, 143, 144. Sketes were monastic communities.

60. As Costlow discusses, critics and historians disagree on the role played by Melnikov's first-hand ethnographic observations in his fiction: some have stressed his use of published sources such as folklore compilations, while others emphasize his experience gathering materials from Old Believers in the 1850s. Jane Costlow, *Heart-Pine Russia: Walking and Writing the Nineteenth-Century Forest* (Ithaca, NY: Cornell University Press, 2013), 65. This distinction matters little for my argument here.

61. Melnikov's 1875 speech to the Society of Lovers of Russian Literature, cited in Costlow, *Heart-Pine Russia*, 78.

62. J. G. A. Pocock, "Modes of Political and Historical Time in Early Eighteenth-Century England," in *Virtue, Commerce, and History: Essays on Political Thought and History, Chiefly in the Eighteenth Century* (Cambridge, UK: Cambridge University Press, 1985), 91.

63. Richard Brodhead, *Cultures of Letters*, 121. For a rich account of American regionalism's cultural work, see Brodhead's ch. 4, "The Reading of Regions."

64. In the nineteenth century, writing about Old Believers almost inevitably implied an ideological stance because Old Belief itself signified powerfully and very differently for different political factions: for the radical intelligentsia, it represented "'Protestant' opposition

and potential; for conservatives, . . . Old Russian virtue and resistance to the West." Costlow, *Heart-Pine Russia*, 56.

65. Evgenii Tolmachev, *Aleksandr III i ego vremia* (Moscow: Terra, 2007), 52.

66. Brodhead, *Cultures of Letters*, 121.

67. Costlow, *Heart-Pine Russia*, 54, 60.

68. Costlow, *Heart-Pine Russia*, 54, 60.

69. Hoisington, "Melnikov-Pechersky," 688; Costlow, *Heart-Pine Russia*, 60.

70. Pavel Mel'nikov-Pecherskii, *V lesakh*, in *Sobranie sochinenii v 6-i tomakh*, 2:7–8.

71. See, for example, Mel'nikov, *SS*, 2:61, 40–43. Characters note the difference between *tysiachniki* (rich peasants, but still technically peasants) and *kuptsy* (members of the merchant class who live in towns; 61).

72. Mel'nikov, *V lesakh*, 84, 251, 29, 110, 193–95.

73. I. A. Goncharov, *Sobranie sochinenii v 8-i tomakh*. (Moscow: Gosudarstvennoe izdatel'stvo khudozhestvennoi literatury, 1953), 4:108.

74. Mikhail Bakhtin, "Forms of Time and Chronotope in the Novel," in *The Dialogic Imagination: Four Essays by M. M. Bakhtin*, ed. Michael Holquist, trans. Caryl Emerson and Michael Holquist (Austin: University of Texas Press, 1981), 99.

75. Moretti, *Atlas of the European Novel*, 22. See also Bakhtin, "Forms of Time and Chronotope," 90–101.

76. Moretti, *Atlas of the European Novel*, 23–24.

77. This argument is more pertinent to *In the Hills* (the sequel to *In the Forests*), in which the main protagonists are agents of the region's rapid and "chaotic economic *development*"—development in the sense of both change and progress—in the second half of the nineteenth century. Rozanna Kazari [Rosanna Casari], "Russkii provintsial'nyi gorod v literature XIX v. Paradigma i varianty," in *MTR*, 168. Hoisington sees the protagonists of *In the Hills* (who are foreshadowed a bit by Kolyshkin of *In the Forests*) as "idealized Russian businessmen combining the virtues of an old-fashioned upbringing with Western entrepreneurism." Hoisington, "Melnikov-Pechersky," 683.

78. Mel'nikov, *V lesakh*, 305.

79. Mel'nikov, *V lesakh*, 2, 305–6.

80. Mel'nikov, *V lesakh*, 2, 305–6.

81. Mel'nikov, *V lesakh*, 2, 432; see also 105, 479, 578.

82. Mel'nikov, *V lesakh*, 159.

83. Mel'nikov, *V lesakh*, 363–66.

84. Mel'nikov, *V lesakh*, 166, 159, 184–85.

85. Mel'nikov, *V lesakh*, 155.

86. Mel'nikov, *V lesakh*, 154. *Rogozhskii poselok* was a center of Old Belief practice in Moscow.

87. Mel'nikov, *V lesakh*, 222, 264.

88. Anne L. Hollander, *Seeing Through Clothes* (Berkeley: University of California Press, 1993 [1975]), 362, 363, emphasis mine.

89. Luba Golburt, *The First Epoch: The Eighteenth Century in the Russian Cultural Imagination* (Madison: University of Wisconsin Press, 2014), 206.

90. Hollander, *Seeing Through Clothes*, 364.

91. Mel'nikov, *V lesakh*, 200–201, 207.

92. I. A. Goncharov, *Polnoe sobranie sochinenii i pisem v 20-i tomakh*. (St. Petersburg: Nauka, 1997), 1:299, 239.

93. Costlow, *Heart-Pine Russia*, 54.

94. Quoted in Costlow, *Heart-Pine Russia*, 58.

95. Janet Sorensen, "'I talk to everybody in their own way': Defoe's Economics of Identity," in *The New Economic Criticism: Studies at the Intersection of Literature and Economics*, ed. Martha Woodmansee and Mark Osteen (London: Routledge, 1999), 82.

96. As noted above, the protagonists of *In the Hills* have even been described as entrepreneurs, "virtuous, honest, educated, Westernized, tolerant, Old Believer-nurtured merchants." Thomas Hoisington, "Melnikov-Pechersky," 683, 690. If one accepts this interpretation, then Melnikov's final work suggests that the future lies with men of the marketplace, and with the connective spatial networks the marketplace creates—networks that spell the end of the intensely regional identities that are the focus of *In the Forests*.

97. N. S. Leskov, *Sobranie sochinenii*, ed. V. G. Bazanov et al. (Moscow: Gosudarstvennoe izdatel'stvo khudozhestvennoi literatury, 1956–58), 4:354. Melnikov is cited in Costlow, *Heart-Pine Russia*, 76.

98. Nick Baron, "New Spatial Histories of 20th-Century Russia and the Soviet Union: Exploring the Terrain," *Kritika* 9, no. 2 (Spring 2008): 444n8.

99. Leskov, *SS*, 7:125–31. First published in *Novoe vremia* no. 2453 (Dec. 25, 1882) with the title "Rozhdestvenskaia noch' v vagone (Puteshestvie s nigilistom)."

100. The compartment was also useful to writers as a space where characters could engage in solitary contemplation and free-thinking, thanks to the temporary removal of certain social constraints (which is why it is in a train compartment that Anna Karenina first ponders illicit love, for example). And it could also be a site of the kind of obsessive, trapped-in-one's-own-head thinking that occupies Dostoevsky's narrator in *Winter Notes on Summer Impressions*. On the latter, see Anne Dwyer, "Of Hats and Trains: Cultural Traffic in Leskov's and Dostoevskii's Westward Journeys," *Slavic Review* 70, no. 1 (Spring 2011): 67–93.

101. Leskov, *SS*, 4:323.

102. As a result even when railroads were linking places together, they did so by destroying the lived reality of space between points (which is to say almost everyplace). Wolfgang Schivelbusch, *The Railway Journey: The Industrialization of Time and Space in the Nineteenth Century* (Berkeley: University of California Press, 1986), 37.

103. Leskov, *SS*, 7:432. The narrator attributes this insight to Pisemsky.

104. James H. Billington, *The Icon and the Axe: An Interpretive History of Russian Culture* (New York: Vintage Books, 1970 [1966]), 382–84.

105. *No Way Out* (*Nekuda*, 1864) and *At Daggers Drawn* (*Na nozhakh*, 1870–71).

106. Baron, "New Spatial Histories," 446.

107. As Dwyer writes, "Leskov's railroad hardly seems a marvel of modern technology" ("Of Hats and Trains," 90).

108. Thus Leskov pointedly rejects the genre designation "novel" for *Cathedral Folk*, insisting that it is instead a "chronicle." He claims that his texts, unlike novels, *unfold* the way real life does, "like a scroll unwinding from a spool"—or, one might also say, like a winding road or a circuitous path. Leskov, *SS*, 5:279. Quoted and translated in Irmhild Christina Sperrle, *The Organic Worldview of Nikolai Leskov* (Evanston, IL: Northwestern University Press, 2002), 116, emphasis mine.

109. Sperrle, *The Organic Worldview*, 3 (emphasis mine). Sperrle is echoing many Leskov scholars when she laments that Leskov "has not received the scholarly attention he deserves." Sperrle, *The Organic Worldview*, 3. *The Cambridge Companion to the Classic Russian Novel* claims that only those with an "intimate knowledge of the [Russian] tradition" would rank Leskov among the "great" Russian writers. See Malcolm V. Jones and Robin Feuer Miller, "Editors' Preface," in *The Cambridge Companion to the Classic Russian Novel*, ed. Malcolm V. Jones and Robin Feuer Miller (Cambridge, UK: Cambridge University Press, 1998), xiii.

110. Gorky, quoted in Knut Andreas Grimstad, *Styling Russia: Multiculture in the Prose of Nikolai Leskov* (Bergen, Norway: Slavica Bergensia 7, 2007), 17.

111. Irina Stoliarova, quoted in Grimstad, *Styling Russia*, 18.

112. Grimstad, *Styling Russia*, 17–18; Kuzmin, quoted in B. M. Eikhenbaum, "O proze Kuzmina," in *O literature* (Moscow: Sovetskii pisatel', 1987), 348. Accessed July 31, 2017, http://philologos.narod.ru/eichenbaum/eich_kuzmin.htm. Grimstad marshals a great many more comments along these lines.

113. Jane Costlow, *Heart-Pine Russia*, 58, 59. Among the writers who acknowledged drawing on Melnikov were Andrei Belyi and Andrei Remizov.

114. Mirsky, cited in Costlow, *Heart-Pine Russia*, 59.

115. Kaganskii, "Tsentr-provintsiia-periferiia-granitsa. Osnovnye zony kul'turnogo landshafta," *Kul'turnyi landshaft: voprosy teorii i metologii issledovaniia*, edited by V. V. Valebnyi et al. (Moscow: Izd. SGU, 1998), 76; see also Vasilii Shchukin, "Krizis stolits ili kompleks provintsii?" *Novoe literaturnoe obozrenie* 34 (1998): 350–54, which describes *provintsiia* as "eternal and indestructible."

116. From an interview with Nabokov conducted on September 25, 27, 28, 29, 1966, at Montreux, Switzerland. Interview by Alfred Appel, Jr., *Wisconsin Studies in Contemporary Literature* 8, no. 2 (Spring 1967), accessed March 10, 2017, http://lib.ru/NABOKOW/Inter06.txt_with-big-pictures.html. Second quote is from Vladimir Nabokov, *Speak, Memory: An Autobiography Revisited* (New York: Vintage International, 1989), 160.

117. Roberto Maria Dainotto, "'All the Regions Do Smilingly Revolt,'" 486.

118. Milan Kundera, "Die Weltliteratur: European novelists and modernism," *New Yorker* (January 8, 2007), accessed March 10, 2017, http://www.newyorker.com/magazine/2007/01/08/die-weltliteratur.

119. Mordovtsev, "Pechat' v provintsii," *Delo* 9, 51; B. M. Eikhenbaum, "O proze Kuzmina," 348.

Chapter Nine

1. F. M. Dostoevskii, *Polnoe sobranie sochinenii v 30-i tomakh* (Leningrad: Nauka, 1974), 6:115. Hereafter all Dostoevsky citations are from this edition and appear parenthetically in main text.

2. Cited in Stephane Gerson, "Parisian Litterateurs, Provincial Journeys and the Construction of National Unity in Post-Revolutionary France," *Past and Present* 151, no. 1 (May 1996): 168–69.

3. Napoleon's empire was itself "deeply centralized," as Kokobobo writes: "It has been described as revolving around three concentric circles structured 'hierarchically in terms of [. . .] dependence on the center [. . .].' The first and innermost circle constituted the French empire in the strictest sense although certain parts of France deemed peripheral did not make it into this space; the second circle was made up of the satellite kingdoms that France had conquered, whereas the third circle consisted of countries with which Napoleon had alliances. From this perspective, Russia fell on the third concentric circle— and Napoleon expected the Russians as allies to wholeheartedly assist his geopolitical interests. . . . From this perspective, Napoleon's invasion of Russia was in many ways centripetal, or an attempt to force an ally to submit to the power of the center." Ani Kokobobo, "Tolstoy as Literary Cartographer of the Napoleonic Wars: Mapping the Human Geography of *War and Peace* through Digital Technology" (unpublished ms., forthcoming in *Russian Literature: Special Issue: Digital Humanities and Russian and East European Literature*, no page number; cited by author's permission). Kokobobo is citing Thierry Lentz, "Imperial France in 1808 and Beyond," in *The Napoleonic Empire and the New European Political Culture*, ed. M. Broers, P. Hicks, and A. Guimera (New York: Palgrave-Macmillan, 2012), 26.

4. Kokobobo, "Tolstoy as Literary Cartographer," no page number.

5. Leonid Gorizontov, "The 'Great Circle' of Interior Russia: Representations of the Imperial Center in the Nineteenth and Early Twentieth Centuries," in *Russian Empire: Space, People, Power, 1700–1930*, ed. Jane Burbank, Mark von Hagen, and Anatolyi Remnev (Bloomington: Indiana University Press, 2007), 68.

6. N. V. Gogol', *Polnoe sobranie sochinenii* (Moscow: Akademiia Nauk SSSR, 1937–52), 6:206. Baffling, that is, because Moscow and Petersburg are separated by four hundred miles.

7. Gary Saul Morson, *Narrative and Freedom: The Shadows of Time* (New Haven, CT: Yale University Press, 1994), 184.

8. L. N. Tolstoi, *Polnoe sobranie sochinenii v 90-i tomakh* (Moscow: Gosudarstvennoe izdatel'stvo khudozhestvennoi literatury, 1958), 12:17. Here Tolstoy refers to Voronezh as being *v provintsii*, and on the previous page he speaks of *gubernskaia zhizn'*—a sign that the two words are still quite interchangeable during this period. Very rarely does Tolstoy use forms of *provintsiia* metaphorically, to indicate lack of sophistication. In *War and Peace*, in addition to the passage cited here, he does so only one other time, when he describes the Moscow-based Rostovs as "provincials" in relation to Petersburg high society. Kokobobo's mapping of *War and Peace* reveals that characters who travel to and through provincial places achieve fuller development than those who are confined to the capitals.

9. In some texts an estate is interesting to Tolstoy chiefly because it stands for something larger. Both "Childhood" and the early fragment "Morning of a Landowner," for example, are set on self-enclosed estates whose locations are left entirely unspecified; what is important about each of these places is not geographic location but rather the set of questions the place allows Tolstoy to address (the family as it stretches over time, the question of serfdom, etc.).

10. Alexander M. Martin argues persuasively that Tolstoy's view of Moscow in 1812 is distorted by his disregard for what Martin calls the "middling sort" who even then were the backbone of urban life. See his *Enlightened Metropolis: Constructing Imperial Moscow, 1762–1855* (Oxford: Oxford University Press, 2013), esp. ch. 5: "Government, Aristocracy, and the Middling Sort."

11. Tolstoi, *PSS*, 18:178.

12. D. Mordovtsev, "Pechat' v provintsii." *Delo* 9 (September 1875): 44.

13. A. S. Gatsitskii, *Smert' provintsii ili net?* (Nizhnii Novgorod: Tip. Nizh. gub. pravleniia, 1876), 7.

14. Dostoevsky was living in Dresden when he learned of the Nechaev Affair in the Russian press, which he followed almost obsessively while abroad. The writing of *Demons* (which was serialized in *The Russian Herald* from January 1871 through December 1872 before being published as a book in 1873) largely predated detailed newspaper accounts of Nechaev's crime, but once these accounts appeared in the papers—in July of 1871, after about half the novel had already been serialized—Dostoevsky declared that he had been successful in imagining the kind of person who would be capable of such an act. For a detailed account of Dostoevsky's use of the press while writing *Demons*, see Dostoevskii, *PSS*, 12:192–218. On Dostoevsky's reaction to the Nechaev Affair, see Joseph Frank, *Dostoevsky: The Miraculous Years, 1865–1871* (Princeton, NJ: Princeton University Press, 1995).

15. See notes in Dostoevskii, *PSS*, 12:223–24.

16. As Melissa Frazier has pointed out, in the earlier decades of the nineteenth century the place name "Tver" was at times used simply to stand for a "quintessentially average address . . . an abstraction, the imaginary home of a Russian Everyman who does not really exist." Melissa Frazier, *Romantic Encounters: Writers, Readers, and the "Library for Reading"* (Stanford: Stanford University Press, 2007), 181.

17. As one scholar has written of Skotoprigonevsk, "the action in *The Brothers Karamazov* could have developed in any other town of a similar size and location . . . Skotoprigonevsk stands for the province, it is the small town typically opposed to the metropolis, to the urban area traditionally well-known to Dostoevsky's readers. The geographical description of Skotoprigonevsk is deliberately vague, place-names are very general (*Bol'shaia ulitsa, Bazarnaia ploshchad', Sobornaia ploshchad'*)." Thus the town "has little significance of its own," just as it has "no boundaries, no historic centre, no particularly relevant or evocative monuments for the action to revolve around. There is only a monastery, but at about a verst or more away, immediately suggesting, in fact, that it belongs to another world." Furthermore, much as in *Demons*, in *Brothers Karamazov* "the characters' movements are almost entirely confined to the territory of the town," a fact that intensifies our sense of the town's isolation. Gian Piero Piretto, "Staraia Russa and Petersburg; Provincial

Realities and Metropolitan Reminiscences in *The Brothers Karamazov*," *Dostoevsky Studies* 7 (1986): 82–83.

18. Dostoevskii, *PSS*, 14:463, 252. N. V. Zhivolupova argues that the setting of *Brothers Karamazov* is what we immediately recognize as "the deeply 'material' world of the 'little provincial town'" ("sgubo 'material'nyi' mir 'provintsial'nogo gorodka'"). Fyodor Karamazov is "deeply immersed in [this] heavy corporeality," whereas his sons only *appear* in it; their fates and actions are not at all in keeping with the chronotope of the sleepy, event-less *gorodok*. Zhivolupova theorizes that Smerdiakov's evil may be tied to the chronotope of stagnant and grossly corporeal *provintsiia*. N. V. Zhivolupova, "Skotoprigon'evsk kak nazaret i mifologema provintsii v Russkoi kul'ture," in *ZP*, 195.

19. I should note here that this characterization holds true only for the more or less "educated" minority who make up nearly the whole cast of *Demons*. Peasants—who have their own culture, in Dostoevsky's estimation—would be another matter entirely.

20. See, for example, how the final chapter of *Demons* recalls *Dead Souls* by dwelling not on the resolution of the plot, but on the swirl of wild rumor and uncertainty that persists after the cabal is "revealed" (e.g., 10:508–9).

21. *No mne nikto eshche* tam *ne zakazyval vashego kharaktera, i nikakikh podobnykh zakazov* ottuda *ia eshche ne bral na sebia.* Dostoevskii, *PSS*, 10:278, emphasis in original.

22. Stepan Trofimovich, too, is known for his associations "*there*—that is, abroad" (again with *tam* in italics), since he is famous among the locals for having published a politically sensitive poem decades earlier in a foreign journal. Dostoevskii, *PSS*, 10:10.

23. Mikhail Epstein, *Bog detalei: Narodnaia dusha i chastnaia zhizn' v Rossii na iskhode imperii* (New York: Slovo, 1997), 35.

24. Pertinent words related to *set'* include *setka* (grid, coordinates) and *setevoi* (netting, mesh).

25. Gogol', *PSS*, 6:220.

26. Quoted in Christopher David Ely, *This Meager Nature: Landscape and National Identity in Imperial Russia* (DeKalb, IL: Northern Illinois University Press, 2002), 146–47. Ely's chapter "Outer Gloom and Inner Glory" analyzes many landscapes of this type.

27. But as *Demons* makes clear, these linked nodes can also act as what might be described as disease vectors, a distribution network facilitating the "viral" spread of noxious ideas. Here one recalls the epilogue to *Crime and Punishment*, with Raskolnikov's nightmare of an ideology epidemic in which a terrible "pestilence" attacks the world's whole population, "infecting" people with the conviction that their ideas are infallible. See Dostoevskii, *PSS*, 6:419.

28. Donald Fanger, *The Creation of Nikolai Gogol* (Cambridge, MA: Harvard University Press, 1979), 135, 133.

29. Epstein, *Bog detalei*, 32.

30. A more positive interpretation of this image of Russian towns as *uzly* is found in the (pre-railroad) "travel notes" published by V. V. Passek in 1834. Passek described Moscow, for example, as only one of several important "nodes of nationality" (*uzly narodnosti*), and he claimed that Russia "possesses a series of centers or points of concentration that operate

as the very source of its life, the hearts of its circulatory system." Passek, cited in Gorizontov, "The 'Great Circle' of Interior Russia," 71.

31. Dostoevskii, *PSS*, 10:287, 303, 304, 488.

32. Jean Cocteau, *Opium: The Illustrated Diary of His Cure* (London: Peter Owen, 1990 [1929]). For a discussion of the role played by the railroad in *The Idiot*, see David M. Bethea, "*The Idiot*: Historicism Arrives at the Station," in *Dostoevsky's* Idiot: *A Critical Companion*, ed. Liza Knapp (Evanston, IL: Northwestern University Press, 1998), 130–90. According to Bethea's fascinating and persuasive analysis, trains are closely linked to the apocalyptic vision that structures *The Idiot*.

33. Kokobobo, "Tolstoy as Literary Cartographer," no page number.

34. And while stasis surrounded by movement would normally suggest an orbit and a gravitational pull, in *Demons* the opposite seems to occur: the inert object (the provincial place) is subject to, or affected by, the pull of surrounding movement. Thus the province becomes a kind of absent center, much like the character of Stavrogin.

35. Wolfgang Schivelbusch, *The Railway Journey: The Industrialization of Time and Space in the Nineteenth Century* (Berkeley: University of California Press, 1986), 37.

36. Quoted in Schivelbusch, *The Railway Journey*, 37–38.

37. Schivelbusch, *The Railway Journey*, 39.

38. P. Ia. Chaadaev, "Lettres philosophiques adressées à une dame. Lettre première," *Polnoe sobranie sochinenii i izbrannye pis'ma* (Moscow: Nauka, 1991), 1:90.

39. Epstein, *Bog detalei*, 30, 35.

40. Bethea, "Historicism Arrives at the Station," 142–43.

41. Billington, *The Icon and the Axe: An Interpretive History of Russian Culture* (New York: Vintage Books, 1970 [1966]), 384, emphasis mine. Within a few years of making his hopeful declaration, Kibalchich had become a revolutionary terrorist dedicated to blowing up trains—a fact that reveals how important railroads were not just to progressives but to various political factions and their contradictory visions of Russian historical development.

42. In *The Idiot*, too—despite the fact that here the image of the locomotive is far more significant than that of the tracks—the network of railway lines carries sinister implications. Characters in *The Idiot* ponder whether "the network of railways [*set' zheleznykh dorog*] spread across Europe" might be the fulfillment of Biblical prophecies concerning the Star of Wormwood that falls to earth and poisons the waters of life (Revelation 8:11–12). As one character asks, "so do you think that the railroads are cursed, that they are the bane of humanity, a plague fallen upon the earth to muddy the 'waters of life'?" Dostoevskii, *PSS*, 8:254, 309, 310–11.

43. In *The Idiot* this climax is death (as in Cocteau's "express train racing towards death"), and perhaps the unnarratable possibility of what comes after. See Bethea, "Historicism Arrives at the Station," 135, 160, 175. Dostoevsky's notebooks for *The Idiot* confirm Bethea's argument about this narrative's end- and death-directed quality. For example, despite Dostoevsky's early uncertainties about how the plot of *The Idiot* would develop, he seems always to have known that Nastasia Filipovna would die; in fact, the climactic scene of Myshkin and Rogozhin confronting each other over her corpse appears in his notebooks very early on. See Frank, *Dostoevsky: The Miraculous Years*, 286, 290.

Chapter Ten

1. A. P. Chekhov, *Polnoe sobranie sochinenii i pisem v 30-i tomakh* (Moscow: Nauka, 1974–83), 13:120. Hereafter Chekhov texts will be referenced parenthetically by volume and page number of this edition. Volumes 19 through 30 of this edition contain Chekhov's letters and are numbered separately: *Pis'ma v 12 t.*, t. 1–12.

2. Cited in Emma Polotskaya, "Chekhov and his Russia," in *The Cambridge Companion to Chekhov*, ed. Vera Gottlieb and Paul Allain (Cambridge, UK: Cambridge University Press, 2000), 19.

3. S. A. Vengerov, "Gogol' sovershenno ne znal real'noi russkoi zhizni," in *Sobranie sochinenii*, vol. 2: *Pisatel'-grazhdanin. Gogol'* (St. Petersburg: Prometei, 1913). Vengerov claims that not only did Gogol spend less than two weeks of his life in the Russian countryside, but that most of this time was spent inside a moving carriage.

4. Cited in Polotskaya, "Chekhov and his Russia," 20.

5. N. D. Khvoshchinskaia [V. Krestovskii, pseud.], "Pansionerka," in *Povesti i rasskazy* (Moscow: Khudozhestvennaia literatura, 1963), 180, 182.

6. Sollogub, "Aptekarsha," in *Povesti i rasskazy* (Moscow: Gosudarstvennoe izdatel'stvo khudozhestvennoi literatury, 1962), 83.

7. N. V. Gogol', *Polnoe sobranie sochinenii* (Moscow: Akademiia Nauk SSSR, 1937–52), 6:9.

8. Khvoshchinskaia, "Pansionerka," 134.

9. Khvoshchinskaia, "Pansionerka," 185.

10. For several reviews expressing this view, see Anton Chekhov, "Nevesta," in *Polnoe sobranie sochinenii*, vol. 10 (Moscow: Nauka, 1986). Accessed December 11, 2016, http://az.lib.ru/c/chehow_a_p/text_1903_nevesta.shtml.

11. V. A. Sollogub, *Povesti i rasskazy*, intro. E. Kiiko (Moscow: Gosudarstvennoe izdatel'stvo khudozhestvennoi literatury, 1962), 180.

12. At the end of *A Boring Story*, too, Kharkov is where Chekhov deposits his dying protagonist to face death in squalor: "Kharkov" for Chekhov perhaps represents the ultimate in provinciality, provinciality in the sense of death, "the end of the line"—rather like what "America" represents for Dostoevsky.

13. M. M. Bakhtin, "Forms of Time and Chronotope in the Novel," in *The Dialogic Imagination*, ed. Michael Holquist, trans. Caryl Emerson and Michael Holquist (Austin: University of Texas Press, 1981), 247–48.

14. Mikhail Epstein, *Bog detalei: Narodnaia dusha i chastnaia zhizn' v Rossii na iskhode imperii* (New York: Slovo, 1997), 30.

15. James H. Billington, *The Icon and the Axe: An Interpretive History of Russian Culture* (New York: Vintage Books, 1970 [1966]), 384.

16. Willard Sunderland, *Taming the Wild Field: Colonization and Empire on the Russia Steppe* (Ithaca, NY: Cornell University Press, 2004), 181; see also 141ff. Of course Russians had largely created this emptiness by settling, eradicating, and strategically forgetting about the land's nomadic inhabitants, in a version of the same process that unfolded in the United States and Canada, Argentina and Australia: first colonizers imagine the land as unpeopled, and then they go about peopling it.

17. Sunderland, *Taming the Wild Field*, 202. In 1870 there were opera houses in Odessa and Piatigorsk, universities in Kharkov and Odessa, "a nice boulevard" in Stavropol, fancy shops and a "decent central avenue" in Orenburg. Sunderland, 159. And by now the steppe was also far from foreign as well: as Sunderland writes, "by the dawn of the twentieth century, the steppe had been so profoundly transformed by Russian imperialism that it was difficult for contemporaries to determine whether it constituted a borderland, a colony, or Russia itself." Sunderland, 223.

18. I am grateful to Vadim Shneyder for this insight (in a personal communication).

19. Quoted in Wolfgang Schivelbusch, *The Railway Journey: The Industrialization of Time and Space in the Nineteenth Century* (Berkeley: University of California Press, 1986), 37–38.

20. Cited in Polotskaya, "Chekhov and his Russia," 19. A city as far east as Perm (in the Urals, which were at one time considered to be on the edge of Siberia) might be expected to have a slightly exotic or at least distinctive identity in comparison to the emphatically and exclusively *Russian* provincial towns of European Russia.

Chapter Eleven

1. M. E. Saltykov-Shchedrin, *Sobranie sochinenii v 20-i tomakh* (Moscow: Khduozhestvennaia literature, 1965–77), 18:1:111.

2. Saltykov-Shchedrin, *SS*, 2:7.

3. Saltykov-Shchedrin, *SS*, 2:225.

4. Saltykov-Shchedrin, *SS*, 2:79.

5. Saltykov-Shchedrin, *SS*, 2:78.

6. Milton Ehre writes, "the novel itself is organized around the action of dying." Milton Ehre, "A Classic of Russian Realism: Form and Meaning in *The Golovliovs*," *Studies in the Novel* 9 no. 1 (Spring 1977): 7.

7. William Mills Todd, III, "The Anti-Hero with a Thousand Faces: Saltykov-Shchedrin's Porfiry Golovlev," *Studies in the Literary Imagination* 9, no. 1 (Spring 1976): 90. In this chapter I have made use of Natalie Duddington's translation of *The Golovlyov Family*, intro. James Wood (New York: NYRB, 2001). Page numbers for the English refer to this edition.

8. Kyra Sanine, *Saltykov-Chtchedrine: sa vie et ses oeuvres* (Paris: Institut d'études slaves de l'Université de Paris, 1955), 223; quoted in Ehre, "A Classic of Russian Realism," 5.

9. Saltykov-Shchedrin, *SS*, 13:78; Duddington, *The Golovlyov Family*, 201.

10. Saltykov-Shchedrin, *SS*, 13:21; Duddington, *The Golovlyov Family*, 21.

11. Saltykov-Shchedrin, *SS*, 13:54, 46, 145, 47; Duddington, *The Golovlyov Family*, 68, 54, 188, 55.

12. Saltykov-Shchedrin, *SS*, 13:47, 54, 228, 107; Duddington, *The Golovlyov Family*, 56, 65, 292, 134.

13. Saltykov-Shchedrin, *SS*, 13:47, 228, 48; Duddington, *The Golovlyov Family*, 54, 293, 56.

14. Saltykov-Shchedrin, *SS*, 13:30; Duddington, *The Golovlyov Family*, 33.

15. Nikolai Berdiaev, *Sud'ba Rossii. Opyty po psikhologii voiny i natsional'nosti* (Moscow: Izdatel'stvo G. D. Lemana i S. I. Sakharova, 1918), 71–72.

16. N. V. Gogol', *Polnoe sobranie sochinenii* (Moscow: Akademiia Nauk SSSR, 1937–52), 6:220.

17. Saltykov-Shchedrin, *SS*, 13:104; Duddington, *The Golovlyov Family*, 131.

18. Saltykov-Shchedrin, *SS*, 13:251; Duddington, *The Golovlyov Family*, 321.

19. Saltykov-Shchedrin, *SS*, 13:104; Duddington, *The Golovlyov Family*, 131; Ehre, "A Classic of Russian Realism," 4.

20. Saltykov-Shchedrin, *SS*, 13:95; Duddington, *The Golovlyov Family*, 120.

21. Saltykov-Shchedrin, *SS*, 13:31; Duddington, *The Golovlyov Family*, 34.

22. Saltykov-Shchedrin, *SS*, 13:96; Duddington, *The Golovlyov Family*, 120.

23. Saltykov-Shchedrin, *SS*, 13:49, 96; Duddington, *The Golovlyov Family*, 57–58, 121.

24. Saltykov-Shchedrin, *SS*, 13:31; Duddington, *The Golovlyov Family*, 34.

25. Saltykov-Shchedrin, *SS*, 13:49; Duddington, *The Golovlyov Family*, 57–58.

26. Saltykov-Shchedrin, *SS*, 13:49; Duddington, *The Golovlyov Family*, 58.

27. Saltykov-Shchedrin, *SS*, 13:256; Duddington, *The Golovlyov Family*, 326.

28. Saltykov-Shchedrin, *SS*, 13:49–50; Duddington, *The Golovlyov Family*, 58–59.

29. Saltykov-Shchedrin, *SS*, 13:50; Duddington, *The Golovlyov Family*, 58–59.

30. Saltykov-Shchedrin, *SS*, 13:161, 174; Duddington, *The Golovlyov Family*, 206, 222–23.

31. Ehre, "A Classic of Russian Realism," 11.

32. Saltykov-Shchedrin, *SS*, 13:51; Duddington, *The Golovlyov Family*, 60.

33. Saltykov-Shchedrin, *SS*, 13:69; Duddington, *The Golovlyov Family*, 84.

34. Saltykov-Shchedrin, *SS*, 13:70; Duddington, *The Golovlyov Family*, 85.

35. A. I. Gertsen, *Sobranie sochinenii v 30-i tomakh* (Moscow: Izd. Akademii Nauk SSSR, 1954), I: 293, IV: 40.

36. Saltykov-Shchedrin, *SS*, 13:29; Duddington, *The Golovlyov Family*, 31–32.

37. Saltykov-Shchedrin, *SS*, 13:34, 46, 99, 144; Duddington, *The Golovlyov Family*, 38, 53, 124, 184.

38. Saltykov-Shchedrin, *SS*, 13:44; Duddington, *The Golovlyov Family*, 51.

39. Saltykov-Shchedrin, *SS*, 13:45; Duddington, *The Golovlyov Family*, 52.

40. M. E. Saltykov-Shchedrin, *Poshekhonskaia starina* (Moscow: Gosudarstvennoe izdatel'stvo khudozhestvennoi literatury, 1950), 12. Cited in Alexander Gerschenkron, "Time Horizon in Russian Literature," *Slavic Review* 34, no. 4 (December 1975): 704.

41. Compare here Goncharov's *Oblomov*: the rural gentry of Oblomovka gorge themselves regularly but they never spend money, because for them "the only way of using capital is to keep it locked up in a chest." I. A. Goncharov, *Sobranie sochinenii v 8-i tomakh.* (Moscow: Gosudarstvennoe izdatel'stvo khudozhestvennoi literatury, 1953), 4:132.

42. V. F. Odoevsky, "Sil'fida" (1837), accessed June 28, 2017, http://rulibrary.ru/odoevskiy/silfida/3.

43. Osip Mandelshtam, "On the Nature of the Word," in *Osip Mandelshtam: Selected Essays*, trans. Sidney Monas (Austin: University of Texas Press, 1977), 75, emphasis mine.

44. V. Sh. Krivonos, "Gogol': Mif provintsial'nogo goroda," in *PKR*, 112.

45. Gogol', *PSS*, 6:692.

46. Saltykov-Shchedrin, *SS*, 13:31; Duddington, *The Golovlyov Family*, 34.

47. Saltykov-Shchedrin, *SS*, 13:30; Duddington, *The Golovlyov Family*, 33.

48. Saltykov-Shchedrin, *SS*, 13:48; Duddington, *The Golovlyov Family*, 56.

49. Saltykov-Shchedrin, *SS*, 13:249; Duddington, *The Golovlyov Family*, 318.

50. Saltykov-Shchedrin, *SS*, 13:250; Duddington, *The Golovlyov Family*, 319, emphasis mine.

51. Fyodor Sologub is not to be confused with the earlier Count Vladimir Sollogub, no relation, whose works are the subject of ch. 3.

52. S. D. Cioran, Introduction to Fyodor Sologub, *The Petty Demon*, intro. and trans. S. D. Cioran (Woodstock, NY: Ardis Publishers, 2006), 15. In this chapter I have made use of Cioran's translation and scholarly apparatus while also consulting the Russian text of the novel.

53. Cioran, Introduction to Sologub, *The Petty Demon*, 15. See Cioran's Introduction for an overview of the novel's complicated publication history.

54. F. K. Sologub, *Melkii bes* (St. Petersburg: Nauka, 2004), 9.

55. Sologub, *Melkii bes*, 87.

56. Murl Barker, "*The Petty Demon* and the Critics," in S. D. Cioran, trans., *The Petty Demon*, 294. Barker is quoting Ivanov-Razumnik's assessment of the novel.

57. Irene Masing-Delic, "'Peredonov's Little Tear'—Why Is It Shed? (The Sufferings of a Tormenter)," in S. D. Cioran, trans., *The Petty Demon*, 334.

58. A. P. Chekhov, *Polnoe sobranie sochinenii i pisem v 30-i tomakh* (Moscow: Nauka, 1974–83), 10:46.

59. Cf. in Chekhov's *My Life (A Provincial's Story)*, where the main character laments, "I couldn't understand why and how these 65,000 people were living. . . . What our town was and what it was doing, I did not know." Chekhov, *PSS*, 9:205.

60. Mikhail Bakhtin, *Rabelais and His World* (Bloomington: Indiana University Press, 2009), 40.

61. Saltykov-Shchedrin, *SS*, 13:119.

62. Ani Kokobobo, *Russian Grotesque Realism: The Great Reforms and the Gentry Decline* (Columbus: The Ohio State University Press, 2018).

63. Diana Greene, *Insidious Intent: An Interpretation of Fedor Sologub's* The Petty Demon (Columbus, OH: Slavica, 1985), 28.

64. Evgeny Zamyatin, *A Soviet Heretic: Essays by Evgeny Zamyatin*, ed. and trans. Mirra Ginsburg (Chicago: University of Chicago Press, 1970), 221.

65. See Kate Holland, "The Russian *Rougon-Macquart*: Degeneration and Biological Determinism in *The Golovlev Family*," in *Russian Writers and the Fin de Siècle: The Twilight of Realism*, ed. Ani Kokobobo and Katia Bowers (Cambridge, UK: Cambridge University Press, 2015). Sologub, *Melkii bes*, 422.

66. Diana Greene, "Structure and Meaning in Sologub's 'Petty Demon,'" *Ulbandus Review* 1, no. 2 (Spring 1978): 27.

67. Greene, "Structure and Meaning in Sologub's 'Petty Demon,'" 28.

68. Greene, "Structure and Meaning in Sologub's 'Petty Demon,'" 31.

69. Sologub, *Melkii bes*, 198 (Peredonov's "spells"), 413 (Prepolovensky's retellings); the character Tishkov also speaks in compulsive rhymes and repetitions (*boiko proiznosimykh skorogovorok*, 444–45). Words that recur in the narrative to describe Peredonov include sluggish, spiteful, suspicious, sullen, and angry.

70. Sologub, *Melkii bes*, 174, 198; Saltykov-Shchedrin, *SS*, 13:161.

71. Sologub, *Melkii bes*, 89.

72. Sologub, *Melkii bes*, 34.

73. Sologub, *Melkii bes*, 396–97.

74. Sologub, *Melkii bes*, 74.

75. Sologub, *Melkii bes*, 74, 34.

76. *Boloto, tina, pyl', sliakot', luzh, nemoshchenye, neprokhodimye.*

77. M. L. Lur'e, "'Ves'egonsk gorodishko prebedneishii' (Vzgliad na uezdnyi gorod v putevykh zametkakh XIX veka)," in *PKR*, 132.

78. Andrei Bely, *The Silver Dove*, trans. John Elsworth (Evanston, IL: Northwestern University Press, 2000), 80–81.

79. William James, *The Varieties of Religious Experience: A Study in Human Nature* (New York: The Modern Library, 1929); Mary Douglas, *Purity and Danger: An Analysis of Concepts of Pollution and Taboo* (London: Routledge and Kegan Paul, 1966).

80. Sologub, *Melkii bes*, 75, 90.

81. V. A. Sollogub, "Aptekarsha," in *Povesti i rasskazy*, intro. E. Kiiko (Moscow: Gosudarstvennoe izdatel'stvo khudozhestvennoi literatury, 1962), 83; Saltykov-Shchedrin, *SS*, 8:407.

82. Sologub, *Melkii bes*, 50.

83. Sologub, *Melkii bes*, 74, 445, 515–16

84. Sologub, *Melkii bes*, 73, 69. Characters treat each other as objects too, as when Peredonov sees the servant girl Marta being just like "all the [other] objects" with which he has established minimal relations.

85. Linda J. Ivanits, "The Grotesque in Fedor Sologub's *The Petty Demon*," in S. D. Cioran, trans., *The Petty Demon*, 302. Ivanits continues, "In *The Petty Demon* one can see the continuation of the tradition in Russian literature which perceives evil as petty; Peredonov may legitimately be considered a relative of both Gogol's Chichikov and Dostoevsky's Smerdyakov." Ivanits, 313–14.

86. Svetlana Boym, *Commonplaces: Mythologies of Everyday Life in Russia* (Cambridge, MA: Harvard University Press, 1995), 41.

87. Vladimir Nabokov, *Strong Opinions* (New York: McGraw-Hill, 1973), 100; Vladimir Nabokov, *Nikolai Gogol* (New York: New Directions, 1944), 70.

88. Saltykov-Shchedrin, *SS*, 13:31; Duddington, *The Golovlyov Family*, 34.

89. J. G. A. Pocock, "Modes of Political and Historical Time in Early Eighteenth-Century England," in *Virtue, Commerce, and History: Essays on Political Thought and History, Chiefly in the Eighteenth Century* (Cambridge, UK: Cambridge University Press, 1985), 91.

90. Ehre, "A Classic of Russian Realism," 11.

91. P. Ia. Chaadaev, "Lettres philosophiques adressées à une dame. Lettre première," *Polnoe sobranie sochinenii i izbrannye pis'ma* (Moscow: Nauka, 1991), 1:90–91. For the English, see *Philosophical Works of Peter Chaadaev*, ed. T. J. Blakeley, Guido Küng, and Nikolaus Lobkowicz (Netherlands: Springer Netherlands, 1991), 1:86–205.

92. Chaadaev, "Lettres philosophiques adressées à une dame. Lettre première," 89; Mikhail Bakhtin, "Forms of Time and Chronotope in the Novel," 247.

93. Chaadaev, "Lettres philosophiques adressées à une dame. Lettre première," 89.

94. Iurii Lotman, "'Pikovaia dama' i tema kart i kartochnye igry v russkoi literature nachala XIX veka," in *Izbrannye stat'i*, 3 vols. (Tallinn: Aleksandra, 1992), 2:397. See also ch. 2 ("Chance and Historical Necessity") in Svetlana Evdokimova, *Pushkin's Historical Imagination* (New Haven, CT: Yale University Press, 1999), and Alexander Dolinin, "Historicism or Providentialism? Pushkin's *History of Pugachev* in the Context of French Romantic Historiography," *Slavic Review* 58, no. 2, Special Issue: Aleksandr Pushkin 1799–1999 (Summer 1999): 291–308. For more on this topic, see ch. 2.

Chapter Twelve

1. Victor Terras, ed., *Handbook of Russian Literature* (New Haven, CT: Yale University Press, 1985), 70.

2. F. Sologub, *Sobranie stikhotvorenii v 8-i tomakh* (St. Petersburg: Nav'i Chary, 2002), 7:624.

3. Anton Chekhov, *The Complete Plays*, trans., ed., and annot. Laurence Senelick (New York: W. W. Norton, 2007), 815. Kharkov fulfills more or less this role in *The Seagull* (the provincial audiences there love Arkadina's acting), *Uncle Vanya* (it is the destination of Elena and the professor), *Cherry Orchard* (Lopakhin runs off to do business there at the end of the play), *A Boring Story* (where the dying protagonist ends up in squalor), and other texts.

4. L. O. Zaionts, "Russkii provintsial'nyi 'mif' (k probleme kul'turnoi tipologii)," in *Geopanorama russkoi kul'tury: Provintsiia i ee lokal'nye teksty*, ed. L. O. Zaionts, V. V. Abashev, A. F. Belousov, and T. V. Tsivian (Moscow: Iazyki slavianskoi kul'tury, 2004), 427.

5. A. A. Akhmatova, "Pridu tuda, i otletit tomlenie," *Sobranie sochinenii v 6-i tomakh* (Moscow: Ellis Lak, 2000), 4:117–18. The word *khranilishche* (repository) recurs in critical discussions of Leskov's and Melnikov's texts as well.

6. See N. Gumilev, *Koster* (Berlin: Izdatel'stvo Z. I. Grzhebina, 1922), 13–14.

7. "Gde tina na parchu pokhozha." Akhmatova, "Pridu tuda, i otletit tomlenie," 117–18.

8. Zaionts, "Russkii provintsial'nyi 'mif,'" 429. As Zaionts shows, these decades also witnessed a boom in archaeology, folklore studies, ethnography and *kraevedenie* ("studies aiming to 'uncover' spaces and places"), as well as new museums, dictionaries, and geographic reference works, all of which enjoyed remarkable popularity.

9. Zaionts, "Russkii provintsial'nyi 'mif,'" 428.

10. Yuri M. Lotman, *Universe of the Mind: A Semiotic Theory of Culture*, trans. Ann Shukman (London; New York: I. B. Tauris, 2001), 192.

11. Zaionts, "Russkii provintsial'nyi 'mif,'" 434, 432,

12. A. A. Litiagin and A. V. Tarabukina, "Zritel'nyi obraz malen'kogo goroda," in *PKR*, 55.

13. M. L. Lur'e, "'Vesegonsk gorodishko prebedneishii' (Vzgliad na uezdnyi gorod v putevykh zametkah XIX veka)," in *PKR*, 136. As I. Gauner wrote of Vesegonsk in 1902, "Anything you might say about Vesegonsk might be said about hundreds of other small [*uezdnykh*] Russian towns." Thus the town of Vesegonsk is useful as a "case study." Lur'e, 136.

14. Zaionts, "Russkii provintsial'nyi 'mif,'" 435. "In the Symbolist period an absolutely new understanding of the classic Russian estate took shape, in which they began to see 'a poetic hypostasis of Russia.'"

15. F. M. Dostoevskii, *Polnoe sobranie sochinenii v 30-i tomakh* (Leningrad: Nauka, 1972–1990), 23:6–7.

16. Zaionts, "Russkii provintsial'nyi 'mif,'" 428.

17. This is how Nick Baron sums up Paperny's schema. Nick Baron, "New Spatial Histories of 20th-Century Russia and the Soviet Union: Exploring the Terrain," *Kritika* 9, no. 2 (Spring 2008): 444n8. See Vladimir Paperny, *Architecture in the Age of Stalin: Culture Two* (Cambridge, UK: Cambridge University Press, 2011).

18. Baron, "New Spatial Histories of 20th-Century Russia and the Soviet Union," 444n8.

19. V. Maiakovskii, "Prochti i katai v Parizh i v Kitai," in *Polnoe sobranie sochinenii Maiakovskogo v 13-i tomakh* (Moscow: Gosudarstvennoe izdatel'stvo khudozhestvennoi literatury, 1955), 10:257. The poem dates to 1927.

20. Cited and translated in Yuri Slezkine, *The House of Government: A Saga of the Russian Revolution* (Princeton, NJ: Princeton University Press, 2017), 317, emphasis mine.

21. Quoted in Slezkine, *The House of Government*, 598, emphasis mine.

22. P. Ia. Chaadaev, "Lettres philosophiques adressées à une dame. Lettre première," *Polnoe sobranie sochinenii i izbrannye pis'ma* (Moscow: Nauka, 1991), 1:90.

23. Slezkine, *The House of Government*, 56. The Bolsheviks' adoption of the swamp image may well have been encouraged by Chernyshevsky's *What Is to Be Done?* In Vera Pavlovna's second dream, the coming revolution appears as a new "drainage system" (*drenazh*) promising to clean out the stagnant, poisonous waters of the old world, rendering them pure and productive. N. G. Chernyshevskii, *Chto delat'? Iz rasskazov o novykh liudiakh* (Leningrad: Nauka, 1975), 124.

24. Slezkine, *The House of Government*, 57. Fascists, too, have found the swamp image congenial: Mussolini called on Italians to "drenare la palude," or "drain the swamp." Robin Wright, "Madeleine Albright Warns of a New Fascism," *New Yorker* (April 24, 2018), accessed July 30, 2018, https://www.newyorker.com/news/news-desk/madeleine-albright -warns-of-a-new-fascism-and-trump.

25. Slezkine, *The House of Government*, 57, 195.

26. Slezkine, *The House of Government*, 57, 56.

27. Thomas Newlin, "The Return of the Russian Odysseus: Pastoral Dreams and Rude Awakenings," *Russian Review* 55, no. 3 (July 1996): 449.

28. Slezkine, *The House of Government*, 196.

29. Voronsky, cited in Slezkine, *The House of Government*, 623.

30. *Pravda* and *Literaturnaia gazeta* quotes are from the introduction to *MTR*, 9. *Literaturnaia gazeta* quote is from 1933.

31. M. Gor'kii, "Pis'ma nachinaiushchim literatoram," *Sobranie sochinenii v 30-i tomakh* (Moscow: Gosudarstvennoe izdatel'stvo khudozhestvennoi literatury, 1953), 25:141, 135. Gorky made similar charges elsewhere, for example in "O prose," "Po povodu odnoi dis-kussii," "Otkrytoe pis'mo A. S. Serafimovich," "O iazyke," and "Literaturnye zabavy." See vols. 26 and 27 of his *Sobranie sochinenii.*

32. Gor'kii, "Doklad na pervom vsesoiuznom s'ezde sovetskikh pisatelei, 17 avgusta, 1934-ogo goda," Gor'kii, *SS,* 27:328.

33. Emily D. Johnson, *How St. Petersburg Learned to Study Itself: The Russian Idea of Kraevedenie* (University Park, PA: Penn State University Press, 2006), 178. Vladimir Ka-gansky also makes this point: "Tsentr-provintsiia-periferiia-granitsa. Osnovnye zony kul'turnogo landshafta," *Kul'turnyi landshaft: voprosy teorii i metologii issledovaniia,* edited by V. V. Valebnyi et al. (Moscow: Izd. SGU, 1998), 91, 96–7.

34. Quoted in Ia. E. Akhapkipa, "Provintsiia, periferiia—problema nominatsii," in *PKR,* 10. For the original, see Nikolai Pogodin, *Malen'kaia studentka,* in *Sobranie sochinenii v 4 tomakh* (Moscow: Izd. "Iskusstvo," 1973), 3:219–84.

35. On contradictory representations of *provintsiia* in the post-Soviet period, see Ly-udmila Parts, "Topography of Post-Soviet Nationalism: The Provinces—the Capital—the West," *Slavic Review* 74, no. 3 (Fall 2015): 508–28.

36. Pascale Casanova, *The World Republic of Letters* (Cambridge, MA: Harvard University Press, 2004), 87–88.

37. Casanova is drawing on Immanuel Wallerstein's "world systems theory" as articu-lated in his works including *The Modern World-System I: Capitalist Agriculture and the Origins of the European World-Economy in the Sixteenth Century* (New York: Academic Press, 1974).

38. Fredric Jameson, "Third-World Literature in the Era of Multinational Capitalism," *Social Text* 15 (Autumn 1986): 65.

39. See index of *The Routledge Companion to World Literature,* ed. Theo D'haen, David Damrosch, Djelal Kadir (New York: Routledge, 2012).

40. See John Burt Foster, Jr., *Transnational Tolstoy: Between the West and the World* (New York: Bloomsbury, 2013), for an examination of Tolstoy's place in a "globalized" liter-ary world.

41. Arjun Appadurai, *Modernity at Large: Cultural Dimensions of Globalization* (Min-neapolis: University of Minnesota Press, 2000), 30.

42. Casanova, *The World Republic of Letters,* 93.

43. Casanova, *The World Republic of Letters,* 92–93. For Paz's complete text, see Octavio Paz, "In Search of the Present," *Inti: Revista de literatura hispánica:* 32, Article 3 (Autumn 1990), 16–17. Available at: http://digitalcommons.providence.edu/inti/vol1/iss32/3, ac-cessed July 17, 2017.

44. Casanova, *The World Republic of Letters,* 93.

45. Casanova, *The World Republic of Letters,* 87–88.

46. Mikhail Epstein, *Bog detalei: Narodnaia dusha i chastnaia zhizn' v Rossii na iskhode imperii* (New York: Slovo, 1997), 30. Furthermore, as new scholarship on the Soviet and post-Soviet literary sphere has begun to demonstrate, other "worlds" of literature have at

times been imagined and constructed. Unlike Casanova's model, which is centripetal and tightly focused on centers, Russian and Soviet versions of World Literature have tended instead to be centrifugal, often focused on peripheries, boundaries, and "contact zones." See Kate Holland, "Narrative Tradition on the Border: Alexander Veselovsky and Narrative Hybridity in the Age of World Literature," *Poetics Today* 38, no. 3 (September 2017): 429–51; Ilya Kliger, "World Literature beyond Hegemony in Yuri M. Lotman's Cultural Semiotics," *Comparative Critical Studies* 7, no. 2–3 (2010): 257–74, and "Historical Poetics between Russia and the West: Toward a Nonlinear Model of Literary History and Social Ontology," *Poetics Today* 38, no. 3 (September 2017): 453–83; Galin Tihanov, "The Location of World Literature," *Canadian Review of Comparative Literature* 44, no. 3 (September 2017): 468–81.

47. Casanova, *The World Republic of Letters*, 94.

48. Luce Irigaray, *Ce sexe qui n'en est pas un* (Paris: Minuit, 1977).

49. Lotman, *Universe of the Mind*, 198.

50. Arthur Rimbaud, *A Season in Hell and Illuminations*, trans. Bernard Mathieu (Rochester, NY: BOA Editions, 1991), 22.

51. Lotman, *Universe of the Mind*, 192; Mikhail Epstein, *Bog detalei*, 35.

52. P. Ia. Chaadaev, "Apologie d'un fou." *Polnoe sobranie sochinenii i izbrannye pis'ma* (Moscow: Nauka, 1991), 1:289–304. For the English, see Peter Chaadaev, "Apologia of a Madman," *Philosophical Works of Peter Chaadaev*, ed. T. J. Blakeley, Guido Küng, and Nikolaus Lobkowicz (Netherlands: Springer Netherlands, 1991), 102–11.

53. Leon Trotsky, *History of the Russian Revolution* (Chicago: Haymarket Books, 2008), 4–5.

54. Michael Holquist, *Dostoevsky and the Novel* (Evanston, IL: Northwestern University Press, 1977), 16.

55. Holquist, *Dostoevsky and the Novel*, 15–16, 30–31. Cf. Appadurai: "Modernity belongs to that small family of theories that both declares and desires universal applicability for itself. What is new about modernity (or about the idea that its newness is a new kind of newness) follows from this duality. Whatever else the project of the Enlightenment may have created, it aspired to create persons who would, after the fact, have wished to have become modern." Appadurai, *Modernity at Large*, 1.

56. Monika Greenleaf, *Pushkin and Romantic Fashion* (Stanford: Stanford University Press, 1994), 15–16. Greenleaf is referring to the Romantic period, but her insights shed light on the tradition as a whole.

57. Pavel Mel'nikov-Pecherskii, "Krasil'nikovy," in *Sobranie sochinenii v 6-i tomakh* (Moscow: Knizhnyi Klub Knigovek, 2010), 1:17.

58. N. V. Gogol', *Polnoe sobranie sochinenii* (Moscow: Akademiia Nauk SSSR, 1937–52), 6:95.

59. Gogol', *PSS*, 8:369.

60. Edward Said, *Culture and Imperialism* (New York: Vintage Books, 1994), xxv.

61. Donald Fanger, *The Creation of Nikolai Gogol* (Cambridge, MA: Harvard University Press, 1979), 30.

62. Salman Rushdie, *In Good Faith* (London: Granta, 1990), 4.

63. I. A. Razumova and E. V. Kuleshov, "K fenomenologii provintsii," in *PKR*, 19, 13.

64. P. Ia. Chaadaev, "Lettres philosophiques adressées à une dame. Lettre première," 92.

65. Chaadaev, "Lettres philosophiques adressées à une dame. Lettre première," 89.

66. Of Platonov, for instance, Seifrid writes, "Platonov hardly qualifies as a modernist in the effete, aestheticist sense that applies to a Joyce, a Belyi, or even a Khlebnikov. . . . He is rather a kind *de facto* modernism developed, at a remove from the centers of Russian modernist culture, out of the satirical-grotesque tradition of Gogol', Leskov, and Saltykov-Shchedrin and emphatically preserving the 'crude' perspective of the semi-literate provincial masses." Thomas Seifrid, *Andrei Platonov: Uncertainties of Spirit* (Cambridge, UK: Cambridge University Press, 1992), 18.

67. Platonov, quoted in Seifrid, *Andrei Platonov*, 9; Andrei Platonov, *"Ia prozhil zhizn',"* Pis'ma 1920–1950 (St. Petersburg: Astrel', 2013), 182.

68. Platonov, quoted in Seifrid, *Andrei Platonov*, 9; Platonov, *"Ia prozhil zhizn',"* 215.

69. Seifrid, *Andrei Platonov*, 9; Platonov, *"Ia prozhil zhizn',"* 215.

70. Abram Terts [pseud. Andrei Siniavskii], *V teni Gogolia* (London: Collins, 1975), 434.

71. Thus it is probably no accident that among cultural theorists, it is Russians who have most clearly perceived the complicated nature of center-periphery literary dynamics. Lotman, for instance, notes that Peter's transfer of the capital to "the geographical frontier" was one manifestation of a more general and ongoing process "whereby the periphery of culture moves into the center, and the center is pushed out to the periphery." Lotman, *Universe of the Mind*, 141. As Kate Holland writes, for Russian thinkers like Lotman, Bakhtin, and Veselovsky (and one might add here Tynianov), "the boundary rather than the center is the site of hybridization and thus literary and cultural transformation." Kate Holland, "Narrative Tradition on the Border," 429.

72. Epstein, *Bog detalei*, 33.

BIBLIOGRAPHY

Abashev, Vladimir. *Perm' kak tekst. Perm' v russkoi kul'ture i literature XX veka*. Moscow-Berlin: Direct Media, 2014.

Abrams, H. *A Glossary of Literary Terms*. New York: Harcourt Brace, 1999.

Akhapkipa, Ia. E. "Provintsiia, periferiia—problem nominatsii." In *Provintsiia kak real'nost'*, edited by Belousov, Stroganov, and Sorochan, 6–11.

Akhmatova, A. A. "Pridu tuda, i otletit tomlenie." In *Sobranie sochinenii v 6-i tomakh*, edited by N. V. Koroleva, 4:117–18. Moscow: Ellis Lak, 2000.

Allen, Elizabeth Cheresh. *Beyond Realism: Turgenev's Poetics of Secular Salvation*. Stanford: Stanford University Press, 1992.

Alvarez, Al. "The Long Road Home." *The Guardian*, September 11, 2004. Accessed July 21, 2017. http://donswaim.com/guardian.uk.rothprofile.html.

Anderson, Benedict. *Imagined Communities: Reflections on the Origin and Spread of Nationalism*. London: Verso, 1991. First published 1983.

Appadurai, Arjun. *Modernity at Large: Cultural Dimensions of Globalization*. Minneapolis: University of Minnesota Press, 2000.

———. "Disjuncture and Difference in the Global Cultural Economy." In *Colonial Discourse and Post-Colonial Theory: A Reader*, edited by Patrick Williams and Laura Chrisman, 324–39. New York: Columbia University Press, 1994.

Austen, Jane. *Mansfield Park*. New York: W. W. Norton, 1998.

Bakhtin, Mikhail. *Rabelais and His World*. Translated by Helene Iswolsky. Bloomington: Indiana University Press, 2009.

———. "Forms of Time and Chronotope in the Novel." In *The Dialogic Imagination: Four Essays by M. M. Bakhtin*, edited by Michael Holquist, translated by Caryl Emerson and Michael Holquist, 84–258. Austin: University of Texas Press, 1981.

Balzac, Honoré de. "La Femme de Province." In *Les Français peints par eux-mêmes: Encyclopédie morale du dix-neuvième siècle*. Vol. 6. Paris: Louis Curmer éditeur, 1841. Accessed July 31, 2017. http://www.bmlisieux.com/curiosa/balzac01.htm.

———. *Lost Illusions*. Introduction by Richard Howard, translation by Kathleen Raine, notes by James Madden. New York: Modern Library, 1997.

Baranets, N. G. "Faktor provintsializma v universitetskoi filosofii v Rossii kontsa XX-ogo veka." In Poltoraka, *Tsentr-provintsiia*, 177–80.

Barker, Murl. "*The Petty Demon* and the Critics." In Sologub, *The Petty Demon*, 306–10.

Baron, Nick. "New Spatial Histories of 20th-Century Russia and the Soviet Union: Exploring the Terrain." *Kritika* 9, no. 2 (Spring 2008): 433–48.

Bassin, Mark. *Imperial Visions: Nationalist Imagination and Geographical Expansion in the Russian Far East, 1840–1865.* Cambridge, UK: Cambridge University Press, 1999.

Belinskii, V. G. *Polnoe sobranie sochinenii v 13-i tomakh.* 13 vols. Moscow: Akademii Nauk SSSR, 1953–59.

Belousov, A. F., M. V. Stroganov, and A. Iu. Sorochan, eds. *Provintsiia kak real'nost' i ob"ekt osmysleniia.* Tver': Tverskoi gosudarstvennyi universitet, 2001.

Belousov, A. F., T. V. Tsivian, and V. N. Sazhin, eds. *Russkaia provintsiia: mif—tekst—real'nost'.* Moscow: Nauchnyi sovet po istorii mirovoi kul'tury Rossiiskoi Akademii Nauk, 2000.

———. "Simvolika zakholust'ia (oboznachenie rossiiskogo provintsial'nogo goroda)." In Zaionts, Abashev, Belousov, and Tsivian, *Geopanorama russkoi kul'tury*, 457–82.

Bely, Andrei. *The Silver Dove.* Translated by John Elsworth. Evanston, IL: Northwestern University Press, 2000.

———. *Petersburg.* Translated and edited by Robert A. Maguire and John E. Malmstad. Bloomington: Indiana University Press, 1978.

Berdiaev, Nikolai. *Sud'ba Rossii. Opyty po psikhologii voiny i natsional'nosti.* Moscow: Izdatel'stvo G. D. Lemana i S. I. Sakharova, 1918.

Bethea, David M. "*The Idiot*: Historicism Arrives at the Station." In *Dostoevsky's Idiot: A Critical Companion*, edited by Liza Knapp, 130–90. Evanston, IL: Northwestern University Press, 1998.

———, and Sergei Davydov. "The History of the Village Gorjuxino: In Praise of Puškin's Folly." *Slavic and East European Journal* 28, no. 3 (Autumn 1984): 291–309.

Biggs, Michael. "Putting the State on the Map: Cartography, Territory, and European State Formation." *Comparative Studies in Society and History* 41, no. 2 (April 1999): 374–405.

Billington, James H. *The Icon and the Axe: An Interpretive History of Russian Culture.* New York: Vintage Books, 1970. First published 1966.

Blacker, Uilleam. "Blurred lines: Russian literature and cultural diversity in Ukraine." *The Calvert Journal*, March 14, 2014. Accessed February 12, 2017. http://calvertjournal.com/comment/show/2176/russian-culture-in-ukraine-literature?hc_location=ufi.

Bojanowska, Edyta M. *Nikolai Gogol: Between Ukrainian and Russian Nationalism.* Cambridge, MA: Harvard University Press, 2007.

———. *A World of Empires: The Russian Voyage of the Frigate Pallada.* Cambridge, MA: Harvard University Press, 2018.

Bourdieu, Pierre. *The Rules of Art: Genesis and Structure of the Literary Field.* Stanford: Stanford University Press, 1996.

———. *The Field of Cultural Production: Essays on Art and Literature.* New York: Columbia University Press, 1993.

———. "Deux impérialismes de l'universel." In *L'Amérique des Français*, edited by Christine Fauré and Tom Bishop, 149–56. Paris: François Bourin, 1992.

———. *Distinction: A Social Critique of the Judgement of Taste*. Translated by Richard Nice. Cambridge, MA: Harvard University Press, 1984.

Boym, Svetlana. *Commonplaces: Mythologies of Everyday Life in Russia*. Cambridge, MA: Harvard University Press, 1995.

Brodhead, Richard. *Cultures of Letters: Scenes of Reading and Writing in Nineteenth-Century America*. Chicago: University of Chicago Press, 1993.

Broomfield, William F. "Dvorianskaia idiliia. Neoklassicheskaia arkhitektura v epokhu Ekateriny Velikoi." In Fortunatov, *Zhizn' provintsii*, 188–92.

Brower, Daniel R. *The Russian City between Tradition and Modernity, 1850–1900*. Berkeley: University of California Press, 1990.

Campbell, Donna M. "Regionalism and Local Color Fiction, 1865–1895." *Literary Movements*. Department of English, Washington State University. Last modified October 10, 2017. Accessed July 29, 2018. http://public.wsu.edu/~campbelld/amlit/lcolor .html.

Casanova, Pascale. *The World Republic of Letters*. Cambridge, MA: Harvard University Press, 2004.

———. *La république mondiale des lettres*. Paris: Editions du Seuil, 1999.

Chaadaev, P. Ia. *Polnoe sobranie sochinenii i izbrannye pis'ma*. Vol. 1. Moscow: Nauka, 1991.

——— [Peter Chaadaev]. *Philosophical Works of Peter Chaadaev*. Edited by T. J. Blakeley, Guido Küng, and Nikolaus Lobkowicz. Netherlands: Springer Netherlands, 1991.

Chekhov, Anton. *The Complete Plays*. Translated, edited, and annotated by Laurence Senelick. New York: W W. Norton, 2007.

———. "Nevesta." In *Polnoe sobranie sochinenii*, vol. 10. Moscow: Nauka, 1986. Accessed December 11, 2016. http://az.lib.ru/c/chehow_a_p/text_1903_nevesta.shtml

———. *Polnoe sobranie sochinenii i pisem v 30-i tomakh*. 30 vols. Moscow: Nauka, 1974–83.

Chernetsky, Vitaly, Nancy Condee, Harsha Ram, and Gayatri Chakravorty Spivak. "Are We Post-Colonial? Post-Soviet Space." *PMLA* 121, no. 3 (May 2006): 828–36.

Chernyshevsky, Nikolai. *What Is to Be Done?*. Translated by Michael R. Katz, introduction by Michael Katz and Michael G. Wagner. Ithaca, NY: Cornell University Press, 1989.

——— [N. G. Chernyshevskii]. *Chto delat'? Iz rasskazov o novykh liudiakh*. Leningrad: Nauka, 1975.

Cioran, S. D. Introduction to Sologub, *The Petty Demon*. Edited by Murl Barker, introduced and translated by S. D. Cioran. Woodstock: Ardis Publishers, 2006, 8–33.

Cocteau, Jean. *Opium: The Illustrated Diary of His Cure*. London: Peter Owen, 1990. First published 1929.

Cohen, Margaret. *The Sentimental Education of the Novel*. Princeton, NJ: Princeton University Press, 1999.

Costlow, Jane Tussey. *Heart-Pine Russia: Walking and Writing the Nineteenth-Century Forest*. Ithaca, NY: Cornell University Press, 2013.

———. *Worlds Within Worlds: The Novels of Ivan Turgenev*. Princeton, NJ: Princeton University Press, 1990.

Dainotto, Roberto Maria "'All the Regions Do Smilingly Revolt': The Literature of Place and Region." *Critical Inquiry* 22, no. 3 (Spring 1996): 486–505.

Dal', V. I. "Bedovik." In *Russkie povesti XIX v., 20-kh–30-kh godov.* Vol. 2. Edited by B. S. Meilakh, 515–82. Moscow: Izdatel'stvo khudozhestvennoi literatury, 1950.

Debreczeny, Paul. "Nikolay Gogol and his Contemporary Critics." *Transactions of the American Philosophical Society* 56, no. 3 (1966): 1–68.

Denby, David. "A Fine Romance: The New Comedy of the Sexes." *The New Yorker*, July 23, 2007. Accessed July 28, 2018. https://www.newyorker.com/magazine/2007/07/23/a -fine-romance.

D'haen, Theo, David Damrosch, and Djelal Kadir, eds. *The Routledge Companion to World Literature.* New York: Routledge, 2012.

Dickinson, Sara. *Breaking Ground: Travel and National Culture in Russia from Peter I to the Era of Pushkin.* Amsterdam: Rodopi, 2006.

Didenko, P. I. "Istoricheskie formy oppozitsii 'tsentr-provintsiia.'" In Poltoraka, *Tsentr-provintsiia*, 3–5.

Dolgorukov, I. M. *Povest' o rozhdenii moem.* Vol. 1. Edited by N. V. Kuznetsova and M. O. Mel'tsin. St. Petersburg: Nauka, 2004.

———. "Zhurnal puteshestviia iz Moskvy v Nizhnii 1813 goda." In *Chteniia v Imperatorskom Obshchestve Istorii i Drevnostei Rossiiskikh* 1 (1870): 1–117.

———. "Slavny bubny za gorami, ili puteshestvie moe koe-kuda 1810 goda." In *Chteniia v Imperatorskom Obshchestve Istorii i Drevnostei Rossiiskikh* 2: Materialy otechestvennye (April–June 1869): 1–170.

Dolinin, Alexander. "Historicism or Providentialism? Pushkin's *History of Pugachev* in the Context of French Romantic Historiography." *Slavic Review* 58, no. 2. Special Issue: Aleksandr Pushkin 1799–1999 (Summer 1999): 291–308.

Dostoevskii, F. M. *Polnoe sobranie sochinenii v 30-i tomakh.* 30 vols. Leningrad: Nauka, 1972–1990.

Douglas, Mary. *Purity and Danger: An Analysis of Concepts of Pollution and Taboo.* London: Routledge and Kegan Paul, 1966.

Dumm, Thomas L. *A Politics of the Ordinary.* New York: New York University Press, 1999.

Dwyer, Anne. "Of Hats and Trains: Cultural Traffic in Leskov's and Dostoevskii's Westward Journeys." *Slavic Review* 70, no. 1 (Spring 2011): 67–93.

Edelman, Lee. *No Future: Queer Theory and the Death Drive.* Durham, NC: Duke University Press, 2004.

Ehre, Milton. "A Classic of Russian Realism: Form and Meaning in *The Golovliovs*." *Studies in the Novel* 9, no. 1 (Spring 1977): 3–16.

———. *Oblomov and his Creator: Life and Art of Ivan Goncharov.* Princeton, NJ: Princeton University Press, 1974.

Eikhenbaum, B. M. "O proze Kuzmina." In *O literature*, 348–51. Moscow: Sovetskii pisatel', 1987. Accessed July 31, 2017. http://philologos.narod.ru/eichenbaum/eich_kuzmin .htm.

Eliot, T. S. "What is a Classic?" In *Selected Prose of T. S. Eliot*, edited by Frank Kermode, 115–31. New York: Farrar, Straus, and Giroux, 1975.

———. "Turgenev." *The Egoist* 4 (December 1917): 167.

Ely, Christopher David. *This Meager Nature: Landscape and National Identity in Imperial Russia*. DeKalb, IL: Northern Illinois University Press, 2002.

Epstein, Mikhail, *Bog detalei: Narodnaia dusha i chastnaia zhizn' v Rossii na iskhode imperii*. New York: Slovo, 1997.

———. "Good-bye to Objects, or, the Nabokovian in Nabokov." In *A Small Alpine Form: Studies in Nabokov's Short Fiction*, edited by Gene Barabtarlo and Charles Nicol, 217–24. New York: Garland, 1993.

Etkind, Alexander. *Internal Colonization: Russia's Imperial Experience*. Cambridge, UK: Polity Press, 2011.

Evdokimova, Svetlana. *Pushkin's Historical Imagination*. New Haven, CT: Yale University Press, 1999.

Evtuhov, Catherine. *Portrait of a Russian Province: Economy, Society, and Civilization in Nineteenth-Century Nizhnii Novgorod*. Pittsburgh, PA: University of Pittsburgh Press, 2011.

———. "The Provincial Intelligentsia and Social Values in Nižnij Novgorod, 1838-91." *Slavica Lundensia* 22 (2005): 79–98.

Fanger, Donald. *The Creation of Nikolai Gogol*. Cambridge, MA: Harvard University Press, 1979.

Fazolini, Marica. "Vzgliad na usad'bu, ili predstavlenie provintsialov o russkoi stolichnoi zhizni." In Belousov, Tsivian, and Sazhin, *Russkaia provintsiia*, 176–85.

Fet, A. A. "Dve lipki." In *Sochineniia v dvukh tomakh*. Vol. 1, 487–99. Moscow: Khudozhestvennaia literatura, 1982.

Fisher, Philip. *Still the New World: American Literature in a Culture of Creative Destruction*. Cambridge, MA: Harvard University Press, 1999.

Fortunatov, N. M., ed. *Zhizn' provintsii kak fenomen dukhovnosti*. Nizhnii Novgorod: izd. Vektor T i S, 2004.

Foster, John Burt, Jr. *Transnational Tolstoy: Between the West and the World*. New York: Bloomsbury, 2013.

Frank, Joseph. *Dostoevsky: The Miraculous Years, 1865–1871*. Princeton, NJ: Princeton University Press, 1995.

Frazier, Melissa. *Romantic Encounters: Writers, Readers, and the "Library for Reading."* Stanford: Stanford University Press, 2007.

Gan, E. A. "Ideal." In *Russian Women's Shorter Fiction: An Anthology, 1835–1860*, translated by Joe Andrew, 1–49. Oxford: Oxford University Press, 1996.

———. "Sud Sveta." In *Dacha na Petergofskoi doroge: Proza russkikh pisatel'nits pervoi poloviny XIX veka*, edited by V. V. Uchenova, 147–212. Moscow: Sovremennik, 1986.

———. "Ideal." In *Russkaia Romanticheskaia povest'*, compiled by Vsevolod Sakharov, 435–80. Moscow: Izd. Sovetskaia Rossiia, 1980. Accessed May 30, 2017. http://az.lib.ru/g/gan_e_a/text_0010.shtml.

Gatsitskii, A. S. *Liudi Nizhegorodskogo Povolzh'ia*. Nizhnii Novgorod: Tip. Nizh. gub. pravleniia, 1887.

———. *Smert' provintsii ili net?* Nizhnii Novgorod: Tip. Nizh. gub. pravleniia, 1876.

Gerschenkron, Alexander. "Time Horizon in Russian Literature." *Slavic Review* 34, no. 4 (December 1975): 692–715.

Gerson, Stephane. "Parisian Litterateurs, Provincial Journeys and the Construction of National Unity in Post-Revolutionary France." *Past and Present* 151, no. 1 (May 1996): 141–73.

Glinka, F. N. *Pis'ma k drugu*. Edited by V. P. Zverev. Moscow: Sovremennik, 1990.

Glushkova, M. A. "Mir russkoi usad'by v lirike Afanasiia Feta." In Fortunatov, *Zhizn' provintsii*, 237–42.

Gogol, N. V. *The Collected Tales of Nikolai Gogol*. Translated by Richard Pevear and Larissa Volokhonsky. New York: Vintage Classics, 1998.

———. "The Carriage." In *The Collected Tales of Nikolai Gogol*, translated by Richard Pevear and Larissa Volokhonsky, 327–39. New York: Vintage Classics, 1998.

———. *Dead Souls*. Translated by Richard Pevear and Larissa Volokhonsky. New York: Vintage Books, 1997.

——— [Gogol']. *Polnoe sobranie sochinenii*. 14 vols. Moscow: Akademiia Nauk SSSR, 1937–52.

Golburt, Luba. *The First Epoch: The Eighteenth Century in the Russian Cultural Imagination*. Madison: University of Wisconsin Press, 2014.

Goncharov, I. A. *Polnoe sobranie sochinenii i pisem v 20-i tomakh*. 20 vols. St. Petersburg: Nauka, 1997.

———. *Oblomov*. In *Sobranie sochinenii v 8-i tomakh*. Vol. 4.

———. *Sobranie sochinenii v 8-i tomakh*. 8 vols. Moscow: Gosudarstvennoe izdatel'stvo khudozhestvennoi literatury, 1952–55.

Gorizontov, Leonid. "The 'Great Circle' of Interior Russia: Representations of the Imperial Center in the Nineteenth and Early Twentieth Centuries." In *Russian Empire: Space, People, Power, 1700–1930*, edited by Jane Burbank, Mark von Hagen, and Anatolyi Remnev, 67–93. Bloomington: Indiana University Press, 2007.

Gorky, Maxim. "On the Russian Peasantry." *Journal of Peasant Studies* 4, no.1 (October 1976): 11–27. First published in Berlin, 1922.

——— [Gor'kii]. *Sobranie sochinenii v 30-i tomakh*. 30 vols. Moscow: Gosudarstvennoe izdatel'stvo khudozhestvennoi literatury, 1949–55.

Greene, Diana. *Reinventing Romantic Poetry: Russian Women Poets of the Mid-Nineteenth Century*. Madison: University of Wisconsin Press, 2014.

———. *Insidious Intent: An Interpretation of Fedor Sologub's* The Petty Demon. Columbus, OH: Slavica, 1985.

———. "Structure and Meaning in Sologub's 'Petty Demon.'" *Ulbandus Review* 1, no. 2 (Spring 1978): 26–36.

Greenleaf, Monika. *Pushkin and Romantic Fashion*. Stanford: Stanford University Press, 1994.

Griboedov, A. S. *Sochineniia v stikhakh*. Leningrad: Sovetskii pisatel', 1967.

Grigoryan, Bella. *Noble Subjects: The Russian Novel and the Gentry, 1762–1861*. DeKalb, IL: Northern Illinois University Press, 2018.

Grimstad, Knut Andreas. *Styling Russia: Multiculture in the Prose of Nikolai Leskov*. Slavica Bergensia, Volume 7. Bergen, Norway: Department of Foreign Languages, University of Bergen, 2007.

Guizot, M. [François]. *General History of Civilization in Europe: From the Fall of the Roman Empire to the French Revolution*. 9th American Edition. Notes by C. S. Henry. New York: D. Appleton, 1869.

Gujarawala, Toral. "Nagarjun's World Literature and the Problem of Fiction as Theory." Conference Paper, delivered at conference "World Literature and Its Discontent," NYU Abu Dhabi, March 31, 2016.

Gumilev, N. *Koster*. Berlin: Izdatel'stvo Z. I. Grzhebina, 1922.

Gutsche, George J. "Puškin and Belinskij: The role of the 'Offended Provincial.'" In *New Perspectives on Russian Nineteenth Century Prose*, edited by George J. Gutsche and Lauren G. Leighton, 41–59. Columbus, OH: Slavica, 1982.

Herzen, Alexander. *My Past and Thoughts*. Translated by Constance Garnett, introduction by Isaiah Berlin. Berkeley: University of California Press, 1973.

—— [Aleksandr Gertsen]. *Byloe i dumy*. Part 4: *Moskva, Peterburg i Novgorod (1840–1847)*. Moscow: Gosudarstvennoe izdatel'stvo khudozhestvennoi literatury, 1958. Accessed July 31, 2017. http://az.lib.ru/g/gercen_a_i/text_0130.shtml.

——. *Sobranie sochinenii v 30-i tomakh*. 30 vols. Moscow: Izd. Akademii Nauk SSSR, 1954.

Hoisington, Thomas H. "Melnikov-Pechersky: Romancer of Provincial and Old Believer Life." *Slavic Review* 33, no. 4 (December 1974): 679–94.

Holland, Kate. "Narrative Tradition on the Border: Alexander Veselovsky and Narrative Hybridity in the Age of World Literature." *Poetics Today* 38, no. 3 (September 2017): 429–51.

——. "The Russian *Rougon-Macquart*: Degeneration and biological determinism in *The Golovlev Family*." In *Russian Writers and the Fin de Siècle: The Twilight of Realism*, edited by Ani Kokobobo and Katia Bowers, 15–32. Cambridge, UK: Cambridge University Press, 2015.

Hollander, Anne L. *Seeing Through Clothes*. Berkeley: University of California Press, 1993. First published 1975.

Holquist, Michael. *Dostoevsky and the Novel*. Evanston, IL: Northwestern University Press, 1977.

Hoogenboom, Hilde. "The Importance of Being Provincial: Nineteenth-Century Russian Women Writers and the Countryside." In *Gender and Landscape: Renegotiating Morality and Space*, edited by Josephine Carubia, Lorraine Dowler, and Bonj Szczygiel, 240–53. London: Routledge, 2009.

——. "The Society Tale as Pastiche: Mariia Zhukova's Heroines Move to the Country." In *The Society Tale in Russian Literature from Odoevskii to Tolstoi*, edited by Neil Cornwall, 85–97. Amsterdam: Rodopi, 1998.

Il'f, Il'ia, and Evgenii Petrov. *Dvenadtsat' stul'ev*. Moscow: Vagrius, 1998.

Irigaray, Luce. *Ce sexe qui n'en est pas un*. Paris: Minuit, 1977.

Ivanits, Linda J. "The Grotesque in Fedor Sologub's *The Petty Demon*." In Sologub, *The Petty Demon*, 312–23.

James, William. *The Varieties of Religious Experience: A Study in Human Nature*. New York: The Modern Library, 1929.

Jameson, Fredric. "Third-World Literature in the Era of Multinational Capitalism." *Social Text* 15 (Autumn 1986): 65–88.

Jeanneret, Michel. *A Feast of Words: Banquets and Table Talk in the Renaissance*. Chicago: University of Chicago Press, 1991.

Johnson, Emily D. *How St. Petersburg Learned to Study Itself: The Russian Idea of Kraevedenie*. University Park, PA: Penn State University Press, 2006.

Jones, Malcolm V., and Robin Feuer Miller. "Editors' Preface." In *The Cambridge Companion to the Classic Russian Novel*, edited by Malcolm V. Jones and Robin Feuer Miller, xi–xv. Cambridge, UK: Cambridge University Press, 1998.

Kaganov, Grigory. *Images of Space: St. Petersburg in the Visual and Verbal Arts*. Translated by Sidney Monas. Stanford: Stanford University Press, 1997.

Kaganskii, V. L. "Tsentr-provintsiia-periferiia-granitsa. Osnovnye zony kul'turnogo landshafta." In *Kul'turnyi landshaft: voprosy teorii i metologii issledovaniia*, edited by V. V. Valebnyi et al., 72–101. Moscow: Izd. SGU, 1998.

Karmannyi pochtovyi atlas vsei Rossiiskoi Imperii, razdelennoi na gubernii s pokazaniem glavnykh pochtovykh dorog. St. Petersburg: Sobstvennyi Ego Imperatorskogo Velichestva Departament Kart, 1808.

Kazari, Rozanna [Rosanna Casari]. "Russkii provintsial'nyi gorod v literature XIX v. Paradigma i variant." In Belousov, Tsivian, and Sazhin, *Russkaia provintsiia*, 164–69.

Kelly, Catriona. *A History of Russian Women's Writing, 1820–1992*. Oxford: Clarendon Press, 1994.

Khvoshchinskaya, Nadezhda. *The Boarding School Girl*. Translated by Karen Rosneck. Evanston, IL: Northwestern University Press, 2000.

——— [Khvoshchinskaia; V. Krestovskii, pseud.]. "Pansionerka." In *Povesti i rasskazy*, 92–188. Moscow: Khudozhestvennaia literatura, 1963, 92–188.

Kirichenko, Evgeniia, and Elena Shcheboleva. *Russkaia provintsiia*. Moscow: Nash dom, 1997.

Kivelson, Valerie Ann. *Cartographies of Tsardom: The Land and Its Meanings in Seventeenth-Century Russia*. Ithaca, NY: Cornell University Press, 2006.

Kliger, Ilya. "Historical Poetics between Russia and the West: Toward a Nonlinear Model of Literary History and Social Ontology." *Poetics Today* 38, no. 3 (September 2017): 453–83.

———. "Hegel's Political Philosophy and the Social Imaginary of Early Russian Realism." *Studies in East European Thought* 65, no. 3–4 (2013): 189–99.

———. "Genre and Actuality in Belinskii, Herzen, and Goncharov: Toward a Genealogy of the Tragic Pattern in Russian Realism." *Slavic Review* 70, No. 1 (Spring 2011): 45–66.

———. "World Literature beyond Hegemony in Yuri M. Lotman's Cultural Semiotics." *Comparative Critical Studies* 7, no. 2–3 (2010): 257–74.

Klubkov, P. A. "'Zamkami slaven Tver', a Novgorod syrtiami.'" In Belousov, Stroganov, and Sorochan, *Provintsiia kak real'nost'*, 47–52.

Klubkova, T. V., and P. A. Klubkov. "Russkii provintsial'nyi gorod i stereotipy provintsial'nosti." In Belousov, Tsivian, and Sazhin, *Russkaia provintsiia*, 20–29.

Kokobobo, Ani "Tolstoy as Literary Cartographer of the Napoleonic Wars: Mapping the Human Geography of *War and Peace* through Digital Technology." Unpublished manuscript, forthcoming in *Russian Literature: Special Issue: Digital Humanities and Russian and East European Literature*, no page numbers.

———. *Russian Grotesque Realism: The Great Reforms and the Gentry Decline*. Columbus: The Ohio State University Press, 2018.

Kokovina, I. Z. "Provintsial'nyi byt v strukture khudozhestvennogo proizvedeniia XIX veka," In Belousov, Stroganov, and Sorochan, *Provintsiia kak real'nost'*, 101–9.

Kolchin, Peter. *Unfree Labor: American Slavery and Russian Serfdom*. Cambridge, MA: Harvard University Press, 1987.

Koshelev, V. A. "O 'literaturnoi' provintsii i literaturnoi 'provintsial'nosti' novogo vremeni: Zametki." In Belousov, Tsivian, and Sazhin, *Russkaia provintsiia*, 37–54.

Kotsonis, Yanni. *Making Peasants Backward: Agricultural Cooperatives and the Agrarian Question in Russia, 1861–1914*. New York: Palgrave Macmillan, 1999.

Krivonos, V. Sh. "Gogol': Mif provintsial'nogo goroda." In Belousov, Stroganov, and Sorochan, *Provintsiia kak real'nost'*, 110–17.

Kudriashchov, I. V. "Khronotop 'lesov' i 'gor' v filosofskom kontekste dialogii P. I. Mel'nikogo-Pecherskogo." In Fortunatov, *Zhizn' provintsii*, 252–55.

Kul'chitskii, A. Ia. *Neobyknovennyi poedinok* (1845). Accessed July 31, 2017. http://homlib.com/read/kulchickiy-aya/neobyknovennyy-poedinok.

Kundera, Milan. "Die Weltliteratur: European novelists and modernism." *The New Yorker*, January 8, 2007.

Lentz, Thierry. "Imperial France in 1808 and Beyond." In *The Napoleonic Empire and the New European Political Culture*, edited by Michael Broers, Peter Hicks, and Agustín Guimerá, 24–37. New York: Palgrave-Macmillan, 2012.

Lermontov, Mikhail Iurevich. *Polnoe sobranie sochinenii v 6-i tomakh*. Moscow: Akademiia Nauk SSSR, 1954–57.

Leskov, N. S. *Sobranie sochinenii*, edited by V. G. Bazanov et al. 11 vols. Moscow: Gosudarstvennoe izdatel'stvo khudozhestvennoi literatury, 1956–58.

Lincoln, W. Bruce. *In the Vanguard of Reform: Russia's Enlightened Bureaucrats 1825–1861*. DeKalb, IL: Northern Illinois University Press, 1982.

Litiagin, A. A., and A. V. Tarabukina. "Zritel'nyi obraz malen'kogo goroda." In Belousov, Stroganov, and Sorochan, *Provintsiia kak real'nost'*, 53–63.

Lofland, Lyn. *A World of Strangers: Order and Action in Urban Public Space*. New York: Basic Books, 1973.

Lotman, Yuri M. *Universe of the Mind: A Semiotic Theory of Culture*. Translated by Ann Shukman. Introduction by Umberto Eco. London; New York: I. B. Tauris, 2001.

—— [Iu. M. Lotman]. "'Pikovaia dama' i tema kart i kartochnye igry v russkoi literature nachala XIX veka." In *Izbrannye stat'i.* 2:389–415. Tallinn: Aleksandra, 1992.

—— [Iurii Lotman]. "The Poetics of Everyday Behavior in Eighteenth-Century Russian Culture." In *The Semiotics of Russian Cultural History*, edited by Alexander D. Nakhimovsky and Alice Stone Nakhimovsky, 67–94. Ithaca, NY: Cornell University Press, 1985.

Lounsbery, Anne. Review of *Internal Colonization: Russia's Imperial Experience*, by Alexander Etkind, *The Russian Review* 72, no. 1 (January 2013): 157–60.

——. "The World on the Back of a Fish: Mobility, Immobility, and Economics in *Oblomov*." *The Russian Review* 70, no. 1 (January 2011): 43–64.

——. "'Russia! What Do You Want of Me?': The Russian Reading Public in *Dead Souls*." *Slavic Review* 60, no. 2 (Summer 2001): 367–89.

Lur'e, M. L. "'Ves'egonsk gorodishko prebedneishii' (vzgliad na uezdnyi gorod v putevykh zametkakh XIX veka)." In Belousov, Stroganov, and Sorochan, *Provintsiia kak real'nost'*, 124–40.

Maiakovskii, V. "Prochti i katai v Parizh i v Kitai." In *Polnoe sobranie sochinenii Maiakovskogo v 13-i tomakh*, 10:257–63. Moscow: Gosudarstvennoe izdatel'stvo khudozhestvennoi literatury, 1955.

Majumdar, Saikat. *Prose of the World: Modernism and the Banality of Empire.* New York: Columbia University Press, 2013.

Mandelshtam, Osip. "On the Nature of the Word." In *Osip Mandelshtam: Selected Essays*, translated by Sidney Monas, 65–79. Austin: University of Texas Press, 1977.

Maiorova, Olga. *From the Shadow of Empire: Defining the Russian Nation through Cultural Mythology, 1855–1870.* Madison: University of Wisconsin Press, 2010.

Martin, Alexander M. *Enlightened Metropolis: Constructing Imperial Moscow, 1762–1855.* Oxford: Oxford University Press, 2013.

Masing-Delic, Irene. "'Peredonov's Little Tear'—Why Is It Shed? (The Sufferings of a Tormenter)." In Sologub, *The Petty Demon*, 333–43.

McDonald, David MacLaren. "Razmyshleniia o poniatii 'glush'": provintsiia, gosudarstvo i dvoriantsvo v Rossii." *Russkii sbornik. Issledovaniia po istorii Rossii.* Vol. 5. Edited by O. R. Airapetov et al. Moscow: Modest Kolerov, 2008. Accessed April 4, 2018. http://nlr.ru/domplekhanova/dep/artupload/dp/article/70/NA1914.pdf.

Mel'nikov, Pavel [Mel'nikov-Pecherskii]. *Sobranie sochinenii v 6-i tomakh.* 6 vols. Moscow: Knizhnyi Klub Knigovek, 2010.

Merezhkovskii, Dmitrii Sergeevich. "Turgenev." *Rech'* 51 (February 22, 1909). Accessed July 31, 2017. http://dugward.ru/library/merejkovskiy/merejkovskiy_turgenev.html.

Michelet, Jules. *Tableau de la France. Géographie physique, politique et morale.* Paris: A. Lacroix et Cie, 1875.

Mink, Louis. "Narrative Form as a Cognitive Instrument." In *The Writing of History*, edited by Robert H. Canary and Henry Kozicki, 129–49. Madison: University of Wisconsin Press, 1978.

Mordovtsev, D. "Pechat' v provintsii." *Delo* 10 (October 1875): 1–32.

——. "Pechat' v provintsii." *Delo* 9 (September 1875): 44–74.

Moretti, Franco. *Atlas of the European Novel, 1800–1900*. London: Verso, 1998.

Morrison, Toni. *Playing in the Dark: Whiteness and the Literary Imagination*. New York: Vintage, 1993.

Morson, Gary Saul. *Encyclopædia Britannica*, s.v. "Russian literature." Accessed February 9, 2017. https://www.britannica.com/art/Russian-literature.

———. *Narrative and Freedom: The Shadows of Time*. New Haven, CT: Yale University Press, 1994.

Nabokov, Vladimir. *Speak, Memory: An Autobiography Revisited*. New York: Vintage International, 1989.

———. *Strong Opinions*. New York: McGraw-Hill, 1973.

———. Interview by Alfred Appel, Jr. *Wisconsin Studies in Contemporary Literature* 3, no. 2 (Spring 1967). Accessed March 10, 2017. http://lib.ru/NABOKOW/Inter06.txt_with-big-pictures.html.

———. *Nikolai Gogol*. New York: New Directions, 1944.

Nadezhdin, N. "Zdravyi smysl i Baron Brambeus." *Teleskop*, 21 (1834): 329–30.

Nairn, Tom. "The British Political Elite." *New Left Review* 23 (January–February 1964): 19–25.

Newlin, Thomas. "Rural Ruses: Illusion and Anxiety on the Russian Estate, 1775–1815," *Slavic Review* 57, no. 2 (Summer 1998): 295–319.

———. "The Return of the Russian Odysseus: Pastoral Dreams and Rude Awakenings." *The Russian Review* 55, no. 3 (July 1996): 448–74.

Novikov, N. I. "Pis'mo uezdnogo dvorianina k ego synu." Accessed April 15, 2018. http://rvb.ru/18vek/novikov/01text/01prose/05.htm.

Odoevsky, V. F. "Sil'fida" (1837). Accessed November 1, 2016. http://rulibrary.ru/odoevskiy/silfida/1.

Osterhammel, Jürgen. *The Transformation of the World: A Global History of the Nineteenth Century*. Princeton, NJ: Princeton University Press, 2014.

Ostrovskii, A. N. *Beshenye den'gi* (1870). Accessed April 16, 2018. http://rushist.com/index.php/rus-literature/5184-ostrovskij-beshenye-dengi-chitat-onlajn-polnostyu.

Paperno, Irina. *Chernyshevsky and the Age of Realism: A Study in the Semiotics of Behavior*. Stanford: Stanford University Press, 1988.

Paperny, Vladimir. *Architecture in the Age of Stalin: Culture Two*. Cambridge, UK: Cambridge University Press, 2011. First published in Paris, 1982.

Parts, Lyudmila. "Topography of Post-Soviet Nationalism: The Provinces—the Capital—the West." *Slavic Review* 74, no. 3 (Fall 2015): 508–28.

Paz, Octavio. "In Search of the Present." *Inti: Revista de literatura hispánica* 32, article 3 (Autumn 1990): 13–22. Accessed July 17, 2017. http://digitalcommons.providence.edu/inti/vol1/iss32/3.

Persi, Ugo. "Russkaia stolitsa i russkaia provintsiia v memuarnykh tekstakh Ivana M. Dolgorukova." In Belousov, Tsivian, and Sazhin, *Russkaia provintsiia*, 56–64.

Peterson, Dale. *The Clement Vision: Poetic Realism in Turgenev and James*. Port Washington, NY: Kennikat Press, 1975.

Piatnitskii, V., and N. Dobrokhotova-Maikova. "Parodii na Kharmsa o Turgeneve" (1971–72). Accessed July 31, 2018. http://nasledie.turgenev.ru/stat/smeh/Peredelka/Harms/har.html.

Pickering-Antonova, Kate. *An Ordinary Marriage: The World of a Gentry Family in Provincial Russia.* Oxford: Oxford University Press, 2013.

Piretto, Gian Piero "Staraia Russa and Petersburg; Provincial Realities and Metropolitan Reminiscences in *The Brothers Karamazov.*" *Dostoevsky Studies* 7 (1986): 81–6.

Platonov, Andrei. *"Ia prozhil zhizn'." Pis'ma. 1920–1950.* St. Petersburg: Astrel', 2013.

Platt, Jonathan, ed. "Empire, Union, Center, Satellite: The Place of Post-Colonial Theory in Slavic/Central and East European/(Post-) Soviet Studies." *Ulbandus: The Slavic Review of Columbia University* 7 (2003).

Pleshcheev, A. N. *Zhiteiskie tseny.* In *Russkie povesti XIX veka 40–50-x godov,* edited by B. S. Meilakh. Vol. 2. Moscow: Gosudarstvennoe izdatel'stvo khudozhestvennoi literatury, 1952. Accessed July 31, 2017. http://az.lib.ru/p/plesheew_a_n/text_0130.shtml.

Pocock, J. G. A. "Modes of Political and Historical Time in Early Eighteenth-Century England." In *Virtue, Commerce, and History: Essays on Political Thought and History, Chiefly in the Eighteenth Century,* 91–102. Cambridge, UK: Cambridge University Press, 1985.

Pogodin, N. F. *Malen'kaia studentka.* In *Sobranie sochinenii v 4-i tomakh.* 3:219–84. Moscow: Izd. "Iskusstvo," 1973.

Polotskaya, Emma. "Chekhov and his Russia." In *The Cambridge Companion to Chekhov,* edited by Vera Gottlieb and Paul Allain, 17–28. Cambridge, UK: Cambridge University Press, 2000.

Poltoraka, S. N, ed. *Tsentr-provintsiia. Istorichesko-psikhologicheskie problemy. Materialy vserossiiskoi nauchnoi konferentsii, 6–7 dekabria 2001 g.* St. Petersburg: Nestor, 2001.

Pushkin, A. S. *Eugene Onegin: A Novel in Verse.* Vol. 2: *Commentary and Index.* Translation and commentary by Vladimir Nabokov. Princeton, NJ: Princeton University Press, 1990.

Pushkin, Alexander. *Eugene Onegin.* Translated by James E. Falen. Oxford: Oxford University Press, 1990.

———. *Alexander Pushkin: Complete Prose Fiction.* Translated by Paul Debreczeny. Stanford: Stanford University Press, 1983.

———. *Polnoe sobranie sochinenii v 10-i tomakh.* 10 vols. Leningrad: Nauka 1977–79.

———. *Polnoe sobranie sochinenii v 17-i tomakh.* 17 vols. Moscow; Leningrad, 1937.

Randolph, John. *The House in the Garden: The Bakunin Family and the Romance of Russian Idealism.* Ithaca, NY: Cornell University Press, 2007.

Rankine, Claudia, and Beth Loffreda. "On Whiteness and the Racial Imaginary." *Literary Hub,* April 9, 2015. Accessed March 9, 2017. http://lithub.com/on-whiteness-and-the-racial-imaginary/.

Razumova, I. A., and E. V. Kuleshov. "K fenomenologii provintsii." In Belousov, Stroganov, and Sorochan, *Provintsiia kak real'nost',* 12–25.

Reyfman, Irina. *How Russia Learned to Write: Literature and the Imperial Table of Ranks.* Madison: University of Wisconsin Press, 2016.

Rimbaud, Arthur. *A Season in Hell and Illuminations.* Translated by Bernard Mathieu. Rochester, NY: BOA Editions, 1991.

Roosevelt, Patricia. *Life on the Russian Country Estate.* New Haven, CT: Yale University Press, 1995.

Roosevelt, Priscilla R. "Tatiana's Garden: Noble Sensibilities and Estate Park Design in the Romantic Era." *Slavic Review* 49, no. 3 (Autumn 1990): 335–49.

Rushdie, Salman. *In Good Faith.* London: Granta, 1990.

Russ, Joanna. *To Write Like a Woman: Essays in Feminism and Science Fiction.* Bloomington: Indiana University Press, 1995.

Ryleev, K. F. "Provintsial v Peterburge." In *Polnoe sobranie sochinenii*, edited by A. G. Tseitlina, 299–304. Moscow: Academia, 1934.

Said, Edward. *Culture and Imperialism.* New York: Vintage Books, 1994.

Saltykov-Shchedrin, M. E. *The Golovlyov Family.* Translated by Natalie Duddington with an introduction by James Wood. New York: NYRB, 2001.

———. *Sobranie sochinenii v 20-i tomakh.* 20 vols. Moscow: Khudozhestvennaia literatura, 1965–77.

———. *Sobranie sochinenii.* Vol. 2: *Gubernskie ocherki, 1856–1857.* Moscow: Khudozhestvennaia literatura, 1965. Accessed July 31, 2017. https://rvb.ru/saltykov-shchedrin /tocvol_02.htm.

———. *Poshekhonskaia starina.* Moscow: Gosudarstvennoe izdatel'stvo khudozhestvennoi literatury, 1950.

Sanine, Kyra. *Saltykov-Chtchedrine: sa vie et ses oeuvres.* Paris: Institut d'études slaves de l'Université de Paris, 1955.

Savkina, Irina. *Provintsialki russkoi literatury (zhenskaia proza 30–40-kh godov XIX veka).* Wilhelmshorst, Germany: Verlag F. K. Göpfert, 1998.

———. "Kto i kak pishet istoriiu russkoi zhenskoi literatury." *Novoe literaturnoe obozrenie* 24 (1997): 359–72.

Schivelbusch, Wolfgang. *The Railway Journey: The Industrialization of Time and Space in the Nineteenth Century.* Berkeley: University of California Press, 1986.

Schjeldahl, Peter "Mystery Train. Martin Ramirez, Outsider." *The New Yorker*, January 9, 2007. Accessed July 28, 2018. https://www.newyorker.com/magazine/2007/01/29 /mystery-train.

Schor, Naomi. *Reading in Detail: Aesthetics and the Feminine.* London: Routledge, 1987.

Scott, Bonnie Kime, ed. *The Gender of Modernism: A Critical Anthology.* Bloomington: Indiana University Press, 1990.

Seifrid, Thomas. *Andrei Platonov: Uncertainties of Spirit.* Cambridge, UK: Cambridge University Press, 1992.

Senkovskii, O. I. "Pervoe pis'mo trekh tverskikh pomeshchikov k baronu Brambeusu." *Biblioteka dlia chteniia* 22, section 1 (1837): 65–96.

Shchukin, Vasilii. "Krizis stolits ili kompleks provintsii?." *Novoe literaturnoe obozrenie* 34 (1998): 350–54.

Shelgunov, Nikolai. *Ocherki russkoi zhizni*. St. Petersburg: O. N. Popova, 1895.

Showalter, Elaine. *A Literature of Their Own: British Women Novelists from Bronte to Lessing*. Princeton, NJ: Princeton University Press, 1999. First published 1977.

Slezkine, Yuri. *The House of Government: A Saga of the Russian Revolution*. Princeton, NJ: Princeton University Press, 2017.

Smith-Peter, Susan. *Imagining Russian Regions: Subnational Identity and Civil Society in Nineteenth-Century Russia*. Leiden: Brill, 2017.

———. "Making Empty Provinces: Eighteenth-Century Enlightenment Regionalism in Russian Provincial Journals." *REGION: Regional Studies of Russia, Eastern Europe, and Central Asia* 4, no. 1 (2015): 7–29.

———. "The Russian Provincial Newspaper and Its Public, 1788–1864." *The Carl Beck Papers in Russian & East European Studies* 1908 (2008).

———. "Defining the Russian People: Konstantin Arsen'ev and Russian Statistics before 1861." *History of Science* 45, no. 1 (2007): 47–64.

———. "How to Write a Region: Local and Regional Historiography." *Kritika* 5, no. 3 (Summer 2004): 527–42.

Sobol, Valeria. "The Uncanny Frontier of Russian Identity: Travel, Ethnography, and Empire in Lermontov's 'Taman.'" *The Russian Review* 70, no. 1 (January 2011): 65–79.

Sollogub, V. A. *Povesti i rasskazy*. Introduced by E. Kiiko. Moscow; Leningrad: Gosudarstvennoe izdatel'stvo khudozhestvennoi literatury, 1962.

———. "Aptekarsha." In *Povesti i rasskazy*, 83–133.

———. "Serezha." In *Povesti i rasskazy*, 17–37.

———. *Tarantas*. In *Povesti i rasskazy*, 158–303.

Sologub, F. K. *Melkii bes*. St. Petersburg: Nauka, 2004.

———. *The Petty Demon*. Edited by Murl Barker, introduced and translated by S. D. Cioran. Woodstock, NY: Ardis Publishers, 2006.

———. *Sobranie stikhotvorenii v 8-i tomakh*. St. Petersburg: Nav'i Chary, 2001–3.

Somov, O. M. *Roman v dvukh pis'makh*. In *Selected Prose in Russian*, edited by John Mersereau and George Harjan, 39–76. Ann Arbor: University of Michigan, 1974.

Sorensen, Janet. "'I talk to everybody in their own way': Defoe's Economics of Identity." In *The New Economic Criticism: Studies at the Intersection of Literature and Economics*, edited by Martha Woodmansee and Mark Osteen, 75–94. London: Routledge, 1999.

Sperrle, Irmhild Christina. *The Organic Worldview of Nikolai Leskov*. Evanston, IL: Northwestern University Press, 2002.

Spieker, Sven, ed. *Gogol: Exploring Absence: Negativity in Nineteenth-Century Russian Literature*. Bloomington, IN: Slavica, 1999.

———. "Esthesis and Anesthesia: The Sublime in *Arabesques*." In Spieker, *Gogol: Exploring Absence*, 161–70.

Spivak, M. L. "'Zavetnye griazishchi' i 'slavnyi gorod Likhov' (provintsiia v tvorchestve Andreia Belogo)." In Belousov, Tsivian, and Sazhin, *Russkaia provintsiia*, 241–56.

Stroganov, M. V. "Provintsializm/provintsial'nost': opyt definitsii." In Belousov, Tsivian, and Sazhin, *Russkaia provintsiia*, 30–36.

Stroganova, E. N. "'Miniatiurnyi mir': provintsiia v russkoi proze 1830-kh–pervoi poloviny 1840-kh gg. Ekskiz." In Belousov, Tsivian, and Sazhin, *Russkaia provintsiia*,
196–204.

Sunderland, Willard. *Taming the Wild Field: Colonization and Empire on the Russia Steppe.*
Ithaca, NY: Cornell University Press, 2004.

Terras, Victor, ed. *Handbook of Russian Literature.* New Haven, CT: Yale University Press,
1985.

Terts, Abram [pseud. Andrei Siniavskii]. *V teni Gogolia.* London: Collins, 1975.

Tihanov, Galin. "The Location of World Literature." *Canadian Review of Comparative Literature* 44, no. 3 (September 2017): 468–81.

Todd, William Mills, III. *Fiction and Society in the Age of Pushkin: Ideology, Institutions, and
Narrative.* Cambridge, MA: Harvard University Press, 1986.

———. "The Anti-Hero with a Thousand Faces: Saltykov-Shchedrin's Porfiry Golovlev."
Studies in the Literary Imagination 9, no. 1 (Spring 1976): 87–105.

———. "Pushkin's *History of Pugachev* and the Experience of Rebellion." Unpublished paper, in the author's possession.

Todorova, Maria. *Imagining the Balkans.* Oxford: Oxford University Press, 1997.

Tolmachev, Evgenii. *Aleksandr III i ego vremia.* Moscow: Terra—Knizhnii klub, 2007.

Tolstoi, L. N. *Polnoe sobranie sochinenii v 90-ti tomakh.* Moscow: Gosudarstvennoe
izdatel'stvo khudozhestvennoi literatury, 1929–64.

Tomei, Christine D., ed. *Dictionary of Russian Women Writers.* Vol. 1. New York: Garland,
1999.

Trotsky, Leon. *History of the Russian Revolution.* Chicago: Haymarket Books, 2008.

Trumpener, Katie. *Bardic Nationalism: The Romantic Novel and the British Empire.* Princeton, NJ: Princeton University Press, 1997.

Turgenev, I. S. *Smoke.* Translated by Michael Pursglove. Surrey, UK: Alma Classics, 2013.

———. *Virgin Soil.* Translated by Constance Garnett. New York: NYRB Classics, 2000.

———. *Fathers and Sons.* Translated by Michael Katz. New York: W. W. Norton, 1995.

———. *Nest of the Gentry.* Translated by Richard Freeborn. New York: Penguin, 1987.

———. *Polnoe sobranie sochinenii i pisem v 30-i tomakh.* Moscow: Nauka, 1978.

———. *Rudin.* Translated by Richard Freeborn. New York: Penguin, 1975.

———. *Sketches from a Hunter's Album.* Translated by Richard Freeborn. New York: Penguin, 1967.

Ushakov, V. A. "Tsentr-provintsiia v SShA: put' preodoleniia razlichii." In Poltoraka, *Tsentr-
provintsiia*, 26–29.

Vajskopf, Mixail. "Imperial Mythology and Negative Landscape in *Dead Souls*." In Spieker,
Gogol: Exploring Absence, 101–12.

Vengerov, S. A. "Gogol' sovershenno ne znal real'noi russkoi zhizni" (1911). *Sobranie sochinenii.* Vol. 2: *Pisatel'-grazhdanin. Gogol'.* St. Petersburg: Prometei, 1913.

Wallerstein, Immanuel. *The Modern World-System I: Capitalist Agriculture and the Origins of the European World-Economy in the Sixteenth Century.* New York: Academic
Press, 1974.

White, Hayden. "The Value of Narrativity in the Representation of Reality." In *On Narrative*, edited by W. J. T. Mitchell, 1–24. Chicago: University of Chicago Press, 1981.

Williams, Rosalind H. *Dream Worlds: Mass Consumption in Late Nineteenth-Century France*. Berkeley: University of California Press, 1982.

Wright, Robin. "Madeleine Albright Warns of a New Fascism." *New Yorker*, April 24, 2018. Accessed July 30, 2018. https://www.newyorker.com/news/news-desk/madeleine-albright-warns-of-a-new-fascism-and-trump.

Zagoskin, M. N. "Tri zhenikha (provintsial'nye ocherki)." In *Russkie povesti XIX v., Vol, 2: 20-kh–30-kh godov*. Edited by B. S. Meilakh, 451–511. Moscow: Izdatel'stvo khudozhestvennoi literatury, 1950.

———. "Bogotonov ili provintsial v stolitse." In *Sobranie sochinenii M. N. Zagoskina*, vol. 11: *Dramaticheskiia proizvedeniia*, 121–206. St. Petersburg: Izdanie Tovarishchevstva M. O. Vol'f, 1901.

Zaionts, L. O. "Istoriia slova i poniatiia 'provintsiia' v russkoi kul'ture." *Russian Literature* 53, no. 2–4 (February–April 2003): 307–30.

———. "'Provintsiia' kak termin." In Belousov, Tsivian, and Sazhin, *Russkaia provintsiia*, 12–9.

———. "Russkii provintsial'nyi 'mif' (k probleme kul'turnoi tipologii)." In Zaionts, Abashev, Belousov, and Tsivian, *Geopanorama russkoi kul'tury*, 427–56.

Zaionts, L. O., V. V. Abashev, A. F. Belousov, and T. V. Tsivian, eds. *Geopanorama russkoi kul'tury. Provintsiia i ee lokal'nye teksty*. Moscow: Iazyki slavianskoi kul'tury, 2004.

Zamyatin, Evgeny. *A Soviet Heretic: Essays by Evgeny Zamyatin*. Edited and translated by Mirra Ginsburg. Chicago: University of Chicago Press, 1970.

Zhivolupova, N. V. "Skotoprigon'evsk kak nazaret i mifologema provintsii v Russkoi kul'ture." In Fortunatov, *Zhizn' provintsii*, 193–201.

Zhukova, M. S. "Naden'ka." In *Serdtsa chutkogo prozren'em: Povesti i rasskazy russkikh pisatel'nits XIX v.* Moscow: Sovetskaia Rossiia, 1991.

———. "Provintsialka." In *Vechera na karpovke*, 186–251. Moscow: Izdatel'stvo Sovetskaia Rossiia, 1986.

INDEX

Page numbers in italics indicate illustrations.

bureaucrats (*continued*)
  in Gogol, 84, 87, 126, 284n16
  in Herzen's memoirs, 65, 88
  in "On Official Business," 1–2, 11, 222
byt, 240–41, 243, 244, 245, 249, 254

C

capital, capitalness. See stolitsa, stolichnost'
Capital and Estate, 17, 245, 264n70
Captain's Daughter (Pushkin), 34, 46–48, 51–53,
    273n49
  estate in, 34, 46–47, 49, 52
  steppe in, 34, 46, 47, 48–52
Casanova, Pascale
  World Republic of Letters, 28, 120, 144,
    249–51, 268n131, 268n137,
    289n38, 289n41, 314n37,
    315n46
Catherine II, 37, 48–49, 52, 53, 123
  in *Captain's Daughter*, 48, 52
  provincial information gathering under,
    18, 48
  provincial reforms/urban planning under,
    22, 25, 55, 83, 85
Caucasus, 13, 35, 227, 269n4, 275n72
center-periphery, 10, 120, 175, 187, 236, 255,
    316n71
Chaadaev, Pyotr, 123–24
  "First Philosophical Letter," 19, 44, 61, 205,
    241, 247n48, 251, 252, 253, 254,
    278n37
Chekhov, Anton, 29, 209–10, 215, 216, 218, 237,
    243, 280n102, 281n108
  "At Home," 223–25, 226, 227
  Boring Story, 307n12, 312n3
  "Champagne," 226
  Cherry Orchard, 12, 202, 224, 225–28, 234,
    312n3
  Duel, 226, 227
  "Fiancée," 212–16, 218, 222, 226, 227
  "In the Ravine," 226
  Kharkov in, 24, 219, 227, 244–45, 307n12,
    312n3
  "Lady with a Little Dog," 212
  "Lights," 226, 227
  "Man in a Case," 236, 237

"Murder," 226
My Life (A Provincial's Story), 211–12, 220,
    226, 283n136, 310n59
"On Official Business," 1–2, 8, 10, 11, 19,
    221–23
Peasants, 226
provincial sameness in, 24, 55, 209
provintsiia-stolitsa in, 1–2, 9–10, 11, 21,
    95, 126, 181, 209, 212–13, 218–19,
    222–23, 227
railway in, 12, 181, 202, 211, 214, 224, 226
Seagull, 220, 312n3
Three Sisters, 9–10, 77, 95, 126, 182, 208–9,
    217, 218–19, 220–21, 223, 225–26,
    227, 251
Three Years, 216–18
Uncle Vanya, 24, 219, 312n3
"Ward No. Six," 79, 209–11
Chernyshevsky, Nikolai, 215
  What Is to Be Done?, 158, 313n23
Cherry Orchard (Chekhov), 12, 202, 224,
    225–28, 234, 312n3
Chulkov, Mikhail, 55
Contemporary, 113, 121
Cossacks, 51, 124, 215, 270n10, 275nn71–72
  in *Captain's Daughter*, 46, 47, 50–51
  in *History of Pugachev*, 274–75nn70–71
Crime and Punishment (Dostoevsky), 20, 24, 64,
    186, 194, 265n79, 305n27

D

Dal, Vladimir
  dictionary, 262n53
  Unlucky One, 57, 75–77, 219, 237, 282n127
Dead Souls (Gogol), 37, 53, 75, 80, 83, 84, 86–88,
    90, 94, 98, 99, 121, 236, 237, 253, 254,
    279n69, 284n11, 285n20, 285n21
  estates in, 16, 29, 39, 40, 84, 92, 93
  gorod N in, 21, 24, 29, 33, 78, 80, 84–86,
    91–92, 94, 95, 108, 223, 240
  provincial emptiness in, 78, 95, 198, 232,
    235, 242
  provincial materiality/thingness in, 78,
    96–98, 99, 130, 213, 235, 242,
    285n32, 288n16
  provincial sameness in, 108

Siberia, 12, 13, 23, 81, 209, 261n27, 308n20
Silver Age, 243, 245–46, 249, 252, 254
Sinyavsky, Andrei, 79, 98–99, 255
Slavophilia, 10, 70, 135, 136, 259n9
Smith-Peter, Susan, 18, 25, 168, 171, 261n27,
266n103, 284n15
Smoke (Turgenev), 27, 120, 125, 136–38, 140
Smolensk, 188, 270n8
"Society's Judgment" (Gan), 145–46, 147
Sollogub, Vladimir, 67, 74, 80, 123–24, 213, 248,
292n4, 310n51
Apothecary's Wife, 57, 65, 66–67, 70–71, 240,
279n69, 280n73
"Serezha," 57, 64, 68–69, 71, 93
Tarantas, 24–25, 29, 55, 56, 57, 58, 63–65,
69, 70, 71–73, 77, 91, 97, 109, 217,
234, 279n51, 281n102
Sologub, Fyodor, 21, 235–36, 310n51
Bad Dreams, 236
paean to Kostroma, 244–45, 246
Petty Demon, 21, 79, 229, 236–40, 241, 242,
244, 311n69, 311nn84–85
Sweeter Than Poison, 236
"Something about Nothing" (Belinsky), 100–
101, 111–13, 114–16, 117, 289n34
Somov, Orest
Novel in Two Letters, 15, 27, 57, 63, 66,
67–68, 70, 279n51, 280n82
St. Petersburg
in *Boarding School Girl*, 155, 159–60, 162,
212, 216
conflated/paired with Moscow, 2, 9–10, 11,
84, 94, 188, 200, 222, 303n6
contrasted with Moscow, 9, 188, 266n98,
303n8
in *Crime and Punishment*, 20, 24, 64, 186, 194
in *Demons*, 196, 197, 199, 200, 201
in Dostoevsky, 20, 186, 192–93, 194, 196,
197, 199, 201, 207
in *Eugene Onegin*, 36, 39, 40–41, 188, 270n8,
270n10
Falconet's monument to Peter, 86
in "Fiancée," 212, 214, 216, 222
as goal/touchstone/model, 9–10, 25, 32, 84,
86, 196, 199, 212, 219, 266n98
in Gogol, 9–10, 93–94, 95, 108, 126, 188, 209
Hermitage, 159, 160

in *Inspector General*, 9, 77, 89, 93–94, 196,
199
as modeled on Europe, 10, 11, 25, 84
in *Mr. Bogotonov*, 61
Nevsky Avenue, 62, 150
in *Ordinary Story*, 102–9, 117
Poltava as miniature, 25, 60
provinces vs., 2–3, 11, 14, 17, 103–4, 113,
139, 140, 188, 197, 212, 222, 266n98,
279n51, 282n199
as provincial, 11, 200, 251
transfer of capital to, 9, 10, 316n71
Tverskoi Boulevard, 279n51
in *Virgin Soil*, 138, 139, 140
in Zhukova, 148, 149, 150, 152, 154
steppe, 61, 62, 67, 77, 84, 113, 231, 232, 248
in "At Home," 223–24, 227
in *Captain's Daughter*, 34, 46, 47, 48–52
in Dolgorukov, 60–61, 277n31
domestication of, 11–12, 23, 34, 46, 48–49,
52, 224, 269n2, 307–8n16, 308n17
emptiness of, 12, 48, 61, 123–24, 223, 224,
274n58, 280–81n102, 307–8n16
in *Family Chronicles*, 81, 124, 225
in "Hamlet of Shchigrov," 123, 124–26, 127,
130, 132, 133, 136
horizontality of, 50, 280n102
in *King Lear of the Steppe*, 124
liminality of, 34, 46, 48
in "Nadenka," 153
in *Nest of the Gentry*, 132, 133, 134
provincialization of, 34, 52, 53, 67, 124–25,
224, 225, 227, 228
in Pushkin, 34, 53
as repository of Russianness, 23, 34, 81
in *Smoke*, 137, 140
as un-Russian, 11–12, 13
stolitsa, stolichnost'/capital, capitalness, 16, 39,
93, 94, 152–53, 216–17
estates as mirror of, 16–18, 40, 60, 132, 148,
264n69
provintsiia-stolitsa/province-capital binary
in Chekhov, 1–2, 9–10, 11, 21, 95, 126, 181,
209, 212–13, 218–19, 222–23, 227
in Dolgorukov, 17, 25, 58, 59–61, 64, 266n98
in Dostoevsky, 18, 20, 115, 186–87, 192–96,
199, 205, 207, 246, 266n96, 304n17

CPSIA information can be obtained
at www.ICGtesting.com
Printed in the USA
FSHW012243280919
62472FS